W9-BSP-065

700 475633

FEB 15 1994

Hoffa

Arthur A. Sloane

The MIT Press
Cambridge, Massachusetts
London, England

© 1991 Massachusetts Institute of Technology

All rights reserved. No part of this book may be reproduced in any form by any electronic or mechanical means (including photocopying, recording, or information storage and retrieval) without permission in writing from the publisher.

This book was set in Bembo by Achorn Graphics, Inc. and was printed and bound in the United States of America.

Library of Congress Cataloging-in-Publication Data

Sloane, Arthur A.
 Hoffa / Arthur A. Sloane.
   p.   cm.
 Includes bibliographical references and index.
 ISBN 0-262-19309-4
 1. Hoffa, James R. (James Riddle), 1913–   . 2. Trade-unions—
United States—Officials and employees—Biography.
3. International Brotherhood of Teamsters, Chauffeurs, Warehousemen,
and Helpers of America. I. Title.
HD6509.H6S56 1991
331.88'11388324'092—dc20
[B]   90-26137
                                                                    CIP

To Louise,
best of wives

BELMONT COMMUNITY COLLEGE
LINE MAXON MAXICE LIBRARY

Contents

Preface

I first met James R. Hoffa in 1962, when I was a Harvard Business School student in search of a doctoral dissertation topic and with the brashness of youth asked him if I could follow him around the country. For the next several months I was basically a full-time Hoffa watcher, and the written product of this experience got me my doctorate the following year. It was entitled "Union-Employer Relations in the Over-the-Road Trucking Industry," but it could just as accurately have been called "Jimmy Hoffa at Work," so totally did the colorful head of the Teamsters dominate the labor relations of that pivotal sector.

Years after his presumed 1975 murder, Hoffa's name continues to be remembered and to fascinate. It is known to millions who could not, if their lives depended on it, identify the current presidents of such major unions as the Automobile Workers, the Steelworkers, and indeed the Teamsters. It has been my experience, too, that a labor relations professor who can say that he knew Hoffa has to this day at least one entirely positive factor going for him in the classroom. Three years ago, in even more of a testimonial, a reporter for the University of Delaware student newspaper informed me that I had been selected as the subject of a feature story strictly on the strength of my long-ago trucking industry study: "No other professor here has ever done anything as interesting," he told me.

This last tribute to Hoffa's continuing hold was undoubtedly too generous. But it provided all the motivation that I needed. From that day on, the writing of this full-scale biography was, I think, inevitable.

In returning to the Hoffa scene, I have interviewed, often at great length, most of the key people in the Teamster leader's life who are still around. In particular, the considerable cooperation that I received from the following should not go unrecognized: Murray Chodak, Barbara Hoffa Crancer, Robert E. Crancer, Richard Fitzsimmons, James P. Hoffa, Robert Holmes, Joseph Konowe, Rolland McMaster, Ralph Orr, Angeline Pall, Vincent Piersante, Sr., Larry Steinberg, and Jack Wood.

I have also drawn on the printed work of many others in this project. I have possibly read every word that appeared on Hoffa between 1952 and 1975 in the *New York Times,* the *Wall Street Journal, Time, Newsweek, U.S. News & World Report,* and *Business Week* and have religiously scrutinized both the McClellan committee record and the records of Hoffa's court cases. In addition, numerous books, articles, and other documents that could shed light on specific aspects of the unionist's life were read: all are cited in the note section at the end of this volume. I found the contributions by Ralph and Estelle Dinerstein James, Steven Brill, Jim Clay, Dan Moldea, Lester Velie, and Walter Sheridan especially valuable. Nor has "Union-Employer Relations in the Over-the-Road Trucking Industry" been ignored; portions of three of the sixteen chapters (chapters 8, 9, and 10) bear, in fact, a definite indebtedness to it.

I would also be remiss if I did not extend my gratitude to my faculty colleagues at the University of Delaware, for their encouragement of and interest in this project (and most especially to William V. Gehrlein, acting chairman of the Business Administration Department, during the time that I took the sabbatical that brought much of this work to its fruition); my graduate assistant Gina Gempesaw, who aided immeasurably in bringing much of the source material together; and University staffers Nancy Sanderson and Myrt Werkheiser, who cheerfully and competently provided a variety of secretarial services.

In addition, Rita M. Beasley typed every word of the manuscript and contributed many suggestions to make me look better, and her daughter, Amy C. Beasley, made this a family affair by ably compiling the index. Members of The MIT Press staff also in various ways rendered considerable help. Most of all, I appreciate the support that the other members of my family—my wife, Louise, and my daughters Amy and Laura—gave to me throughout the process.

Hoffa

The Early Years

1

More than once, he said that no one would remember him ten years after his death. But well beyond this decade, Jimmy Hoffa's name is undoubtedly more familiar to most Americans than that of any present-day labor leader. Quite possibly it is better known than the names of all but a relative handful of twentieth-century personalities of any kind. In this matter, as in some others, the man who once told one of his many attorneys that "I may have faults, but being wrong ain't one of them" has been proven wrong.

To be sure, much of Hoffa's posthumous image is, as it was in his lifetime, both highly simplistic and quite negative. Hoffa is believed by many to have been a kind of latter-day Al Capone who lived by the sword and ultimately, by presumed Mafia murder in 1975, died by it. His name conjures up widespread impressions of a dictator-president of a scandal ridden and overly powerful Teamsters Union (itself, in this popular conception, the deserved object of such jibes as "How many Teamsters does it take to screw in a light bulb? Ten. You got a problem with that?"). He is viewed in many quarters as the entirely worthy, and eventually twice-convicted, recipient of Attorney General Robert F. Kennedy's prosecutorial attention.

Others, however, to this day see Hoffa in a more favorable light. To some, he was a hero-villain in the mold of a Jimmy Cagney, operating on instinct whether pushing a half grapefruit into his girl friend's face (as Cagney did in the classic movie *Public Enemy*) or rabbit-punching his enemies ("You dirty rats") and invariably in the process exuding self-confidence and courage. The name Hoffa invokes visions, too, of a workaholic union president who was both amazingly accessible to his hundreds of thousands of truck driver constituents ("You got a problem. Call me. Just pick up the phone") and hugely successful in improving their incomes and working conditions.

Also part of the image is, often, Hoffa as a highly intelligent, perhaps even brilliant labor leader with a total grasp of trucking industry economics. And so is an impression of a devoted husband and father who more than made up in the quality of his relationship with his family what the demands of his union work denied the latter in terms of quantity of time spent.

Hoffa's middle name was Riddle, and more than a few observers have pointed out that he was in fact a mass of contradictions. He possessed a considerable temper and thought nothing of publicly tongue-lashing some of his closest associates. But he was capable of enormous kindness, was consistently financially generous to a fault, and as Teamster president seemed to be constitutionally unable to fire anyone. He prided himself on being an outstanding character reader and evaluator of people. But he was in fact, as one of his best friends could say long after his death, "one of the world's worst" such assessors. He was an unpolished speaker who regularly mangled the English language, although he improved to some extent through the years. But his effect on Teamster audiences was frequently little short of spellbinding (a close adviser once told him when Hoffa proudly pointed out that in a just-concluded speech he had received five standing ovations, "Jimmy, if you said 'Goddam you, lie down and die,' you'd get a standing ovation"), and he could electrify non-Teamster, and nonunion, audiences as well. He was intellectually curious and had a voracious appetite for news. Yet he apparently never read a book in adulthood ("I don't read books. I read union contracts") until his prison years, when his daughter convinced him to embark on a reading program in an effort to stave off boredom.

He was also, despite his celebrity status, a very private person who did not like anyone outside of his immediate family, especially women, to touch him. He was capable of great affection, although he used it sparingly. He regularly expressed hostility toward the media and academia, but few leaders at any level have ever been as unstinting of their time to interviewers from both quarters. His closest friends and advisers included both dedicated socialist intellectuals and dedicated gangsters. He could say, after learning of John F. Kennedy's assassination, "I hope the worms eat his eyes out," yet he also sent one hundred baskets of fruit, costing $75 each in late 1971, to the families of people who had been in the federal penitentiary in Lewisburg, Pennsylvania, with him. Whatever else might be said of him, he was interesting.

Quite fittingly, James R. Hoffa's entrance into the world—on February 14, 1913, in Brazil, Indiana—contained its own element of color. The sole general practitioner in that small central-western Indiana town had consistently maintained during Viola Riddle Hoffa's pregnancy that the swelling in her abdomen was a tumor, and the arrival of the Valentine's Day baby therefore came as a definite surprise. The third of four children—two boys and two girls all born within a four-year span—the future Teamster chief executive was named after his father's brother James and was given his mother's family name as his middle name. But for the first few days of his life he was apparently known simply as "The Tumor."

Hoffa's father, John Cleveland Hoffa, was a coal driller of Pennsylvania Dutch lineage. He and his two brothers constituted the third generation of his family to live in the western part of Indiana after their grandparents migrated there from Pennsylvania in the mid-1830s. He was a handsome six-footer with powerful shoulders and a brawny frame, and his son Jimmy could point with pride years after his death to snapshots of him that corroborated the general family claims that he was a "striking man, strong yet graceful."[1] Following completion of the ninth grade, he went to work for a coal prospector who needed an assistant to help him operate his steam-powered drilling rig and with the latter traversed several western Indiana counties, itinerants searching for mines. In the summer of 1908, as a twenty-eight-year-old boarder at a farmhouse near Jessup, Indiana, he met a quiet, attractive eighteen-year-old Irish-American neighbor, Viola "Ola" Riddle. He married her the following spring.

His chosen career took John away from his wife and, in short order, his four young children much of the time. But he was by all accounts a loving husband and a devoted father. As Jimmy Hoffa could later say of his parent,

When he was home [in Brazil] it was like Fourth of July every day. When he took a breather from work, he cast it aside entirely. My sisters and brother and I recall that he seemed to get a lot of enjoyment out of us kids. He actually played with us—played our games: hide 'n' seek, and tag, and marbles. And he'd take us fishing out near Harmony, in Fish Creek. We'd stop at Grandpa Hoffa's blacksmith shop and . . . drop in at the drugstore for a phosphate drink. Whenever a circus or a carnival or a medicine show came to town he'd be sure to take us if he was home.

He had big, hard, comfortable hands that made you feel secure when you crossed the street, and he had a deep resonant voice that, though seldom raised, commanded attention.[2]

These happy memories were, unfortunately, based upon very few years. In 1920, when the younger Hoffa was seven years old, his father died—"a victim of the mines" because of "coal dust [poisoning]" according to official Teamsters Union publicity but more probably because of a major stroke. And Viola, who was already taking in laundry to supplement her husband's relatively meager income, was now forced to take on additional employment to support her family and to serve as both mother and father as well.

Nothing if not strong-willed, the new widow attempted to keep the family together in Brazil by cooking in a restaurant on Main Street, doing housework for the wealthier townspeople, and accepting even more washing. Her older daughter Jennetta helped her with the ironing while her two sons did the delivering. Jimmy and his one-year-older brother Billy also helped the family finances in other ways: to augment the food supply at the Hoffa table, the two typically barefooted small-town boys stole apples and pears, shot rabbits and trapped birds, and strung clam lines in the local river.

Opportunities remained limited and the pay modest in the drab mining town, however, and Viola was finally forced to move her brood—first to Clinton, Indiana, in 1922, and two years later to the West Side of Detroit, where boom times in the automobile industry were attracting thousands of immigrants from the rural Midwest and South. After first working in a Detroit laundry, she took a job in an automotive parts production line and eventually became a polisher of radiator caps in the Fisher Body Fleetwood plant. As her son Jimmy saw her, she "worked damned hard and always looked tired."[3]

One of her daughters-in-law was later to say of her, frequently, "Oh, she's mean!" And a granddaughter remembers her as being "kind of sour," while one of her grandsons has described her as a "selfish old frontier woman who looked as though she came across the country in a stagecoach." But whatever the later Viola Riddle Hoffa was like, there is no question that she held her family together in these critical years and that she ingrained in her children a respect for hard work. Unwilling to risk spoiling her offspring by sparing the rod, she used both the razor strop and castor oil as weapons of discipline for all of them, but particularly her two sons, when they failed to live up to her Protestant ethic. All four children played meaningful roles at early ages in generating the family's income—the eleven-year-old Jimmy by bagging groceries at C. L. Smith's grocery store every weekend and by cleaning basements, loading and unloading trucks, and doing a variety of other odd jobs after school.

Academically, the four Hoffa children were enrolled at Detroit's Neinas Intermediate School, whose records show James R. Hoffa to have been a low B student who excelled only in gymnastics and track. At Neinas, the future labor leader was also remembered as a boy who, as many others in that era, had won social acceptance from his classmates with his fists after having been scoffed at by them for being a "hillbilly."

According to the official Teamsters Union publicity, Hoffa "finished the ninth grade" and "never went back to school again."[4] At least at one time in adulthood, on the other hand, Hoffa claimed just seven school grades, insisting that the other two grades existed only in the mind of "some sharp public relations man, trying to make me look educated." And the mystery is compounded by the fact that years later, on at least one occasion, Hoffa specifically referred to his graduation from the ninth grade,[5] while on another he stated that he completed his education in 1927, "when I was fourteen and was to enter ninth grade."[6]

Under any circumstances, he dropped out of school at least three years short of being a high school graduate and with no more education than the relatively modest amount that his coal driller father had achieved more than thirty years earlier in Indiana. As he could say of his decision in later years, he had simply "had it" as far as formal schooling was concerned: he had enjoyed making money from his after-school and weekend pursuits; now he wanted to earn a full-time income.

Hoffa's first posteducational position, nonetheless, hardly overwhelmed him with riches. For working as a stock boy at the downtown Detroit department store of Frank & Cedar's ten hours a day and six days a week, he received a weekly paycheck of $12. Even for a young teenager, the pay was skimpy, but he enjoyed the work and liked his co-workers and supervisors. Moreover, he had few material wants at the time (fishing, walking, and reading newspapers and magazines were his major hobbies, and he rarely dated). And living at home, as he continued to do, effected a mutually beneficial financial arrangement for Viola and himself: he gave his mother his entire paycheck, and she returned to him what he needed for his personal expenses.

He was often to refer to his two years at Frank & Cedar's as a happy time. He gave serious thought while there to the possibilities of becoming a clerk and even, despite his limited education, to joining ultimately the ranks of the Frank & Cedar's management—a goal that in fact might have been realized had he maintained it, for the hard-working and bright teenager was well thought of by his superiors.

The stock market crash of 1929 and the arrival of the Great Depression, however, ended any chance that Hoffa would become a department store tycoon. Almost overnight, the pleasant working environment of Frank & Cedar's deteriorated into one of significant job insecurity. The good-natured employee bantering that had greatly appealed to Hoffa and that he had constantly participated in was now replaced by seriousness. Layoffs took place, followed by the imposition of far greater work loads for those retained and a consequent mass plummeting of morale. The sixteen-year-old stock boy decided to look elsewhere.

His search was particularly influenced by two considerations. One was the sheer logic of the advice given him by an older friend, Walter Murphy: "Get into the food business. No matter what happens, people have to eat." And the other, not inconsistent with the first, was the fact that Hoffa had a considerable number of contacts at the Kroger Grocery and Baking Company. He had worked at Kroger stores on several occasions during his school days. Moreover, the company's main offices and warehouses were located just a few blocks from his home on the West Side, and many friends and neighbors were also Kroger employees.

One of these friends was Kroger warehouse worker James Langley, a boarder at the Hoffa home, who had fallen in love with Hoffa's sister Jennetta and would eventually marry her. When Hoffa expressed an interest in entering the food industry, Langley took his future brother-in-law down to the Kroger warehouse at Fort and Green streets and told the night foreman there that Hoffa was eighteen years of age. On the strength of the contact, the lie, and Hoffa's muscular appearance (although only five feet, five and one-half inches, he weighed a solid 170 pounds and had arms like shovels), he was hired to unload railroad cars full of lettuce, carrots, and strawberries for 32 cents an hour.

The hourly rate, even considering that two-thirds of it was paid in scrip redeemable for food at Kroger's markets, was considerably better than the 20 cents that he had been making at the department store. But the job also carried with it some definite negatives. Although the warehouse workers had to report in at 4:30 P.M. for the twelve-hour shift, they were paid only for the time that they actually worked unloading the boxcars, and sometimes worked as few as three hours a day (although at other times they could in fact be held over and given as much as twenty hours of work). The rest of the time, they would merely sit around, idle and unpaid, waiting to be called. While they could earn over $15 for a forty-eight-hour week, they typically had to be around for sixty hours at the very least to receive this kind of money.

The other negative of consequence was the presence of night shift foreman Al Hastings—"the kind of guy," Hoffa was to tell an interviewer three decades later, "who causes unions."[7] Hastings, Hoffa recalled, "was called 'the Little Bastard' by all the men. This guy was a real sadist. He thoroughly enjoyed screaming out commands and then cursing a man and threatening to fire him if he didn't move quick enough. He was a little tin Jesus in the warehouse and the only time he smiled was when he had fired somebody. Nor, at that time, was there any appeal, any form of job security."[8]

In fact, the level of job insecurity was enormous, given the economic conditions of the period. Long lines of unemployed men, hoping to be chosen to fill the positions of those whom Hastings and the other foremen fired, regularly stretched around the warehouse, and the company was thus invariably freed from the need to worry about replacements. Rubbing salt into the workers' wounds was the fact that relatives of the Kroger's foremen were routinely given priority when the work was assigned. Often, employees (who were frequently husbands and fathers) were simply fired, summarily and without any other reason, to create jobs for these relatives.

Hoffa and his friends on the shift bided their time. As one of these friends—Bobby Holmes, who would rise with Hoffa through the Teamster hierarchy in Detroit—would subsequently recall, they didn't at first specifically talk much about unionism even in the face of this "enormous cruelness." Strikes were illegal in Michigan at the time, and the huge pool of unemployed could be freely tapped as strikebreakers to replace permanently those out on strike in any event. But they ultimately concluded that forming a labor organization was the only logical course for them to follow. They quietly talked up the benefits of unionism among their 175 fellow warehousemen. Five of them agreed to be union leaders: in addition to the now eighteen-year-old Hoffa and Holmes, one year Hoffa's senior, these included Hoffa's equally youthful brother-in-law-to-be, Langley, another late teenager, Frank Collins, and Sam Calhoun, at thirty-six the elder statesman of the group. And one night, in the spring of 1931, shortly after two men were discharged for following their longstanding practice of going to a nearby food cart for their midnight meal, they acted.

Just as a truck filled with highly perishable Florida strawberries pulled into the warehouse, the new union leaders called a work stoppage. Faced with the need to get the cargo unloaded and refrigerated quickly, the management capitulated within an hour. On condition that the strikers go back to work, it agreed to meet with the leaders the next morning, and, following several days of negotiations, Hoffa and his colleagues had a union contract. It included a pay raise of 13 cents an hour, the guarantee of at least half a day's pay, a modest insurance plan, and the designation of an eating room for the workers. It also granted recognition to the union, which shortly thereafter applied for and received a charter as Federal Local 19341 of the American Federation of Labor.

Calhoun, whose age stood him in good stead among his younger cohorts and who also gained respect from the fact that he had been an active unionist when he worked for the Railway Express Agency, was the most influential single leader throughout this sequence of events at Kroger's. Proud of his sense of timing, he had successfully restrained the others from going out on strike until what constituted in his opinion the ideal moment. And his general bargaining sophistication had combined with a calm temperament to make him an effective chief spokesman in the subsequent contract negotiations. He was elected president of the new little single-company union by acclamation, with Hoffa as his vice-president and Holmes as secretary-treasurer.

But Hoffa, who readily acknowledged an indebtedness to Calhoun all of his life, also played a major role in the Kroger happenings. Clay, whose research into these days remains definitive, has concluded that "in the last days before the strawberry strike Jimmy displayed uncanny ability in enlisting the support of his fellow workers. He was a born organizer. [As] William Crow, one of his earliest recruits, said: 'He stood right close up to you and looked right at you. He can really look at you. His face was, well, open. He was the sincere-est little guy I've ever seen. He gave me confidence. Up to then I'd been scared to join a union but Jimmy made me feel that it was just the right thing to do.' "[9]

A year later, Hoffa, who had continued to work at Kroger's nights while working for his fledgling union during the day, was out of a job at the grocery company. The "Little Bastard," who had never forgiven him for his role in the strawberry incident, finally goaded the quick-tempered Hoffa into an act of insubordination (throwing a crate of vegetables on the floor at Hastings's feet, causing it to break and to shower the foreman with its contents). Hoffa would afterward insist that he had quit before Hastings could fire him, but in any event his Kroger days were abruptly over. Within twenty-four hours, he had accepted a job offer that his growing reputation as an effective union organizer had generated for him: as a full-time organizer for Joint Council 43, the Detroit jurisdictional unit of another American Federation of Labor affiliate, the International Brotherhood of Teamsters.

The union whose name would be inextricably linked with that of J. R. Hoffa, and which would within a relatively few years become the nation's largest and strongest labor organization, was anything but large and strong when Hoffa went to work for it in 1932. It remained a small and rather inconspicuous craft union made up primarily of drivers of such specialized products as coal, foodstuffs, and ice a third of a century after its founding as an international. Indeed, its membership had actually declined somewhat over the previous eleven years—from eighty-three thousand in 1921 to seventy-eight thousand in 1932—and now included not significantly more than the fifty-six thousand members whom the Teamsters had counted as far back as 1904.

Established in 1899, when nine midwestern locals requested and received a charter from the AFL as the Team Drivers International Union, the new organization was originally plagued by a severe internal cleavage. In an 1899 compromise, its executive board had agreed to accept as members along with employee-drivers all men owning no more than five teams of horses. The owners quickly made use of their superior numbers to control the union, and employee interests were sufficiently overlooked to foster a large and disgruntled employee-driver minority.

In 1902 the teamster locals in Chicago, representing the bulk of this opposition, disgustedly withdrew from the Team Drivers and launched a new organization. Their Teamsters National Union limited membership solely to nonowner teamsters, teamster helpers, and owners of no more than one team. Attracting a new market by such a policy, the TNU actually surpassed the parent international's enrollment of fourteen thousand members within a few months.

The Chicago Teamsters pressed much more vigorously for higher wages and shorter hours than the Team Drivers had done, although earnings of $12 for an eighty-hour workweek were still common. They also developed the concept of the teamster as a skilled craftsman, to be distinguished from the thousands of unskilled workers who were flocking to Chicago from the rural Midwest and Europe at this time. Both of these doctrines—called, collectively, "wage and trade" unionism—were strongly to shape the direction of future Teamster leadership.

There was a less commendable side to Teamster activities in

Chicago, however. Much racketeering and collusion with employers accompanied the new unionism. The great labor economist John R. Commons, in fact, declared that it was not until 1903 that teaming in the city could be studied as an economic rather than a criminal phenomenon.[10] And another scholar wrote, "In Chicago, the teamsters' badge is still as it has been for years, to a considerable extent an insignia of criminal association."[11]

In 1903, exerting the pressure of his office, AFL president Samuel Gompers persuaded the two rival internationals to merge. A new body, the International Brotherhood of Teamsters, was thereupon awarded an AFL charter and opened its first headquarters in Indianapolis. The founders of the Teamsters National Union, by virtue of their now greater membership, won the issue over which they had originally seceded: owners of more than one team could not join the IBT. Now in a conciliatory mood, however, the union elected as its first president the former Team Drivers Union president, Cornelius P. Shea of Boston.

Shea's regime was a short one. Soon controlled by the Chicago crowd, he won little respect among more law-abiding Teamsters. He was indicted for conspiracy, and acquitted only to find himself under sustained attack by the press as a racketeer. He was also threatened with secession by still-dissatisfied reform elements. At the 1907 convention, with one large local having left the international the previous year following a disastrous strike in Chicago and with his treasury showing a significant deficit, he was defeated for the presidency by another Bostonian, Daniel J. Tobin.

The garrulous Tobin had presided over the union ever since and had established the Teamsters on a permanent footing in these years, which saw local truck driving almost completely displace local horse team cartage. That his first twenty-five years in office showed little more accomplishment than this, however, has generally been attributed to four factors, three of them directly involving Tobin himself:

1. The second Teamster president had remained every bit as craft-conscious as the old Chicago Teamsters had been. He had, with an absence of diplomacy perhaps rivaled only by Marie Antoinette, deemed unskilled workers to be "rubbish" and "riffraff." And he had constantly warned his membership against accepting any but the most highly skilled trucking company employees, in

the interests of a cohesive union. This attitude, by definition, had lowered the IBT's organizational potential.

2. Tobin had guarded the union's funds as closely as he had his own. While he was ever the conservative, this policy did not rest primarily on parsimony. The international was far from wealthy at the time, but its president's repeated attempts to increase per capita monthly dues payments were regularly rebuffed at Teamster conventions: he had, in fact, been able to raise the amount only once since 1907, in 1920, when the original 15 cents had been doubled. Hence, the IBT leader was merely recognizing an obvious necessity for caution. His unwillingness to spend in such directions as organizational campaigns (even among the highly skilled unorganized), however, did not forward the Teamster membership size.

3. At least as important as any other factor during the last decade of this 1907–1932 period had been the early attitude of the international's leadership toward the fast-growing intercity or "over-the-road" trucking sector. Tobin and his key lieutenants had viewed these long-distance operations with suspicion. They saw in the new activities only a serious threat to the market and competitive standards of their local cartage employers, whose drivers formed the heart of the Brotherhood at this time. That the newer drivers might also be converted into Teamsters seemed to escape them entirely. Moreover, the traditional localized joint council structure of the IBT provided no easy method of organizing workers whose jobs carried them across the jurisdictions of several joint councils.

4. Excepting only the World War I period (1916–1920), this period had been one of the low gains for all of organized labor. Concerted employer resistance and governmental antipathy allowed total U.S. union membership to rise only from 1,824,000 to 2,560,000 between 1903 and 1916. And in the 1920s and early 1930s these two adverse elements had combined with employer-sponsored welfare programs and a decline in price levels to cause a major decrease in the labor membership totals: from 4,722,000 in 1921 to 3,226,000 by 1932. There had been no special reason for the Teamsters to escape this pattern.

Teamster resources in Detroit in 1932 were even more modest than those of the national organization. They were, in fact, almost nonexistent. In the entire city, there were only five hundred IBT members, in just two locals.

One of these locals was the debt-ridden Commission House Drivers, Warehouse, Produce, and Fish Employees Local 674. It had just lost a long and bitter strike in the fish industry and was near extinction when new organizer Hoffa, in return for taking the Kroger union with him into it, was given its charter. The other, whose three hundred members Tobin had placed under national Teamster trusteeship (or direct administrative control from Indianapolis) because of financial and electoral improprieties, was the even more impoverished union of General Truck Drivers, Local 299. Not a single labor agreement covered its constituents, and few of these members were paying any dues to the union at all in this Depression period.

As an organizer, Hoffa received no salary. His sole remuneration was a small percentage of the dues of each new dues payer whom he recruited for the Teamsters.

Nor were his working conditions any more attractive. Union organizers were made to feel anything but welcome by the Detroit employers of the early 1930s. It was not for nothing that the city was then known as the "open shop capital of America": Henry Ford, who had called labor unions "the worst thing that ever struck the earth, because they take away a man's independence," reportedly kept a pool of five thousand toughs, many of them ex-convicts, on hand at his motor company to be used as strikebreakers; and most employers of any size were prepared to repel unionization by physical force if necessary.

Hoffa, universally remembered by his associates from these days as having been absolutely fearless, received several beatings, at least one of them severe enough to require stitches. But within a year he had organized the rest of Kroger's workers, some four hundred who worked away from the Fort and Green Streets loading dock, as well as several hundred other Detroit area dockworkers.

He also, between 1933 and 1935, made visible inroads in organizing the truck drivers who were transporting new automobiles from Detroit to dealerships all over the country—the so-called "truckaway, driveaway, and car hauler" group. In this case the general approach of the indefatigable and well-informed Hoffa was to travel up and down the highways leading out of Detroit, pull up at the side of the road alongside sleeping truck drivers, wake them up, and give his sales pitch. One veteran car hauler of these days would subsequently describe a typical Hoffa performance:

I was about half way between Detroit and Cleveland. Guess I'd been sawing the wood for about twenty minutes when the door opening woke me up. I was still half asleep. This little guy looked up at me, grinning. I thought he was a bum looking for a ride. But he said, "My name is Hoffa. Can I talk with you about the Teamsters?" I said, "No, you can't. Now get out of here and let me sleep." He said, "Just five minutes; that's all I ask." Well, I was awake anyhow so I told him to go ahead.

He really bore in on me. I told him I was scared I'd get fired if I joined a union. He said by the time I got back to Detroit everybody would have joined. I told him I couldn't afford the dues. He said if we got organized I'd make it up in pay raises and more besides. I told him I didn't like unions anyhow. Them union guys was always causing trouble. He said in the Teamsters' Union I would be invited to all the meetings and the members called the shots. He had an answer for everything and he never let up. If I hadn't signed that membership card we'd still be there.[12]

None of this escaped the attention of Ray J. Bennett, a general organizer for the International and the man who had originally enticed Hoffa into becoming a Teamster organizer. In 1935, now the trustee for the bankrupt general freight Local 299, he appointed the twenty-two-year-old Hoffa that local's business agent, and thus its major day-to-day administrator, at a salary of $25 per week.

The promotion was, however, more apparent than real. Local 299 was, if anything, in even worse shape in 1935 than it had been three years earlier. Ten thousand dollars in the hole, it owed everyone money—even its landlord, who was threatening to evict it from its small, drab office on his premises for nonpayment of rent. Most of its membership, which had actually shrunk a bit, to 250 in 1935, was not working because of a strike. And even those who did have jobs supported their unit at best with indifference. The new business agent soon discovered that he would be lucky if the local's checkbook allowed him to pay himself even ten dollars weekly from its accounts; frequently, in his early months on the job, he could justify the issuance of only a $5 salary to himself.

Given the situation, as Bennett had recognized in advancing a young man with such strong organizing skills, Hoffa's obvious priority had to be placed on increasing the local's minuscule membership, thereby bolstering its untenable financial status through initiation fees and dues payments. And Hoffa and a close friend, the intelligent and tough Owen Bert Brennan, in short order embarked on an extensive program of trying to organize anyone who either drove a truck or worked on a loading platform: Local 299's General Truck Driver charter made all of them logical candidates. "We'd go out," Hoffa would recall, "hit the docks, talk to drivers, put up picket lines, conduct strikes, hold meetings day and night, convince people to join the union. . . . Pretty soon Local 299 was collecting dues all the way down to Evansville."[13]

As the Teamster successes grew, however, so did the need on the part of Hoffa and Brennan (and their cohorts, some of them the original "Strawberry Boys" from Kroger's) to fight it out with what the former called "hired thugs who were out to get us." As Hoffa subsequently reported,

Our cars were bombed out. Three different times, someone broke into the office and destroyed our furniture. Cars would crowd us off the streets. Then it got worse.

. . . Brother, your life was in your hands every day. There was only one way to survive—fight back. And we used to slug it out on the streets. They found out we didn't scare.

The police were no help. The police would beat your brains in for even talking union. The cops harassed us every day. If you went on strike, you got your head broken. The whole thing didn't take months—it took years.[14]

Hoffa in later years frequently declared that in his first year as a business agent alone, he was beaten up by policemen or strikebreakers "at least two dozen times" and that, in a sharp acceleration of these statistics from his pre-299 days, his scalp was laid open sufficiently as to necessitate stitches on no fewer than a half-dozen occasions. "I was hit so many times with night sticks, clubs, and brass knuckles," he once reminisced, "[that] I can't even remember where the bruises were."[15] He did remember, though, that more than once he and his fellow organizers were required to pay cash in advance for emergency room treatment at hospitals, a condition that was rarely extracted from people in other kinds of occupations and that served as one more indignity.

He charged, too, that the son of the owner of the General Tobacco Company, which was being peacefully picketed by the Teamsters in this momentous year, shot his brother Billy Hoffa in the stomach in the mistaken belief that he was shooting the head of Local 299.

It is also a matter of record that Hoffa's Teamsters freely also used their own muscle not just defensively but offensively in these days. Hoffa himself bragged that in the 1930s he had a list of arrests for picket-line fighting and similar union duty misconduct "that's maybe as long as your arm." He often described with pride the physical damage that he and his friends inflicted on strikebreakers and, on occasion, members of competitive unions ("I can hit back and I did. Guys who tried to break me up got broken up").[16] He was once put in jail eighteen times within a twenty-four-hour period during a strike—most probably a North American record ("Every time I showed up on the picket line, I got thrown in jail. Every time they released me, I went back to the picket line")—although Hoffa appears to have been guiltless in this situation and the sequence was very likely nothing more than the extreme use of a common police harassment tactic of the day.

A close associate from these days even claims that he saw the young Local 299 leader run over an adversary who wouldn't get out of the way of his automobile, thereby breaking one of his legs. "Jimmy did whatever he had to do," says this old colleague, with admiration. And while Hoffa was generally armed only with his fists, as were his fellow Teamsters ("In that era, it was considered a disgrace if you used anything other than your hands," a charter member of Hoffa's local recently explained), on at least one occasion he used a baseball bat to emphasize a point to a Sears Roebuck company strikebreaker. He was also once identified as one of four men who beat up a rival labor union organizer with automobile tire chains. In 1937, he was convicted of assault and battery on a picket line and fined $10.

Over the next nine years, Hoffa was, indeed, to receive two more convictions. In 1940 he had to pay $500 when he pleaded *nolo contendere* to a charge of conspiracy to monopolize the wastepaper trades in cooperation with several unionized companies. (His plea of no contest, he said, was "nothing against a man. Even General Motors has pleaded *nolo*."[17]) And in 1946 he was charged with extortion for demanding that a variety of small retail grocers buy permits from the Teamsters to operate their own trucks while bringing goods from the markets to their stores: he pleaded guilty to a lesser labor law misdemeanor, was placed on two years' probation, fined $500, and ordered to return the $7,600 he had already collected from the grocers. In these years, he was also arrested on thirteen other occasions, not even counting those related to the picket lines, on charges such as participation in an assault and shooting, but all of these other charges—each of them also directly related to his union activities—were dismissed.

Hoffa bore all as a badge of competence. In his opinion, any labor organizer in Detroit in those days "who didn't get in trouble with the police was either buying them off or he wasn't doing his job."[18]

He was also quite intolerant of those who by his definition lacked physical courage. "Once a bunch of dissidents," a veteran of this period recalled not long ago, "came up to 299 for one purpose, to whip our ass. There were four or five of us—including a guy named Brady, an ex-prize fighter—in the union office and maybe ten or twelve of them and they were getting the best of us for a while, although we finally got them out in the street and won that brawl. But Brady didn't perform well; he showed some cowardice. Jimmy said 'You son of a bitch; you don't work here no more.' And Brady was finished as far as his days with the union were concerned."

Not that the youthful organizer was completely foolhardy. As he later observed, "For sport sometime you should go around trying to wake up a sleeping [car hauler] truck driver, preferably some fellow with a couple of thousand miles of hard driving stretching before him. He's not noted for cordiality and hospitality."[19] Drivers in those Depression days, well aware that they were natural targets for thieves as they catnapped alone in their vehicles, frequently slept with tire irons or spanner wrenches in their hands and were quite willing to use them at the slightest sign of an intruder. Hoffa learned to identify himself "with a rapid-fire introduction": "Hi-I'm-Jimmy-Hoffa-Organizer-for-the-Teamsters-and-I-wonder-if-I-could-talk-to-you. Then I'd duck back."[20]

Sometimes, the lack of hospitality that greeted Hoffa at this point was such that he would abort his overture on the spot. More than once, the seemingly innocuous cab turned out to be occupied by employer-hired thugs who emerged, billy clubs swinging, to convey a "warning" to the Local 299 leader (not long afterward the Teamsters implemented a policy of having their Detroit organizers travel in pairs). And, always, such police tactics as the unwarranted issuance of traffic violation tickets, accompanied by a full search of Hoffa's vehicle for "dangerous weapons," had to be reckoned with.

But the ambitious, aggressive Hoffa was not easily deterred. And, as they already had done with so many drivers and other workers, his persuasiveness and tirelessness combined with a dedication to the Teamsters Union that seemed to be quite sincere to win him, with the help of Brennan and the others, many converts. By the end of 1937, not only were the car haulers substantially organized but several thousand additional warehousemen and local truck drivers also were. And Hoffa was free to turn the bulk of his attention to the rapidly increasing number of over-the-road truck drivers, Tobin's lack of enthusiasm for organization of these drivers notwithstanding.

In this newer effort, Hoffa was significantly influenced by a highly unlikely source—Teamster Local 574 in Minneapolis, which was controlled by a group of dissident Communists.

The Minneapolis Teamster unit hardly typified the conservative IBT at the time. Its leaders—the brothers Vincent, Grant, and Miles Dunne, a former lumberjack named Karl Skoglund, and the young organizer, Farrell Dobbs—were all followers of Leon Trotsky, while most Teamsters preferred Franklin D. Roosevelt. It enthusiastically favored organizing unskilled workers, Tobin's "rubbish" and "riffraff." And it advocated maximum use of the strike weapon, which Tobin had tried to exercise only as a last resort.

Particularly inspired by the creative Dobbs, the five men first set out, in 1933, to organize all Minneapolis coal yard workers, regardless of skill or the jurisdiction of other unions. They quickly realized this goal, although only after a bitter strike which resulted in at least two deaths and sixty-seven injuries.

Their attention then moved to over-the-road trucking. As their newspaper asserted, "With the [intercity] trucking industry rapidly replacing the railroads in the handling of freight, the truckdrivers' union becomes the dominating factor in labor organization." They also recognized in these columns, far-sightedly, that it was impossible "to have an island of truckdrivers isolated in one place like the workers of a coal tipple or a woolen mill."[21]

The Trotskyites initially made use of their existing control of the Minneapolis truck terminals. By refusing to let Local 574 men unload incoming trucks unless fellow Teamsters were driving them, they soon forced the out-of-town owners to bargain with them. The newly-enrolled Teamsters then went on to organize the next terminal, and the "leapfrogging" spread.

But the imagination of these Teamsters did not stop here. The Minneapolis leaders organized the warehousemen by restricting the services of their drivers to Teamster-represented warehouses. Then they prohibited the warehousemen from accommodating goods that had not been union made (and union delivered), thereby recruiting a large variety of factory workers as well.

By 1937 many thousands of midwestern members had been won for the Teamsters by this process, and the Trotskyites were generally, if quite begrudgingly, being recognized by other Teamsters as having been the greatest single cause of the appreciable IBT growth in this period—from 75,000 in 1933 to 277,000 in 1937.

One problem remained for the Minneapolis Teamsters. The new over-the-road drivers (as well as the other worker types) had, through diplomatic necessity, been shared with many other IBT locals scattered throughout the Midwest. All such locals were now vulnerable, if they continued to bargain separately, to the lowest wage scale in any of the cities. In the low-investment intercity trucking industry, the owner could easily benefit from wage differentials by moving his terminals to the low-wage areas.

Dobbs therefore, in 1937, took the lead in joining together for contract negotiations for all affected Teamster locals. The first such organization, the North Central District Drivers Council, soon became the Central States Drivers Council. As such, it represented most over-the-road drivers in the twelve midwestern states, and Dobbs was attempting to have it sign a master regional contract establishing identical wages and other conditions of employment throughout this area, notwithstanding the fact that there was no such centralized authority on the employer's side: he would devise some pressure tactic to drive the employers together.

Hoffa watched all of this in fascination. He developed a particular admiration for the innovative Dobbs, whom he was later to laud as a "very far-seeing individual . . . the draftsman and architect of our road operations" and of whose area-wide bargaining he would say, "I realized how right he was and it had an impact on my mind as to the fact that you could no longer live, no matter how well organized, in a particular city or state."[22]

The Detroiter was not at all sympathetic to Dobbs's political views (he steadfastly maintained all his life that Communists were "screwballs" and "nuts"). Nor would he find the Socialist Worker party activities that his fellow organizer would shortly thereafter embrace in lieu of his communism and, ultimately, of his labor movement leadership to be any more commendable (Dobbs was to be the Socialist Worker nominee for the U.S. presidency in four different national elections, ending in 1960). But he was willing to overlook what he considered Dobbs's ancillary values given what he saw as an overriding strength: "Farrell was," he thought, "a hell of an organizer."[23] Years later, he offered Dobbs an attractive salary, in vain, to get him to return and recruit more workers for the union.

Hoffa was not by any means the only admirer of Dobbs within the Teamsters. The craft-conscious Tobin regarded the latter with a conspicuous absence of enthusiasm, to be sure, and so did the majority of Teamster local leaders throughout the country. But Dobbs and his basic concepts of road driver strategic importance, leapfrogging, and areawide bargaining received backing from the influential IBT leadership in Chicago—and, in Detroit, from both of Hoffa's two superiors at the time, Bennett and the now-ranking Teamster in that city, Joseph "Red" O'Laughlin. Anxious to learn more directly from the master, Bennett and O'Laughlin invited themselves to Minneapolis in late 1937. They took with them their feisty young assistant, Jimmy Hoffa.

Hoffa sat and listened to Dobbs as he set forth his views by the hour and found his high second-hand opinion of the latter only confirmed by first-hand observation. "I was studying," he would often say later, "at the knees of a master." Dobbs in turn was impressed by Hoffa's intelligence, capacity for hard work, and own record of organizing successes. The Detroiter, Dobbs subsequently wrote, was "eager to learn and quick to absorb new ideas." Dobbs welcomed the chance to use Hoffa's talents briefly a few months later, when Bennett and O'Laughlin sent their subordinate back to Minneapolis—together with several of Hoffa's Strawberry Boy colleagues—to help Dobbs in his campaign to recruit those of the long-distance midwestern drivers who still remained outside the Teamster fold.

Hoffa remained to participate in Dobbs's ambitious 1938 attempt to have the seventy locals under the umbrella of his Central States Drivers Council negotiate a master regional agreement with the several hundred trucking employers in the twelve states.

The major national employer organization, the American Trucking Associations, had refused to enter this bargaining, claiming that it lacked authority to do so, and no other such centralized employer group existed. But in a brilliant move, Dobbs decided first to concentrate the negotiations on the key city of Chicago, which virtually all midwestern truck routes included, and then to try to implement whatever Chicago conditions he might extract here throughout the rest of the Midwest. The strategy, which Hoffa would subsequently copy, worked because the great majority of the employers wanted to be in on the critical Chicago bargaining that would affect them whether or not they participated in it, as would the general trucking strike that Dobbs was not at all hesitant in threatening. In short order, the managers had banded together in four associations comprising the Central States Employers Negotiating Committee.

Not long afterward, a historic areawide Central States agreement was signed by the parties. All road drivers were granted 2.75 cents per mile and 75 cents per hour for time lost due to pickups and deliveries, vehicle breakdowns, traffic congestion, and other delays—substantial increases over the terms of the expiring local contracts that the regional agreement replaced. Owner-operators, drivers of their own trucks, were to be paid for the rental of their equipment in addition to their wages as drivers. The union was granted a modified closed shop in which all drivers were required to belong to the Teamsters as a condition of their employment. And a grievance committee, with Dobbs as its chairman, was established to enforce these stipulations uniformly over the twelve-state area.

In the immediate aftermath of these 1938 negotiations, Dobbs did something else that was to remain etched in Hoffa's mind and that the latter would later emulate. In Omaha, the trucking employers had voiced their displeasure with the new contract by refusing to sign it and instead, in a move that threatened to undo much of Dobbs's work, locked out their employees. A strong state antipicketing law made it possible for the union to counter this tactic effectively, but Dobbs once again exhibited his prolific imagination.

After a thorough review of the companies' routes, Dobbs concluded that the friendlier city of Kansas City was the key to a solution: if the flow of trucking between Omaha and the Missouri city could be stopped, the Omaha truckers would have to come to terms with the Teamsters. The leading Teamster in Kansas City was another admirer of Dobbs and quickly agreed to strike the employers in his jurisdiction unless they suspended their dealings with Omaha. And the Nebraskans, thus isolated, soon withdrew their resistance to the master regional agreement. This secondary boycott approach (the exercise of economic pressure against one target to get it to exert pressure on another target that is actually the subject of the union's concern) was to become another Hoffa trademark ("You push a button in Kansas City and Omaha jumps," as he was to phrase it) in his own efforts toward other regional trucking agreements, and ultimately a nationwide one.

In point of fact, Dobbs was not the first person to consummate an areawide trucking agreement on behalf of the Teamsters. An aspiring IBT general organizer from Seattle, David D. Beck, had done so two years earlier, his master freight contract covering over-the-road drivers in Washington, Oregon, Idaho, and Montana. And while Beck was by his own admission indebted to the novel policies of the Local 574 leaders, in the same year that Dobbs and his colleagues were implementing their Drivers Council he actually introduced an even more significant bargaining device. He formed the Western Conference of Teamsters, encompassing the eleven western states and British Columbia. Both his 1936 Northwest agreement and the 1938 Central States contract constituted major departures from the traditional IBT practice of local autonomy. But Beck's new creation was the first administrative body to arise between the joint council and the international on an avowedly permanent basis.

The conference was, in turn, subdivided into twelve trade divisions (e.g., bakery, beverage, general hauling) to provide specialized organizing help to the various member joint councils and local unions. Joint council and local membership in both the conference and the divisions was, however, at first voluntary.

Although he frequently pointed to the economics of intercity trucking as the primary justification for the conference concept, Beck, as head of the structure, gained an efficient vehicle for exercising control over all Teamsters in the region. He could also make use of its new components to expand his membership in all fields.

In 1938, the conference's general hauling division, by far the largest trade unit, effected an eleven-state agreement bringing higher wages to the over-the-road drivers of 175 local unions. The pact was reportedly signed by two thousand employers. In other trades, however, contract negotiation remained on a local basis, as did the industries negotiated for.

Nineteen years older than Hoffa, the vain, portly Beck had come a long way from his economically depressed childhood by the later 1930s. He had sold newspapers in downtown Seattle when he was seven and, not unlike Hoffa, had dropped out of school early—in his case, at the age of sixteen to join his mother as an employee in a laundry. The efforts of both mother and son were needed to keep the wolf from the Beck family's door: Beck's father, a carpet cleaner, was unable to make ends meet by himself.

Beck had soon thereafter become both a laundry truck driver and a Teamster, had quickly decided on union leadership as a career, and had never looked back. In 1925, he had been elected president of his Seattle laundry drivers' local; the following year, as an official host for the IBT's national convention being held in Seattle, he had made a favorable impression on Tobin, who had appointed him to the general organizer's position.

Tobin's faith in Beck was almost immediately rewarded. By 1930, the former laundry driver had just about completely organized all Seattle truck drivers. He then expanded both the scope of his geography and his membership, using a paradoxical mixture of conservative "business unionism" to win over reluctant employers and physical violence to subdue rival unionists. He also stressed—to the West Coast longshoremen, Brewery Workers, and Newsboys' Union, many of whose members he recruited for the IBT—that while the Teamsters could do without their help in times of driver work stoppages, their (remaining) members depended greatly on Teamster support when they instituted picket lines. For over-the-road driver organization, his use of the "leapfrog" process was no less intensive than that of the Trotskyites. By 1936, few truck drivers on the entire West Coast remained for him to organize. His domain now also included more truck drivers "allied to truckdriving"—in the distributive, food, and dairy industries primarily—than did any other part of the IBT.

The carpet cleaner's son had also achieved by this time something that he had been completely denied in childhood and had avidly coveted ever since: social respectability. Although he frequently defined unions as "marketing cooperatives established to sell so many head of labor to employers at the highest market price," the fact that this price invariably also considered the employer's ability to pay won him many supporters in the business community. So did his almost obsessive identification with successful business executives as role models. (Later he would say, "I run the Teamsters the way Charley Wilson runs General Motors," and he more than once announced in his speeches, "For every enemy I make in the ranks of labor, I make two friends in the Chamber of Commerce.")

He cheerfully accepted and even solicited invitations to speak before management groups and counted some of Seattle's leading executives among his best friends. He was a prominent Elk and American Legionnaire, a major figure in the Veterans of Foreign Wars, and by the end of the 1930s had also served as Seattle boxing commissioner, chairman of the Seattle Civil Service Commission, and member of Washington State Board of Prison Terms and Paroles. In 1937, the mayor of Seattle said of him, "Dave Beck runs this town and it's a good thing that he does."

Tobin had by this time become somewhat ambivalent about the rising star in the West. He continued to value Beck's considerable competence as an organizer and had no quarrel with the latter's attainment of community status, although there is no evidence that he particularly prized this attainment, either. But he had come to have serious misgivings about Beck's creation of the Western Conference, officially because he viewed it as a "breeding ground for jealousy and internal politics" but more basically because Beck's new influence threatened his own. On the other hand, Tobin was realistic enough to recognize both the conference's role in expanding Teamster membership and Beck's deeply entrenched position. He therefore maintained a *modus vivendi* with his former appointee and even lavishly praised Beck's proven administrative competencies on occasion. And while the Western Conference was not formally recognized by the IBT constitution until 1947, it was effectively an autonomous unit controlled by Beck and not Tobin from the date of its founding. In 1940, with the full support of Tobin, Beck was elected an international vice president of the Teamsters Union. His new position and his existing West Coast power base made him a heavy favorite to succeed the old Bostonian as IBT president whenever Tobin decided to step down.

Being loaned out to Dobbs did not constitute the first special project that the Local 299 business agent had been assigned. Indeed, since accepting Bennett's offer almost three years earlier, Hoffa had been called upon to help a variety of people anxious to organize but not within the logical jurisdiction of his General Truck Drivers local—among them, grocery store clerks, brewery workers, department store employees, and laundry workers. The experience and contacts would in all cases be of value as he extended his influence both geographically and occupationally. In one case, the value had already been huge: helping a group of nonunionized but striking laundry employees on a cold March morning in 1936, he had met the eighteen-year-old Josephine Poszywak, whom he would shortly thereafter make Mrs. James R. Hoffa.

Even by the standards of the day, employment conditions at the downtown Detroit laundry had left much to be desired. The jobs paid a paltry seventeen cents an hour when the laundering machines were in operation and nothing at all when they were not. In a situation not unlike that which Hoffa himself had experienced a few years earlier as a boxcar unloader at Kroger's, moreover, the all-female laundry room labor force on some days could get only two or three hours of work. Nor could these employees leave the premises until the machines had sufficient bundles in them to justify turning them on: as in the situation at Kroger's and countless other workplaces in these depression years, a substantial pool of unemployed workers waited in the wings, allowing the employer to insist on terms that in the later twentieth century would seem absolutely draconian.

The women had first approached the International Laundry Workers Union, which had responded by encouraging them to go out on strike. With replacements for the strikers already hired, however, the laundry union had decided—on the grounds that the laundry's four drivers were members of the Teamsters Union—to request the assistance of the IBT.

The twenty-three-year-old Hoffa arrived on the scene with a set of "Management Unfair" signs. He then established a standard double-ringed picket line, those in the outer circle moving clockwise and those in the inner circle walking counterclockwise. He assumed a place in the outside line and as he passed the women walking counterclockwise tried to give each one a smile of encouragement. Then, as he later wrote, "it happened": "I was looking into the brightest pair of blue eyes I'd ever seen. They crinkled in the corners when she smiled back at me. Her hair was shining blond and although she was small and looked frail she walked erect and proud. I felt like I'd been hit on the chest with a blackjack."[24]

There appears to be little hyperbole here. Hoffa, who did in fact know how it felt to be hit on the chest with a blackjack, invited the attractive young Polish-American woman to go with him to the movies that night. From then on, he and Josephine Poszywak went together on a regular basis. The Teamster organizer, who had dated quite infrequently to that point and who is known to have had anything more than a tepid interest in only two other females—some three years earlier he had considered a young woman named Eileen to have been his "girl" for a short while and not long thereafter he had had a brief affair with a union clerical employee, Sylvia Pigano—proposed to Josephine a few months later. They were married by a justice of the peace in Bowling Green, Ohio, on September 24, 1936—a Saturday, following which they drove back to Detroit so that the bridegroom could be at work on Monday morning.

In many ways, the two Hoffas were exact opposites. The groom exuded physical well-being and strength ("He set a pace that needed, and got, a first-rate body," a lifelong friend has said). The bride was far from robust ("I was a skinny, scrawny little thing," she later told her daughter. "I don't know why Dad picked me with all of those prettier girls at the laundry to choose from"). She was, in fact, to be plagued all her life by poor health: rheumatic fever had damaged her heart when she was a young girl, and the drinking of unpasteurized milk had subsequently further weakened these muscles by giving her undulant fever; she was also prone to as many as four or five fainting spells a year, which were effectively countered by the administration of smelling salts but never satisfactorily explained.

In addition, the groom, although he had attended Sunday school at the Christian Church of Brazil, whose services were patterned after those of East Coast Congregational churches, was an atheist. The bride had been brought up as a devout Catholic and continued to think of herself as one even after she was excommunicated for having married outside the church.

In contrast to the groom's complete fearlessness, the bride was a constant worrier. Although he was a tightly wound man who was temperamentally unable to relax, he tended not to fret about things over which he had no control and would say, "If you see ten troubles coming down the road, don't worry about them. Nine will vanish before they ever get to you and the tenth won't turn out to be much of anything at all." A Hoffa friend of long standing remembers him as being, above all, a fatalist. She, among many other fears, would develop a phobia about being poor once again and would, in fact, sometimes have nightmares on this subject during their marriage. She also, after the Hoffa Detroit residence incurred a small fire caused by children playing with matches next door, worried constantly that there would be another fire and claimed that from that day on she was always frightened by the sound of a siren.

More than this, Josephine's Polish-American roots ran very deep. She had been educated in Polish-sponsored parochial schools in the Polish language and had an abiding affection for both Polish music and Polish weddings (one friend from her laundry worker days has described her as "strictly ethnic"). Her husband's Irish-American mother never quite forgave her son for having married such a "foreigner," and the relationship between the two women was distant from the beginning. Friends and relatives often described Josephine as "sweet"; insofar as is known, the adjective was never applied to her aggressive, two-fisted husband. If the groom was the complete professional, absolutely dedicated to his union, the bride was the complete homebody—never happier than when cooking, cleaning, and, starting in 1938 with the birth of Barbara, bringing up her two children. And while his desire to investigate and to learn about the larger world in which he operated was constant, the same could not be said of her.

The marriage of "Jo" and "Jimmy," as they called each other (he sometimes called her "Josie" or "Josephine," but she did not particularly like either of these names), would nonetheless be an unusually happy one for both of them. As Josephine's sister Angeline would say, "Jo really doted on Jim: he was the star performer in her life"; and she would always be what he often described as his "anchor . . . my whole life . . . the custodian of my happiness." That the two people were entirely devoted to each other would never be doubted by anyone in a position of intimacy with the Hoffa family: the husband and wife relationship would from beginning to end be, in the words of one of these intimates, "a very smooth-running operation."

Whatever else could be said of Hoffa as an evaluator of people, he could not be faulted in his choice of a mate.

Hoffa's relationship with Farrell Dobbs did not, in contrast, end at all happily.

Tobin's misgivings about the Minneapolis Trotskyites had never resulted in much concrete action by the Teamster president. The International Brotherhood of Teamsters was in these days not so much an international union, its title notwithstanding, as a collection of all-powerful local unions, each brooking no interference from the international headquarters within its own geographic area. Beck's West Coast empire hardly stood alone among the local fiefdoms, even though it was by far the largest of these. On the infrequent occasions when Tobin had tried to impinge on any of the strongly entrenched local autonomy (for example, in raising the per capita dues payments), he had generally been rebuffed.

In addition, the Local 574 leaders, especially the three Dunne brothers, remained enormously popular with their own rank and file. The international chief executive's only two real moves against the Communists had, in fact, both resulted in complete failure: in 1936 Tobin had established a rival Local 500 to win over the Local 574 membership; after this effort had culminated in no measurable success, he had merged the two locals into a new Local 544, which, however, was immediately dominated by Dobbs, the Dunnes, and Skoglund.

But by early 1941, Tobin was prepared to take stronger action. He had been granted somewhat greater power over the local unions by amendments made to the IBT constitution at the 1940 Teamster convention. Much more than this, he was becoming increasingly embarrassed, as a close friend of Franklin D. Roosevelt, by the Trotskyites' shrill opposition to Roosevelt's World War II preparedness program. (The Tobin-Roosevelt association was, indeed, sufficiently intimate that Roosevelt would four years later announce his candidacy for a fourth White House term at a Teamster testimonial banquet honoring Tobin, an action that the U.S. President defended by explaining that "truck drivers have such big hands.")

There was also a pressing pragmatic reason. Dobbs and his colleagues had recently voted to secede from the Teamsters and join the more aggressive, and more left-leaning, Congress of Industrial Organizations, founded in 1935 by John L. Lewis after Lewis had himself withdrawn from the American Federation of Labor. Excited by the Minneapolis move, Lewis had immediately issued a CIO charter for a new local of truck drivers in the Minneapolis area. He had also placed his brother Denny in charge of the CIO's ambitious and well-financed organizing drive not only there but in the nearby Michigan cities of Detroit, Pontiac, and Flint.

Fearing wholesale Teamster losses, Tobin turned to a man who had had experience in Minneapolis: James R. Hoffa, who at first declined. Even aside from his indebtedness to Dobbs, Hoffa had developed a respect for the cohesiveness and dedication of the dissident Communists. He had also formed personal friendships with Vincent Dunne and other Local 544 leaders. He was to tell a television interviewer more than three decades later,

I think that [Tobin] used our relationship because I had refused to go on request, or on an order. When he ordered me to go to Minneapolis, I said I wouldn't go and it was none of my business. And then he put it on a

personal basis, as a request, and brought up what he'd done for me and so forth, and what he was gonna do for me. And once the old man made a personal request at his age [Tobin was sixty-six years old at the time], you couldn't very well turn him down. Recognizing he was the General President, I went . . . into Minneapolis . . . took over the office, brought in a hundred crack guys, had the war. We won every battle. And we finally took the union over and then Farrell left and went with the Socialist Party.[25]

Dobbs had somewhat different memories of the 1941 events:

Now it is true that Hoffa was among the IBT goon squads that Tobin sent into Minneapolis. . . . But he . . . says in effect there he whipped us. For instance, he was helped by the Minneapolis Police Department, the courts . . . the mayor, the governor and an antilabor law that had been rigged and put through by the Republican governor of the state, and by the Federal Bureau of Investigation, the United States Department of Justice and Franklin Delano Roosevelt, who then happened to be President of the United States. . . . Under those circumstances you got to admit Hoffa had just a little help, didn't he? The man exaggerates on this point. He exaggerates.[26]

What is irrefutable is that, with or without significant help, the Hoffa forces resoundingly defeated the rebels in Minneapolis and St. Paul in mid-1941—physically, on the streets, with many injuries on both sides resulting from fights with both fists and sticks ("I took enough men with me," Hoffa would later explain, "to make sure we could handle it"). Whatever his motives for breaking with Dobbs and the others—it has been suggested that the Denny Lewis incursion on Hoffa's own Michigan turf may have been the real reason—the Hoffa participation in the Minnesota purge was a willing and an active one. It may have helped to generate the reputation for ruthlessness that was in later years to surround the famous Teamster leader. But as Ralph and Estelle James have noted in evaluating Hoffa's performance on the Minnesota battleground, "That he did his job so effectively is evidence that he already possessed substantial qualities of the trait."[27]

The final chapter in the lives of the Trotskyites as labor leaders was written only a few weeks later. In an action that Dobbs may have been thinking of when he cited the "help" that Hoffa received,

Dobbs, the Dunnes, and five other Local 544 officers were indicted by the U.S. Department of Justice under the 1940 Smith Act. They were charged with conspiring both to overthrow the U.S. government by force or violence and to create insubordination in the armed forces. Dobbs and Vincent Dunne were found guilty and sentenced to twelve to eighteen months in prison, the first people imprisoned under the 1940 sedition law. Grant Dunne committed suicide while in the throes of a nervous breakdown, and Skoglund, a noncitizen, was deported.

Replacing Dobbs as vice-president of the Central State Drivers Council that he had been so instrumental in creating, a relieved Tobin named James Riddle Hoffa, who had already (in 1940) replaced Dobbs as the CSDC negotiating chairman. Bennett was once again made the ranking Teamster in Detroit, a primacy that he had temporarily yielded to O'Laughlin. And, in a final insult that was to be inflicted on the departed Dobbs by his old union, O'Laughlin was himself stripped of all of his Teamster authority in Detroit and given instead a minor IBT organizer's job in North and South Dakota—in recognition of the fact that he had refused to do battle with Dobbs as Hoffa (and Bennett) had.

Denny Lewis remained a force to be reckoned with. Arguing that since Detroit's automobile factories were now fully organized by the CIO (in its United Automobile Workers affiliate, under Walter Reuther), the people who drove the cars away from these factories should also be CIO members, the CIO had embarked on an aggressive campaign to wean away Hoffa's car haulers and assigned Lewis to lead this effort. Hoffa returned to Detroit from Minneapolis to find scores of strong-arm goons roughing up his organizers and threatening his truckaway employers with both strikes and physical violence.

"We needed some [more] husky guys around," Bennett later reminisced. "What the hell, I didn't need no college graduates. I wanted someone who wasn't afraid to use his dukes."[28] He gave Hoffa the authority to hire a variety of such tough specimens for the Teamsters.

One of these specimens, whom Hoffa soon thereafter made a Local 299 business agent (by 1941, the local had several such positions, under Hoffa's clearly established control), remembers:

I'd never seen a pistol prior to then, when Denny Lewis's thugs used them. We had several of our stewards beat up, sometimes in their own houses. . . . We never got no support from the Police Department. Never.

I remember Jimmy once calling up the head of the Detroit police and saying to him, "I want to tell you right now that I'm arming every one of my business agents. We're going to defend ourselves." But Jimmy himself never had anything like that [a pistol]. . . .

I remember once, right out in front of our place [Local 299's first permanent headquarters, now shared with six other locals in downtown Detroit] Lewis sent a car with real hoods strictly to beat Brennan, Tom Burke [another Teamster official] and me up while we were in our car. . . . The guys in the Lewis car jumped out with baseball bats. One of them hit me in the groin. . . . I'm a pretty good sized guy [in his peak years, he was almost six feet, five inches and weighed a solid 250 pounds]. . . . They were unconscious when we left. One of them died.

It was not to be quite that simple, however. Fighting between the Lewis and the Bennett-Hoffa forces went on for months; fist-fights became so common, Bobby Holmes would later recall, "that pedestrians couldn't walk down the street without seeing a couple of union guys rolling around, thrashing each other."[29] The twenty-five CIO organizers especially assigned to Detroit for the Hoffa-raiding project made some headway by freely offering their target employers substandard or "sweetheart" contracts that were less costly than the Hoffa agreements. The fact that the CIO budget allowed the hiring of considerably more thugs than did Hoffa's also gave the Lewis campaign an edge.

Needing more help, Hoffa in late 1941 requested support from the same quarter that many employers, for strikebreaking, and other unionists, for a variety of organizational projects, had already turned to throughout the first several decades of the twentieth century: organized crime. According to people who were closely associated with him in those days, he paid visits to the reputed top mob figures in the city. Santo Perrone, "Scarface Joe" Bommarito, Frank Coppola, and others—known as members of the "East Side crowd" to many Detroiters in recognition of the part of the city in which most of them resided—were asked to provide reinforcement manpower.

The underworld leaders were no less obliging to Hoffa than they had been to their other allies—including, it should be noted, many politicians. ("The mobsters have always been wedded to the political system," as a veteran criminologist observed not long ago, "That's how they survive. Without that wedding, they'd be terrorists—and we'd get rid of them.") No deep labor relations philosophy prevented them from extending such aid to a Teamster, even though some of them already sat on the employer side of the bargaining table in some Teamster-employer relationships: the Detroit mob owned, for example, a significant slice of the Detroit laundry and soft drink industries by this time. Lewis would soon thereafter tell the *Detroit Free Press* that "professional hoodlums and gangsters" were intimidating truck drivers into "joining the AFL Teamsters Union."[30] And within a matter of a few months the threat of Denny Lewis was over.

From then on, Hoffa's relationship with the underworld was to be an ongoing one. From his liaisons with the Detroit gangsters came introductions and often strong social ties to mobsters around the country—in Cleveland, New York, Chicago (where many of Hoffa's allies had close connections to the old Capone organization) and, ultimately, in just about every major city. Nor did he ever, remotely, try to conceal these relationships. Thirty-three years after his initial visits to the East Side crowd, he would tell an ABC-TV News interviewer that "these [organized crime figures] are the people you should know if you're going to avoid having anyone interfere with your strike. And that's what we know them for. I can pick up a phone in Detroit and call anybody and have a meeting with them. . . . We make it our business, and the head of any union who didn't would be a fool. Know who are your potential enemies and know how to neutralize 'em."[31] And another mid-1970s reporter would be offered a similar statement: "I don't deny the fact that I know, I think, what's going on in most of the big cities of the United States. And that means knowing the people, uh, who are in the big cities. I'm no different than the banks, no different than insurance companies, no different than the politicians. You're a damned fool not to be informed what makes a city run when you're tryin' to do business in the city."[32]

He *was* different from banks, insurance companies, and at least the heavy majority of politicians in his degree of familiarity and even close friendships with many criminals. And as Hoffa broadened the initial relationships in the years after 1941 and as he became more famous, his mobster connections were to redound to his considerable discredit. But it should not be forgotten that in originally establishing these relationships, he was merely recognizing a portion of the world in which he and his adversaries lived and walking a road that some of the latter had already taken. He was nothing if not a realist.

The Biggest Small Man in Detroit

2

Hoffa's sense of realism did not preclude him from exercising his fertile imagination to the fullest as far as his own organizing efforts were concerned. He considered a wide variety of unorganized workers to be fair game—among them, employees in breweries, drugstores, packinghouses, warehouses, and department stores—and went so far as to post a sign that said "If it moves, sign it up" in a conspicuous location at his union hall.

Watching from Indianapolis, Tobin tried to discourage such attempts on the entirely logical grounds that they were too far afield from the IBT's traditional and authorized (by the parent American Federation of Labor) jurisdiction of drivers and loading dock employees. But he basically tried in vain. By the end of 1941, employees in many such establishments had been recruited by Hoffa and his colleagues either for Local 299 or for the newer Food and Beverage Drivers Local 337, which worked closely with Hoffa's General Truck Drivers local now headed by Hoffa's close friend Owen Bert Brennan and shared office space with Local 299. The two locals had a total of almost seventy-five hundred members by that time, up substantially from the three thousand figure of four years earlier. With their new dues income, they were able to move to their own building, a nondescript brick one two blocks from Detroit's Tiger Stadium in a modest, litter-strewn neighborhood (where they, more recently created IBT locals, and the parent Teamster Joint Council 43 are lodged to this day).

Although official Teamster publications assert that Hoffa "was elected president of Local 299 in 1937, at the age of 24," it is probable that he was elected to nothing at the local except membership on the 299 board until 1945. The trusteeship imposed under Bennett was not ended until the latter year, and in the long interval Bennett turned a deaf ear to all membership pleas for any kind of broad election. Hoffa was indeed the de facto leader of 299 from 1935 on, and officially both a board member and business agent. But Bennett continually deemed it unwise to hold presidential elections. He argued that if there were such a membership referendum, the organization would "absolutely get out of control," and he was unwilling to risk the defeat of Hoffa, whom he favored over all leadership alternatives, by an unpredictable membership.[1]

Bennett was probably being unduly pessimistic, however. From all of the evidence, Hoffa was highly popular from the very beginning with the 299 rank and file. According to Rolland McMaster, who joined the local in 1936 upon payment of the then-standard $2 initiation fee, "Ninety-nine and nine-tenths per cent of the members loved him . . . we always knew where we stood. We had a continuous growth pattern from the time he came in until the day he left. Every day had a thrill in it." Holmes also remembers his fellow Strawberry Striker as being very well liked in the local, and highly respected for both his intelligence ("It was street intelligence, and he could match wits with the best of them") and his physical strength ("He was strong as a bull and lived for hard work"). Both old associates were also impressed from the beginning by Hoffa's powers of persuasion and his general friendliness. It seems reasonable to assume that the young man from Indiana could have won a Local 299 election at any point before 1945.

He was, in fact, easily elected to one significant leadership position during the years of World War II. Exempted from military service because his union work was considered essential to the trucking industry and, therefore, to national defense, he formed the Michigan Conference of Teamsters in 1942 and was voted its first president. Although the conference began as a tenuously connected association of locals drawn from just six Michigan cities, within a year, helped by pressure applied by the international, Hoffa had pulled all of the Michigan locals into his growing sphere of authority and negotiated a single master contract for all of them.

An impressed Tobin thereupon appointed him, at the age of

thirty, to a vacant international trustee's job. The latter, a part-time position calling for the more or less ceremonial semi-annual auditing of the union's books prior to these books' receiving a full-fledged audit by a certified public accounting firm, by itself meant nothing. But the vacancy was one of only three such posts authorized by the Teamster constitution, and Tobin's naming of Hoffa to it showed how rapidly the young Midwesterner's star was now rising. The trustee's position also gave the alert Hoffa for the first time a clear understanding of the union's financial potential.

After the war, his contacts established and his considerable talents now widely known among Teamsters, Hoffa had little trouble in expanding his influence. He was resoundingly elected Local 299 president in late 1945 and, two years later, was voted into the presidency of Joint Council 43 just as one-sidedly. Even more valuable, for a man who was at this point fully determined to achieve as much national prominence and power as he could get, was the apparatus already at his disposal as negotiating chairman of the Central States Drivers Council.

With the large growth of the trucking industry in the postwar years Hoffa got maximum mileage from his pivotal twelve-state bargaining position. Teamster-organized Midwestern trucking companies that also operated in the nonunion South—an increasing number, attracted by the potential savings in the form of the lower Southern wages—were threatened with strikes unless they employed Teamsters there, too. And if Omaha could be made to jump by pushing a button in Kansas City, so could secondary boycotts also be used below the Mason-Dixon line. There was no reason why a button pushed in, say, Atlanta, might not be able to motivate employers in Birmingham to agree to Hoffa's demands. "Leapfrogging" and secondary boycotts became weapons not only for organizing but for forcing relative uniformity of terms on the Southern labor relationships.

Hoffa then engineered a common expiration date for what were now two Southern Agreements (a six-state Southeast and a four-state Southwest each had one) and his twelve-state Central States contract. And by the end of the 1940s, refusing to sign in the Midwest until a comparable contract was negotiated in the South, he got the Midwesterners who had Southern operations to promise to raise their Southern wage rate to the Central States level within five years. The threat of a strike was generally enough to make the home-grown Southern employers follow suit. Within a very few years, drivers in the South would have their hourly rates rise significantly—in some cases, from seventy-five cents per hour to more than three times that amount.

Not everything was achieved easily, and sometimes goals were not met at all. Ohio employers, in particular, resented Hoffa's intrusion and were willing to pay their drivers a variety of wage rate premiums and special income guarantees to stay outside of the area-wide contract and preserve their local autonomy. Hoffa could offset this approach only by allowing the Ohio drivers a special "Ohio Rider" to the Central States agreement, under which they could keep their advantage indefinitely. In Virginia, Tennessee, and the Carolinas, extreme tenacity on Hoffa's part was required, and several major nonunion companies that operated either exclusively or primarily within those areas—not being susceptible to either strike threats and secondary boycotts—remained unorganized despite the most liberal use of the Hoffa imagination.

But failures such as these were the rare blemishes in an otherwise virtuoso performance. The "little guy" (as he was often referred to by Teamsters in these days and as he would be described by his fellow unionists throughout his career) had come a long way in a short time. He was clearly the ranking member of his international union in the entire midsection of the country by 1952 and the acknowledged leader of the move toward centralized bargaining and uniform standards for the trucking industry coast to coast. He could no longer be remotely ignored by anyone in the Teamsters, and an international vice-presidency was now, given the number of votes that he controlled at the 1952 IBT convention, a foregone conclusion. Daniel J. Tobin, in endorsing him for a vice-presidency at that convention, recognized this and more: "He is the biggest small man in Detroit. When you go to Detroit today you hear about Hoffa, but you do not hear a word about Henry Ford. As I said, he is a very big small man and he is one man we developed in our time. He is pretty nearly civilized now, but I knew him when he wasn't."

In thus joining the international's executive board, the thirty-nine-year-old Hoffa became the youngest man ever elected to it. But this was not his only major accomplishment at the convention.

A few months earlier, the immensely popular Tobin had announced that, at seventy-seven years of age and after forty-five years as IBT president, he would not run for reelection. Instead, he said, he would support Beck, who had become Teamster executive vice-president in 1947, also with Tobin's support. The social climber from Seattle, however, did not inspire the universal support that "Uncle Dan" did, and a stop-Beck movement immediately began, causing Tobin to hint that he might not retire after all and Beck to say that he would be happy to withdraw in favor of Tobin. But Beck would not have been happy to bow out, and when he said this he knew that he would not have to: Hoffa had just informed the executive vice-president that he was pledging all of his Central States, Southern, and Eastern Conference delegates to him, a move that rescued victory for Beck.

Tobin, recognizing that he had indeed come to the end of a career, gracefully if reluctantly withdrew for good within hours. He was made, as a reward for his many services over the years, an "adviser" to the union. He nominated Beck, who was elected unanimously and who from this point on was heavily indebted to Hoffa.

Hoffa proceeded to make the most of the obligation. In the next few years, he seemed as ninth vice-president to be doing exactly as he pleased, the wishes of his official superior notwithstanding.

Beck, courting respectability, was, for example, a major force behind the 1953 expulsion from the AFL of the gangster-ridden International Longshoremen's Association. Hoffa proposed an alliance of the Teamsters and the ILA that would result in joint organizational drives and cooperative action during strikes and announced that three of the four regional groups (the Hoffa-controlled Central, Southern, and Eastern Conferences) were ready to lend the poverty-stricken outcast union more than $400,000; he was persuaded by Beck to shelve the project only with the greatest of difficulty. Beck, moreover, had no particular desire to divert Teamster resources to organize the fifteen thousand warehouse workers at Montgomery Ward, but Hoffa successfully mounted a resource-draining two-pronged attack on the giant corporation: while IBT organizers signed up Ward employees on the company's loading docks, the vice-president made it known that unless incumbent Ward President Sewell Avery signed a companywide contract with the Teamsters, the union would vote its 13,500 shares of union-owned stock in favor of an outside group that was trying to wrest control from Avery.

Beck also seemed to go out of his way to avoid being seen with known racketeers; Hoffa appeared, increasingly, to be flaunting his friendships with such men. Beck wanted to give overall directions for a saturation organizational drive going on in Philadelphia. Hoffa, with an ill-concealed disdain, plunged right ahead on his own in successfully recruiting more than twenty thousand new Teamsters in a twelve-month period. And while Beck, pressured by Teamster officials in New York, would have preferred to let home rule there continue, Hoffa was starting to pick up many of the reins of power in the latter location, too.

The IBT first-in-command, every bit as realistic as Hoffa, regularly responded to questions from reporters about his relations with his aggressive lieutenant with paeans of praise. He knew of no one "with a better future in either the Teamsters or the entire labor movement than Jimmy." Asked if he had any thoughts of "putting the brakes on" Hoffa, Beck said, "Positively not! Why in hell would we want to put the brakes on anybody who is doing that good a job of organizing? I wish I had 40 more like him."[2] Hoffa was a man in whom the Teamsters could "take enormous pride."

Hoffa was not by any means widely known outside of his own professional sphere as yet. Even in late 1955, a *Reader's Digest* article about him could start out, "There have been kings who wielded less power than a labor leader whose name you've probably never heard."[3] Nor was Hoffa, despite Tobin's glowing testimonial to his standing in Detroit, necessarily even the best-known labor leader in his own city. That honor presumably had to be awarded to Walter Reuther, the Hoffa contemporary who had presided over the United Automobile Workers nationally from that union's Detroit headquarters in Solidarity House since 1947 and who, in 1952, also became head of the Congress of Industrial Organizations.

Unlike Hoffa, who tended to express himself succinctly, Reuther was almost a nonstop talker who was given to pious platitudes ("We are not looking for a fight; we are looking for justice"). Where Hoffa could be at times amusing and at other times amused, Reuther was an essentially humorless man, of whom it was once said that he smiled so infrequently that when he did dust came out of his mouth. Hoffa's interest in general social reform was invisible; Reuther stressed "social unionism," or the achievement of social and economic gains benefiting all of society, not just his own membership. Hoffa in these days had no particular desire to participate in politics, and when he did so, his support went strictly to individuals on a highly parochial basis; Reuther was a recognized leader within the liberal wing of the Democratic party. Both of these intense and ambitious men, however, maintained an uneasy truce for years, and Hoffa regularly said that his relations with Reuther were "all right." In 1936, Hoffa had, at Reuther's request, sent a detachment of truck drivers to prevent the Ford Motor Company from removing dies from the plant of a supplier whom the UAW had struck, and Reuther never forgot the favor. In later years, as was not true of most CIO leaders, the latter's comments about Hoffa were models of self-restraint.

Even within American Federation of Labor circles in the Motor City, moreover, Hoffa was not the foremost leader. The autocratic head of the Detroit and Wayne County Federation of Labor, Frank X. Martel, was, and he brooked no opposition from anyone in running his organization. Hoffa first suffered in silence as one Martel decision after another went against the Teamsters, then openly fought with the AFL boss, and finally, in the late 1940s, led a walkout of Teamster and other locals from Martel's labor body. He did not return to the federation umbrella until 1955, when Martel died, and the one-man dynasty automatically ended. And even then Hoffa made known his feelings about his old nemesis by not attending Martel's funeral: "I didn't like him in life," he declared. "And I'm no hypocrite."

But if Reuther was better known and Martel more powerful in Detroit, Hoffa by the early 1950s officially spoke for almost 650,000 Teamsters—he was fond of pointing out that only two international unions in the country, Reuther's Automobile Workers and the United Steelworkers, were any larger—and he was only, relatively speaking, just beginning. If he was not yet a household word, he already wielded unchallenged power in a broad section of America's most strategically potent union and was clearly destined for even bigger things. He was, as he often proudly said himself, "doing okay." He agreed with Beck's statement that his future in the labor movement would be second to no one's.

'53 and 1954, Hoffa received his first attention from the
gress.

'1, Senator Estes Kefauver's Special Committee to Inves-
‿Ɡganized Crime in Interstate Commerce had found that
Detroit's Teamster Local 985 had been used as a front by members
of the underworld to extort money from jukebox distributors. The
latter had been offered the choice of paying an initiation fee and
periodic union dues, thereby becoming "honorary" Local 985
members, or of having a picket line thrown around their locations.
They had, almost without exception, taken the first option.

Nothing much had come of this discovery, a relatively minor
one in the litany of ultimate Kefauver Committee conclusions. But
when a newly elected Republican Congress structured itself two
years later, it decided to pursue the matters of labor racketeering in
general and Detroit Teamster affairs in particular. Joint hearings of
two Special House of Representative Subcommittees—one under
the House Committee on Government Operations, the other under
the House's Education and Labor Committee—were scheduled.
The acid-tongued Clare E. Hoffman, Republican from Michigan
and a long-time Hoffa antagonist, was voted chairman of the new
full investigatory committee.

The Hoffman committee, building on the Kefauver foundation, did not mince words in its evaluation of Local 985's jukebox
activities. The 1953 committee concluded that the local was engaged
in a "gigantic, wicked conspiracy to, through the use of force,
threats of force and economic pressure, extort and collect millions
of dollars" not just from the independent distributors but from
unorganized workers, union members and even, at times, the federal government itself.[4] It found the principal offender in this
conspiracy to be the local's president, William E. Bufalino, a Penn-
sylvania-born lawyer who had moved to Detroit, married the niece
of alleged mobster Angelo Meli (one of the men to whom Hoffa
had turned for help in thwarting the Denny Lewis CIO attacks in
1941), and gone into the jukebox industry.

Given Hoffa's stature as Detroit's most visible, and most powerful, Teamster, it was probably inevitable that he would also be
singled out for congressional scrutiny. And the cantankerous Hoffman did indeed quickly proceed to Hoffa, broadening his line of
inquiry in the process.

Hoffa was hardly intimidated by the hearings, as is evidenced by the following responses on his part to a variety of statements and questions from the Michigan congressman. The exchange also constitutes as good an example as any of the candor that always permeated Hoffa's conversational style. In the years ahead, he would be accused of much, but never of insincerity.

Mr. Hoffman . . . I personally tried to put stuff in a truck off the farm here for the Detroit folks to eat and the union wanted $25.

Mr. Hoffa I dispute that.

Mr. Hoffman You don't know anything about it.

Mr. Hoffa . . . If it happened to the union I know about it.

Mr. Hoffman . . . The teamsters attempted to collect $25 before they would permit me . . . to drive truckloads of apples here, and then also insisted that . . . I hire a union man to unload it.

Mr. Hoffa I don't believe it.

Mr. Hoffman Nobody is talking to you.

Mr. Hoffa It's not true. I resent the fact that you are trying to disturb and embarrass the union by publicity that is not true, and you can't prove it. I defy anybody in this room today to prove that we practiced that way of doing business. . . .

Mr. Hoffman I confine my activities to the job for which the people pay me.

Mr. Hoffa I'm not so sure. . . . For your information, on the investigation of a shooting, my brother was shot by an employer during a strike in absolutely one fit of anger, without him being involved in the strike whatsoever, thinking that it was me. Now, why don't you go and investigate that?

Mr. Hoffman That was a mistake?

Mr. Hoffa It was a mistake.

Mr. Hoffman A mistaken identity. It was your brother that did the shooting?

Mr. Hoffa My brother was shot by an employer, and I repeat it, and nobody to this day ever prosecuted the employer for shooting my brother.

Mr. Hoffman Did they arrest you?

Mr. Hoffa They did not.

Mr. Hoffman How many times have you been arrested [in Detroit] since 1937?

Mr. Hoffa I have been arrested, for a matter of record, numerous times by antiunion police departments, instigated by employers where they use strikebreakers and tactics that need your investigation.

Mr. Hoffman You give us the facts. We will be glad to investigate.

Mr. Hoffa I question it.

Mr. Hoffman I know, but the difficulty there is that your opinion doesn't have too much weight.

Mr. Hoffa That's what I am well aware of.

Mr. Hoffman Do you think it might be because of your record?

Mr. Hoffa You think that is it, or maybe I am a Democrat?

Mr. Hoffman Are you a Democrat?

Mr. Hoffa What do you think I am?

Mr. Hoffman I don't know. There is a gentleman who told me you were a Republican.

Mr. Hoffa I am not. I go by the individual. I wouldn't vote for you. . . . If you were in my district I wouldn't vote for you.

Mr. Hoffman You couldn't be if you wanted to.

Mr. Hoffa I vote for somebody who is up to date.

Mr. Hoffman Don't talk so much. . . . Just one question. In view of the statement that was made by another witness, are you an Italian?

Mr. Hoffa I am not. I am Irish and Dutch.

Mr. Hoffman All right.

Mr. Hoffa You don't want the truth. You would rather have it look like a syndicate.

Mr. Hoffman Don't worry.

Mr. Hoffa I don't worry.[5]

On the other hand, Hoffa did generate bad publicity for himself when he admitted that as Joint Council 43 president he had authorized the Detroit Teamster locals to destroy their financial records each year "to save storage space." Nor, of course, was his public linkage to Bufalino calculated to win him any good citizenship awards.

Hoffman's chairmanship did not last long. The Michigan Republican's committee, abetted by Hoffman's own combativeness, was soon torn by internal wrangling. Hoffman was in short order ousted from the chairman's position, to be replaced by a Kansas Republican, Congressman Wint Smith.

Presumably by no coincidence at all, Hoffa, upon learning of the change in committee leadership from Hoffman to Smith, engaged one of the latter's old associates as a legal consultant. Payne Ratner, who had been the Republican governor of Kansas at the same time that Chairman Smith had headed the Kansas Highway Patrol, was retained to assist Hoffa by, it was widely rumored, getting Smith either to postpone the hearings in Detroit indefinitely or, short of that, to treat Hoffa more favorably than Hoffman had done.

The new regime, nonetheless, began by doing neither. Its Detroit hearings got under way on schedule, in late November 1953. And, if anything, its members (with Hoffman still among them) appeared to be even more threatening to Hoffa than they had been earlier. The Smith committee displayed an active interest in Hoffa's placement of Central States Health and Welfare Fund monies with the Union Casualty and Life Insurance Company, controlled by Paul "Red" Dorfman, a violence-prone major figure in the Chicago mob, and his stepson, Allen Dorfman. It sought to show that Hoffa had taken illegal payoffs from the Dorfmans in return for such a financial plan. And the Dorfmans themselves declined to answer enough Smith committee questions that the committee recommended that they be cited for contempt.

When the Central States employer trustees sought an investigation of Union Casualty's financial soundness on the other hand, reported the committee, "They were successfully resisted by Mr. Hoffa."

The Smith committee also tried to shed light on the formation of the Test Fleet Corporation, a trucking company set up five years earlier by Hoffa and Owen Bert Brennan in their wives' maiden names, allegedly with considerable help from another Michigan trucking company, Commercial Carriers, Inc. Hoffa and Brennan had, the committee indicated, accommodated Commercial Carriers just before this help was given them, by settling a Teamster strike there on terms favorable to the struck company.

Very little light was to be shed on either topic, however. On November 25, the Detroit hearings were interrupted while Chairman Smith left the room to take an important long-distance telephone call. He, soon after returning, informed the Detroit press that he was under strong political pressure to conclude the hearings rapidly ("The pressure comes from way up there, and I just can't talk about it any more specifically than that," he said). And the investigation was indeed terminated not long afterward.

Ratner was generally credited with effecting this happy ending for Hoffa, although some observers attributed the abrupt conclusion of the hearings to a commitment by Hoffa and the Teamsters to support the Republicans in Michigan in 1954. Chairman Smith, beyond denying that any favored treatment was granted Hoffa, steadfastly refused to elaborate on his intriguing original statement.

In 1954, history more or less repeated itself for Hoffa. Congressman Hoffman, never one to accept defeat gracefully, had continued to urge the House to let him conduct another major investigation, this time strictly of the Teamsters. And while he was once again denied his own opportunity of leadership in this case, the House's Government Operations Committee did authorize such new hearings, by a subcommittee to be headed by Ohio Republican Congressman George H. Bender, who was now his party's candidate for the U.S. Senate. In September 1954, Bender opened hearings in Cleveland by summoning for questioning Hoffa's two ranking lieutenants in Ohio, William Presser and Louis M. ("Babe") Triscaro.

Not unlike Detroit's Bill Bufalino, Presser had become interested in the jukebox as a means of income maximization. His Cleveland Teamster Local 410, working in conjunction not only with the jukebox operators association but also the beer delivery drivers, profited by suggesting to tavern owners that they might not receive their requested beer if they did not have an approved jukebox on their premises. He had recently expanded 410's activities into Youngstown, where he had installed as business agent a former bartender who had served a three-year jail sentence for promoting prostitution, and he was generally believed to be quite friendly with the Ohio mob. It was widely rumored that these contacts, in fact, were helping him considerably as he rapidly climbed—as head of Cleveland IBT Joint Council 41, the Ohio Conference of Teamsters, and assorted other Teamster operations—to the status of leading Teamster in Ohio.

Triscaro, Presser's backup as vice-chairman of the council and number two man in the conference, as well as president of the Excavating and Building Materials Teamsters Local 436 in Cleveland, was a former prizefighter who allegedly had even deeper underworld connections than did Presser. He, indeed, was thought to be Presser's major linkage to the mob. For Bender, both men were tempting targets as he strove for the maximum in favorable publicity in his race for the Senate.

After a handful of hearing days in Cleveland, during which both Presser and Triscaro took the Fifth Amendment on questions relating to their personal incomes, and two such days in Washington, in the course of which Presser took the Fifth again, the Bender investigation was, however, abruptly ended. Technically, it was "recessed at the call of the chairman." It was never to be resumed.

Shortly thereafter, the Ohio Conference of Teamsters, which had been actively supporting Bender's Democratic opponent, threw its support to Bender. And a few years later, a highly respected Ohio Teamster leader testified to the McClellan committee that the Teamsters had apparently also spent about $40,000 "to pull certain strings" so as to stop the investigation.

In 1955, George Bender, now U.S. Senator George Bender, was the featured speaker at an Ohio Conference of Teamsters meeting, and Presser had no trouble finding words of praise: "To you George Bender, the Republican whose name has been handed around as an anti-labor Senator, if it weren't for this one man, and his advice and the constant pounding we would have a lot of problems that do not exist . . . and Bill Presser is committed to George Bender anywhere down the line."[6]

It is, of course, absolutely unknown as to what damage either of the two investigations could have done to Hoffa's career. Presumably, Congressman Bender's revelations would have been somewhat less directly negative for Hoffa than Congressman Smith's, since only Hoffa's associates and not the Detroiter himself were at least initially scrutinized by Bender. But it is equally obvious that neither project was welcomed by the Teamsters and that in both 1953 and again in 1954 House of Representative investigating committees had come close to causing Hoffa some problems. A best-selling book a few years later could comment that both times the investigators "had been on the threshold of uncovering major corruption in the Teamsters; corruption involving Mr. Hoffa and some of his chief lieutenants. Both times the investigations had been halted. The congressmen went their way and Mr. Hoffa went his."[7] And, however valid or invalid this statement may have been, it was widely believed.

If the sudden conclusions to the two sets of hearings could be said to have constituted good luck for Hoffa, what might be described as misfortune for the Detroiter was waiting just around the corner.

In January, 1955, the Democrats regained control of the Senate and an austere, schoolmasterish member of the majority party, John L. McClellan of Arkansas, became chairman of the Senate Permanent Subcommittee on Investigations. The new chief counsel of the subcommittee was a brash, Boston-accented young man only four years out of the University of Virginia Law School: one Robert F. Kennedy.

The Harvard College graduate Kennedy, thirty years McClellan's junior, differed from the senior senator from Arkansas in other ways, too. Highly emotional where McClellan was phlegmatic, politically and economically liberal in contrast to the latter's embedded southern conservatism, and inclined to brutal frankness where the Arkansan was very much the diplomat, the twosome constituted a classic study in contrasts. But Kennedy was well known to McClellan and enjoyed his complete confidence. Both men had served together—the new chief counsel in those days as assistant counsel—on the same Permanent Investigations Subcommittee since early 1953. Both had temporarily left it in protest: Kennedy could not tolerate what he saw as the high-handed ways of chief counsel Roy Cohn; McClellan, together with the other Democratic senators on the subcommittee, had walked out because of their unhappiness with the subcommittee's Republican chairman, the controversial Joseph R. McCarthy of Wisconsin. When the minority party members had returned in early 1954, they had convinced Kennedy to come back with them.

There had been no indication whatsoever, at first, that the Mc-

Clellan unit would even investigate labor unions, let alone either the Teamsters Union in general or Hoffa in particular. Counsel Kennedy and his assistants, many of them former agents of the Federal Bureau of Investigation and virtually all of them zealous in their loyalty to their boss, began by concentrating on such nonlabor topics as trade with what was then called Red China and possible conflict of interest situations involving high governmental officials. In the latter effort, particularly, they had made their presence known: in the course of Kennedy's investigations, both the secretary of the Air Force and an assistant secretary of the Army had resigned. The investigators had then, in late 1955, turned their attention to the clothing procurement program of the armed forces and had rapidly discovered that several leading East Coast gangsters had come to dominate both some of the manufacturing and some of the trucking of uniforms.

From this latter finding a consideration of the union that dominated the trucking industry was inevitable. And the fact that several of the leading gangsters appeared to be on a friendly basis with the Midwest's ranking Teamster made Hoffa, in addition to Beck, a logical further topic on the Kennedy team's agenda.

Even then, however, Kennedy seemed unwilling to delve very deeply into the topic of IBT corruption. He was well aware of the failure of the previous congressional investigatory efforts and had no wish to add his name to the list of unsuccessful Teamster investigators. He also had serious doubts that the McClellan subcommittee even had the jurisdiction to conduct such an inquiry, especially since there was a Senate Labor and Public Welfare Committee in existence.

It had taken the persuasiveness of a labor relations reporter to rid the chief counsel of these reservations. Clark R. Mollenhoff, Washington correspondent for Cowles Publications and a union expert of some note, had convinced Kennedy that the 1953 and 1954 congressional investigations were fixed because of political pressure, something that presumably would not be a factor here. A lawyer himself, he had also successfully pointed out to the relatively inexperienced Virginia Law School graduate that Kennedy did have jurisdiction since the Teamsters were tax exempt and, in his opinion, misusing their funds; the operations of two agencies, the Internal

Revenue Service and the Labor Department, were therefore involved, and McClellan's permanent investigating subcommittee had every right to come in.

Kennedy had needed no further coaxing. By the end of 1956, he and his assistants had gone to Chicago, Los Angeles, Seattle, and a variety of other places in search of evidence that could incriminate the Teamster high command, as well as lower-echelon Teamsters. He had also shaken off whatever inhibitions he might have had regarding his pursuing allegations of wrongdoing in other unions —the Plumbers, Steamfitters, Retail Clerks, and Operating Engineers among them. And he had come away persuaded, as he was later to write, that some cases "cried out for an investigation," most especially the circumstances surrounding Dave Beck.[8]

Mollenhoff had been wrong about one thing. The question of appropriate senatorial jurisdiction was not quite as cut and dried as he had made it out to be. The Labor and Public Welfare Committee, as it turned out, quite adamantly resisted the ambitious explorations of the Kennedy personnel into labor racketeering. And the senatorial civil war was resolved in January 1957 only by the creation of an entirely new agency of the Senate to carry on these efforts. The latter was entitled the Senate Select Committee on Improper Activities in the Labor or Management Field. It was made fully bipartisan, with four Democrats and four Republicans constituting its entire membership. In a further display of brotherhood, the eight members were chosen in equal number from both the Labor Committee and the Committee on Government Operations, the parent of McClellan's Permanent Subcommittee on Investigations. McClellan became the chairman of the new body, and Kennedy the chief counsel. The Democratic senators, in addition to McClellan, were John F. Kennedy of Massachusetts, the counsel's older brother, Sam J. Ervin of North Carolina, and Pat McNamara of Michigan. The Republican representation was provided by Irving M. Ives of New York, Karl E. Mundt of South Dakota, Barry Goldwater of Arizona, and Carl T. Curtis of Nebraska.

From then on, Beck's days were numbered. And it would be only a matter of time, and not much time at that, before the Detroiter who even now was widely believed really to run the Teamsters would be back in the investigatory limelight.

On the surface, Beck was anything but a sensible target for an agency concerned with improper union activities. By 1957, the glib seeker of respectability had achieved a good deal of it, even aside from whatever standing might accrue to him as the president of the largest and richest union in the country.

He was now a member of the governing board of the University of Washington, a regular key participant at international labor meetings, and the chairman of an independent trucking industry advisory conference. He was friendly with many leading national politicians, primarily those who shared his own Republican party affinity and not excluding the present incumbent of the White House, Dwight D. Eisenhower. When he endorsed Eisenhower's 1956 Presidential candidacy, in fact, the endorsement (which Beck actually announced on the steps of the White House) had generally been treated as a major news story. He thought of himself as a "labor statesman" and insisted that his public relations staffers build up such an image. He was known within Teamster circles, irreverently, as "His Majesty, the Wheel" in recognition of these many extracurricular activities and the intense pursuit of social applause on his part that accompanied them. But his style did lend prestige, if a superficial kind of prestige, to his union.

Yet, when the McClellan committee focused on Beck, as it did almost immediately after its initial February 26, 1957, hearing, he went quickly. Nor, as indicated above, did his exit come as any surprise at all to Kennedy and his assistants: they had found unmistakable evidence as they prepared for Beck's appearance that the former laundry driver had misused hundreds of thousands of dollars of Teamster funds.

Moreover, nothing that he had done in his almost five years in the president's office became Beck less than his leaving of it. When the committee first asked him to come before it in Washington to testify about his apparently diverting some $370,000 from the Western Conference of Teamsters to finance personal purchases, he declined the invitation. Although he had just returned to his Seattle home following a European trip, his doctor—he said—now advised him not to travel, indefinitely. Three days later, however, he did venture far afield to Miami Beach, to chair a meeting of his union's executive board. He was still in Florida a few days after that, in attendance at an AFL-CIO Executive Council meeting, where he was the only council member to vote against a resolution that would oust any labor leader who took the Fifth Amendment. Then, suddenly, he left the country altogether, fleeing in obvious panic first to the Bahamas and then back to Europe. Traveling under an assumed name, D. David, he had almost overnight become a pathetic figure—a once tough man who, when the going had gotten tough, had gotten going. "He kept on running until he ran out of gas," Hoffa would later say. "When your nerve runs out, you run, then that hole card don't look so good no more."[9]

When he finally did appear before the McClellan committee in March and then May, Beck looked, if possible, even worse. Asked about his use of union funds to pay for such items as (among many others) a sizable collection of expensive undershirts, two boats, a twenty-foot freezer, outboard motors, and costly repairs on his Seattle home, he steadily took refuge behind the Fifth Amendment. In his May appearance alone, he tapped this constitutional guarantee against possible self-incrimination 117 times, using it even when asked if he knew his own son, Dave Beck, Jr. He seemed nervous and tired, and the forced geniality that had been his trademark since his earliest days in Seattle had entirely deserted him. Several journalists pointed out that when he spoke, his voice shook, and it was also noticed that during recesses in the hearings he whistled to himself.

He would be convicted later in 1957 of grand larceny for diverting $1,900 from the sale of a Teamster-owned automobile into his own wallet, and in 1959 for income tax evasion. With appeals, he would not actually go to jail for five more years, until mid-1962. But as of March 1957, the career of the man who had been the first to implement an areawide trucking agreement and then created the imaginative concept of the geographic conference was, for all practical purposes, over, and a replacement for him was needed in the presidential office of the Teamsters.

James and Josephine with their four-and-one-half-month-old daughter Barbara, at Lorch Lake, Michigan, 1938. (Crancer Collection)

Local 299 staff in front of the union building in Detroit, approximately 1942. (Crancer Collection)

With close friend Owen Bert Brennan, approximately 1947. (Crancer Collection)

(above left) With son James, 1950. (Crancer Collection)

(below left) Trip to Israel, 1956. Israeli Foreign Minister Golda Meir is on Hoffa's left, with Barbara Hoffa next to her. (Crancer Collection)

(below) The entire Teamster-sponsored traveling party with Ms. Meir in Israel, 1956. (Crancer Collection)

(above left) With Robert F. Kennedy during a lull in the McClellan Committee hearings, 1957. Hoffa's attorney George S. Fitzgerald is in the background. (AP/Wide World Photos)

(below left) Retiring Teamster president Dave Beck points to the leading candidate to succeed him at the 1957 IBT Miami Beach convention. (AP/Wide World Photos)

(above) Prior to the 1957 convention roll-call voting, vice-president Hoffa is swept across the convention platform on the shoulders of enthusiastic supporters. (AP/Wide World Photos)

International president Hoffa, campaigning for New Jersey Teamster leader
Anthony Provenzano in the latter's home state, 1959. (AP/Wide World Photos)

At Home and Abroad

3

Hoffa once said of his predecessor,

Beck was an iceberg. Very cold. He didn't visit the local unions. . . . I saw Beck come into Chicago once: he got off the plane, and two cars picked him up and he swung over to the hotel. [As] he walked through the lobby, he'd say "Hi fella." [Then] he went up to his room and stayed there till everything was ready. Then he came bustin' in, up on the platform and made a tremendous speech, got down, walked through the crowd, "Hi fella." . . . Hi fella what? You go to hell—if you don't know my name I don't wanta talk to you. You at least got to know who came to your meeting.[1]

Hoffa, throughout his career, was just the opposite, and the difference was appreciated by his constituents. No more than one-third of his working time, indeed, was spent in the office—in Detroit and, after 1957, at the International building in Washington. The rest of the hours found him out in the field—addressing mass meetings, joining the rank and file on picket lines, touring new trucking terminals, and taking a turn behind the wheel of new equipment. As a qualified Teamster staff official could say at the peak of the Detroiter's career, "This union is Jim's whole life. And this is the major secret of his popularity among those who know him."

And as another close adviser could observe at about this same time,

Hoffa is very accessible. He loves direct contact with people, especially his own people. And you can sense the genuine admiration of the truck driver

for him because of this. He has never separated himself from the working Teamster. He knows everybody's name and, at least in a general way, everybody's problems. If he's a politician at all, he's one in a good sense of the word.

In complete contrast not only to Beck but to virtually all other labor leaders, Hoffa often included his office telephone numbers in his speeches to Teamsters and invited the members to call him, boasting that he offered his services "around the clock." Nor was this last phrase much of an exaggeration. His regular workday began at 8 A.M. and was rarely over until 2 A.M. or later. He frequently worked through the night.

For all of this, the union was not "Jim's whole life." He was, by all accounts, a devoted family man who when he was at home, in the words of his daughter, "was there totally."

"Home" was essentially two locations for the Hoffa family. A modest two-story red brick house at 16154 Robson Street in northwest Detroit was purchased for the equally modest price of $6,800 in 1939, one year after Barbara was born. A few years later, the Hoffas bought a two-story frame cottage at Lake Orion, about forty miles north of Detroit. The latter, with its one bathroom and utter absence of luxury, was even less pretentious than the family's urban holding (visitors to it could be heard muttering under their breath, "This is what Hoffa lives in?"). But the cottage, its accompanying three acres, and its swimming facilities amply met the Hoffa needs. And the four Hoffas (a son, James, was born in 1941, completing the family) over the years actually spent almost as much time there as they did in Detroit.

There had been, briefly, another place. In 1940, the labor leader had spent $6,500 to purchase a property in rural Memphis, Michigan, that he hoped to make into a dairy farm. He had added a barn and some stalls, bought livestock and machinery, and fully expected to turn a profit as a weekend farmer. Josephine, however, had hated the Memphis environment, and she had convinced her husband to sell everything. He had acceded to her wishes, making a $4,000 profit in the process. Not long thereafter, the new owners had struck oil on the farm, and *their* profit had been a more gratifying $250,000.

The Teamster chieftain liked his Robson Street home and, for this reason and perhaps also because the Memphis experience still rankled, soon told his wife that he never wanted to sell it. But he found more to occupy himself with at Lake Orion. When he and Josephine first bought the cottage, the three acres contained a considerable amount of brushwood and stumps, and for years he enjoyed the challenge of clearing these away single-handedly. He particularly liked starting fires to burn off the wood once he had collected enough of it, but he was not above reproach in this endeavor. Using gas instead of fuel oil, he created larger fires than he had intended on several occasions. Once, his efforts caused all of the power lines in the neighborhood of the cottage to melt. On another occasion, the nearest fire department was called from its base some forty-five minutes away to avert disaster: an embarrassed Hoffa handed each of its members a $20 bill. With a mixture of love and trepidation, Josephine called him "Gasoline Gus."

But Hoffa's pleasure in his Lake Orion property was far from a selfish one. He thought of it as an ideal weekend and summer residence for his wife and young children and was quite willing on this basis to spend almost two hours daily driving from Lake Orion to his Local 299 offices, when staying on Robson Street would have been much more economical of his time. "I don't mind," he told his children, "when I think of all the fun you kids are having."

Much as he had said of his own father, when Hoffa was at home, whether at Lake Orion or in Detroit, it was "like Fourth of July every day." He told Barbara, Jim, and their friends endless "Freddie the Fox" stories, his own creations, involving a fox who was always getting into trouble with the other animals but who always overcame these troubles and thus each time brought about a happy ending to the story. He took his children to performances of the Detroit Light Opera Company, to appearances by Roy Rogers and Sonja Henie at the Detroit Olympia, and to a myriad of movies (often at the "Blue Skies" Drive-In, not far from the Lake Orion cottage). There were frequent visits to Teamster picket lines, to help Dad inspect the troops, and to "Uncle Bert" Brennan's impressive farm in nearby Plymouth, Michigan, for horseback rides in the warmer months and sleigh rides in the winter ones. There were Sunday drives to the Penn-Mar Restaurant for lunch or supper, to the nearby towns of Mt. Clemens or Port Huron, or just out to the southern Michigan countryside to observe nature in its various seasonal forms. And for Jim, although not Barbara, there were also regular duck-hunting and fishing trips, barbells-and-calisthenics drills, and (later) excursions to health clubs, where father and son would play racquetball together and then sit in the steam baths. (It was particularly important to the father that his son never be thought of as "soft": when Jim was only six years old, the parent left him alone in a duck blind for six hours with nothing more than a gun and a bottle of soda; his boy would never be deficient in toughness if he could help it.)

"He could turn the simplest thing into an adventure," Barbara would later recall of her father. "Even going to the lumber store would be exciting with him." The adventures were also learning experiences, for whenever the senior Hoffa could draw a moral from a situation, he would not hesitate to do so: "If you're going to do something, work at it as hard as you can, day and night"; "It doesn't matter what they say about you as long as you're doing the job that you're supposed to be doing"; "You can learn a lot more by listening than you can by talking"; "Nothing comes easy. For every inch, there is a stone."

Possibly because he was away from home so much, possibly also because it was simply counter to his parental style, the same Hoffa who had used his muscle so freely as a rising labor leader imposed no physical discipline at all on his children. He inspired obedience through respect, not fear. Both of his offspring viewed him with adulation, as a national figure who, in his son's words, "came from nothing and rose as high as he did by sheer force of will, brains and guts." Both were proud of his rapidly growing celebrity status ("It was like walking around with a movie star, everywhere he went," Jim in adulthood reminisced, "People would line up at a restaurant. You could hardly eat"). And they were proud of the devotion that he was so universally accorded by his Teamsters.

His daughter would "die if I ever disappointed him, because he tried his hardest to be the best he could be." His son felt no differently.

Typical of the style of Hoffa père was an incident that took place when Barbara was about fourteen years of age and her brother eleven, at the Hoffas' Upper Michigan retreat, the family's third and only other holding in addition to the aborted dairy farm. Even more modest than the other properties, the retreat consisted of a hunting lodge that lacked electricity, was supplemented by an out-house, and was surrounded by 160 inexpensively purchased acres of woods and hills. It also featured an old Quonset hut and a minuscule honeymoon cottage. It was, in those days, twelve hours from Detroit and thus not particularly convenient, but Hoffa enjoyed its opportunities to hunt deer, to fish, and generally to enjoy its outdoors. Josephine always lamented its isolation but agreed to go there with the children if she could simultaneously invite friends and relatives. And the retreat, accordingly, usually housed a dozen or so people when the Hoffas stayed at it.

On this occasion, both Hoffa children had accompanied their father on a fishing excursion out to the middle of a nearby lake one evening, and Barbara, in an unlikely action, had cast and caught the senior Hoffa squarely on the lid of his right eye with her fly. Bleeding profusely and with the hook remaining embedded on the lid, Hoffa said only, "We'd better get out of here." Despite his obvious pain, he calmly rowed all the way back across the lake to the lodge, got his car, and, spurning an impassioned insistence by a resident brother-in-law that he let the latter drive him the twenty-six miles to the nearest hospital, no less stoically proceeded to drive himself and his children there.

The guilty Barbara to this day remembers crying "I'm sorry, I'm sorry" almost constantly to her father until the town's sole physician extracted the hook. And, just as vividly, she remembers Hoffa consistently reassuring her during the entire seemingly endless episode, "I know you are. Of course you are." "His theory was that I felt badly enough," she says of a memory that will never leave her. "And he just didn't want me to feel bad or stupid. He did that on instinct and pure love."

In only one way, in fact, did the professionally belligerent Hoffa generate fear in his children, and it was obviously an unintentional one. He was a heavy-footed automobile driver who thought nothing of reaching speeds of one hundred miles per hour (as he did on such roads as the Tamiami Trail in Florida), consistently tailgated, and was never happier on the highways than when passing every car within passing range. Amazingly, he never got either a speeding ticket (troopers would invariably recognize him and dismiss him with a "Slow down, Jim") or into an accident. He did, however, once wind up in a cornfield after knocking down some twenty fence posts during a blizzard. On another occasion, his vehicle went out of control at the top of a steep hill and came to a stop on some railroad tracks at the hill's bottom ("We were all day getting a tow truck to pull us out," recalls his son). With his typical recklessness, he never wore a seat belt.

It was left to Josephine to administer what punishments were needed as her children grew up. Her family, in recognition of this role, sometimes called her "the sergeant" and to embellish the private joke once bought her a whistle to wear around her neck. The good-natured mother announced, upon receiving it, that she was "going to go back to the laundry."

But the required acts of discipline were few and far between. Generally, instead, the two younger Hoffas were sources of pride to their parents.

Barbara, always an honors student, became president of her large high school class, and graduated from Albion College in Michigan with high enough grades to earn her membership in Phi Beta Kappa. As her father often boasted, her completion of college marked the first time that either a Hoffa or a Poszywak had done so. She became a successful schoolteacher and, in 1961, married Robert E. Crancer, a wealthy St. Louis businessman whom she met on a blind date while both were attending the 1961 Miami Beach IBT convention (he as a "company representative"). The mother and father of the bride hosted a lavish three-day Polish wedding, to which eight hundred people were invited and over two thousand came. Barbara would remember these festivities for many things: a ten-foot-high cake, provided by the Bakery and Confectionery Workers Union; Frankie Yankovich and his Polish music; the presence of the noted New York restaurateur, Toots Shor; the attendance of a wide variety of Michigan political figures; and, by no means the least of these memories, her father's not only wearing a tuxedo but also dancing: he had, to her knowledge, never before done either.

James P. Hoffa, frequently if erroneously referred to in media coverage of the Hoffa family as "Jimmy Hoffa, Jr.," was an all-state football player at Detroit's Cooley High School, as well as a member of that high school's honor society. He rejected scholarship offers of one kind or another from almost one hundred colleges in favor of attending Michigan State, where he pledged Alpha Tau Omega fraternity and made both the freshman and varsity football teams. During his sophomore year, he got injured, and his father (who had never been sufficiently excited by his son's football prowess to see him play at either high school or college) convinced him to give up the sport: "I didn't send you to school to get hurt," he told his offspring. "I sent you to get an education. If you want to keep playing football go out and get yourself a job and send yourself to college. If you want me to send you, forget football and get your education." The son took the advice, concentrated on the books, and graduated with a B plus average. He went on to the University of Michigan Law School, married a young woman whom he had met at college football practice, and became a respected attorney at law in his home town of Detroit.

The Hoffa household also contained, much of the time, two other residents. Sylvia Pigano, James R. Hoffa's old girl friend for a brief period in the early 1930s, was also a longtime friend of Josephine's who had walked picket lines with her in her laundry worker days. An outgoing brunette of ravishing beauty, she had left Detroit for Kansas City and there had married Sam Scaradino, alias Frank O'Brien, the elderly chauffeur for an underworld figure. After her husband's death not long thereafter, she had returned to her home town, married a cleaning establishment executive named John Paris, and upon the demise of this second husband a few years later had been invited to move into the Hoffa home with her young son, Charles. She was good company for Josephine, in particular, but one intimate remembers her as being "bossy from the word 'go,' and an awful know-it-all. Jo relied much too much on her."

Charles "Chuckie" O'Brien (he had taken Scaradino's other name) called James R. Hoffa both "Dad" and "the old man." For this reason, because also of Hoffa's past relationship with Chuckie's mother, and because the Hoffas played a major hand in raising the boy from the time that he was six years old, in 1940, it has been widely rumored but never proven ever since that the Teamster leader did in fact father him in his pre-Josephine era. Far from being resented by Barbara and James P. Hoffa, he was viewed as a fun-loving and personable surrogate older brother who was never too busy to take their mother to the doctor or to do an endless variety of other errands for her and to serve as a traveling companion, when his school schedule allowed, for their father. After he married for the first time, he and his wife both lived in the Hoffa home, and the warm and witty Mary Ann O'Brien became one of Barbara's closest friends.

Chuckie was not, however, destined to achieve the same degree of success that Barbara and James P. Hoffa would. An indifferent student, he enjoyed his union trips with "Dad" and gradually evolved into a full-time jack-of-all-trades business agent for Local 299, more than ever an on-the-road companion of Hoffa's but now being paid for the pleasure. After Hoffa became international president, he made O'Brien a general organizer, a post that came with an almost unlimited expense account as well as a comfortable salary. But O'Brien nonetheless lived well beyond his means and constantly incurred debts that the union could not justify paying for. He, for example, once took the entire Detroit Red Wings hockey team to Detroit's luxurious waterfront Rooster Tail Restaurant and ran up a $1,000 bill in treating the players to ice carvings, expensive drinks, and other items whose connection to collective bargaining was obscure. On several occasions, he wrote checks that were not covered by his bank deposits. Hoffa frequently had to dip into his own pockets to get him off the hook. In his twenties, Chuckie was viewed by the IBT leader as a definite challenge. In some quarters, the latter's infinite patience with him constituted further evidence that he was really Hoffa's son.

Relatives, especially, and close friends were very much a part of the Hoffa family environment in Detroit and at Lake Orion in the 1940s and 1950s no less than they were in these years at the Upper Michigan hunting lodge. But the relatives were virtually all Poszywaks. Viola Hoffa's initially cool attitude toward her "foreigner" daughter-in-law only hardened through the years, and Josephine—a sister would later recall—habitually tended to "wrinkle up her nose" with contempt at the mention of Viola's name.

Relations between the James R. Hoffas and Hoffa's three siblings, influenced to some extent by the stern widow's antagonisms, were also far from close. The Teamster leader found jobs for his two brothers-in-law and often sent money to them—as he did to Viola, who not infrequently received her son James's entire paycheck. But the sisters and brother, in the words of a family intimate, "always figured that Hoffa owed them something" and were not particularly gracious in accepting this aid. With the sole exception of Viola's much younger brother Steve Riddle, the Hoffa side of the family was conspicuous by its absence at the home of the most successful Hoffa.

The Poszywaks, on the other hand, were regular visitors. Josephine was particularly fond of her mother, a pleasant-faced and humorous woman, who wore a hearing aid and in recognition of her handicap was shouted at, but who seemed to her grandchildren "to hear whatever she wanted to hear." Hoffa, who had no father-in-law (Mr. Poszywak having been killed by a bus when Josephine was twelve years old), treated her with considerable devotion and always personally drove her back and forth when she came to visit.

Josephine's two sisters, Angeline and Sophie, her brother Ed, and their families also spent quite a bit of time in the Hoffa home, especially at the cottage, where the master of the house was a friendly and warm host. Hoffa usually grilled steaks for his guests, always purchased large quantities of beer and wine in advance of their arrival, and invariably made sure that everyone had plenty to eat and drink ("If you need something else, just ask, and we'll get it for you even if we have to go out and buy it"). The financial generosity that he granted Hoffas was also freely offered Poszywaks and, without exception, he refused to be paid back. He often told relatives, "You know, when you're with me, you don't need money." "He had a lot of family feeling," says Angeline, "and he helped a lot of people."

He, by the same token, spent very little money on himself. Expensive clothes had no appeal for him—"I don't need to impress anybody," he would often say—and he felt no more favorably disposed toward any kind of jewelry. He didn't even wear a watch for years, and although he did drive a succession of new black Cadillacs in his business agent days (because "it impresses the bosses and the workers when agents drive up in a new car") he was much more at home in a modest Pontiac and drove the latter kind of car once he became national Teamster president. He was a difficult person to buy presents for, since he wanted so little: "We'd buy shirts or something like that for him," his daughter recalls. "He could always use them."

Nor was he much of a gourmet. He had, as a former intimate recently said of him, "a working man's taste in food." In addition to beef (medium well done), he liked spaghetti and seafood (especially red snapper broiled). He asked little else of a chef. In Detroit, Carl's Chop House—a venerable but modest institution a stone's throw from the Teamster office complex on Trumbull Avenue, where many of his fellow IBT officers ate and where the proprietor also, reputedly, kept one table reserved strictly for mobsters—was a favored establishment. In Washington, he frequently ate at the fancier Duke Zeibert's, but this was almost solely due to the urgings of his chief lieutenants at the international headquarters and he never felt fully at home there.

Close friends tended to be old friends, Teamsters who had shared Hoffa's hardship-laden past. "If I'm going fishing and hunting," he said on more than one occasion, "these are the people I'm going with. My friends are the people I came up with." He could trust such people, he would explain. "The others you've got to watch with both eyes."

Bobby Holmes, the scholarly looking English immigrant who had been a Hoffa confidant since the Kroger loading dock days, was one of these friends. So was another "Strawberry Boy," Frank Collins, the mild-mannered, bookish secretary-treasurer of Local 299. The friendship circle also included Frank Fitzsimmons, a chubby, slow-moving former city bus and truck driver six years Hoffa's senior whom Hoffa had allied himself with in 1936 and who was now second-in-command at 299. And Dave Johnson, a jut-jawed Finnish-American who, like Fitzsimmons, had started his union officership career as a 299 shop steward. And, of course, Owen Bert Brennan, the colorful horse-breeding and racetrack-gambling head of IBT Local 337 who shared office space with Hoffa and now administered Joint Council 43 with him. The steely eyed Brennan, who once got sufficiently mad at a Detroit hotel clerk that he pulled out a gun and riddled the premises with bullets, has been described by a Teamster who knew both men well as "Hoffa's mentor in street ways and violence just as the Minneapolis people were Jimmy's mentors intellectually." A short, quiet chain smoker whose admiration for Hoffa's intelligence was unbounded and who was fond of saying that "Jim has the brains for both of us," his equally unquestioned brightness was appreciated by his office mate.

He was the only "best friend" whom Hoffa could ever be said to have had: Hoffa called him his "partner," and Brennan's funeral in 1961 was to mark one of the very few occasions on which the Teamster leader was seen to cry.

Generally, these men led lives that were as family oriented as Hoffa's, and their families often spent time together—usually outdoors and often at Lake Orion or in the Upper Michigan woods. "The best years of my life," Holmes would declare years after Hoffa's death, "were spent working with and being part of his family, and having his family be part of mine."

Jo Hoffa, clearly, occupied the highest niche on her husband's scale of personal values, as he did on hers. A Teamster publicist once quite justifiably wrote that "it is a mutual admiration society with Jimmy and Jo," and they had many shared experiences. She frequently told the children stories about their dad coming home from his work in the 1930s bloodied, and of having to patch and clean him up so that he could go back to work the next day. Her dedication to her children was as strong as his. His friends were her friends.

She could regularly make her husband laugh, often by relaying jokes—never, for the straight-laced Hoffa, off-color ones—that she had heard during the day. And arguments between the two were all but nonexistent. "I figured he argues all day long," she once told a journalist, "so why should he have to argue at home. When he opens that front door at the end of the day he's smiling and I'm smiling."[2] He, in his turn, was unfailingly solicitous of her welfare, invariably telephoned her at least once a day and often more than this when he was out of town, and always sent her red roses on their anniversary.

One of the very few quarrels remembered by their children, indeed, stemmed from a well-intentioned attempt by Hoffa to teach his wife to drive: he quickly abandoned the effort in the face of Josephine's unwillingness to be taught and continued to serve as family chauffeur when he was at home, with Chuckie O'Brien (if available) assuming the role when Hoffa was not in residence. When Barbara turned sixteen, she was immediately given a car so that she could ease her father's burden.

Two potential grounds for marital tension caused none at all. Hoffa had readily acceded to Josephine's desires to keep his side of the family at a safe distance. And the atheistic husband and Catholic wife encouraged their children to attend any church that they preferred. The daughter and son chose a Methodist church that was within walking distance of their Robson Street residence almost strictly on the basis of geographic proximity, and that was just fine with their parents. Hoffa, who thought that religion was important for others even if not for him, easily convinced his wife that "when the kids grow up, they'll find their own religion," and the pragmatic Teamster found his children's reason for favoring the church of John Wesley, at least temporarily, as good as any other.

Josephine, more outgoing than her husband, had a considerable sense of playfulness. She was capable of not only spiking a punch bowl but also of herself answering a letter from Hoffa's former girl friend, Eileen, which the latter wrote the IBT leader after he became famous ("We never heard from Eileen again," she would afterward drily announce). In contrast to the man she married, she greatly enjoyed dancing. She also, lacking his strong puritanical streak, drank, occasionally to excess, and was a heavy cigarette smoker (a weakness that she tried, without much success, to hide from her husband). She loved parties, vacations, and going out to dinner with friends.

The former laundry worker was far from lighthearted, however. She was, as was noted earlier, a constant worrier, in particular about her spouse. She worried about his physical health, although except for a mild diabetic condition he remained in excellent shape throughout these years. She fretted about his recklessness as a driver, his "Gasoline Gus" ways with fuel, and the everyday dangers that he faced as a union officer in a violence-prone era. She was fearful about his failure to properly respect the rays of the sun: once, vacationing in the Virgin Islands, he had fallen asleep on a rock with some rented scuba equipment and had burned his feet so badly that he was unable to wear shoes for several days, as well as painfully burning his arms and legs. She was uneasy about his careless approach to pulling out the Lake Orion property's stumps, a technique that had on one occasion resulted in a tractor's turning over on him and that often caused severe bruises and cuts to his legs. And she worried about the not always so savory professional associates with whom he sometimes aligned himself and about his refusal to provide himself with personal protection of any kind:

"Hoffa don't need no bodyguard," was his standard answer to the frequently made suggestion that he consider such an arrangement, and, similarly seeing no reason why he should own a pistol, he never did so.

Increasingly, along with her husband's mounting legal difficulties, this last dread on Josephine's part assumed dominant proportions. Hoffa himself once told a researcher that he expected to die a "violent, early death"—a belief that accounted, he said, for his unwillingness to have a large family—and Josephine had no reason to omit this possibility from her list of concerns. She often told her spouse that, as frail as she habitually was, she was afraid that he would die first.

But even beyond these burdens, at least on an everyday basis, the wife of Jimmy Hoffa suffered from loneliness. "It wasn't a good way for a couple to have to live," in the opinion of Holmes, in whose lexicon loneliness is "the worst disease." Her husband's dedication to his union kept him away from Detroit for substantial periods long before he went to Washington in 1957, and she did not cope with these absences well. After 1957, she still preferred to spend most of her time in Michigan, surrounded by Poszywaks, on familiar terrain, and knowing that her husband's continuing Teamster positions in Detroit would guarantee her regular and reasonably frequent reunions with him. It was for her the lesser of two evils, however, and virtually every Hoffa family intimate was to comment on this highly visible loneliness factor in the marriage—an aspect that was clearly accentuated by the deep love that Josephine had for her marital partner. The loneliness undoubtedly increased the frequency of her drinking, which ultimately became sufficiently worrisome to her husband that he implemented a policy of having two IBT business agents watch her when she made public appearances and there was liquor around. As he advanced up the Teamster hierarchy and demands upon his professional time became even greater, her sadness from this single negative dimension of an otherwise entirely positive marriage would only grow.

As a consolation for Josephine, on the other hand, there were many moments of enormous pride.

On August 22, 1956, for example, a noteworthy event occurred in the fledgling state of Israel. On one of the terraced hills of Judea, near the site of the birthplace of John the Baptist, the cornerstone was laid for the James R. Hoffa Children's Home of Jerusalem.

The money for this project, which was originally intended to be known as Beth Hoffa ("House of Hoffa," in Hebrew), had in turn been raised some four months earlier. On April 20, 2,650 guests had gathered at Detroit's State Fair Coliseum to honor the IBT's ninth vice-president at a $100-a-plate testimonial dinner.

April 20 had been declared "James R. Hoffa Day" by Detroit's governing body, the Common Council, and the council had passed a resolution in Hoffa's honor that resounded with praise:

He has contributed so much to the cause of humanity and the betterment of the social and economic conditions of all classes of citizens in this city. . . . His untiring efforts and zeal for the welfare of his fellow citizens have aided greatly in the civic and economic development of Detroit as a great metropolitan area. . . . The members of the Detroit Common Council recognize his dynamic leadership, courageous labors, and valuable sense of civic duty.

The participant list at the April banquet was no less impressive, as well as diverse. Bernard J. Sheil, the Roman Catholic auxiliary bishop of Chicago, offered the invocation. Rabbi Aaron Decter of Philadelphia's Temple B'nai Aaron delivered the benediction. Abba Eban, Israeli ambassador to the United States, conveyed his good wishes as one of four featured speakers. So did the eminent University of Wisconsin law professor and former Wage Stabilization Board chairman Nathan P. Feinsinger; an immediate past president of the American Trucking Associations; and Dave Beck. Blocks of tickets were purchased by—among many other corporations—General Motors, Ford, Montgomery Ward, and Sears, Roebuck (all of whom sent ranking vice-presidents) and by an even greater number of unions, not excluding Reuther's UAW (although Reuther himself was not in attendance).

The large Sponsors Committee included, in addition to most top members of the Teamster international hierarchy, many major trucking company owners. Its roster also contained several international union presidents, including A. J. Hayes, who in addition to leading the International Association of Machinists was head of the AFL-CIO's Ethical Practices Committee. The legendary former

Notre Dame football coach Frank Leahy was a sponsor, as were the Chicago mobster Paul "Red" Dorfman and two of the original Strawberry Boys from Kroger's—Holmes and Collins.

The motives for participation in this "Jimmie Hoffa Testimonial Dinner," as the event was officially named notwithstanding Hoffa's lifelong other spelling of his nickname, presumably varied widely. For some, a clear-cut desire to help Israel was, it is fair to suppose, the sole determinant. But undoubtedly a positive regard for the guest of honor dictated other appearances, and even those who came for the crassest of political or economic reasons bore silent testimony to the increasing importance of the combative little Teamster leader.

The selection of a charitable cause was by no means accidental, the obvious public relations benefits of Hoffa's chosen project notwithstanding. Hoffa had long admired the Israelis for their values of survival, pride, and pioneering, which he often likened to the values of organized labor in the United States ("To him, the nation of Israel was very much like a union," in the words of his daughter, "with its concept of brotherhood and its struggling against the bosses—in Israel's case, against the rest of the world—to establish independence."). Nor, at the age of forty-three, had he forgotten what a childhood of poverty had meant, and his Michigan Teamsters had contributed to other children's homes before.

He affirmed both of these beliefs in rising to some eloquence in his dedication speech, delivered just outside Jerusalem on an August day that was uncomfortably hot even by local standards:

We hope this children's home will be a center which symbolizes the spirit of Israel. We know and appreciate what it must mean to be a child who has been uprooted from his family and from surroundings that he has known. We believe that the job that Israel has done in setting up educational centers for young and old alike is unique. As a matter of fact, building this country in the span of a few short years—building its industry, its homes, its schools, its strength—is an undertaking unparalleled in human history.

This is the fifth in a string of children's homes. . . . America sees and admires what you are doing about the problems of your children, and we salute you.

America also sees and admires what you are doing about all the people, from many lands and cultures, who comprise the nation of Israel. Out of an arid land of desert and stone, you are raising up food by the most modern methods of drainage and irrigation. You are seeking and finding natural resources that will in time be a source of trade balance and prosperity. You are building factories and providing jobs. You are building homes and cities. . . .

You are doing these things against many great odds, because Israel is a people of unquenchable spirit. . . .

You are a nation which believes in democracy and lives it. . . . You are a beacon light to the Middle East.

The Teamster chieftain, accompanied by the eighteen-year-old Barbara Hoffa and some twenty-five other labor and business representatives, spent eight days in Israel on this 1956 trip. He met a variety of Israeli luminaries, including Prime Minister David Ben-Gurion and Foreign Minister Golda Meir, both of whom seem to have instantly impressed him by their intelligence as well as by their lack of formality. His first reaction to life on an Israeli kibbutz was something less than positive: pointing out to an assistant the fact that the collective farm residents were enjoying the benefits of electricity, refrigerators, and tractors, he asked, "You call this pioneering?" But his cynicism quickly changed to admiration when he was shown the barbed wire and gun emplacements on the farm's perimeter. He was also impressed by the fact that the kibbutzim had their needs taken care of in return for their giving their labor ("He had known the Dunnes and Dobbs, don't forget," this same assistant not long ago recalled).

The cities of Rome, Paris, and London, which the Hoffa party visited on their way back to the States, produced a less positive opinion from Hoffa, however. His general reaction to Europe was that it was "just a bunch of old buildings"; and his evaluation of Paris, which he offered before retiring to bed early one night was that "there's nothing much going on in this town, anyway."

He really meant what he said about the City of Light. Paris's relaxed attitude toward sex held no attraction whatsoever for a man who had once been so embarrassed by the performance of a stripper at a San Francisco nightclub that he had turned his chair away so as not to have to watch her. He was also known to have walked out of New York's Latin Quarter with his family in protest against the suggestive aspects of an act there. Even the hugs and kisses that he received by the hundreds from admiring Teamster wives invariably made him uncomfortable and often caused him to grimace visibly: it was part of the job and he knew that he had to allow it, but that didn't mean that he had to like it. He was, as more than one of his intimates observed, a "real Boy Scout."

In Rome, he pleased his daughter by taking her to the Opera, but quickly embarrassed her by falling asleep and quite audibly snoring, producing a torrent of hisses from an offended Italian audience. He also caused Barbara a certain amount of consternation in Italy by asking taxi drivers, "What did you think about Mussolini?" and then proceeding to offer his own highly negative opinion of the late Italian dictator. The Fascist premier still had many admirers in the country thirteen years after his death, and the chronically outspoken Teamster was, at least in his daughter's opinion, risking a fight in each instance.

A meeting with the Pope was a less tense feature of the trip. Hoffa, as a nonbeliever, eschewed both bowing to the pontiff and kissing the papal ring. The Pope, who had been briefed about his American visitor, offered his hand to him as a viable alternative.

Hoffa's gift to the Israeli children was very much in character. His financial generosity was, in fact, monumental. "He was probably the most generous, open-handed guy I've ever met," says one Hoffa intimate, explaining that Hoffa was a "sucker for any sad song or hard luck guy." A family friend has described him as "the easiest touch in the world." In his daughter's opinion, "he would give anybody anything."

Some of Hoffa's largesse was formulated strictly on the spur of the moment—rounding up the neighborhood children in the vicinity of the Local 299-Joint Council 43 Teamster complex in Detroit and buying them all ice cream, for example. Old-timers in this decidedly unprosperous section of the city still remember, too, how on several occasions he spent hundreds of dollars of his own money to purchase sports equipment for these boys and girls.

But the Teamster leader also had a variety of special institutionalized causes that could consistently count on his philanthropy. Many were Jewish charities in addition to the Children's Home in Israel: the atheistic Hoffa admired Judaism as much as he admired any religion and also greatly respected the ability of the Jewish people through the ages to overcome hardships. He and his wife also supported numerous Catholic causes. In the latter category, activities that were related to St. Jude, Jo Hoffa's patron saint, were particularly favored with contributions. So, too, was the Holy Trinity church in the Corktown section of Detroit, near Hoffa's Detroit offices: the church's pastor, Father Clement Kern, would regularly tell his neighbor, "Jimmy, I need some help; give me a big one"; and Hoffa would just as regularly comply. (The grateful Father Kern presided over a well-attended wake at the church in honor of his benefactor on the day before Hoffa went to prison in March 1967).

Many more recipients of the Hoffa largesse were individuals who had convinced the union leader of their personal financial need. A Brink's driver down on his luck, for example, got $1,500, which Hoffa patiently counted out for him in one-dollar bills; the driver ultimately repaid the money but only because he insisted on it despite the Teamster leader's attempts to dissuade him. Whitey, an elderly derelict who had been a fixture at Local 299 headquarters for years, was a permanent Hoffa charity, a situation that Hoffa explained to his curious son as stemming from the fact that "Whitey at one time helped the union." A widow whose Teamster husband had been killed in a trucking accident received $400 (and, when she informed the IBT president that she really needed "a job not a handout," also was rewarded with a job through Hoffa's efforts). Sometimes, the IBT leader acted on a misfortune only secondhand, as when he read in a Detroit newspaper of a newsboy who had been run over by a car and badly injured and sent a significant sum of money to the boy's parents to help defray hospital bills. And it was a Christmas tradition that unemployed Local 299 members would line up in front of their president's office in December, when their president was in town, for money: some $15,000 was typically dispensed for the purpose, and while some of the amount came from the local's treasury, Hoffa's own contributions did not go unnoticed.

The family-minded IBT leader was an especially soft touch if the individual's hard luck story involved other members of the family. Once he was told by a young man who was walking down the street not far from the Teamsters' Washington headquarters building that "I need $2 to get home to Virginia for Thanksgiving dinner." Hoffa gave the Virginian much more than this amount—$400—and also some advice: "First thing you do is buy your mother a present. Don't tell her your problems. You go home in style." When another teller of a sad story sought a job from the Teamster boss and said that he did not want any money at all, but happened to mention that he had pawned his wedding ring for $50, Hoffa immediately handed him $50 and told him to "go get it. That's the last thing you should ever do, pawn your wedding ring. Then come back here and I'll find you a job."

Like Confetti at a Country Fair

4

On March 13, 1957, the man who had long ago amassed a list of arrests "that's maybe as long as your arm" was arrested once again. But this time the allegation involved much more than picket-line scuffling and similar union duty misconduct, and the potential consequences for Hoffa were far more serious than they ever had been.

In an action that, befitting Hoffa's current status as the de facto Number Two Teamster (and, as such, the likely heir to the mantle of the now discredited Beck), generally made front page headlines all over the country, he was seized by three FBI agents as he entered an elevator in Washington's Dupont Plaza Hotel. Arraigned a short while later, he was officially charged with having attempted to bribe a lawyer on the staff of the Senate Select Committee headed by John L. McClellan and of conspiring to influence and obstruct the committee's inquiry. More than once, he had said that a sensible rule of life was to "do unto others, first." Now, he had seemingly practiced what he preached.

The lawyer was one John Cye Cheasty, formerly a Secret Service agent, a Naval Intelligence commander (who currently received an 80 percent service connected disability allowance), and an Internal Revenue Service investigator. He had gone to committee counsel Robert F. Kennedy one month earlier and told the latter that Hoffa (originally through a mutual acquaintance intermediary, attorney Hyman Fischbach, and then in person) had offered him $1,000 in cash as a down payment, with $17,000 more to follow, to get a job as an investigator with the committee. From this position, as a spy, he was to furnish Hoffa with secret information from the committee files.

Cheasty, according to the government's version as to what happened after this, had taken the money and run to Kennedy as a matter of both conscience and civic duty. A devout Catholic, he believed, as he later informed the committee counsel, "in right and wrong and that I must answer to God for my conduct. All my life I have regarded good as something to work for, and evil as something to be fought."[1] He told Kennedy that Hoffa was in effect "asking him to betray his country" and he agreed to serve as a "double agent," actually working for the committee while appearing to Hoffa to be working for Hoffa. And, with the cooperation of the FBI, it was agreed that a trap would be set for the Teamster leader when Hoffa came to Washington in March to attend an AFL-CIO Building and Construction Trades conference meeting.

On the night of March 12, with a large number of FBI agents watching from across the street, Cheasty met Hoffa outside Hoffa's hotel at Dupont Circle in the heart of the city. He handed the latter an envelope of confidential documents with which he had been furnished for the purpose by the committee. In return, according to the FBI, he had $2,000 in cash shoved into his hands by a grateful Hoffa. The papers related primarily to Beck, and Hoffa was reported to have said upon perusing them, "It looks like Beck's goose is cooked if that is what they have on him." The Teamster then, according to the indictment, asked for more inside information regarding the Senate's investigation of his international president.

The next night, another meeting between the two men took place, again at Dupont Circle. This time, Cheasty brought more secret papers with him and once more transferred these to Hoffa, although on this occasion Hoffa did not give Cheasty any money. When Hoffa walked back into his hotel on this second night, he was arrested. The FBI, in making its announcement of the arrest, stated that Hoffa had in his possession documents from the committee files "which he had just received."

It was generally believed that Hoffa, now released on $25,000 bail, was by this single sequence of events finished as a rising labor power. If found guilty on all three of the bribery and conspiracy counts on which he had been indicted, he faced up to thirteen years in jail (plus $21,000 in fines).

And it was taken as a given in most quarters that he would in fact be found guilty. Even ignoring Cheasty's very respectable credentials, the fact that the prosecution could so easily produce so many credible witnesses to the two March Cheasty-Hoffa meetings appeared to guarantee an airtight governmental case. Kennedy, who knew also that the FBI had made a film that documented both rendezvous in their entireties and that would be offered to the jury, was himself so optimistic as to the outcome that he announced at a press conference following the Hoffa arrest, "If Hoffa isn't convicted, I'll jump off the Capitol dome."

The defense, on the other hand, also possessed an asset that was of no small worth: the services of Edward Bennett Williams, who at an impressively young thirty-six years of age had established a reputation as one of the nation's ablest criminal lawyers. A tall, handsome, and arguably brilliant courtroom enchanter, he had previously represented clients as diverse as mobster Frank Costello, U.S. Senator Joseph R. McCarthy, and four Minneapolis Teamsters who had been charged with illegally taking a bribe from an employer, attracting widespread favorable publicity for himself in the process. Eddie Cheyfitz, who had served as public relations staffer for Hoffa after being an active Communist in Toledo, then studied under Williams at the Georgetown University Law School and subsequently become the latter's law partner, was one of Williams's greatest fans. At Cheyfitz's request, Williams had agreed to represent Hoffa in the upcoming early summer trial. He would be opposed by attorney Kennedy.

The twelve-person jury that was ultimately charged with deciding Hoffa's fate included, quite unremarkably for a trial held in the heavily black District of Columbia, eight blacks. And Williams quickly proved that he was no ordinary attorney by suggesting to the jurors, in his cross-examination of Cheasty, that Cheasty might be antiblack. In questioning that brought an admonition from the judge on the grounds that it was irrelevant to the trial, Williams asked Cheasty whether he had used a fictitious name when employed by the City of Tallahassee, Florida, to "break the bus boycott" and to investigate the National Association for the Advancement of Colored People there. Cheasty heatedly denied the intimation, apparently with good cause. But the possibility that the double agent was something less than a paragon of virtue had been raised.

Two other actions that seemed calculated to win over the black jurors to the Hoffa side were also credited to the fertile mind of Williams, although he steadfastly denied having had a hand in either of them.

Halfway through the trial, Washington's black newspaper, the *Afro-American,* published an unabashedly pro-Hoffa issue that called Williams the "White Knight" and the "Sir Galahad" of the civil rights movement and described Hoffa as the "hardest-hitting champion" of the Teamsters Union, which "has 167,000 colored truck drivers." The issue included a large picture showing Williams and Hoffa with Martha Jefferson, a black lawyer from Los Angeles who was identified as having joined the Hoffa defense team. It also listed a considerable number of people whom it identified as "champions of Negro rights" and asserted that it was the opinion of these people that Hoffa "had been framed." The judge, upon reading press reports that this issue had been delivered to every juror, locked the jury up for the remainder of the trial to prevent any further such influences.

Nor did it escape the attention of the jurors that the legendary black former heavyweight boxing champion Joe Louis was present in the courtroom for a day and a half near the end of the three-week trial. Louis, who warmly embraced Hoffa in full view of all when he arrived, described the defendant as "my good friend" and said that he had come from Detroit to see what was happening to him.

After less than four hours of deliberation, the jury acquitted Hoffa, essentially accepting his defense that he had hired Cheasty strictly as a lawyer and that he did not know that Cheasty planned to take a committee job. The FBI movie was dismissed as documentation merely of the fact that two men had exchanged an envelope at Dupont Circle, not by itself a crime of any kind. "The basic factor in the verdict," said the jury's foreman, "was the failure of the evidence to prove any conspiracy. That made the crux of the whole thing one man's word against another's—Hoffa's against Cheasty's. And the verdict shows who was believed."[2]

All of the jurors, black and white, said that they had not been influenced in the slightest by racial considerations, and it is entirely possible, of course, that they were not. Kennedy himself was convinced that a combination of Williams's overall courtroom ability, Hoffa's own strong testimony, and the unpreparedness and ineffectiveness of the prosecution—and not the black-oriented tactics—had won Hoffa his acquittal. One juror believed that Hoffa had gained considerable sympathy from the jury through testimony that he had left school at an early age to go to work. The elated defendant, who upon hearing the news slapped his son on the arm so emphatically that the younger Hoffa almost toppled over, explained the favorable verdict even more simply: "It proves once again if you are honest and tell the truth you have nothing to fear."

A commonly held opinion was, however, that the racial tactics had been of some persuasiveness. Few blacks were willing to discount entirely the pro-Hoffa message of the widely read and highly regarded *Afro-American*. And there was considerable agreement with the statement of Senator Barry Goldwater of the Select Committee, which immediately revealed that the Teamsters had paid Joe Louis's hotel bill during his Washington visit, that "Joe Louis makes a pretty good defense attorney. That's all I can say."

Williams, in deference to the 287 feet separating the Capitol dome from the ground below it, told reporters that he would send counsel Kennedy a parachute.

The bribery trial did not, as it happened, serve as the first occasion on which Hoffa and Kennedy had met face to face. On the snowy evening of February 19, 1957—exactly six days after Cheasty had originally gone to the Harvard graduate with his charges concerning Hoffa—the two men had been the only two guests at a dinner party held in the Washington suburb of Chevy Chase, Maryland.

The host for this unlikely event was the ex-Teamster public relations man, Cheyfitz, who had remained a close friend of his former boss and also maintained cordial relations with Kennedy. Cheyfitz and his law partner Williams had, in fact, for some time been trying to entice Kennedy into leaving the government and joining their law firm.

Cheyfitz had also been telling Kennedy that Hoffa was no Beck: the Detroiter, in his opinion, had reformed and could now be a definite force for good within the Teamsters. He hoped that the McClellan committee counsel would agree with this opinion once he had sized up Hoffa for himself by spending an intimate evening with him. Cheyfitz also thought that the two guests might even get to like each other, since the patrician Kennedy and the rough-edged Hoffa actually had a lot in common. Both were ambitious, combative, feisty bantamweights. Each was a confirmed workaholic but also a devoted family man. Both prided themselves on candor. Both were nonsmoking physical fitness addicts. Each demanded, and received, total loyalty from his staff. Each was frequently described as "charismatic" by admirers, and as "ruthless" by detractors.

The meeting, undergirded by Kennedy's secret knowledge of the Cheasty allegations, was nonetheless not a success by any standard. Although he later acknowledged that Hoffa had shown himself to be capable of charm, politeness, and friendliness, Kennedy came away with the impression that Hoffa was "worse than anybody said he was." He thought that the Teamster was a "bully" hiding behind a facade of toughness, compelled to brag and boast about his strength and power because of self-doubts that he really had such an ability to excel. Hoffa, he subsequently recounted, had been quick to tell him, "I do to others what they do to me, only worse." Kennedy also noted Hoffa's readiness to discuss his many fights, with employers and others—"Always he had won," the attorney would later sarcastically write—as a further sign of this insecurity on Hoffa's part.[3]

Kennedy had attempted to joke about Hoffa's toughness—"maybe I should have worn my bullet proof vest"—but the humor "seemed to go over his head."[4] The evening ended early, at about 9:30, when Kennedy's wife telephoned to tell her husband that a driver had skidded into a tree on the Kennedy property in McLean, Virginia, and although not seriously hurt, was now sitting, hysterical, in their living room. Kennedy quickly took advantage of the opportunity, made his apologies, and left.

The memories that Hoffa brought away from this rendezvous were quite different than Kennedy's, but they were no more positive. The only word that could describe his fellow guest, the labor leader was to recall, was "condescending." Kennedy had asked him numerous personal questions concerning how much money he made, how he happened to get into the union, and why he hadn't tried to go to college. "Clearly," Hoffa thought, "he was puzzled over the fact that a kid from a poor family, lacking education, could rise to the top of the largest union in the nation."[5] Hoffa also later told an interviewer, "I can tell by how he shakes hands what kind of fellow I got. I said to myself, 'Here's a fella thinks he's doing me a favor by talking to me,' " and asserted that the chief counsel was "a damn spoiled jerk."[6]

Hoffa also took away from the evening a further impression that was no more scientifically verifiable than any of these others. He was convinced that Kennedy became his "mortal enemy" that night because he—Hoffa—had accepted a challenge from Kennedy to Indian hand wrestle and had then proceeded to beat the younger man, not once but twice, at it. In a description remarkably reminiscent of the one that Kennedy had selected to describe him, Hoffa would point out that Kennedy was "a man who always made a big thing out of how strong and how tough he was, how he had been a football player or something at Harvard, and how he always exercised and kept himself in top shape."[7] Nothing could convince Hoffa that this Indian-wrestle wounding of Kennedy's pride did not contribute to the "vendetta" that from that day on he saw the Bostonian as waging against him.

To the surprise of absolutely no one, Beck had announced that he would not be a candidate for reelection. And, a mere seven days after his acquittal in the Cheasty case, Hoffa—who until then had been so widely regarded as finished—was catapulted into the position of front-runner to succeed the man from Seattle at the upcoming IBT convention in Miami. Some eight hundred "Friends of Jimmy Hoffa," representing about 75 percent of the delegates at this late September convention, unanimously and enthusiastically endorsed him for the Teamster presidency in a meeting at Chicago's Shoreland Hotel.

The action by the informal "Friends" group was not in the least unexpected. But the size of the turnout, almost double what even the event's most optimistic sponsors had hoped for, did come as a surprise, as did the large numbers of Teamsters who had come from outside the traditionally pro-Hoffa Midwest. Only the Western Conference, under the control of Hoffa's adversary Frank Brewster, was not represented. And many of the largest locals in both the Eastern and Southern Conferences, not wanting to be left off the growing Hoffa bandwagon, sent emissaries.

Upon his arrival in Chicago for this meeting, Hoffa had told the press that it was "too early to make any statements. If they want me, I'll run." But his pretense at indecision had fooled no one. The unionists, who had preceded him into the Shoreland's Louis XVI ballroom and greeted his arrival there with a prolonged standing ovation (and cries of "Atta boy, Jimmy" and "we're with you all the way, Jim"), had expected an acceptance speech after their "spontaneous" demonstration, and they received one: "There's nothing I can do but carry on with your wishes. . . . If I am elected, I will devote my full time and energy . . . in behalf of every . . . member of our union."[8]

Warming to his subject, Hoffa proceeded to read a nine-page "policy statement," copies of which had been distributed to the gathering. Worthy of some attention as one of the few written expositions of the IBT leader's basic thoughts about administering his union, the document called for an enlargement of the labor organization from its present membership of 1.4 million to 2 million workers, with at least 25 percent of the IBT's income to be earmarked for organizing. It also advocated transferring many of the present powers of the general president, including the interpretation of the Teamster constitution, to the general executive board. It recommended that the finances of the IBT locals be audited by certified public accountants, with copies to be mailed to the international. It urged an expansion of the Teamster research unit and the payment of strike benefits for sympathy and recognition strikes as well as for strikes occurring when labor contracts expired. But it opposed the AFL-CIO position that any union official who pleaded the Fifth Amendment be prohibited from holding office, Hoffa stating that "it is one thing to stand for a society of law and order. It is another thing to pursue a shadow cloak of brief popularity, and in so doing lose a right of human liberty."[9]

Hoffa emerged from this July 26 meeting without a serious rival for the presidency. John T. "Sandy" O'Brien of Chicago had harbored hopes of attracting a sizable block of votes as a "reform" candidate. But the Hoffa bandwagon contained many O'Brien defectors, effectively dashing these aspirations and, recognizing the inevitable, O'Brien withdrew from the race, declaring, "It kind of breaks your heart a little bit." He asked his supporters to vote instead for Hoffa. None of the half-dozen or so remaining candidates appeared to present Hoffa with anything other than token opposition.

It was not, however, to be quite that easy for the ninth vice-president. In the next few weeks several developments cast a definite cloud over Hoffa's prospects.

The first of these was a four-day appearance, starting on August 20, 1957, by the Teamster presidential candidate before the McClellan committee

In actions that received nationwide headlines (and, for an estimated 1.2 million East Coast homes, live television coverage) from start to finish, the committee linked Hoffa's name to an extensive list of activities that appeared to be at best questionable and at worst illegal. And while in responding to the various charges Hoffa did not once invoke his constitutional right against self-incrimination, he was sufficiently vague and evasive in his responses as to cause one senator, Irving M. Ives of New York, to tell him, "You haven't taken the Fifth but you're doing a marvelous job of crawling around it." Senator McClellan himself was aroused enough to ask the Justice Department to see whether or not Hoffa's faulty memory constituted grounds for perjury charges.

At these hearings, which were held in the red-carpeted, marble-columned Caucus Room of the old Senate Office Building, the major witness exhibited a broad band of personality characteristics. He exuded his normal cockiness and breeziness throughout much of his testimony, but he was at other points surprisingly—for him—subdued. He was generally quite respectful, invariably calling the senators on the committee "Sir" or "Senator," but he was at times both flip and combative with the committee's chief counsel, calling Kennedy either "Bob" or "brother" (as in "You are so right, Bob" and "I gave you my answer, brother") in what were often quite terse replies to Kennedy's questioning. He was usually entirely affable, but he displayed flashes of the well-known Hoffa temper. He was both witty and serious, poised and fumbling, relatively (for him) relaxed and visibly tense. (In a matter of days, Kennedy wrote in his journal, the Teamster was alternately "arrogant, angry, pleasant, antagonistic. Tuesday . . . he looked awful. Thursday morning he did well for himself. He is difficult to figure out unless he's slightly mad which I think he might very well be."[10] The one constant impression that he left on the standing-room-only crowd in the Caucus Room and on the millions who watched the proceedings on television (live and taped) was, however, that he was not an entirely cooperative witness, presumably because he had something to hide.

At one point following a line of inquiry into Hoffa's labor philosophy, Kennedy said, "I hate to take you back from being a labor leader to a business man," and the witness retorted, "Go right back; don't worry about it." At several points, when he thought that Kennedy was pressing him too closely for an answer, Hoffa curtly commanded, "Just a minute now." And Hoffa frequently replied to the counsel's questioning rather insolently in the eyes of some observers, by saying "You didn't ask me to bring it so I haven't got it," or "I couldn't tell you offhand." Hoffa also, several times, told Kennedy that the information he was seeking was in the record of the "Hoffman hearings." (Each time Kennedy pointed out, appropriately enough in view of the abrupt conclusion of these 1953 proceedings, that the Hoffman hearings were "incomplete.") Hoffa's whole demeanor was, in the eyes of at least one observer of his performance, that of a man who was "determined to brazen it out."

When, however, the questions rather abruptly turned, on the second day, to the single subject of Hoffa's relationship with one Johnny Dio, the witness appeared to lose at least some of his aplomb.

Dio, born John Ignazio Dioguardi in 1914, was a long-time New York City racketeer. He had gone to Sing Sing prison in 1937 for extorting money from truck operators in the garment industry and in 1956 had become infamous on a national basis by being charged with the acid blinding of labor columnist Victor Riesel (although he was never prosecuted in this case). In the 1930s New York District Attorney Thomas E. Dewey had called him a "young gorilla" who "by the time he was twenty had become a major gangster."

In the field of labor-management relations, he had not proven himself to be a friend of the workingman. He had operated a nonunion dress shop in Pennsylvania and then taken an $11,200 bribe upon selling it, to use his connections to ensure that it would stay nonunion. He had, ironically, been convicted under New York State laws of failing to report this money as income.

He was also a director of the United Automobile Workers Union, AFL, in New York (not to be confused with Walter Reuther's Detroit-based UAW-CIO) and as such had hired as labor officials for the fifteen UAW-AFL locals in New York some forty thugs who had been convicted a total of seventy-seven times for crimes that included robbery, burglary, extortion, possession of stolen mail, and accessory to murder. Often, these men had taken payoffs from employers in return for demanding less than competitive wages for the workers whom they represented.

One of them, Anthony "Tony Ducks" Corallo, was paid by an employer simply to come into the latter's plant on a reasonably regular basis and "glare at the employees" to keep them in line. He had been arrested thirteen times, starting with a grand larceny charge when he was fifteen years old, but had somewhat lowered the two-to-one ratio of convictions to Dio-hired thugs by having only been convicted once, for unlawful possession of narcotics. He had derived his colorful sobriquet from his reputation for "ducking" convictions, and he was now believed to control at least five IBT locals, to be quite friendly with Hoffa, and to be an even more powerful underworld figure than Dio.

Dio had appeared before the committee some two weeks before Hoffa testified. He had taken the Fifth Amendment on all questions, including whether or not he knew Hoffa. Making his message entirely clear, he had even, after an exasperated Senator Ives had announced, "I would like to ask Mr. Dioguardi if there is anything he ever did from the time he was born until the present moment that would not incriminate him," conversed briefly with his lawyer and then responded, "I respectfully decline . . ." In his two hours on the stand, he had invoked the constitutional provision 140 times.

Hoffa, who had seriously considered taking the Fifth himself but finally decided not to, was a model of forgetfulness in his answers to committee questions regarding his dealings with Dio. Even when the committee played a series of recordings of wire-tapped 1953 telephone conversations between Hoffa and Dio, showing rather conclusively that Hoffa had tried to pressure Beck into letting

Dio organize the thirty thousand taxicab drivers in New York as a newly appointed Teamster against the wishes of a fellow Teamster vice-president (but Hoffa enemy) Thomas L. "Honest Tom" Hickey, Hoffa's memory seemed to have failed him. He asserted, in one way or another more than one hundred times, "to the best of my recollection, I can't recall." At one point, seemingly quite rattled by the irrefutable evidence on the tapes, he hit somewhat of an oratorical nadir: "To the best of my recollection I must recall on my memory, I cannot remember." Chairman McClellan, obviously irritated, retorted, "If these recordings do not refresh your memory, it will take the power of God to do it. The instrumentalities of man apparently can't do it."

Nor could Hoffa remember whether or not he had arranged through Dio to smuggle some miniature recording devices, called Minifons, into a grand jury hearing so that he would have recorded evidence of the testimony of his union subordinates at the hearing. Here, however, he seemed to have recovered some of his original brashness:

Mr. Kennedy What did you do with the Minifons you purchased?

Mr. Hoffa What did I do with them? Well, what did I do with them?

Mr. Kennedy What did you do with them?

Mr. Hoffa I am trying to recall . . .

Mr. Kennedy You know what you did with the Minifons. . . .

Mr. Hoffa What did I do with them?

Mr. Kennedy What did you do with them?

Mr. Hoffa Mr. Kennedy, I bought some Minifons, and there is no question about it, but I cannot recall what became of them. . . .

Mr. Kennedy You wore a Minifon yourself.

Mr. Hoffa I cannot recall doing it, and I may have.

Mr. Kennedy Did you ever wear one?

Mr. Hoffa You say "wear." What do you mean by "wear"?[11]

The chairman not long thereafter exclaimed, "We have proceeded to the point where the witness has no memory and he cannot be helpful even when his memory is refreshed." He then called for a recess, but only after reading on behalf of the committee a list of forty-eight points of "conflict of interest and questionable actions"

---

ascribed to the ninth vice-president. The last of these points was somewhat conjectural: "Mr. Hoffa has not taken the Fifth Amendment, but Mr. Hoffa either avoided or equivocated the answers to 111 questions at Thursday's session and today, although we are adjourning early, I think that he broke that record." All of the other points had been established as "facts," McClellan asserted, either in the course of the hearings or through "information the committee has, and we are not disclosing all of the information."[12]

The listing included a summary of monies that Hoffa had, between 1952 and 1956, borrowed from union officials "whose jobs depend on [his] good will" and from businessmen with Teamster contracts. These loans totaled some $120,000, and Hoffa had obtained most of them, the committee pointed out, without collateral, without notes, and without interest payments. (Hoffa, on the stand, had admitted all of this. He said that the money, some $70,000 of which had not yet been repaid, was used for a variety of ventures. He had lost, he said, some $20,000 in an investment in a brewery and $10,000 in an oil exploration company.)

The Senate panel also charged that Hoffa had spent $150,000 from the funds of his home Local 299 and Brennan's Local 337 to purchase the five-acre Indiana estate of Paul "The Waiter" Ricca, a notorious Al Capone lieutenant who had been ordered deported from the United States. (Hoffa had said here that the union had bought the property, including tennis courts and a swimming pool as well as a two-story house that could sleep twenty people, as a proposed school for union business agents, and conducted this business with a trust company. He stated that he hadn't asked who the actual owner was.)

An old skeleton in the Hoffa closet also came back to haunt the Teamster vice-president in these hearings: as the hearings chaired by Kansas Congressman Wint Smith almost four years earlier had done, the McClellan committee focused upon Hoffa's relationship to the Test Fleet Corporation. But where the Smith investigation of this topic (and, of course, all others) had been quickly aborted by what Smith had called the "pressure [that] comes from way up there and I just can't talk about it any more specifically than that," Chairman McClellan's summary of this alleged Hoffa activity was far more tangible.

McClellan claimed on behalf of the committee that Josephine

Hoffa and Owen Bert Brennan's wife, Alice, had made a profit, as co-owners of Test Fleet between 1949 and 1956, of $125,000 on an original investment of a mere $4,000. And he had a ready explanation for this highly impressive financial result: Hoffa's 1948 intercession to settle a Teamster strike against the large Michigan trucking company, Commercial Carriers, Inc., on terms favorable to the employer had so pleased the latter that it had generously reciprocated in helping both Hoffa and his close friend Brennan. The Smith investigation, it will be remembered, had indicated this much originally, but McClellan put considerable meat on the Smith bare bones. Specifically, he charged, the general counsel of Commercial Carriers had incorporated Test Fleet in Tennessee under his name, and the Commercial Carriers owner had signed a $50,000 note for equipment for Test Fleet—following which the stock was quietly transferred into the maiden names of the two wives. In addition, the accountant for Commercial Carriers had kept the books and records of Test Fleet for four years at no salary. And, most significantly, Commercial Carriers had handed the Hoffa-Brennan operation lush contracts for the transportation of Cadillacs. The owners could not have lost money on this arrangement had they tried to, McClellan hinted broadly.

In this case, witness Hoffa had attributed his intercession to the fact that the strike was illegal. His settlement with Commercial Carriers was designed to avoid a "very serious lawsuit," he said. And there was no connection, he had told the committee, between his intercession and the subsequent helpful actions of Commercial Carriers.

Nor, he had testified, was there anything wrong with a labor leader or his family having an ownership interest in the same industry that his union had organized. Committee member Senator John F. Kennedy's questioning of him on the subject elicited the following response from Hoffa:

I find nothing wrong with [such an ownership interest] because it has been my experience that if you can be corrupt for a very small amount of money or a very large amount of money, there isn't much difference. My record speaks for itself, and my contracts speak for themselves, that they are equivalent to anything that has ever been negotiated in any industry without strikes, Senator. . . .

. . . I believe that, if there is uniformity of payment and the contracts speak for themselves in the matter of handling grievances, in the matter of keeping the equalization of wages in line with other industries, it should not be construed as . . . illegal [to have such an ownership interest] . . . because it is my firm belief as a labor leader that, if you know the business that you are negotiating in, and if you have some touch of responsibility, you will be in a better position at the bargaining table to get more for your men when it comes time to bargain.

My experience [of having some ownership in a number of trucking businesses] has saved our drivers throughout the entire central conference from having any strikes and [let them] get at the same time the prevailing wage scales, prevailing increases, in many instances much higher and better fringe benefits, than the average union that takes the position that they don't want to know what the employer's business is about.[13]

No amount of verbal aptitude could offset the very telling evidence amassed by the committee regarding Hoffa's relationship with Dio, however. The several tape recordings of phone conversations between the two men, played over the vigorous objections of Hoffa's normally unruffled lawyer George S. Fitzgerald, confirmed Hoffa's attempts to put the thirty thousand New York taxicab drivers under the leadership of the convicted labor extortionist. They also bore witness to the Detroiter's large role in conspiring with Dio to set up a group of "paper" locals in an apparent effort to gain for himself control of New York City Teamster affairs.

In this latter case, the committee charged, Hoffa had talked Beck's administrative assistant Einar Mohn, after Beck had told Mohn that it was all right to do so, into chartering seven bogus locals in New York. The "locals," which had no members, existed only to the extent of having "officers"—many, according to the committee, Dio's henchmen in the UAW-AFL. Other officers were, in the committee's judgment, lieutenants of "Tony Ducks" Corallo, the practitioner of employee intimidation through glaring.

With the illicit votes of these locals, Hoffa had then tried to get his handpicked candidate, John J. O'Rourke, elected president of Teamster Joint Council 16, the organizational umbrella for the 125,000 truck drivers in the New York City area. (Ironically, O'Rourke, who took the Fifth Amendment in replying to all

McClellan committee questions dealing with his union activities, did win this 1956 election, but he did so without the paper locals' votes. Beck refused, on appeal from O'Rourke's opponent, Martin Lacey, to count them. Beck did, however, award sixteen other challenged votes to O'Rourke, and even though a subsequent court decision dislodged the latter in favor of Lacey, Lacey shortly after this event withdrew and O'Rourke—and the Hoffa forces—took over New York.)

Hoffa was not completely bereft of explanations regarding his relationship with Dio. His position in the taxicab matter, he said, probably stemmed from a misunderstanding. He had felt, he testified, that the Teamsters and not the UAW-AFL should have jurisdiction over the cab drivers but that to get the best organizers available the IBT should take in the UAW-AFL executive board. This position, he admitted, may have made it appear that he was trying to place the thirty thousand drivers under Dio. But, he argued, Dio was not a member of the executive board and therefore would not himself be taken into the Teamsters at all. As for the issuance of the "phony" local charters, Beck was the person entirely responsible, although Hickey, as the IBT vice-president whose sphere of authority embraced all Teamster activities in the New York area, was derelict in his duty in not reporting the bogus quality of these locals to the international president.

Basically, however, Hoffa fell back here on his professed inability to recall the circumstances involving Dio. And this hardly redounded to his credit. Dio's nationwide notoriety, particularly in view of his indictment in the acid blinding of labor columnist Riesel only a few months earlier, made the vagueness of many of the Hoffa answers highly suspect ("Mr. Hoffa," counsel Kennedy had exploded after the witness had said he couldn't recall whether Dio had been in his hotel room recently, "I bet anybody in this country can remember what conversation they had with Johnny Dio or whether Johnny Dio was in their room 2 months ago."[14])

Nor did Hoffa's clear antagonism toward Hickey help his case. The committee had described the latter as one of the few honest Teamster leaders. Committee member Senator Karl E. Mundt had told the New Yorker, "You have the face of an affidavit." And Hickey appeared from all of the evidence to have earned his "Honest Tom" nickname entirely on merit.

And above all of these considerations loomed, of course, the quite persuasive evidence that had been provided by the tapes.

There was no question that Hoffa's first appearance before the Senate Select Committee had bruised him badly. The unknown dimension, as the combative Teamster left the hearing room at the close of the four days, with a subpoena from Chairman McClellan to appear again at an unspecified date, was how much the forty-eight committee charges had combined with his own embarrassing performance to hurt his Teamster presidential prospects.

The general verdict was that he would still arrive at the Miami Beach convention on September 30 as an overwhelming favorite. For one thing, five weeks after O'Brien's late July withdrawal as a candidate, no meaningful competition for Hoffa had arisen. For another, there was no sign that the negative McClellan publicity had cost Hoffa any significant defections among his large army of supporters.

But this prognosis assumed no further problems for Hoffa, and by the end of September four more of them had arisen.

First, the AFL-CIO's Ethical Practices Committee had issued a scathing attack on the Teamsters in general and on Hoffa in particular. And it had clearly indicated that if Hoffa were elected to the IBT presidency, the Teamsters would be expelled from the federation at the latter's early December convention. Basing its report heavily on the McClellan committee findings, the AFL-CIO unit had concluded that "unrefuted . . . evidence shows that the Teamsters Union continues to be dominated, controlled, or substantially influenced by corrupt influences." Hoffa, it had reported, was guilty of a variety of "inherently evil" and "improper" misdeeds, including using union funds for personal purposes and associating with and sponsoring "notorious labor racketeers." One week later, on September 25, 1957, the twenty-nine-member AFL-CIO executive council had approved this Ethical Practices Committee document, with only one dissenting vote (that of the Teamster representative on the council, IBT secretary-treasurer John F. English).

Second, on the same date as this executive council action, a federal grand jury had indicted Hoffa for perjury. It had charged him with lying five times in another grand jury investigation. The latter, a few months earlier, had looked into reports that Hoffa had conspired with Owen Bert Brennan and also with wiretap specialist Bernard Spindel to conduct illegal wiretaps in the union's Detroit headquarters to keep tabs on employees. (Hoffa's alleged purpose there was to find out what information the latter were giving to governmental rackets investigators.) October 15 was set as the date for Hoffa, who faced up to twenty-five years in prison if found guilty of all five perjury counts, to plead to these latter charges. It was the same date that had been tentatively established for his trial in the wiretap case.

Third, as if these problems were not enough, Senator McClellan on behalf of his select committee, two days before the September 30 start of the Teamster convention, had issued thirty-four new charges against the front-running presidential candidate. In an ill-camouflaged attempt of its own to thwart Hoffa's presidential prospects, the committee had reconvened on September 24, on short notice, to hear new allegations against the Teamster vice-president. It had been meeting all week long, frequently from early in the morning until after nine in the evening (in contrast to the normal banker's hours of Senatorial hearings), and this second wave of charges had stemmed from the testimony of almost forty witnesses in this time frame.

The new allegations essentially condemned Hoffa on three grounds. Twelve of the charges accused him of having manipulated some $2 million of Teamster funds to his own advantage. The primary thrust of the others had been indicated by two less than flattering summary statements: 1) "James R. Hoffa has taken the part of employers and convicted extortionists against members of his own union"; and 2) "James R. Hoffa has constantly defended and given aid and comfort to Teamster Union officials who were selling out the interests of Teamster Union members by setting themselves up in highly improper business activities and by entering into collusive agreements with employers."

The long litany of specific charges included assertions that Hoffa had transferred $500,000 in IBT funds to a Florida bank on an interest-free basis to ensure that the bank would loan $500,000 to Sun Valley, a Florida land development scheme in which Hoffa and Brennan had an unpublicized option of purchasing 45 percent for the original cost of the land. The land, near Orlando, had been bought by a former Teamster organizer, Henry Lower, with almost

$200,000 borrowed from the union. He had received his loan after he had allegedly lent $25,000 to Hoffa. Lower had then, the committee charged, remained on the Local 299 payroll for eighteen months and drawn at least $59,000 in salaries and expenses during this period from this and other Detroit locals while working on the land promotion project. Counsel Kennedy, leaving nothing to the imagination, pointed out in a press conference accompanying the issuance of this second battery of charges that Hoffa and Brennan stood to make "a tremendous killing" if the project succeeded and to lose absolutely nothing if it did not.

Another charge contended that Hoffa had loaned $1 million in Teamster welfare funds to the John W. Thomas department store in Minneapolis "despite the fact that a top store official had admitted the concern was near bankruptcy." Here, no elaboration was furnished the public, but the committee clearly believed that if the former wanted to assume the worst of the lender, such an assumption was all right with it.

Hoffa also stood accused of having ordered a Teamster lieutenant to "hide out William Hoffa, his [Hoffa's] brother, while the latter was being sought by the police on an armed robbery charge," of having used union money to pay his brother's hotel bill and $75 a week in expenses during this period, and of having sent another underling to California to find William's runaway wife "at a cost to the union of some $5,000 to $7,000."

Among the many other improper activities attributed to Hoffa was the appointment of Zigmont Snyder, "a notorious hoodlum," as a Local 299 business agent. Another "notorious . . . hoodlum," John Bitonti, received "either $40,000 or $50,000 of union dues money" from Local 299 and through Hoffa's direct efforts, after Bitonti had been denied loans from more orthodox lending institutions "because of his poor character, reputation, and long criminal record." Hoffa was also responsible, according to the committee, for spending $170,000 in union money to pay the legal expenses of Midwestern Teamster leaders accused of bombing and extortions, and to pay the salaries of these men after they had been convicted.

The new assault upon him from the Senate, certainly when combined with his condemnation by the AFL-CIO and his perjury indictment, clearly created for Hoffa a situation that only a Job could have contemplated with equanimity. But on top of all this had come, on the eve of the Teamster convention, a threat that if the convention did go ahead and elect the ninth vice-president as Beck's successor, the election might actually at some later date be invalidated by the courts.

Generating this fourth significant problem for the presidential candidate from Detroit, thirteen New York area rank-and-file Teamsters, claiming that the IBT and its leaders had violated the union's constitution by improperly selecting convention delegates, had filed suit in Washington's Federal District Court. They had specifically contended that 80 percent of the nearly nineteen hundred delegates had been handpicked to rig the election for Hoffa by "fraud and deception," thereby violating the union's "contract" with them. They had asked the judge to delay the convention and election until new, untainted delegates could be chosen under court supervision.

The judge—F. Dickinson Letts, an eighty-two-year-old appointee of Herbert Hoover—had not taken long to comply with the plaintiffs' request. Within hours, he had issued a temporary restraining order enjoining the election. The Teamster laywers had immediately appealed this action to the appellate court for the District of Columbia, however, and in equally short order had been rewarded with a reversal of the Letts decision. But this reversal had contained its own uncertainties: even though the election could now proceed, the three-judge court of appeals had ruled, it could count votes only from delegates who had been "properly selected according to the Teamsters constitution"; the action of the convention's credentials committee in seating all delegates would be subject to a full subsequent review by the courts. The union could, in short, go ahead with the election, but it did so at its own risk.

As Hoffa's attorney Fitzgerald could lament, "Everything has been happening on the eve of the convention," with problems for his client "dropping like confetti at a country fair."[15] And it is conceivable that Hoffa, who was said by one close observer to "be drawn as tight as a bowstring" at this point, might have been successfully challenged by some newly declared candidate for the presidential office.

As the long-awaited 1957 convention opened in Miami Beach, Teamster vice-president William A. Lee of Chicago appeared to some to be that man. Unsullied by even the whisper of scandal and generally regarded for both this reason and for his universally acknowledged leadership talents as Hoffa's strongest potential competitor (an opinion that was shared by Lee himself), he had for months been under considerable pressure from the anti-Hoffa forces to enter the race. His close friend Brewster of the Western Conference had assured him that he could immediately count on over four hundred West Coast delegates should he run. And he had received pledges of support from a variety of scattered locals in other parts of the country, not excluding his own bailiwick of Chicago, as well. He had insisted, however, that he would not seek the presidency "under any circumstances."

That he now declared his candidacy, only hours before the convention's call to order, apparently stemmed from two considerations on his part, both of them attributable to the fast-changing circumstances. First and foremost, Lee believed that, with so many major problems suddenly surrounding Hoffa, there was an excellent chance that the Miami Beach delegates would now turn to him. But, second, he was also not unaware that even a Hoffa victory might allow him to preside over a Teamsters Union—one that the AFL-CIO would charter after expelling the Hoffa-led Teamsters in December—if he positioned himself for this office by making a strong showing at Miami Beach.

In his primary hope, Lee was assuming that Hoffa's three other declared opponents, none of them individually regarded as a credible threat, would support him. And here he envisioned one or the other of two scenarios in operation. Ideally, the three opponents would now recognize his stronger candidacy and, in the interests of thwarting a common enemy, throw their support to him. He had no objection, however, to an alternative sequence of events, wherein the three other candidates would endorse him on a second or third ballot, after their delegates and his had combined on the first ballot to stop Hoffa and create a wide-open convention.

Neither of these developments took place. One of the opponents, Democratic Congressman John Shelley of California (a longtime Teamster from San Francisco), did drop out shortly after Lee's entrance into the race, declaring that "a united opposition to the forces of Hoffa must take place." But Lee gained essentially nothing from this occurrence. Shelley controlled only a handful of delegates and, at that, he not only refused to back Lee but further muddied the waters by asserting that his fellow West Coaster Einar Mohn would make the best candidate.

A second opponent, Chicago's Thomas J. Haggerty, adamantly refused to withdraw. Greeting visitors at his Fontainebleau Hotel convention headquarters (which was, unlike the headquarters of the puritanical Hoffa, well supplied with both liquor and attractive women), he thought that he still had a chance, albeit a remote one, to win. He publicly claimed to have almost half of the convention's delegates, and privately counted over one-quarter of the votes as his. In addition, he planned to challenge the credentials of 177 Hoffa delegates and hoped to gain some additional votes for himself through this action.

And while the third anti-Hoffa candidate, "Honest Tom" Hickey, ultimately joined Shelley in withdrawing, and in this case did give his endorsement to Lee, he did so only on the fourth day of the scheduled five-day convention, long after it was apparent to everyone that no one would be able to stop Hoffa.

The evidence that the heavy majority of the delegates would be voting for Hoffa was, in fact, unmistakable to all objective observers from the convention's very beginning. The Detroiter received far more applause when he entered the hall and made his way to the stage on September 30 than did his three remaining rivals combined when they arrived. The delegates vociferously shouted down the AFL-CIO corruption charges against Hoffa when these were read out, and voted to expunge them from the convention's records. The Central Conference, following an endorsement of Hoffa at its caucus by the venerable IBT secretary-treasurer English (who announced, "We don't care what anybody says about Hoffa. I love this little fellow"), gave all but two of its almost seven hundred votes to the conference president, an unexpectedly one-sided margin.

And, as the *Wall Street Journal*'s reporter on the scene could comment,

Walk into any hotel in Miami Beach and you see Jimmy Hoffa in one form or another, picture or banner. Or walk along almost any street here and you see cars with bumper stickers reading "Jimmy for President." . . . *Contrast all this with Jimmy's opponents.* . . .

If the public display of Hoffa buttons means anything, Mr. Hoffa doesn't even need to go through the formalities of being elected. Everywhere, Hoffa buttons, three inches in diameter, stare out at you. Some delegates wear papier-mache derbies with vivid signs repeating the slogan, "Hoffa for President."[16]

Even the Teamster security guards at the convention wore Hoffa buttons, this newspaperman informed his readers, and they defined their assignment somewhat more broadly than people in their position normally do. While candidate Lee was giving a speech to the Chicago Joint Council caucus, they passed the time by tearing down the "Lee for President" cards tacked up in the hallway outside.[17]

Hoffa came to Miami Beach with not the slightest doubt that the convention would elect him. He thought, in fact, that he might garner as many as 75 percent of the votes, primarily because of a membership backlash to the McClellan committee's aggressive onslaught on him. (Years later, he was to write in regard to Robert Kennedy, "I think that all he did was clinch the election for me. He went too damned far. Our guys were starting to get mad as hell at all this pressure."[18]) He now had so many votes to spare, he told reporters, that the credentials committee could disallow some of his delegates without his raising any objection at all.

But while this last statement symbolized his optimism as to the presidential election, it also bore witness to his fear that the federal judiciary might not allow his victory. The court of appeals decision was never far from his thoughts. And, knowing that any actions of the credentials committee would be tested in the courts, he sought to maximize the chances of success in the latter forum. He instructed his supporters who passed on credentials to be "exceptionally careful," and they took his charge so seriously that, of the 1,868 delegates who sought accreditation, 115 delegates (all but a handful of them pledged to Hoffa) either were denied such approval or simply withdrew from the convention in anticipation of rejection. And the committee members could hardly be accused of impulsive actions even in seating the remaining 1,753 delegates: they proceeded so diligently that over 100 delegates still remained to be ruled on well into the convention's fourth day.

Hoffa won the election as handily as he had expected that he would. A three-hour roll-call saw him receive 1,208 votes, with Lee getting 313 votes and Haggerty (the liquor and women notwithstanding) coming in third with 140 votes. If there was ever any question that the forty-four-year-old Detroiter would prevail, it was removed when the pivotal Los Angeles Joint Council (with 123,000 members) joined the Hoffa bandwagon and thereby made a sizable dent in the Western Conference's formerly almost solidly anti-Hoffa front. In the eyes of many, it had been removed even earlier, when the widely respected and scrupulously honest English had nominated Hoffa "for what he has done for the organization" and assured the delegates that there "may be a little trouble going on here and there, but he will take care of that."

The margin of victory was so large that the delegates did not even wait for the official announcement before embarking on a half-hour demonstration that appeared to be heartfelt. Hoffa stood up, in the words of one observer, to "thunderous applause. Then he called Jo up and kissed her and put an arm around her, and there was more thunderous applause. She was in tears."[19] The applause was so thunderous, in fact, that for a few moments authorities feared that the floor of the big Miami Beach Auditorium might collapse, and one security officer raced up to the platform and excitedly asked convention presiding officer Dave Beck to do whatever he could to bring the cheering to an end. Beck did his best to comply.

The convention then gave its new president-elect an executive board that was very much tailored to do his bidding. It was headed by the new first vice-president Harold J. Gibbons, who from this position would become acting president of the Teamsters should Hoffa's wiretapping and/or perjury charges send the latter to jail. Owen Bert Brennan was also elected to a vice-presidency, as were ten other Hoffa choices. One of the latter, in an action that surprised no one, replaced Frank W. Brewster, who was dropped from the board (while Mohn, as a reward for his last-minute influence in bringing Los Angeles into the Hoffa camp, succeeded Brewster as head of the Western Conference). Hickey was replaced by O'Rourke, and English, in another forgone conclusion, was re-elected secretary-treasurer.

In his acceptance speech, the president-elect (he would officially assume the office on October 15) pledged to do everything that he could to remain within the AFL-CIO. He felt, he said, that the Teamsters had complied "fully and properly with [the] proper ethical demands" of the federation at the convention, and asked for time to prove that he could make the IBT a "model of trade unionism." He promised, he said, "to do all in my power to lead you and this organization to a position of respect and honor in the eyes of the rank and file of labor, in the eyes of the nation, in the eyes of the world." But if the organization that was presided over by George Meany did expel the Teamsters and then attempted to raid its membership, he declared, the union would defend itself "with every ounce of strength we possess."

In an emotional statement, he also asserted,

To say that I do not feel deeply about the charges that have been made against me would be untrue. To say that it has not been tough would be untrue. I am a family man. I have a wife and children. I am proud of my family, and they are proud of me. They know how I believe in the cause of labor. They know this is my life's work and I am not ashamed to face them at any time for anything I have ever done. I will fight to defend myself and to keep the name of Jimmy Hoffa as a symbol of good trade unionism and as a symbol of devotion to the cause of labor.

And he had something to say about the ongoing congressional investigation:

I have no fight with the McClellan Committee, nor have I any desire to obstruct a true and honest investigation. Investigations by committees of Congress to aid in legislation have a useful and proper place in America. But when a Congressional committee concentrates on a personal attack or misuses its power, it can be dangerous for all of us. Something is wrong when a man may be judged guilty in a court of public opinion because some enemy or some ambitious person accuses him of wrongdoing by hearsay or inference. What is happening to our historic principle that a man is innocent until proven guilty?

. . . Destruction of the basic principles of due process and the use of the lawmaking function to smear a man's reputation without the protection of judicial processes is one of the greatest threats to freedom and the rights of the individual that America has faced in our lifetime. I want to say that a great injustice has been done to the individual members of the Teamsters Union. You are the people whose good name has been smeared.

Five days later, the triumphant Hoffa flew back to his home city and received a hero's welcome. Some two thousand Local 299 members greeted him at Detroit's Willow Run Airport with cheers and noisemakers. Many of them also had paper streamers, which they threw at the object of their affection and his wife as the two Hoffas walked down a line of Teamster stewards to an impromptu platform on the rear of a truck trailer.

The general motif of this event was the American Indian, and many in the assemblage wore a feather and an Indian headdress. Fittingly, a Teamster official presented Beck's successor with a headdress of his own—that of an Indian chief, with several white feathers and orange tips. He informed a rather embarrassed Hoffa that it was being given by the Indians to "our big chief Jimmy Hoffa." In accepting it, Hoffa said that it was a pleasure to be home again among the "honest members" of Local 299, people who understood his problems and those of the Teamsters.

They might have understood them, but this was hardly tantamount to resolving them for Hoffa. And the problems continued to mount. Even before the voting for Teamster president, the McClellan committee had subpoenaed all of the documents of the credentials committee and placed itself on record as believing that over half of the delegates had been improperly chosen. It thereby joined the thirteen rank-and-file Teamster dissidents who had failed to stop the convention from being held but who were now claiming that the convention violated the order of the court of appeals.

The subpoenaed records were turned over to the committee, but not without some difficulty. A maid at the Eden Roc Hotel had accidentally thrown them into a trash receptacle. She had then, quite suddenly, died of a heart attack, and therefore was unable to testify to her error of commission.

The records were recovered after a thorough search of the hotel floor where the credentials committee had kept them, but only after the issuance of more negative national publicity for Hoffa by a highly suspicious Senator McClellan.

The select committee's chairman, not one to take explanations from the Hoffa camp at face value, told reporters that the Eden Roc incident was either just another of the many "strange coincidences" that the committee had encountered in trying to procure IBT records or a "willful defiance" of the committee and an effort to obstruct its activities. He had in mind at least two experiences. When the committee had previously sought the records of a Portland, Oregon, local, it had been informed that a janitor had thrown them out. And Johnny Dio had phlegmatically told McClellan's investigators that a thief had broken into his automobile and stolen some of *his* records.

Much worse for the new Teamster president, within hours of receiving the subpoenaed documents, McClellan announced that they proved that Hoffa had been improperly elected. They revealed some actions that were "just plain scandalous," the chairman said, in pointing out that under the Teamster constitution delegates had to be selected before September 1, and this selection had to be made at a general membership meeting. Even a brief sampling of the records clearly showed, he declared, that both of these commandments had been violated, Hoffa's instructions to the credentials committee to be "exceptionally careful" notwithstanding. He used as an illustration Hoffa's own Detroit Local 299, whose delegates had apparently been chosen between September 8 and September 11, 1957, and at meetings not open to the general membership. He also pointed to a Missouri IBT local that had tampered with its delegates' printed credentials so "it would appear that the delegates had been properly elected."[20] Kennedy underscored this theme in asserting that "I don't believe we have found one local that elected its delegates properly."[21]

Particularly galling to the committee was evidence that convention chairman Beck had exercised his vested authority as outgoing Teamster president to "interpret" the IBT constitution by blandly declaring the constitutional requirements to be "not mandatory but directory." In line with this rather imaginative interpretation, he had instructed the credentials committee to seat delegates "pursuant to by-laws, rules, or motions which were adopted by membership vote authorizing such method of selection."

McClellan quickly made the subpoenaed documents available to the lawyers for the thirteen dissidents. The latter, in equally rapid fashion, convinced Judge Letts on October 14 that Hoffa should not be allowed to officially assume the office the next day, as he was scheduled to do. The elderly jurist issued his second temporary restraining order for Hoffa, and this time it was not reversed in higher court. Nine days later, he signed a new injunction forbidding the president-elect (and all of the other Teamsters elected to office at the convention) from taking office until the suit of the rank-and-file Teamsters had been judicially resolved. Until that time, the District Court judge mandated in his order, Hoffa and the other newly chosen officials could receive no salary or other compensation in their new roles. Nor could they spend any union funds or make any policy decisions on behalf of the union.

The besieged Hoffa did get a badly needed respite on one front. His October 15 wiretapping trial was postponed so that the federal judge assigned to that case could consider a claim by Hoffa's lawyers that, in the current atmosphere of publicity surrounding their client, he could not receive a fair trial. The judge informed Hoffa that a new date would be set for the trial on October 25, the same date on which the Teamster leader would learn when he would be tried on the five perjury charges (to which, on October 15, he had pleaded innocent).

But no relief was provided Hoffa by the AFL-CIO. On the same day that Judge Letts signed his injunction, the federation's executive council rubbed salt in the president-elect's wounds by voting to suspend the Teamsters from its membershisp. It also went on record as recommending that the IBT be expelled from the federation entirely at the December AFL-CIO convention. Only if the federation's largest affiliated international union met two conditions, the council decreed, would these actions be negated: the Teamsters must bar Hoffa (and certain other individuals named in September by the Ethical Practices Committee as also having engaged in "corrupt practices") from all international union offices; and the union must allow a special committee appointed by the executive council to clean up its administration.

The action was expected, but the strength of the anti-Teamster forces came as a surprise. Only four of the twenty-nine council members voted against the actions. And two of the four—the IBT's own English and the former president of the Bakery and Confectionery Workers Union, which itself had already been found guilty of corruption by the executive council—cast ballots that were essentially automatic. Hoffa, who had consistently maintained that the federation needed the Teamsters and the more than $800,000 in dues that they annually paid to the AFL-CIO far more than the Teamsters needed the federation, stomped out of the AFL-CIO headquarters building as soon as the council voting was announced. He offered a curt "No comment" to the reporters who awaited him. His face was, in the words of one of the latter, "tense with anger." And his action, combined with that of the council, left little doubt in anyone's mind as to what would happen at the convention.

The long-awaited second biennial convention was called to order in early December at the cavernous Convention Hall in an icy, wind-swept Atlantic City. The U.S. Secretary of Labor, James P. Mitchell, greeted the two-thousand-odd delegates and, in a thinly veiled reference to the main item on the convention's agenda, announced that President Dwight D. Eisenhower would soon propose legislation to protect union members from "crooks and racketeers." The blunt and implacable Meany, in his Bronx-accented, gravel-voiced keynote speech, was more explicit: Teamster expulsion could only be averted, the AFL-CIO president said, if Hoffa were to resign as president-elect; Hoffa was not the only problem the IBT had ("God knows, they've got plenty of problems"), but the others, in his opinion, could be ironed out inside the AFL-CIO framework. The October report of the executive council was then read.

Hoffa was unable to attend the sessions. His wiretapping trial had now begun, ninety miles away in New York City, and his presence was required there. The case for Teamster retention was to be presented by the distinguished looking vice-president of the IBT, Einar Mohn, and by the popular Teamster secretary-treasurer, John F. English.

Mohn led off, reminding the delegates that the Teamsters had always been available for help when other unions had needed them. "It has become traditional and customary," he asserted, "for labor unions in practically all industries to call upon the Teamsters . . . for assistance when they have disputes, and in organizing campaigns. . . . Nothing can change the strategic importance of the Teamsters, and nothing can change the dependence that the local unions affiliated with the other organizations that are in the Federation will continue to have on Teamsters locals throughout the country." As for the charges of corruption, the IBT was simply too large and its power too widely dispersed, he said, for it to be dominated by corrupt influences and anyone who made such a charge failed to understand the union's make-up. He sat down to tepid applause.

The lean, leathery English (whom reporters had so often described with the adjective "venerable" that some people may well have thought that this word was part of his name) echoed the same themes but with somewhat more eloquence and far more truculence:

Regardless of what you or anybody says, deep down in your hearts you know there is not a union connected here that is better than the Teamsters. . . . For fifty years, when you were on strike . . . when you knocked at the Teamsters' door, they helped you. . . .

We ask for one year, after giving you fifty years. We ask for one year to clean up our house. Beck is gone. Brewster is gone. And Brennan [Sidney Brennan, another IBT executive board member who had been named in the original corruption charges and who also, as Beck and Brewster, was not reelected at Miami Beach] is gone. There is only one man—Jimmy Hoffa. And Jimmy Hoffa has done more for our international union than anybody connected with it, including myself. How in the hell can we kick him out? Does he deserve that? He is fighting to clear himself, and if he can't be cleared, then that is up to us. . . .

Oh, it makes my blood run cold. I am coming near the end of my days. I never thought I would live to see this . . . the Teamsters will get along. We won't forget our friends. Teamsters never forget their friends. As far as our enemies are concerned, they can all go straight to hell. . . .

English asked for understanding, too, from the delegates:

We have $40-million and I wish to God we didn't have it, because when we had only $1.50 we never had any trouble. But the minute we get a dollar in the treasury all these lawyers are taking it.

How in the hell did we run our organization when there weren't any attorneys? There's seven or ten of them now robbing us, a hundred bucks a day, and they can't agree among themselves. How in hell can we win these cases?

Several other delegates spoke on behalf of the Teamsters. Two of them, in particular, came from unions that were universally respected for their long-established membership democracy and high moral standards. The president of the International Typographical

Union, the only union with a formalized two-party system in its structure, argued against expulsion. So did the head of the Upholsterers Union, one of only two labor organizations to have established an independent appeals board of distinguished private citizens to protect its members against unwarranted actions by the union leadership.

But not a single delegate took the floor to speak in favor of the motion to expel. Except for the chairman of the federation's appeals committee, who made it clear that he was against only Hoffa and not the Teamster members (whom he described as the principal victims of the corruption at the top), the forces favoring the IBT's ouster remained quiet. "No one," in the words of one of the three hundred journalists in attendance, "would bell the cat."[22] Meany, never in doubt as to what had to be done, grimly took the microphone to call for the expulsion himself.

Not even his worst enemies had ever accused the Irish-American plumber of insincerity. Whether railing against college professors ("College professors, when offered a choice of publish or perish, usually make the wrong decision") or making known his opinion of sociopolitical theories ("Ideology is baloney"), Meany's words harmonized totally with his thoughts. Once, when asked on a nationally televised interview program to say why he refused to elaborate on a view that he had just expressed, he had explained, "Because I don't want to."

Now, the head of the federation vented his full fury on an errant member union. In strident tones, he pointed out that the Teamsters had done nothing about the "crimes against the labor movement" that their leadership had committed. He reminded the delegates, his voice heavy with emotion, that the Miami Beach conventioneers had instead voted to expunge the charges against Hoffa and the others from the records. He hoped, he said, that the Teamsters would be back in the federation soon. They would be welcome as soon as they had complied with the clean-up order. But since they had chosen now not to clean their own house, the AFL-CIO had to do the job for them, had to "free the membership . . . from this dictatorship. The secretary will call the roll. You vote yes or no."

A two-thirds vote was required to oust the federation's largest affiliate, and the delegates gave Meany considerably more than this margin. Ballots representing 10,458,598 AFL-CIO members were cast for expulsion, with 2,266,497 votes being registered for retention. Many of the latter votes came from three large unions themselves under investigation by the McClellan committee: the Carpenters, the Sheet Metal Workers, and the Hod Carriers. Of the 128 international unions that were (unlike the Teamsters) entitled to participate in the balloting, 95 voted with the majority, 21 supported the Teamsters, 4 split their votes, and 8 abstained. In New York, Hoffa received the expected news matter-of-factly, declaring that the AFL-CIO "didn't build us and they won't weaken us."

We Admire the Man
Who Can Deliver

5

The specific consequences, for both the Teamsters and the federation, of the expulsion from the AFL-CIO remained to be seen. The Hoffa-led Teamsters had obviously been branded, in the full glare of national publicity, the pariah of the labor movement. But, a few months before the expulsion, it had been widely believed that ousting the big union would touch off a ruinous civil war between the two organizations. Now this was not so certain.

Meany, normally a relentless noncompromiser, informed Hoffa's union that at least for the time being no rival union would be chartered. He recognized the possibility that Hoffa might in fact be ousted by reform elements within the IBT or that the Teamster might by dint of imprisonment or other court ruling become otherwise unable to preside over the Teamsters. And the AFL-CIO leader preferred not to inherit all of the sticky jurisdictional questions that the existence of an IBT clone within the federation would pose.

In addition, an AFL-CIO decision on whether or not to cancel some half-dozen mutual assistance pacts between federation affiliates and the Teamsters would be postponed for a while. This latter decision, too, recognized the tenuousness of Hoffa's position. Hoffa, here today, might conceivably be gone tomorrow.

If so, this departure would not be caused by Hoffa's current New York wiretapping trial, however. In late December 1957, after deliberations lasting more than thirty hours, the seven-man, five-woman jury in that case told the judge that it was "hopelessly deadlocked," and the judge thereupon discharged it without a verdict. Eleven members had favored conviction. But the twelfth, a broker in syrups and sugar, had concluded that the government had not proven beyond a reasonable doubt that Hoffa had conspired with Brennan and the wiretap specialist Spindel to conduct the illegal wiretaps of Hoffa's Detroit subordinates.

"I conscientiously kept my mind open, looking for proof," the broker informed reporters, and he hadn't been furnished such proof. He had even returned to the judge during the deliberations to ask for guidance: the judge had suggested that if you are in a subway and people enter with wet clothing, you can infer that it is raining, but the evidence is merely circumstantial. And the broker had found the evidence against Hoffa and the others to be of this caliber—not, in his mind, enough to justify a finding of guilt.

The hung jury allowed the chunky president-elect to walk out of the courtroom, on $2,500 bail. But it lifted this one of many weights on Hoffa's shoulders only temporarily. U.S. Attorney Paul W. Williams, the government's chief prosecutor in the case, immediately announced that he would bring the wiretap conspiracy charge back to court "as soon as it is practicably possible." Most observers interpreted this to mean that a new Hoffa trial, together with the threat for Hoffa of a maximum prison sentence of five years should he be found guilty on this second occasion, would take place sometime during the following spring.

On the other hand, another of Hoffa's problems seemed now to have been permanently resolved in his favor. Also in December 1957, the U.S. Supreme Court ruled that evidence obtained by telephone wiretaps could not be used in federal courts. And this meant, realistically, that the government would have to drop its perjury indictment against Hoffa: the bulk of the proof that Hoffa had lied in the original grand jury wiretapping investigation had been obtained through the tapping of his own telephones by the government. The case technically remained outstanding, but it was now obvious that only a prosecutor with a suicidal instinct would ever bring it before a jury.

Hoffa's impressive batting average in the courts improved even further, a month later, when the thirteen dissident Teamsters ended their suit to prevent him from assuming the presidency. In an unprecedented compromise, which Judge Letts termed a "magnificent disposition" of the litigation, they agreed to let a three-man board of monitors scrutinize the affairs of the union. One monitor would be appointed by the union; a second by the dissidents; and a third, who would serve as chairman, would be chosen by the first two monitors, with Judge Letts making this last selection should the two be unable to agree. The court would determine the monitors' compensation, which would be paid by the union.

The monitors would be responsible for protecting the rights granted individual members of the union by the union's constitution, and Hoffa was in addition obligated to heed their advice: if he ignored it, they could go to Letts, who would retain jurisdiction, and ask him to reopen the case. The monitors would also have the authority to recommend that a new union election be held at any time after one year. And Hoffa was given the lesser title of "Provisional President," rather than "President," under the terms of this compromise.

But, by the same token, the president-elect was now the official leader of the Teamsters—in a form that was still quite acceptable to him. He would be drawing his $50,000 annual salary and be entitled to all the other perquisites of his position, including a basically limitless expense account. Under the IBT's constitution, ample powers of the purse and of patronage would be available to him. He would control the union's extensive publications and be able to impose trusteeships on local unions if they, among other possibilities, were "being conducted in such a manner as to jeopardize the interests of the International Union." His judicially sanctioned domain would now be nationwide. Where the case of the thirteen plaintiffs against him could have been drawn out for as much as eighteen more months in the courts (and even, at that, been resolved against him) it was now—suddenly—over.

Hoffa did not, moreover, expect to have any real trouble with the monitors. One of them would by definition be a Hoffa man, and this union appointee would have as much say in the selection of the chairman as would the dissidents' agent on the board. He was confident that the advice of the monitors would be both minimal and sympathetic. And he, in any event, expected that the monitorship would be ended in not much more than a year, following which a new IBT convention would elect him to a no-longer-challenged bona fide "presidency."

The "magnificent disposition" had, in fact, been primarily engineered by Hoffa's own attorney Edward Bennett Williams, the lawyer who had so adroitly extricated Hoffa from his problems in the Cheasty bribery case and who had continued to serve his client with distinction in the latter's other court battles. Eddie Cheyfitz, Hoffa's friend and Williams's law partner, had also had a hand. The two primary lawyers for the plaintiffs, Godfrey P. Schmidt and Thomas J. Dodd, had initially resisted the proposed compromise. They had ultimately gone along only when they were persuaded that, if they did not, the case could indeed be drawn out in the courts for months—something for which they neither had time nor, since the dissidents had already spent most of their money, any expectation of being meaningfully compensated. Schmidt, a New Yorker who had generally represented employers rather than union members in court before this, also was assured by the thirteen rank-and-filers that he would be named as their representative on the board.

As the *New York Times* observed in an editorial critical of the settlement:

Surely, the thirteen must be deeply dissatisfied. Their aim in bringing suit was to prevent Mr. Hoffa and his crew from taking office and to bring about a new and free election of officers at a new and freely elected convention. But Mr. Hoffa is now president. His reputation for surmounting all obstacles has been given a mighty boost. The clean-up efforts of the insurgents within his union have had a corresponding setback. . . .

The A.F.L.-C.I.O. has also grounds for complaint. The elimination of Mr. Hoffa had been made the first requirement for readmission of the expelled I.B.T. Now he is, if anything, more firmly in the saddle than ever before, even though the reins can be pulled by others.[1]

To represent its interests on the board, the union selected L. N. D. Wells, Jr., a Dallas lawyer who was already on the Teamster payroll as counsel for the Southern Conference. Schmidt, as he had been promised, was the appointee of the anti-Hoffa Teamsters. Named as chairman, after no less a person than former U.S. President Harry S Truman rejected an overture to consider the job, was Nathan L. Cayton, a retired Washington, D.C., judge. And, with the players thus in place, the era of the monitors began in January

1958—just as amicably as the IBT's provisional president had expected that it would.

Hoffa, who had immediately pledged full cooperation with the three men, seemed determined to avoid any criticism from these watchdogs of Teamster constitutional rights and financial honesty. To absolutely ensure that the new presidential election would be held a year hence, he went out of his way to be seen as being above reproach. Within six months, he had restored self-government to almost 50 locals (out of some 104) that had been under international union trusteeship and scheduled a similar change of status for some 20 other such Teamster affiliates. He had reinstated several rank-and-file rebels who had been suspended from the IBT for various political reasons. And he announced that he had substantially liquidated the outside business interests that had gotten him into so much hot water with both the Senate and the AFL-CIO. He preferred not to provide details on the latter topic, claiming it to be a personal matter. But it was generally believed that Test Fleet, the organization that his wife and Alice Brennan had jointly owned, had been given priority among the business liquidations.

In these early months, he met frequently with the monitors, accepted essentially all of their relatively modest suggestions, and freely shared union records with them. A two-hundred-page six months' summary report issued by the board indicated that he and the union had complied with all but two of what the board in this report deemed its "orders" in this period of time.

Chairman and neutral board member Cayton, whom one Teamster watcher had likened to a "Daniel in the lion's den," had resigned from the board shortly before the publication of this mid-1958 report. But even he, in leaving, had attributed his exit strictly to the overly burdensome demands of the job and had praised the "distinguished cooperation" of the union leadership. Moreover, his successor as jointly selected chairman seemed to augur an even greater era of Hoffa-monitor good fellowship, since Washington attorney Martin F. O'Donoghue—a former law professor at Georgetown University and long-time counsel for the Plumbers Union—had represented the Teamsters Union on several occasions in the past. O'Donoghue had, in fact, served as lawyer for the union in the early stages of the suit against it by the thirteen rank and filers.

But what was past was not, in the case of the new chairman, prologue. The tall, amiable O'Donoghue quickly made it clear that he was beholden to no one. In short order, he had teamed up with the anti-Hoffa appointee Schmidt to pursue a far more activistic approach than his predecessor had taken. Within weeks, the two-to-one monitor majority had called upon the Teamster provisional president to remove a variety of IBT officials, many of them Hoffa's close allies, who had been accused of various illegalities by the McClellan committee.

Conspicuous among these allies were two Philadelphia union officers and Hoffa friends: Local 107 head Raymond P. Cohen, who had refused to tell the senate committee how he had spent $491,000 in union funds; and Local 929 leader Samuel "Shorty" Feldman, who had served three years in Sing Sing for burglary, whose uncomplicated philosophy was that "a man learns to respect people who break his neck for him," and who had taken the Fifth Amendment when asked by the committee whether he had solicited a $50,000 bribe from an employer to settle a labor dispute. Even more prominent was Hoffa's best friend and business partner, Teamster Vice-President Owen Bert Brennan, who had also invoked the Fifth at the senate hearings in refusing to explain testimony that he had used thousands of dollars of union monies for personal gain.

The monitor majority had also proceeded to denounce as slipshod the union's record-keeping system and to declare that inadequate membership lists could lead to a plundering of the union's $39 million treasury unless controls were implemented. It had requested Hoffa to set up election rules designed to keep convicted criminals out of union office, to investigate local IBT officials who had been already challenged by the monitors for past activities, and to dissolve an allegedly illegal merger of two locals in Alaska. It had asserted that the board wanted full, not token, compliance with its recommendations: in fact, the monitors would go back, they had said, to Judge Letts to ask that he spell out their powers more explicitly and, in so doing, force Hoffa to comply with their recommendations.

The O'Donoghue-Schmidt tandem, further, had implemented its own personnel to receive and deal with membership complaints. And, by far most jarring to the provisional head of the Teamsters, it had announced that there was "a lot still to be done" before there could be any guarantee of democratic practices in the union and, therefore, that it had absolutely no intention of calling for a new Teamster presidential election in the near future. First, said Chairman O'Donoghue, the union must: adopt model by-laws designed to safeguard membership rights; establish an effective reporting control system between the international and the local unions; release the more than fifty locals that remained under trusteeship; and amend the IBT constitution to reflect all of this housecleaning. "We've got quite a lot of work to do before there'll be a convention," the new neutral member of the three-man panel asserted.[2]

Hoffa continued to profess a desire to cooperate fully. He suspended the philosopher Feldman. He approved a three-man special hearing board (with one public member) to investigate not only Cohen but all officials of Local 107 (although, in announcing this action, he stressed that the panel's appointment was not to be taken as "any acceptance of statements . . . that there is anything wrong with the operation of Local 107"). As an outgrowth of this latter activity, he established a three-man antiracketeering commission, to be financed by Teamster money, to investigate all racketeering within the union and to be headed by the same George H. Bender who as a congressman had chaired the abortive 1954 investigation of the Teamsters and then, from 1955 to 1957, been a U.S. senator. And he avoided anything that could be construed as direct defiance of the monitorship, even though he was assured by his knowledgeable chief counsel Williams that if the union chose to refuse an order from the monitors "there would be nothing they could do about it."

But with his hopes for an early election now so completely dashed and with Brennan and other close friends now becoming prime targets of the monitors, Hoffa at this point refused to do anything more to accommodate O'Donoghue and Schmidt. Months after the two-man monitor majority (invariably, with Teamster appointee Wells vigorously dissenting) had begun issuing its spate of requests to Hoffa, Feldman remained the only IBT official to have been ousted, and both of Hoffa's investigatory panels appeared to be proceeding sluggishly at best.

In mid-September, moreover, the provisional president publicly went on the offensive. Complaining that he was being persecuted and made the target of "unfair and poisonous propaganda," he—with the full support of the Teamster executive board—called for a new election at a special February 1959 convention. The date was the earliest one possible under the original order of Judge Letts, and the entire action was justified by monitor Wells as being fully consistent with the judge's mandate. Nothing in the order, Wells argued, prevented the union from calling an election at any time. In fact, the habitual minority of one contended, the judge in issuing his order fully expected that an election would be held after one year, to be followed by an immediate termination of the monitorship. The February convention date was soon changed to March, in recognition of the advance notice needed for delegate selection and hotel reservations. But otherwise the head of the Teamsters was adamant regarding his convention plans.

O'Donoghue and Schmidt rapidly responded by asking Letts to give them more time to clean up the union—at least until September, 1959. O'Donoghue contended, among other specifics, that the Hoffa stewardship had now refused to comply with ten out of twenty-one reform directives. Schmidt asserted that "nothing effective has been done" since the dissident Teamsters had first filed their charges in federal court over a year earlier.

Hoffa also now openly took on Schmidt, whom he regarded as his primary enemy on the board. Through his attorneys, he asked Letts to remove the intense, serious appointee of the anti-Hoffa forces on the grounds of "conflicts of interest." His petition to the court charged that Schmidt had continued to represent employers in labor negotiations with the Teamsters and that he had illegally solicited and received large contributions from employers who were parties to IBT contracts. For good measure, Schmidt was also condemned in the petition for filing expense claims that were double those of the other monitors.

The accused monitor denied all charges of wrongdoing and could not resist adding that he was "sure that Mr. Hoffa and his associates are experts in padding expenses." Schmidt also asserted that Hoffa and his associates were "trying to ditch me because they can't frighten me or buy me off." The latter comment referred to an offer of $100,000 that the attorney from New York claimed had been offered him to resign from the board.[3]

This $100,000 might have represented, not an outright bribe as Schmidt interpreted it to be, but payment of the fees (actually,

$105,000) that Schmidt contended that he was now owed by the union for handling the suit brought against it by the thirteen rank and filers. With relations between the lawyer and the Hoffa forces now so strained, there was minimal communication. Therefore, there were ample grounds for misunderstanding. It is a matter of record, however, that the fertile Hoffa mind had also explored three additional routes, beyond the payment of the $100,000 and the removal request to Judge Letts, that might lead to an ex-monitor's status for Schmidt.

One of these, as the Teamster president readily acknowledged, was the hiring of a private investigator in an effort to unearth personal information that would be damaging to the monitor appointed by the rank and file. This avenue was apparently not pursued very far, very possibly because the habits of the clean-living Schmidt afforded little prospect of success in this endeavor.

A second was the withholding of other monies due the monitor from the IBT, some $25,000 in fees and $3,500 in expenses for serving as a monitor since the activation of the board on January 31. In his countersuit to the Teamster removal suit, the earnest New Yorker contended that he had not yet been paid and that, since he had given up his law practice to work on the monitorship, the receipt of dollars to which he was rightfully entitled would be both appreciated and very much welcomed.

Finally, the man who originally led the thirteen rank-and-file insurgents in their suit against Hoffa, and as such had been Schmidt's most prominent single client in this affair, now filed a separate suit against his old attorney. John R. Cunningham, a New York truck driver, charged that Schmidt had misappropriated $50,000 in rank-and-file funds that had been collected for the legal proceedings and was refusing to give an accounting of this money. Hoffa and his primary lawyer Williams disavowed any connection with Cunningham's action. But the quickly discovered fact that the Teamsters had been paying some of Cunningham's Washington, D.C., hotel bills made the disavowal ring hollow.

His patience exhausted, Schmidt now issued and publicly released a scathing memorandum to his two colleagues on the panel of monitors. In it, he accused Hoffa and other top IBT officials of "corruption, incompetence, unfitness, non-compliance [with the monitors] and lack of cooperation." He said that Hoffa should be removed from even provisional leadership given the sorry record of his administration. And, joining O'Donoghue in requesting Judge Letts to rule on the legality of the January 1958 settlement in view of the fact that the full Teamsters membership was never notified of the terms of this settlement, Schmidt minced no words in arguing that "to leave [the question of legality] unsettled at this time is to provide irresponsible characters like Hoffa with an obvious legalistic 'out' at some future time when it suits their convenience and the exigencies of their dictatorial conspiracy."[4]

In December, Judge Letts issued his findings on these several matters before him, and they overwhelmingly supported the monitors. Henceforth, he ruled, the Teamsters would take "orders" from the board and not treat the panel's "orders of recommendation," as the board had taken to calling its fiats, simply as "recommendations." Far from being limited to a "merely advisory" role, the monitors in the jurist's opinion had available to them "every known method" to guarantee an honest presidential election and democratic procedures in the union. They had not only the "grant of express powers" contained in his original January ruling, Letts declared, but "all other powers reasonably necessary." Moreover, since Teamster obstruction had "completely destroyed" the consideration upon which the January reference to a one-year minimum monitorship had rested, this one-year minimum was now rescinded and the monitors could recommend the timing of the convention completely as they saw fit.

As for the Teamster requests to remove Schmidt from the board on conflict of interest grounds, it was rejected because the union had simply failed to show such a conflict. And, unwilling to stop here in voicing his dim view of the Hoffa administration, Letts reprimanded the IBT further by finding that after its initial cooperation with the monitors, it had "ceased cooperation . . . or refused or ignored the reasonable and relevant requests of the monitors." It had refused to comply in good faith with its end of the "magnificent disposition" and rather had frustrated and blocked the monitors in their efforts.

Hoffa announced that he would appeal this lower court ruling to higher judicial authority and airily told the press, "What the hell. It just means another fight." Privately, however, he was deeply disappointed. He had expected a better fate at Letts's hands.

Hoffa was acquitted in his second wiretapping trial, held in the late spring of 1958 in New York City. The eight men and four women on the jury were apparently most influenced by the twenty-seven defense witnesses who testified that on the date in question—July 9, 1953—Hoffa had been in Seattle attending a union convention and therefore could not also have been in Detroit. (The government, while acknowledging that no one could be in two places simultaneously, had argued that the Local 299 leader could have flown back to Detroit and then back to Seattle on this date.) Word of the event was passed in a note bearing the three words "Hoffa was acquitted" to Kennedy in the middle of McClellan committee hearings and, according to several reporters present, he turned ashen upon receiving the information.

According to Kennedy, the defendant himself had been uneasy about the situation here. Kennedy wrote subsequently that he had met Hoffa, purely by accident, in the elevator of the courthouse building where the trial was being held. Minimal pleasantries had been exchanged: "Hello, Jimmy"—"Hello, Bobby"—"How does it feel to be president of the Teamsters Union?"—"Greatest job in the world. But it's keeping me busy." Then the lawyer had asked how the trial was going, and Hoffa had responded, "You never can tell with a jury. Like shooting fish in a barrel."[5] (Hoffa, on the other hand, remembered nothing about this encounter except that he had said, "Hello, Bobby. How are you getting along?" and that Kennedy "gave me that silly smile and went on about his business."[6])

But, to balance this good wiretapping trial news for Hoffa, another threat to the Detroiter's control of the Teamsters had soon thereafter arisen to haunt him. In August, seeking to oust the provisional head of the IBT by showing close connections between him and a myriad of racketeers and gangsters well established within the union hierarchy, the McClellan committee reconvened after a recess and again focused on the Teamsters.

This time, the gloves were clearly off from the beginning. Chairman McClellan, in his opening statement, said

At the time Mr. Hoffa appeared before this committee last year, he did not hold the top position in the Teamsters Union. Since then, however, at a convention in Miami, Fla., he was elected to the presidency with attending

circumstances that raised serious questions of the propriety and validity of his selection. . . .

On the basis of previous testimony before this committee, replete with improper practices and conduct on the part of Mr. Hoffa and some of his associates, a serious question has arisen in the minds of the committee as to Mr. Hoffa's motivation and the direction and leadership he proposes to give this great and important union.

As spelled out in the committee's interim report, the evidence had shown that in numerous instances Mr. Hoffa has alined [sic] himself with certain underworld characters, who are a part and parcel of the criminal elements and most sinister forces in this country. . . .

It will be recalled that when Mr. Hoffa testified before, he suffered seriously from "lack of memory," and thus avoided answering many pertinent questions seeking information, about which he had knowledge and in which the committee was interested.

It is to be hoped that his memory has improved and that he can now give the committee the cooperation and assistance it is entitled to receive. . . .

It is unthinkable that the leaders of any such powerful organization should have an alliance or understanding in any area of its activities with racketeers, gangsters, and hoodlums. . . .

Notwithstanding Mr. Hoffa's reported remarks of contempt for the committee, its source of authority, the United States Senate, and the purposes and objectives for which the committee labors, the committee will pursue its duty and carry out the mandate in the resolution creating it.[7]

And Hoffa, having been so welcomed, was also anything but amiable even at the start:

Mr. Kennedy Mr. Hoffa, did you know Mr. Joseph Holtzman?

Mr. Hoffa Yes, I did.

Mr. Kennedy He was a close friend of yours, was he?

Mr. Hoffa I knew Joe Holtzman.

Mr. Kennedy He was a close friend of yours?

Mr. Hoffa I knew Joe Holtzman.

Mr. Kennedy He was a close friend of yours?

Mr. Hoffa I knew Joe Holtzman.

Mr. Kennedy He was a close friend of yours?

Mr. Hoffa Just a moment. I knew Joe Holtzman, and he wasn't any particular friend of mine.[8]

Two Hoffa associates in particular received widespread television and other media coverage this time.

The first of these got the bulk of his publicity posthumously. Frank Kierdorf had served twenty-seven months in a Jackson, Michigan, prison for armed robbery. Released in 1945, he had in short order been hired by Hoffa as business agent in charge of Teamster Local 332 in Flint. His management of the five-thousand-member local had been marked by widespread allegations of dynamitings and physical beatings of employers who had resisted his bargaining demands. Once he had tried to run over an obstinate proprietor. Another manager had said of him, "You don't give him arguments." Above all, he had favored arson as a labor relations weapon: the premises of recalcitrant owners received personal late-night visits from the Flint business agent and were reduced to ashes.

On the night of August 3, 1958, while torching a cleaning and dyeing establishment, Kierdorf accidentally set fire to himself and was horribly burned over 85 percent of his body. Sometime thereafter, he staggered through the front door of St. Joseph's Mercy Hospital in the nearby city of Pontiac—a zombielike figure with his face grotesquely swollen, his hair completely gone, and scores of blackened blisters from his head to his ankles. He insisted that he was "John Doe of Washington," but a police check of his fingerprints (preserved only because he had clenched his fists amid the anguish of his burning) quickly identified him.

He was given blood and plasma and survived in agony for four more days. As he lay in his hospital bed, the prosecuting attorney—a devout man—told him, "You have only a few hours to live, you are about to face your Maker, your God. Make a clean breast of things. Tell me what happened." Kierdorf was silent for a moment. Then, through lips burned beyond recognition, he uttered what was to be his final sentence: "Go fuck yourself."

Hoffa himself was at this same time back in the Senate Office Building Caucus Room. Under his continuing subpoena, he was undergoing another series of interrogations from the McClellan committee. Kierdorf, in fact, died on the same day that committee counsel Kennedy, not entirely by accident, was questioning the head of the Teamsters about why he had hired the now-deceased human torch shortly after Kierdorf's parole from prison. And Hoffa's explanation that he had done so because Kierdorf "was an experienced organizer" simply was not a credible one. It prompted Kennedy to assert that "the only experience we can find is experience in armed robbery" and confirmed the worst fears that millions of Americans, many of whom had seen photographs of the charred body of the Flint Teamster in newspapers all over the country, already had about criminal infiltration of the nation's biggest union.

Hoffa had exuded confidence a few days earlier when he had entered the Caucus Room to start the first of his several days of testimony. When a reporter had complimented him on how well he looked, he had grinned and sarcastically commented to the many media people who had surrounded him, "I tell ya, I'm worried—I got troubles." His lame explanation for Kierdorf's employment and his weak insistence that he knew nothing about the alleged Kierdorf reign of terror in Flint because "I asked him about it and he said he didn't do it" had to have caused the intelligent IBT leader some concern, however.

(Two decades earlier, Hoffa had also hired Frank's uncle Herman Kierdorf as a business agent for Joint Council 43 in Detroit shortly after Herman had spent two years in Leavenworth Prison for impersonating a federal officer. Herman had subsequently exhibited what seemed to be a family trait by engaging in armed robbery himself and had returned as a Teamster official in 1949 after Hoffa had interceded with the Ohio parole board for his release. Although the Detroiter now told the McClellan committee that he could not remember such an intercession, letters from Hoffa to the parole board proving such action on his part were immediately produced by the committee's staff, and Hoffa's reputation was further tarnished by *this* revelation. It was bad enough that Hoffa had already told the committee that Herman was "a very good friend of mine.")

The second Hoffa associate to receive exhaustive media treatment was a genuine American primitive, a colorful ex-convict who seemed to have almost been expressly invented for these televised hearings. Obese Robert "Barney" Baker, although urged by his attorneys to take the Fifth Amendment, freely talked for two days about his mobster friends in language that was nothing if not wry:

Mr. Kennedy [Committee Counsel] Did you know Cockeyed Dunn?

Mr. Baker I didn't know him as Cockeyed Dunn. I knew him as John Dunn.

Mr. Kennedy Where is he now?

Mr. Baker He has met his Maker.

Mr. Kennedy How did he do that?

Mr. Baker I believe through electrocution in the City of New York of the State of New York. . . .

Mr. Kennedy What about Squint Sheridan? Did you know him?

Mr. Baker Andrew Sheridan, Sir?

Mr. Kennedy Yes.

Mr. Baker He has also met his Maker.

Mr. Kennedy How did he die?

Mr. Baker With Mr. John Dunn.[9]

And, referring to an ambush in which he, Hoffa's New York City lieutenant John J. O'Rourke, and one Joe Butler were shot at, he told the investigators, "All I heard was a lot of noise and I hit the pavement. They shot myself, Mr. O'Rourke and Mr. Butler. . . . Mr. Joe Butler passed away."[10]

He liberally shared his beliefs with his audience ("Little white lies don't mean nothing, not when you are not under oath") and proudly declared that, at separate sittings, he had devoured thirty-eight pounds of meat and four pounds of spaghetti.

But the questions and answers quickly established that the committee had not reserved two days for this 284-pounder (down from 420 pounds five years earlier) merely because of his gift for interesting gab. They also revealed that, for the past two decades, Baker had been a strong-arm man and enforcer for what amounted to a Who's Who of the United States underworld: Meyer Lansky, Joe Adonis, "Bugsy" Siegel, "Scarface Joe" Bommarito, Joe Vitale, "Trigger Mike" Coppola, and others. ("Everywhere you go," counsel Kennedy commented, "there has been violence.")

And, of particular relevance to the main item on the committee's agenda, Baker had for some time worked for the Central Conference of Teamsters as an "organizer" under the direct orders of James R. Hoffa. His duties were not fully defined and included a variety of smallish odd jobs: it was Baker, for example, who had actually paid Joe Louis's Washington hotel bill on behalf of Hoffa one year earlier. But primarily, in the style of "Tony Ducks" Corallo, these duties seemed to have had physical intimidation as their centerpiece: Kennedy was later to write in summing up what the committee had found out about Baker, "Sometimes the mere threat of his presence in a room was enough to silence the men who otherwise would have opposed Hoffa's reign."[11]

Hoffa sat in the hearing room throughout most of Baker's testimony, smiling broadly at his employee's particularly humorous remarks. When, back on the witness stand himself, he was asked if Baker's admitted associations with the heaviest hitters of organized crime bothered him, his reply was, "I am quite sure, hearing him testify here that he knew every one of them . . . it doesn't disturb me one iota."[12]

The committee's effort to show that Hoffa was continuing to keep ex-felons and labor racketeers on the Teamster payroll hardly stopped with its focus on Kierdorf and Baker. The IBT's provisional president was confronted with charges, made primarily but not solely by the relentless counsel Kennedy, that he had taken no steps at all in his over six months in office against the scores of possessors of police records who had infiltrated his union. Many of these alleged infiltrators—including Dioguardi and Corallo—had already been named in prior committee sessions. Many others were now made known to a fascinated American public for the first time: Joey Glimco, the head of Chicago Teamsters Local 777 and a man who had been arrested thirty-six times, two of them in connection with killings; Glenn W. Smith, a Tennessee Teamster official who had twice served terms for burglary and robbery before joining the union; Bernard Adelstein, a ranking New York Teamster with five arrests to his credit; Frank Matula of California, a convicted perjurer; Gus Zapas, a power in the Indiana Conference of Teamsters, despite a record of forty-five arrests; and a large and unsavory collection of others whose aggregate criminal box score was undoubtedly impressive enough to blur the distinction between "Teamster" and "hoodlum" in the minds of many Americans. As a widely circulated witticism of this period had it, the International Brotherhood of Teamsters was an organization that had dropped the "brother" and kept the "hood."

An old problem for the Teamsters was also now trotted out

for renewed public consumption. The committee charged that the IBT's placement of Central States Health and Welfare Fund monies had been, as the aborted 1953 Detroit hearings led by Congressman Wint Smith had initially hinted, marked by scandal. The $1 million paid in fund commissions over the past seven years to the Union Casualty and Life Insurance Company run by Al Capone gang alumnus Paul "Red" Dorfman and his stepson Allen exceeded by a striking $1 million the commission that, in the opinion of the committee, should have been paid. A further and equally damning charge was that the Teamsters, by awarding the business in the first place to the Dorfman operation—though it was not the lowest bidder—had caused the fund to suffer a loss of some $600,000 in the first three years of its operation.

To millions of television viewers and newspaper readers, one man bore the blame for such a scandalous situation. The chunky, combative forty-five-year-old who now led the union and who remained the committee's most prominent witness in his several appearances on the stand throughout these two weeks of hearings was very much the person at whose desk the buck-passing stopped. Himself an Al Capone reincarnated, he was unwilling to move against the gallery of criminals who formed such a prominent part of his hierarchy because his code of values was not significantly different from theirs.

Unless he was afraid of these people, that was. And counsel Kennedy, with the conspicuous lack of subtlety that characterized his general approach to questioning Hoffa, left open this possibility:

Mr. Kennedy Are you frightened of these people, Mr. Hoffa?

Mr. Hoffa I am not frightened of anybody, Mr. Kennedy, and I don't intend to have the impression left, as has been stated publicly, that I am controlled by gangsters. I am not controlled by them but by the same token I do not intend to go around and evade provisions of the constitution of the international constitution which you accused Mr. [Dave] Beck of doing by having dictatorial powers. I want to be able to follow the constitution in due time. This situation will be cleared up. If you recall I took office almost just about February 1. Then I went through a long trial in New York which tied me up. I had the question of monitors which tied me up. . . .

Mr. Kennedy You have people in Detroit, at least 15, who have police records. . . . I say you are not tough enough to get rid of these people, then.

Mr. Hoffa I don't propose to be tough.

Mr. Kennedy You haven't moved against any of them.

Mr. Hoffa I don't propose to act tough. I will follow the constitution of the international union. In due time the situation where necessary, will be corrected.[13]

Hoffa's line of testimony hardly disposed of the doubts that had been raised regarding his criminal connections. At the very least, Senator McClellan's rhetorical (and sarcastic) question to the union leader—"This extraordinary care that you are exercising perpetrates these crooks in office; does it not?"[14]—had to be answered in the affirmative. At the most, the head of the largest, strongest, and richest union in the country came out of this fortnight's battle of wits far more badly tarnished as a willing associate of gangsters than he had been even when he had appeared before the committee one year earlier. He was now much better known than he was in August 1957, to some large extent because of his previous committee testimony but also through his several other pressing problems. He was, therefore, considerably more newsworthy. The made-for-television drama that was again being played out in the floodlighted Senate Office Building room was, accordingly, all the more widely watched. And a public that had basically not heard of him at all not many months before now knew him well, and quite unfavorably.

Nor did Hoffa's own techniques as a witness help him here. Consistent with his established past practice, the president of the Teamsters continued to avoid taking the Fifth Amendment. He was not unaware of the advantages of claiming this constitutional right against self-incrimination. On the other hand, he believed that if he did so now the monitors might seek to oust him from his presidency on that ground alone. And he was quick-witted enough to realize that he might achieve the same result by adopting any of three alternative approaches in giving his answers to the committee's questions. That he might suffer in his public relations by pursuing them was for him a consideration that was definitely secondary.

One of these avenues constituted what counsel Kennedy called "taking the Fifth by proxy." Hoffa would reply to a query that might prove personally embarrassing by saying that while he himself couldn't remember the specifics, the committee should "ask Bert Brennan" (or some other relevant individual). The recommended person would then claim the Fifth while on the witness stand. (On occasion, this proxy pleading was engineered directly by Hoffa: several times he looked toward the witness and held up the five fingers of one hand in a signal that left nothing to the imagination; and at least once he whispered to a person about to testify, "Take five.")

At one point, Senator John F. Kennedy reproached Hoffa for using such a strategy, eliciting from Hoffa's chief counsel Edward Bennett Williams the comment that "this is the first time I've heard guilt inferred by some other person's taking the Fifth Amendment" and a deadpanned rejoinder from the senator, "Well, I'm putting it forward as an original thesis."

A second course of action involved what might be called "the use of stout denial." Hoffa, after listening to a summary of some previous witness's testimony, would simply assert, "That isn't in the record. I have read the record and nothing like that is in there." As Kennedy later would write in his book, *The Enemy Within*, "If the Chairman decided to take the time to call this bluff, twenty minutes would be lost digging into the record that had just been summarized."[15] Often, the Hoffa statement was allowed to go unchallenged simply in the interests of time, and Kennedy begrudgingly later admitted that the Teamster leader had developed this ploy "to perfection."

The third Hoffa approach was, for him, now an old one. Frequently in answering the questions he merely went off on a vague, irrelevant, unenlightening, and long tangent, highlighted by protestations that he just couldn't remember the details. He adopted, in other words, the same oratorical weapon that had caused Senator Ives one year earlier to tell him that while he hadn't taken the Fifth he was "doing a marvelous job of crawling around" the latter.

Actually, a fourth Hoffa stratagem was also utilized, although it was reserved strictly for people named Kennedy and did not involve the use of a single word. The committee counsel, who claimed to have first observed it on the last day of the 1957 hearings, called it "the look" and described it in the following graphic language:

[Hoffa] was glaring at me across the counsel table with a deep, strange, penetrating expression of intense hatred. . . . It was the look of a man obsessed by his enmity, and it came particularly from his eyes. There were times when his face seemed completely transfixed with this stare of absolute evilness. It might last for five minutes—as if he thought that by staring long enough and hard enough he could destroy me. Sometimes he seemed to be concentrating so hard that I had to smile, and occasionally I would speak of it to an assistant counsel sitting behind me. It must have been obvious to him that we were discussing it, but his expression would not change by a flicker.

During the 1958 hearings, from time to time, he directed the same shriveling look at my brother. And now and then, after a protracted, particularly evil glower, he did a most peculiar thing: he would wink at me. I can't explain it. Maybe a psychiatrist would recognize the symptoms.[16]

The IBT president later explained that the winking was just a form of enjoyment for him: "I used to love to bug the little bastard. Whenever Bobby would get tangled up in one of his involved questions, I would wink at him. That invariably got him."[17] And he often said that "there's no way that I could ever afford all the publicity that the committee is giving me for absolutely nothing." But the bravado fooled no one. Hoffa did not remotely enjoy being so widely depicted as either a willing associate or an unwilling dupe of mobsters. And, as a documentably devoted family man, he liked even less being portrayed as a heavy in a major media event that was so widely interpreted as a battle between the forces of good and evil.

Even worse for the union chieftain, the committee's second round of Hoffa interrogations did not confine itself to establishing Hoffa's gangster connections. As it had in 1957, the Senate subgroup also focused on its star witness's personal financial affairs. Here, it alleged that there had been a series of ill-gotten gains by Hoffa, and made the three following points, among others, concerning these gains:

1. In a sworn affidavit that had been furnished committee investigators, former Detroit laundry owner William Miller said that in 1949 he and the other laundry owners in the city had averted a Teamster truck driver strike by contributing $17,500 to a purse that was being raised for Hoffa by two officials of the industry's trade

association, the Detroit Institute of Laundering. At least $10,000 of this money, the ex-owner further stated, definitely found its way to Detroit's premier Teamster, through the good offices of a Detroit labor consulting firm headed by two close Hoffa friends, Jack "Babe" Bushkin and the late Joe Holtzman. Two other laundry owners had orally confirmed Miller's story to the investigators.

On the stand, Hoffa conceded that he had gotten $10,000 in "loans" from Bushkin and Holtzman. But, with the faulty memory that rarely seemed to leave him for long as he testified, he could furnish no additional information. He could neither recall any specifics about repaying the loans nor produce any written evidence to show that he did repay them.

And Miller, to the committee's disappointment, now testified that he really wasn't at all sure that Hoffa ever got any of the money. One possible explanation for his retraction, the committee contended, was that Hoffa had accompanied the two Detroit Institute of Laundering officials on their flight to Washington to attend the hearings and reminded them that the late Holtzman, not he, actually got the money. Bushkin took the Fifth Amendment.

2. Between 1948 and 1956, Hoffa listed a total of $60,322 as "collections" and "miscellaneous earnings" on his federal income tax returns. Despite the committee's strong suggestion that this money should properly have been attributed to "bribes from employers," Hoffa explained that the true source was racetrack betting. "There is racetracks in Detroit," he told the committee, "and [Owen 'Bert' Brennan] has some horses and he places some bets and we are fortunate to win some money." He and Brennan split the gains on a fifty-fifty basis, he said, in return for his giving Brennan half of the money gambled by the latter.

Asked if he had any documentation to support his racetrack story, Hoffa stated that Brennan kept the records. In his turn, Brennan took the Fifth Amendment on the stand—prompting Chairman McClellan to ask him, "Is the taking of the Fifth . . . one of the prerequisite qualifications for advancement [in the Teamsters Union]?" In answer to this latter question, Brennan took the Fifth again.

3. A former heavyweight boxer named Embrel Davidson informed the committee that he had been paid seventy-five dollars a week for two years by the Teamsters Union as an IBT welfare fund

investigator although he had done no investigating at all. Instead, he had helped feed the racehorses on Brennan's farm and trained for his prizefights. In his boxing endeavors, Davidson told the committee, he was under the management of Hoffa and Brennan.

Hoffa, Chairman McClellan pointed out, had testified in his committee appearance a year earlier that he had known nothing of this arrangement and its use of union funds for a private Hoffa-Brennan investment. The Justice Department would accordingly, the senator from Arkansas declared, be asked to investigate this inconsistency. McClellan warned that there were potential consequences for Hoffa of a perjury indictment here.

And more damaging publicity awaited Hoffa in mid-September, when he returned to the Caucus Room for a third round in his Senate appearance. The committee, now in the full glare of national media attention, reintroduced a subject that it had first dealt with in 1957: the Sun Valley, Florida, land development scheme and Hoffa's role in it. With Hoffa now present, as he was not when the committee had first alleged Sun Valley improprieties on his part, the unionist was asked why he had transferred $500,000 in union funds to a Florida bank on an interest-free basis. Even at 2 percent interest, the account would have earned the Teamsters Union $10,000 annually, it was pointed out. And, once again, the assertion that the bank would now (with the interest-free transfer but not without it) loan $500,000 to this scheme into which Hoffa and Brennan had a hidden option to buy was made by the investigators.

This third round also featured an assertion by committee investigator Pierre Salinger that 57.6 percent of the votes cast for Hoffa at the 1957 convention had been illegally cast. Another highlight was the appearance of Hoffa's pudgy, jewelry-bedecked Ohio lieutenant William Presser, who ducked most questions seeking to link him to vending machine industry racketeering by taking the Fifth Amendment (once, however, he departed from predictability by promising the committee, "I'll tell you the truth if you let me get out from under the oath").

"No family in this country," asserted Chairman McClellan at the conclusion of this September round of hearings, "can escape the repercussions. All of our lives are too intricately interwoven with this union to sit passively by and allow the Teamsters under Mr. Hoffa's leadership to create such a superpower in this country—a power greater than the people and greater than the Government. This situation even now is critical for the nation."[18]

And committee member Sam J. Ervin, Jr. soon thereafter was even harsher in his comments. Avoiding direct reference to the IBT's provisional president but leaving no doubt at all as to whom he primarily had in mind, he observed that the conduct of some Teamster bosses "makes Attila the Hun appear by comparison to be a very mild-mannered and benevolent individual."[19] The colorful senator from North Carolina was known as one of the better quipsters on Capitol Hill: he had, for example, not long before this informed Teamster witness Rolland McMaster after McMaster had taken the Fifth Amendment when asked whether Yvonne McMaster was his wife, "I will leave it up to you to answer her when you get home." And in his Attila comment he was obviously only kidding. It is probable, however, given what had now been publicly stated about Hoffa, that the senator's words were taken literally by a large number of people.

By late 1958, then, James R. Hoffa had in one way or another been attacked as an adult delinquent on four highly visible national fronts. The AFL-CIO had expelled his union solely because of his leadership. Although he had been found innocent in his bribery case and his wiretapping trials had culminated first in a hung jury and then in an acquittal, there was a chance that he would now face prosecution in the federal courts for alleged perjury in his Embrel Davidson testimony. The monitors, now armed with the favorable decision of Judge Letts, were waging war with him on a third battleground. And the McClellan committee, having already issued its cornucopia of charges against him, gave no impression whatsoever that it had spoken its last negative piece on the president of the Teamsters. Sparked by its relentless chief counsel Kennedy, in fact, it seemed to have many more damaging revelations in its system.

A logical hypothesis, given this potent combination of anti-Hoffa forces, would be that Hoffa's own union constituents might now themselves be having severe second thoughts about the man at their helm. No rational rank and file, it could easily be argued, would accept a leader who had been so widely depicted as the hoodlum head of a criminal-infested empire. No self-respecting membership could much longer tolerate a president who—if the McClellan charges were to be believed—had treated the union's treasury as his own private property, made the Teamsters a haven for organized crime, and executed collusive arrangements with employers against the best interests of the membership. Few Teamsters, arguably, could continue to support a president who had seemed to do so little to accommodate the "reasonable and relevant requests of the monitors" to root out corruption and maximize democratic procedures within the union. And just as few, it could also be rationally contended, would want to put up much longer with a president whose sheer position holding had made their union an outcast of the labor movement's mainstream, or with a leader whose troubles, past and pending, with the law had been so significant.

Every one of these assumptions would, however, be wrong. Hoffa remained highly popular with his own unionists despite the serious charges. There had been a few demonstrations of concerted resistance to him—in New York, Cincinnati, Chicago, and San Francisco, in particular. But local opposition was, of course, not unknown in the IBT. Moreover, not one of these revolts could easily be attributed directly to dissatisfaction with the Hoffa code of ethics. Hoffa's ever-widening scope of trucking industry bargaining, resulting in diminished authority for local leaders, seemed to have played a part in all of them.

More apparent to Teamster members than any major moral lapses were the tangible gains that had been steadily realized under Hoffa since his advent to power.

In one of his wiretapped conversations with Johnny Dio, Hoffa had recognized the primacy of this latter factor over all others: ". . . treat 'em right and you don't have to worry,"[20] he had told the extortionist. And Hoffa had delivered for his rank and file in spades. Wages had more than tripled for Teamsters in the Hoffa jurisdiction in the Hoffa years: in many cases, as the Detroiter had widened his bargaining arena, drivers had been brought up from 95 cents an hour to $2.46 hourly in less than four years' time. In some cases, as noted earlier, even more impressive gains had been registered. Pay for each mile traveled in the truck, the alternative and more common way of rewarding long-distance drivers, had shown a similar rise: it had gone from 3 cents at the end of the pre-Hoffa era to more than 9 cents (depending upon the size of the vehicle operated). Overtime was now generally awarded after eight hours a day, rather than after twelve. Liberal vacations, pensions, health and welfare programs now existed in abundance where not so long ago there had been none of these at all. Seniority protection had become highly meaningful under Hoffa, and pay for the time that trucks were inoperable because of mechanical problems, impassable highways, or traffic congestion had been enlarged considerably (or, in some cases, implemented). The IBT president could speak to truck driver constituents in Detroit who once drove their rigs to Chicago for $1.50 and to Toledo for 75 cents; now Chicago commanded $36 and Toledo $17.

Even college professors, with all of their education, often didn't do nearly as well, Hoffa's *International Teamster* once reminded its large readership: "Recently a professor at the ivy-covered Williams College in New England returned to the Teamsters as an over-the-road driver because he could double his salary at Williams."[21] It was hard to be negative toward a leader who could bring about this stunning triumph.

Indeed, as the labor specialist of the *New York Times* discovered in privately talking to Detroit drivers at this time, only two out of nearly two hundred such Teamsters felt that "the union was in a mess. . . . The others declared, with every indication of sincerity, that they felt Hoffa had done a standout job on wages, welfare, grievances and every other phase of union service. They brushed aside the accusations of gangsterism and racketeering as part of an attempt by outside forces to cut Hoffa down to size because he was doing too good a job in defense of the rank and file."[22]

Such sentiments were hardly confined to Detroit. Remarks such as "Jimmy's always been good to us drivers and that's all we care about," and "Everyone has a little bit of the cheater in him. It's just that they're making a scapegoat out of Hoffa because he's been such a successful labor leader" had flowed freely from the mouths of Teamsters throughout the Midwest for some time. Now, with the IBT leader's sphere of authority a nationwide one, these sentiments were generally echoed by Teamsters in all sections of the country.

Hoffa, needless to say, did nothing to discourage such opinions. As he went around the nation talking to his membership, he skillfully converted the widespread attacks on his personal conduct into apparent attacks on all Teamsters ("Well now, you know and

I know that Jimmy Hoffa is nothing—just a name, just an individual. So when Bobby Kennedy talks about me, he talks about destroying the entire Teamsters Union because we've been so successful"). As he once told his Local 299 constituents and repeated literally hundreds of times in almost identical language in other IBT settings, "All this hocus-pocus about racketeers and crooks is a smokescreen to carry you back to the days when they could drop you in the scrap heap like they do a worn-out truck."[23] Such oratory was typically greeted by prolonged hand clapping.

And it was exactly because of this bread-and-butter gratitude of the membership for the gains that their leader had delivered to them that Hoffa had expected to win a clear title to the Teamster presidency at the now-postponed March 1959 convention hands down. In the eyes of most objective observers, he would have needed none of the illegal vote casting that allegedly marked his 1957 convention victory this time (if, in point of fact, the always-popular Hoffa had ever needed this contrived support). With the exception only of the Mine Workers' John L. Lewis, whom Hoffa greatly admired, no other twentieth-century labor leader had ever, indeed, enjoyed such rank-and-file adulation. That he had gained and maintained it simultaneously with being so widely portrayed as a bad citizen said much about his leadership talents.

It also, of course, said a great deal about the values of the huge majority of Hoffa's union constituents and, by justifiable extension, about the values of most workers. As A. H. Raskin could quite accurately generalize in his insightful November 1958 article, "Why They Cheer for Hoffa," "We admire the man who can deliver—how he delivers is much less important."[24]

Hoffa Can Take Care of Hoffa

6

For all of Hoffa's genuine problems, events soon proved that he had absolutely nothing to fear from his own "anti-racketeering" investigatory commission. Almost from the day that former Ohio senator Bender was appointed as the three-man commission's chairman, the ex-legislator's role was ridiculed by the media. A widely reprinted cartoon by the *Washington Post and Times Herald*'s eminent Herblock showed the chubby Bender following the trail of a large number of greenbacks on the street while crouching on all fours and being led on a dog's leash by Hoffa. And a *New York Times* editorial asked if anything could be "more brazen" than the appointment of the commission by "the very man against whom the most serious charges have been made."[1]

The Ohioan quickly justified the absence of faith in him by adopting an investigative method that one observer thought was "roughly comparable to trying to solve a murder case by going to an open window and yelling, 'Is anybody out there guilty?' "[2] Elbowing aside his two colleagues on the panel, a retired Detroit judge and a Washington attorney, Bender proceeded independently to send a form letter to every Teamster local in the country. The letter asked the local officials to supply information on "any racketeering or gangster alliances" of which they might be aware within their respective Teamster subunits.

All of the replies (including those from racket-ridden locals) were in the negative. The secretary-treasurer of a Miami local whose ex-convict leader was quite visibly negotiating sweetheart contracts, shaking down employers, and freely consorting with known racketeers responded, "There are no cases of racketeering or gangster alliances in this local union. We will give you full cooperation on any investigation of this local union." (Bender thereupon wrote the Miamian, "The fine report you give of your organization is most gratifying to the Commission. The officials and members of your local are to be commended upon it. Thank you sincerely for your fine spirit of cooperation."[3]) The secretary-treasurer of another highly suspect IBT local—of bakery drivers in Tacoma, Washington—was even more succinct in his answer: he simply returned the letter that he had received from Bender, with a scrawled notation affixed to it in his own handwriting, "No racketeering here."[4]

In December 1958, with his research into the locals completed, Bender reported preliminarily to Hoffa that he had found the International Brotherhood of Teamsters "free of corruption." The ex-senator's two colleagues on the commission almost immediately disclaimed any responsibility for this finding.

Bender continued his "investigation" with the same degree of intensity until early May 1959, charging the Teamsters a formidable $58,636.07 in salary and expenses for his efforts. He failed to recommend the expulsion from the IBT hierarchy of even one hoodlum, and when a puzzled McClellan committee summoned him to its stand as a "voluntary witness" a few months later, he did not cover himself with glory in his testimony:

Mr. Kennedy Has anybody been ousted from the Teamsters Union, Mr. Bender?

Mr. Bender Well, I recall . . .

Mr. Kennedy That is, on your recommendation has anybody been ousted? . . .

Mr. Bender I am not going to go into that. My report is to Mr. Hoffa.

Mr. Kennedy You came as a voluntary witness.

Mr. Bender That is right, but . . . not to discuss my work or what I am doing.[5]

He admitted that he had not taken any action at all in the cases of William Presser and Louis M. "Babe" Triscaro, still Hoffa's two major lieutenants in Bender's own state of Ohio and men whose clear-cut links to the underworld had now been convincingly established by the committee. (Both, it will be recalled, had been the short-lived recipients of some probing by the 1954 Bender investigation before it was abruptly and permanently "recessed at the call of the chairman.")

Nor had the former senator from Ohio taken any kind of stand regarding New York Local 239 leader Sam Goldstein, now serving a jail sentence for extortion but still drawing $375 a week in salary and $25 for expenses. Bender's only direct comment when asked about this state of affairs was that "[Goldstein] is a good man to be able to do that. But I have not—."[6]

And in response to probing by his old Republican legislative colleague, Barry Goldwater of Arizona, Bender could do no better than the following:

Senator Goldwater George, let me ask you a question. Take the case of a man like Goldstein. Suppose you went to Mr. Hoffa and said, "Jimmy, you ought to kick this fellow out." Do you think he would do it?

Mr. Bender Last week, I went to him regarding a man, a matter came to my attention where a man was having relations with a 16-year-old prostitute and speaking very bluntly, he said, "Well, frankly, that son-of-a-bitch should be kicked out." He said, "He is no good. No man should be in this union who is doing that kind of thing."

Senator Goldwater Was he kicked out?

Mr. Bender That I can't tell you. . . .

Senator Goldwater Let's take a man like Glimco in Chicago. He is certainly no credit to the union movement. Have you made any recommendations relative to him?

Mr. Bender Frankly, no. That matter hasn't come to my attention either.[7]

Hoffa would clean up whatever corruption might exist in the Teamsters, Bender insisted, after his reelection. While the Detroiter was still provisional president, in Bender's opinion, he couldn't "go around kicking people in the teeth." In fact, said Hoffa's appointee in an illustration of his own general political philosophy, if cats and dogs could vote, he would personally "shake hands with them."

Commenting that he himself had appointed the "best prostitute" in one of his districts to the post of Republican committeewoman, the former senator explained that "unless you get the votes of the washed and the unwashed you can't win elections. . . . You don't have to become a prostitute yourself, but sometimes you have to get their votes."[8]

Not coincidentally, Bender was asked if he had received any kind of Teamster payoff in return for his lack of aggressiveness in the 1954 congressional investigation, and he heatedly denied the implication as "a damnable lie." "No charges were dropped," he testified. "No strings were pulled with me."[9]

The always candid Senator Goldwater later said that Bender's performance on the witness stand had been a total disgrace. It was almost enough, he told the press, to make him a Democrat. Counsel Kennedy, taking an equally dim view of the man who had served on Capitol Hill for fourteen years as a congressman and two years as a senator, subsequently wrote, "To me, it is incomprehensible that such a man should occupy the Senate seat once held by [Ohio Republican] Robert Taft, a man who was a symbol of integrity and excellence."[10]

To Kennedy, however, there was a clear-cut explanation for Bender's behavior both in 1954 and now: James R. Hoffa, who "believes that money, or influence, or political pressure, or a combination of all three can fix any problem that faces him. As [Hoffa] once said to [a Washington reporter]: 'Every man has his price. What's yours?' " "It must have been a setback to [Hoffa]," Kennedy could not resist adding, "the night he was arrested for attempting to bribe a Committee investigator to find that there was one man in America who was above and beyond a price."[11]

Whatever the validity of these speculations on the part of John F. Kennedy's younger brother, Hoffa definitely suffered two setbacks in the first year of his provisional presidency. Neither of them was at all major, certainly as compared to all of his other troubles and even on an absolute basis. But in both cases Hoffa was forced to rescind ambitious programs that he had only recently announced, and to do so publicly. For a man for whom recantation was all but unknown, the events consequently were noteworthy.

The first of these related to a project that the union leader had announced, with considerable fanfare, in July 1958. He revealed to a well-attended press conference that he was launching an unprecedented league of transportation unions. To be called the "Conference on Transportation Unity," it would initially include the International Longshoremen's Association, which, it will be recalled, Hoffa had wanted to help a few years earlier and which now had in common with the Teamsters the fact that it had been expelled from its parent labor federation (the AFL, in 1953) for alleged corruption. The ILA had, indeed, a few years earlier served as the real life inspiration for crooked unionism in the Marlon Brando movie, "On the Waterfront." The conference would also have as a charter member the National Maritime Union. Ultimately, it would embrace all of the more than fifty unions in the transportation sector under its single Hoffa-managed umbrella: the railroad brotherhoods, the airlines unions, and every other transportation collective bargaining agent. And all of the fifty-plus unions would be invited to an August 1958 meeting to which the Teamsters, Hoffa said, attached so much importance that the union would underwrite the entire cost by itself if necessary.

The public outcry to this revelation had been both immediate and highly negative. George Meany, speaking for the AFL-CIO's Executive Council, had announced that any member international that might join the outcast Hoffa's league could consider itself expelled from the larger federation. ("I expect all AFL-CIO unions to comply," the major force behind the IBT's 1957 expulsion pithily asserted.)

The projected land, sea, and air union program was also quickly attacked as a threat to the country's well-being by members of the U.S. Congress. Some of the latter indicated that, if need be, they would introduce legislation to thwart Hoffa's plans. Hoffa's ongoing nemesis, Senator McClellan, who told journalists that under the conference arrangement "you could have one man with more power over the economy than the Government," was only one of dozens of such potential Hoffa thwarters. And many of these national legislators doubtless fully agreed with the sentiments of McClellan's young chief counsel that the foremost Teamster was already close to holding such sway. "He's not just the most powerful man in labor," Robert Kennedy had said in the wake of Hoffa's announcement; "he's the most powerful man in the country, next to the President."

The last thing that Hoffa, who was surprised by the intensity of the reactions, needed was another battlefront; and more negative publicity was a luxury that he really could not afford. Moreover, Meany's threats seem to have dissuaded the National Maritime Union, still in the AFL-CIO, from continuing to display interest and to have dampened whatever enthusiasm the airline and railroad unions might have had for the idea. A scheduled meeting to get Hoffa's concept off the ground was postponed, by Hoffa, indefinitely. Few people expected a rescheduling any time soon.

The second aborted Hoffa program was a nationwide campaign to bring every policeman in the United States, starting with the twenty-four thousand members of the New York City Police Department, into the Teamsters Union. Most New York policemen already belonged to an independent labor organization, Hoffa recognized. But the latter, the Patrolmen's Benevolent Association, was in his opinion much too "lax" and ineffectual in protecting wages and conditions. The New Yorkers deserved better representation, and he would provide it for them and their hundreds of thousands of counterparts from coast to coast. Where state laws forbade such unionization, the Teamsters would get the laws changed.

Although in making this late 1958 announcement, the nation's most investigated union president had renounced the strike weapon (in favor of arbitration) for the police, he probably would not have precipitated a more negative outcry had he sought to organize the Joint Chiefs of Staff. The New York City police commissioner said that if his subordinates did become Teamsters, he would advise New Yorkers "not to waste their money paying the police commissioner a salary" because Hoffa would then be "the real police commissioner." New York's mayor, Robert F. Wagner, called the campaign both "dastardly" and "a disgrace"; he promised that he would go to court if necessary to stop the Teamster efforts. The city's biggest newspaper warned that public opinion would "approve overwhelmingly any steps—repeat any steps—" that authorities might take to quell the campaign. Teamster monitor Godfrey Schmidt, now buoyed by the favorable ruling from Judge Letts, called Hoffa's project a "piece of unmitigated gall." And the president of the Patrolmen's Benevolent Association said, "We want no part of Hoffa or any of his goon organizers."

Hoffa had expected Schmidt's reaction. And the PBA's angry response was, of course, also highly predictable. But the rest of the sentiments, which were paraphrased by literally hundreds of other influential sources throughout the country, seemed to take him as completely by surprise as he had been in the case of his proposed transportation league. Three weeks after his original announcement of the organizational drive, he called the campaign off.

The nation's police officers, he proclaimed in a statement issued at his Washington headquarters, had every right to want security through collective bargaining. And the Teamsters would not turn a deaf ear to any pleas for organizational help from them. But the police would have to approach the IBT. Police organization, Hoffa announced flatly, "will be undertaken by the Teamsters Union only if they come to us seeking such organization."

These two reversals were, however, the only ones to mar Hoffa's collective bargaining (as opposed to his activities away from straightforward labor relations) record in this period. Otherwise, his efforts as head of the Teamsters brought considerable success. The union's membership grew by some 132,000 (to 1,567,000) in the year preceding May 1959, and this was particularly impressive given the significant membership *losses* suffered by many other unions in this same period of national economic recession. The Teamster treasury, the beneficiary now of the $840,000 annually that the IBT had paid to the AFL-CIO but also as a direct result of this increase in dues payers, contained an all-time-high dollar total of $40 million. With the need to observe AFL-CIO jurisdictional boundaries now removed, the union had registered marked progress in recruiting workers in such nontraditional Teamster populations as retail clerks, airline stewardesses, furniture production employees, and egg farmers. And Hoffa's special area of concentration, the widening of the scope of the over-the-road truck driver bargaining unit, continued to be a fruitful one for him.

Hoffa's area-broadening accomplishments in the central and southern regions of the country had already been pronounced. By 1955, essentially all road drivers in the twenty-two states worked under a single master labor contract, at least for their economic stipulations. But Hoffa was now busy converting the myriad of dissimilar agreements that as provisional president he had inherited in the West and East, too, into a relatively few, comparatively uniform ones.

When Dave Beck made his inglorious exit from union office in 1957, there were still thirty-five road contracts in his old West Coast domain. By the end of the following year, Hoffa had replaced these with a single master contract that paralleled the Central States document in many of its aspects. On the East Coast, also, the new Teamster chief executive officer was making strides. Even though there were still sixteen different trucking contracts there, Hoffa had brought them to a much closer conformity with their non-Eastern counterparts than they had ever had previously. Upon their respective expirations, he fully expected to whittle down their number as well, with an eye toward his ideal total of one: a single nationwide trucking agreement.

In these months, too, despite all of the governmental and other unsought extracurricular demands on his time, Hoffa continued to offer his services to his huge membership virtually around the clock and literally around the country. He was by all accounts, as he frequently boasted, a "working president" and, while he reveled in the popularity that he fully recognized he was receiving from his dedicated constituents, he was intelligent enough to understand that he must continue to earn it. He remained at least as "near as the telephone," as he so often reminded Teamsters. More often, in his constant travels to meet the rank and file in their own territory, he was even nearer to them. "I like this job," he once told a guest; "every hour I work [at it] is an hour of pleasure,"[12] and he was not about to give it up if he could help it.

By most standards, it was in fact nice work if you could get it. The job paid the then-handsome stipened of $50,000 annually, a figure that would be increased in 1961 to make its incumbent the most highly paid union official in the nation. And Hoffa also continued to receive $15,000 a year for simultaneously presiding over Local 299.

No less generously, the Teamster constitution covered "all expenses" for its chief executive. Into this category fell, explicitly, travel expenses without limit "for the purpose of promoting the interests and welfare of the international union and the making of diplomatic contacts for other organizations and for the purpose of conserving his health." So did the taking of "periodic rests" for the president, and allowance for the leader "in his discretion [to] travel in this country or, with the approval of the general executive board, abroad." And, of appeal to a devoted husband like Hoffa, provision was also made for the "full and complete maintenance of [the presidential] wife so that she can accompany the general president."

It was nice, too, to be so well known that airline pilots and flight engineers would leave their cockpits and come back just to sneak a look at the celebrity whom they had been told was among the passengers. And to recognize that one's mere presence in a Chicago hotel lobby or Boston restaurant could be counted upon to generate considerable excitement among the other people in the room. And to be asked to be the guest speaker at university seminars, management conferences, and testimonal banquets honoring people who themselves were major names, all over the country.

Working conditions in Washington were not bad, either. In town, Hoffa supervised Teamster affairs from a magnificent five-story glass-and-white-marble headquarters building, built in 1955 by Beck for what was at the time the princely sum of $5 million. The structure occupied a full block of prime District of Columbia real estate—on Louisiana Avenue, just across the street from the U.S. Capitol with its spacious and well-manicured lawns, picturesque fountains, and attractive dogwoods. It exuded, as it still does (even more so since the doubling of its size in 1977 with the construction of an annex), extreme luxury: bronze-framed floor-to-ceiling picture windows; corridor columns covered with imported Venetian mosaics; a marble-finished hundred-foot lobby; a directors' table in the primary conference room (one of many), which Teamster literature distributed at the building's dedication described as "one of the two largest in the United States"; expensive wall-to-wall carpeting and custom-made draperies throughout; and ornately paneled lounges in abundance.

Its designer had also incorporated in it a penthouse terrace, a variety of private bathrooms complete with built-in showers, and a 474-seat auditorium containing not only elaborate equipment for showing motion pictures (which Beck used to do, free of charge, to building personnel) but a costly lectern duplicated—according to the union—only by another one in the White House. It could have comfortably accommodated at least four hundred persons. Only one-quarter that number did, however, work there, and visitors were invariably impressed by the spaciousness as well as by the opulence of the place.

The Teamsters headquarters building was also, quite probably, the only union base of operations in the United States with a French chef: Jean Grihangne, formerly of Seattle's Olympic Hotel, whose sophisticated offerings even the meat-and-potatoes man Hoffa invariably enjoyed (Hoffa also, as general president, got table service in the dining room, as did the international secretary-treasurer, John English; all others had to serve themselves).

Beck had recruited Grihangne, but Hoffa had soon after his installation added a luxury of his own: a $50,000 tiled gymnasium with a steam room, a large variety of glistening barbells, and the services of a Swedish masseur, John Hansen. For the exercise-conscious Hoffa ("Weight on the seat of my pants slows down my brain" was a favorite Hoffa expression), the latter addition was even more of a contribution to the building than Beck's engagement of the chef had been. But Hoffa seemed to stand alone in this belief, since employee demand for the gym and its offerings invariably lagged way behind the demand for Grihangne's food. Once, indeed, when the IBT leader tried to implement a daily exercise program for all headquarters workers strictly on a voluntary basis, exactly one underling was inspired to participate in it. The idea was quickly shelved.

Hoffa's own office, the walnut-paneled third-floor Suite 305-6, was fully compatible with this luxuriance. Highlighted by a massive, nine-foot mahogany desk and a magnificent Scandinavian chandelier, its vista of the Capitol Hill grounds was by far the best in the building. It came complete with a private elevator, a forty-eight-button intercom system, soundproofed doors, a liberally endowed bar (for guests but not for the teetotaler Hoffa), and built-in highest-quality television and stereo sets. It had inch-thick beige carpeting and expensive burnt-orange drapes. All of these accoutrements, as in the case of the building itself, testified far more to the grandiose lifestyle of the sybaritic Beck than to Hoffa's own more modest values. But for a poor boy from Brazil, Indiana, it was heady stuff, a symbol that he had now totally arrived and yet one more reason for considering each hour as IBT president "an hour of pleasure."

On the many occasions when the "little guy" was away from Washington, there was still another contributory factor to his high level of job satisfaction. The man who actually ran the day-to-day operations of the headquarters, Hoffa's handpicked executive assistant as well as the first vice-president of the union, was an old Hoffa associate who enjoyed the latter's complete confidence. The relationship between Hoffa and the able Harold J. Gibbons was so close, in fact, that when they were both in Washington, the two top Teamsters lived together in an expensive suite at the upscale Woodner Hotel overlooking the District's scenic Rock Creek Park. Gibbons had also served as one of the two most important officials of the 1956 Hoffa Testimonal Dinner in Detroit and as coordinator of the subsequent trip by Hoffa, his daughter, and the many others who accompanied them to Israel and Europe.

The tall, slim, second-in-command Teamster was a former socialist intellectual who had taken Keynesian economic courses at the universities of Chicago and Wisconsin, met his future wife at a socialist-sponsored peace rally, taught English, and gotten his start in the labor movement by organizing a Chicago union made up of his fellow adult education teachers. But he was no effete highbrow: a newspaper reporter had once described him as a man who "uses four-letter words to convey four-syllable ideas," and he had been pleased by what he had considered to be the total accuracy of the statement. He had wound up in St. Louis in 1941 as director of that city's Retail, Wholesale and Department Store Employees Union, and eight years later had merged this operation into the Teamsters.

Gibbons had come to know Hoffa well in the early 1950s, when a group of gangsters (the so-called Irish Buster Workman gang) had threatened to wrest control of his IBT Local 688 away from him, and he had responded by asking the rapidly rising Teamster Hoffa for help in thwarting this project. Hoffa had provided Gibbons not only with advice ("Arm your people. Shoot the first son of a bitch who comes in the door of the union hall to take over") but with an offer of a personal bodyguard to protect the St. Louis leader, and Gibbons had accepted both. But Hoffa had been equally impressed by the toughness of Gibbons: once, when the two men left a particularly acrimonious Teamster-employer bargaining session, Hoffa reportedly said with admiration, "Gibbons, there are some men in Detroit who dislike me—but those fellows back there actually hate you."[13]

Toughness was not the only common denominator for the two men. The youngest of twenty-three children (Gibbons had never met all of them and by the 1960s could not even remember how many of each sex there were), Gibbons was also a coal miner's son whose father had died when he was quite young (fourteen years old, in his case) and whose mother had then moved the family from an impoverished mining town (Archibald Patch, Pennsylvania) to a large city (Chicago). Gibbons was also highly intelligent and a master labor negotiator. Gibbons, like Hoffa, was never said to have been lacking in professional ambition. And the Gibbons family, back in St. Louis, lived in a house that was not appreciably more impressive than the very modest Hoffa residence on Robson Street in Detroit.

But there were many pronounced differences too. Consistent with his socialistic background, and with his present status as a member of the board of the Americans for Democratic Action, Gibbons espoused a brand of social unionism that was very much at variance with the Hoffa bread-and-butter labor philosophy. While leader of Local 688, the St. Louisian had introduced such progressive programs as a comprehensive Labor Health Institute, providing free, prepaid medical and dental care for members and their families years before other unions moved in this direction. There was no charge, either, for the legal advice and home nursing care that Gibbons's rank and file could utilize, and both prescription drugs and groceries (if the latter were bought at the Local 688 grocery store) were offered at cost. A "community steward" system, to forward the complaints of all citizens against the city's administration, was a further hallmark of Gibbons's local, as was an unyielding stand on civil rights. Many foreign labor leaders had come to St. Louis to view this progressive operation in person and had invariably come away impressed. A book had even been written about Local 688 and its social innovations. (Hoffa never held these "egghead" tendencies, as he called them, against Gibbons, and he often told visitors to the Teamster building that "I can get out in the field because Harold is here. We don't let him push his social ideas." He also frequently said with pride that Gibbons was "not a longhair but a practical Teamster.")

And there were other differences. Gibbons also, his status as a husband notwithstanding, had a well-deserved reputation for womanizing (Hoffa used to rib him about his sexual escapades, both frequently and good-naturedly, but he could never fully understand how a married man could engage in them). Where Hoffa considered both drinking and smoking to be "wastes of time," as well as detrimental to physical well-being, Gibbons engaged in both with no self-discipline at all: sustained in his sophisticated drinking tastes (as in most of his other living habits) by a liberal expense account, he imbibed regularly and well, rarely having any problem with alcohol (at least once, however, he did arrive at an important Hoffa-conducted meeting in an obvious liquor-induced glow, causing the ascetic Hoffa to immediately announce, "This meeting is adjourned"); he smoked cigarettes almost continuously. And if Hoffa could only with extreme charity be called even an average dresser—for much of his life, he favored cheap suits, old ties, and white socks (because "dark socks make my feet sweat") and upgraded his wardrobe only when Josephine, embarrassed by the frequent uncomplimentary references to it in the press, finally prevailed on him to do so—Gibbons's tastes in attire ran to the expensive and well tailored.

Gibbons was, in fact, an extreme hedonist. He invariably patronized the best restaurants in town, stayed at the fanciest hotels when traveling, and otherwise tried to live life to the fullest, as his more austere superior did not. And in a way it was this very pursuit of pleasure on his part that, however paradoxically, explained the linkage of the two strange bedfellows. As Brill has pointed out with no little insight,

Jimmy Hoffa offered Gibbons a different class war. With Hoffa he could personally jump right over to the other side of the class barrier. He might have done it by going into business or a profession, but this way he could do it while still fighting for his workers. . . . Hypocrisy and simple greed? Yes. But especially understandable in Gibbons' case. Here was . . . Hoffa, showing him that unionists could be brash and powerful and have lots of pocket money. That he yielded to the temptation to dominate men—and women—and took the chance Hoffa offered to ride high, live well, and play sexual conqueror in a world where he had been born as the last of twenty-three hungry faces in the crowd is not surprising.[14]

Hoffa also had two equally competent lieutenants who could fill in for Gibbons when *he* was away from the District of Columbia.

Joseph Konowe of New York, head of a big merchandising local there, often came to Washington on temporary duty to administer Teamster headquarters affairs. He had first met Hoffa in 1939 and was to know him closely and value this friendship enormously to the end of Hoffa's life, but he was very much of a disciple of Gibbons's social brand of unionism. Lawrence N. Steinberg, from Toledo, another liberal unionist favoring the Gibbons approach, also flew in to pinch-hit when needed at the helm; he, too, developed a strong attachment to Hoffa, gave him total loyalty, and was a close Hoffa confidant—even living with Hoffa and Gibbons for a while. Like Gibbons, neither had been or ever would be tainted by the slightest hint of scandal; like the Teamster first vice-president also, both were idealistic CIO alumni, totally dedicated to both the IBT (into whose ranks they had brought their respective CIO local unions) and the labor movement. Highly literate and relatively urbane men, all three contrasted sharply with the tougher types who were still very much part of the Teamster landscape, and all three were understandably, if unfairly, resented by the latter.

Each of the three had his own style.

Gibbons, convinced of the necessity for a better Teamster image, seldom acted without a regard for the outside world. He set up the IBT's first official public relations department (directed by the man who had handled the same function for him in St. Louis, John McCarthy), and supervised its activities, which included the production of highly favorable biographies of both Hoffa and himself. The monthly *International Teamster* magazine was another particularly important Gibbons concern, and while Gibbons (and Hoffa) allowed it to have relative autonomy, its feelings about the IBT leadership were fully predictable: monitor Schmidt quickly complained of "the blatant manner in which the [magazine had] been used consistently and almost exclusively for the purpose of self-glorification and propaganda."[15] The attractive, college-educated Gibbons also was not averse to boosting the Teamster image by accepting outside speaking invitations and continued to preach his impressive gospel of union values ("Business ethics aren't good enough for trade unions" was a favorite theme) at, among other places, Harvard, throughout his Washington executive assistant days.

Konowe and Steinberg, on the other hand, were very much internalists but with a definite difference in their approach to office management. Konowe was an inveterate hoarder of paper. "Konowe saves everything," a student of the Hoffa headquarters had once tersely observed.[16] The New Yorker had been in charge of the 1957 convention's credentials committee, had suffered personal embarrassment when the Eden Roc Hotel maid had accidentally disposed of his committee records, and was not about to have this happen to him ever again. Steinberg, in stark contrast, found very little that came across his desk worth saving: "Much of it," he recently reminisced, "consisted of letters to Jimmy saying 'If you would believe in Jesus, you wouldn't have all the problems that you do,' and that kind of thing." He was an active user of the wastebasket.

With Gibbons had also come several other able additions to the headquarters staff beside McCarthy. Sidney Zagri, a Harvard Law School product who had headed Local 688's ambitious program of community involvement, was brought in to establish and run a new Teamster legislative department: he launched the latter's activities with a novel approach to fund raising, asking each of the almost 1.6 million Teamsters to contribute, voluntarily, 50 cents monthly for IBT political purposes, and followed this up with invitations to all 435 House of Representatives members to come, two dozen at a time, to breakfast at a leading Washington hotel. From the Gibbons St. Louis operations, also, came Gibbons's former personal secretary there, Yuki Kato Keathley, who now became Hoffa's primary secretary, and her husband, Ferguson, who was promoted to a major position in the union's national warehouse division.

Two other former Gibbons staffers who were thought to be first-rate additions to Hoffa's own entourage were Richard Kavner, made a troubleshooter for the general president, and Peter Saffo, brought to Washington as a somewhat lower-ranking presidential assistant.

For all of the Gibbons imprint, however, Hoffa was quite accurate in asserting, as he often did, that IBT leaders were "not theorists but practical people." With the downfall of the Minneapolis Trotskyites in 1941, the sole noteworthy Teamster effort at social reform was ended. Notwithstanding the influx of theorists into the organization and the increasing interest in political action, the theorists were of little influence in the international's policy determination, and the political action bore a strongly pragmatic flavor. The IBT's overriding avowed goal remained very much in the tradition of Samuel Gompers: in the words of the union's chief economist, "to improve the status of the union's members within the existing social and economic system."

If there was any abiding social philosophy in the general president's office, however, it was not one of liberalism but of mitigated conservation. A description by Zagri might be said to typify a rather generally held sentiment in this regard:

Jim's credo is not too clearly thought through yet, but events are forcing him to think it through. There are times when he sounds like a Marxist, speaking of the class struggle and so on. But he has a great admiration for the rugged individualist who has come to the top in Big Business, and to a large extent he's bought the values of Big Business. He believes in the free enterprise system, the greatest possible business profits, and the survival of the fittest under the rules of the marketplace.

He fears Big Government—particularly the governmental "long-hair"—because he feels that it doesn't understand the problems of industry as well as labor unions or businesses, or the two of these mutually, understand them and each other. In this sense, he's a 19th Century liberal. But he's also pragmatic enough to see that Big Government happens to be necessary in many areas—social security, medicare, automation, unemployment compensation. He can't, for example, see the sense of trucking companies giving a 35-hour week to their workers when these companies have to face fly-by-night competition. He feels that only the Government can do this the right way—for everybody.

Hoffa was also realistic enough to recognize that some political action by his union was necessary as a defensive measure. He sincerely believed that his presidency coincided (not necessarily by accident) with what he called "one of the greatest anti-union crusades in history," and he told his membership that if "we don't fight back, we will die." "What we gain across the bargaining table," he frequently warned, "we could lose by the stroke of the pen of a McClellan."

But the approach was never doctrinaire, always hard-headed and earthy. Zagri's new political arm was diplomatically named Democratic, Republican, Independent Voter Education (DRIVE), and, as Hoffa wrote in one of his monthly *International Teamster* columns,

I say it is time to turn back to the political advise [sic] of . . . Gompers. He didn't advocate that we vote for Democrats. He didn't advocate that we vote for Republicans.

He advocated that we reward our friends and punish our enemies at the polls. . . .

To make our political units at the local union and joint council level effective, I suggest that we ask not whether a man is a Democrat or a Republican, but rather, is he a friend of labor?[17]

And the perspective was anything but far-reaching. The pursuit of such an abstract concept as social justice was for others—for example, the UAW's Walter Reuther, whose management counterpart at General Motors once welcomed him to the bargaining table with the words, "Well, Walter, what's today's burning social issue?" Hoffa told Paul Jacobs, when that ex-socialist writer dared to suggest to him that his leadership horizons were far too narrow, "Don't give me that! What do you think I am, the State Department? I don't want to get into world politics. I have enough trouble taking care of my own members."[18] He did not, as he frequently said, want to change society. Or, as he once stated in a speech to his home Local 299, "Everybody who writes about me seems amazed that I call (the running of a union) a business, instead of a crusade or something. Well, it is a business. We're not labor statesmen here. We're not humanitarians or longhairs. Look, what do you hire us for? Is it to throw a picnic for you? Is it to study the European situation? Or is it to sell your labor at the top dollar?"[19] Dave Beck could not have said it any better.

Hoffa's staff also included a large battery of attorneys, headed by the two men who had done so much to design the "magnificent disposition" that had let him take office, Edward Bennett Williams and his partner Edward T. Cheyfitz, and by respected labor relations practitioner David Previant. Some 150 lawyers, only a few of them working out of the headquarters building, collectively comprised what its members deemed the "Teamsters' Bar Association." Most were specialists in either labor or transportation law, although some, like Williams, were experts in criminal jurisprudence. Hoffa good-naturedly complained that there were so many of them and he paid them so well that he had "singlehandedly doubled the average standard of living for all lawyers in the country."

The septuagenarian international secretary-treasurer, John English, once a driver of teams of coal wagon horses in Boston, was also very much a part of the marble palace's brain trust. He was invariably accorded great respect by the rarely deferential Hoffa, who called him "chief," both out of gratitude for his support and in recognition of English's own huge popularity among the membership. The wooden-legged secretary-treasurer (he had lost a leg to gangrene some years earlier) in turn ensured that the Hoffa presidency would not suffer from a cash flow problem. He guarded the union's treasury so carefully that Hoffa once told a visiting reporter, with a twinkle in his eye, "You'd think the money was his own."[20]

The manager of all of this administrative machinery by and large maintained his considerable aplomb in these days. Perhaps because Hoffa had survived so many outside onslaughts in such a short period of time, perhaps also because he was fully aware that his rise to national prominence had been little short of meteoric, the visible jaunty optimism that had always tended to mark his approach to life never seemed to desert him for long now. A small plaque that he had placed on the nine-foot mahogany desk in his office bore the Latin exhortation, "Illegitimi non Carborundum"—roughly, "Don't let the bastards wear you down." And, despite the monitors (and his deep disappointment at the December ruling of Judge Letts), the courts, the McClellan committee, and the AFL-CIO, Hoffa at least most of the time practiced what it preached.

A visitor who hadn't seen him in almost eighteen months commented, in March 1959, that there was "not much outward change. There's still the same direct gaze, the quick smile, hard handshake and easy conversation. . . . [In] general, he wears an . . . air of confidence that he is firmly in the president's seat—and is there to stay."[21] Another observer thought that "Mr. Hoffa has developed a sense of his own invulnerability to successful prosecution. . . .

[He has] thumbed his nose unconcernedly as he [has] rolled past all his detractors in Government and labor."[22] The Teamster president was frequently described by a national press that was now, understandably, devoting increasing space to his activities as "self-possessed" and "self-confident" and sometimes, less flatteringly, as "cocksure" and "arrogant."

Nor did the owner of this self-esteem ever make any apologies for it. Years later, Hoffa was to say in an interview published, improbably, in *Playboy* Magazine (the prudish union leader had originally refused this interview, claiming that he didn't want to be in a "magazine with tits on the back of my picture," but had finally relented), "Certainly, I got an ego! A man don't have an ego, he don't have any money and he don't have any ambition. Mine's big enough to do the job I wanna do."[23] He often said with obvious pride, in a variant of this same theme, "Hoffa can take care of Hoffa."

He was encouraged by the occasional encomiums that he received from respected labor relations experts—the Harvard Business School's eminent James J. Healy, for example, who asserted in mid-1959 that Hoffa might yet "emerge as one of the outstanding labor leaders of all time . . . some of the greatest saints had their schooling in sin."[24] On the other hand, the negative publicity that he was generally accorded by the media typically seemed to have little, if any, effect on him.

Years earlier, he had been easily upset by journalistic attacks upon either his record or his power. He had actually told one newsman, apparently in all seriousness, that the latter would some day scratch himself on his typewriter and die of blood poisoning. With equal gravity, he could assert to various audiences that the probable reason why he had such a poor press was that his truck drivers tended to make a great deal more than did newspaper reporters. Now only an unusually vitriolic contribution could arouse him. A *Boston Herald* cartoon that depicted him as a club-wielding caveman guarding a skull-littered highway tunnel labeled "Truck Route, U.S.A." and saying "Leave things as they are, or else!!" was of this latter ilk; an enraged Hoffa within hours of its publication told some twenty-five hundred Boston Teamsters, "My responsibility is far and beyond some cartoonists or editorial writers who want to display their high school skills to embarrass you and possibly put you in prison." (The cartoonist, Jim Dobbins, thereupon himself paid a compliment to Hoffa's basic imperturbability: "I'm pleased that I scored—he seemed such a hard guy to penetrate with ridicule."[25]) But this was the exception. Hoffa as Teamster president freely gave interviews, subject only to time constraints, to essentially all comers, perhaps because, as one former key Hoffa aide believes, he "felt that running away from journalists was an admission of guilt."

He appeared, indeed, to be genuinely convinced that he had committed no wrongdoing of any kind. When told on one occasion that he seemed to be leading a charmed life, given the results of his court trials and the many potentially fatal allegations made against him by the McClellan committee, he retorted, "Who's lucky if they can't find anything wrong?"[26] As for the contentions of the AFL-CIO and the monitors that his union was racket ridden, the Teamsters Union "has never been corrupt. Our organization is comparable [in its degree of sinful behavior] to any group of 1,600,000 persons in social, religious or business life in America."[27] He frequently asked visitors, "Why should I be nervous?"

He also believed, and often told his family when unfavorable news about him broke, "The only people that I'm concerned about are the Teamsters. And they like me. So I must be doing something right." And, as he had done for two years, he professed—to his wife, children, and others—actually to be pleased with "the free advertising that Bobby Kennedy is giving me. I couldn't buy that kind of publicity for a million dollars." He was nonetheless sufficiently worried about the effects of the uncomplimentary Hoffa portrayals on his fragile spouse and worshipful children to call them together whenever he could anticipate a major news story about himself and give them the "true" version so that they would not be taken unawares. (One kind of report that invariably surprised the members of his immediate family, on the other hand, involved his use of profanity: four-letter words were second nature to Hoffa, but he never swore at home, and quotations that were quite accurately attributed to him consistently astonished his loved ones.)

Concern for family was always a paramount Hoffa value, of course, and it extended well beyond his own three dependents. Once, two shifty-eyed visitors to the IBT headquarters building told Konowe that they had proof that Robert Kennedy was "picking up bills for women and prostitutes and keeping them in hotels."

For $10,000, they announced to the Hoffa lieutenant, they would hand this proof over to the general president. Konowe relayed the information to Hoffa, who was in the building at the time, and was vehemently directed to "kick them in the ass and send them out." Asked about his reaction later, Hoffa explained that he did not want to embarrass Kennedy's wife and family. The Teamster leader had another reason too: Kennedy had respected Josephine's private life by not forcing the shy wife to testify in any of the Hoffa proceedings, and Hoffa, for all of his negative feelings toward his primary antagonist, very much appreciated this thoughtfulness shown *his* spouse.

Now, generally uncowed by the forces pressing in on him from all sides, the cocky Hoffa set his sights even higher. He waged an ambitious organizational campaign in Florida, bringing upon himself a strong attack by that state's governor ("I wish Hoffa would keep out of Florida. The less we see of him the better"). By such an effort, he also renewed chances of open warfare with the AFL-CIO: the Teamster president staked out, and successfully swept into his union's ranks, such federation-sought employees as Tampa brewery workers, Miami-based Pan American World Airways stock clerks, northern Florida citrus grove workers, and Miami Beach hotel doormen.

Hoffa then announced a plan to battle a new AFL-CIO union for the right to represent thousands of truck drivers and warehousemen in Puerto Rico, publicly vowed to compete against federation unions *wherever* they had been "derelict" in organizing workers in their jurisdictions, and spoke of unionizing almost ten million governmental employees ("It will be necessary to organize the unorganized in toto")—in all cases, without any visible regard for federation sensibilities.

He also, according to the Associated Press, said that if Congress enacted legislation putting unions under the antitrust laws, as Senator McClellan and others were now advocating (to some large extent because of Hoffa himself), the Teamsters might "call a primary strike all across the nation that will straighten out the employers once and for all."[28] Secretary of Labor Mitchell, the same man who had obliquely called Hoffa and his cohorts "crooks and racketeers" at the 1957 AFL-CIO convention, deemed this strike threat "the most arrogant, brazen thing I've ever heard in my life," and Hoffa soon thereafter denied having made it. But the Associated Press stood by its guns.

As for the monitors, the Letts December 1958 decision notwithstanding, Hoffa continued to treat the edicts of the three-member panel strictly as nonbinding recommendations. On more than one occasion, he was reported to have said to the board members, "O.K., you've advised me; your advice is rejected." He was hopeful that the U.S. Circuit Court of Appeals would dissolve Judge Letts's ruling when it rendered its verdict in the near future.

In this latter expectation, he was soon to be disappointed. In mid-June 1959, the three judges of the higher court unanimously upheld almost all of what Letts had ordered. More than that, they gave the monitors a good deal more in the way of specific powers than the Hoover Administration appointee had bestown upon them six months earlier. Now, if Hoffa rejected any recommendations of the panel, the monitors could take the matter to federal court. The court would then investigate the recommendations, amend them where it deemed such modification advisable, and send them back to the provisional president as official court orders. Any subsequent noncompliance would put Hoffa in contempt of court. There was to be no more foot-dragging by the Teamsters.

Warming to their theme, the appellate court judges also mandated that Hoffa now must investigate charges of misuse of union funds outstanding against two of his close associates, and that the Teamster leader had to take appropriate action against each of them as soon as possible. One was the man whom Hoffa considered to be his best friend, union vice-president Bert Brennan, accused by the McClellan committee of wrongly diverting union welfare monies to pay the boxer Embrel Davidson. The other was Ray Cohen of Philadelphia, the Local 107 leader (and international trustee) who had taken the Fifth Amendment before the Senate Select Committee when asked whether he had misdirected thousands of dollars of Teamster money into his own pockets. In Brennan's case, proceedings for discipline "should be instituted forthwith." Cohen had succeeded in blocking the inquiry into his activities by getting a state court injunction. The appeals court judges in this latter situation said that Hoffa "should make a good faith effort" to get the injunction set aside and, assuming that this was done, then get on with the disciplinary process for Cohen.

And the higher court further called for: the expulsion from the IBT of two Chattanooga local union officers, Glenn W. Smith and H. L. Boling, for allegedly using their local's funds to get criminal indictments against twelve other Teamsters quashed (or "fixed") in a Tennessee court; an audit of the books of Teamster Local 245 in Springfield, Missouri, accused of a variety of blatant irregularities; the suspension of convicted extortionist John J. McNamara as an official of two Teamsters locals in New York City; and several other specific actions geared to upgrading the caliber of union officials.

Hoffa remained unruffled. He expressed confidence that the U.S. Supreme Court, with which another Teamster appeal would be filed, would upset *this* ruling. He insisted that the membership was free to elect anyone it pleased to union office. He pointed out that employers with criminal records could (and sometimes did) sit across the bargaining table from him and that "men have walked out of jail and been elected to Congress." And, while none of these freely offered considerations on his part could obviously alter the unwelcome appellate decision a whit, he could even take comfort from one portion of the ruling itself: Schmidt, his foremost opponent on the board of monitors, now had little choice but to resign. The court found that the New York lawyer had indeed, as Hoffa had originally contended, been in a conflict of interest situation because he represented employers in their dealings with the union.

Schmidt, who technically could have remained on the board pending a decision by Letts as to whether the conflict of interest disqualified him as a monitor, did not, however, go quietly. He officially resigned because the union was conducting a "contemptuous" campaign of "retaliations and reprisals" against him. He announced that "there can be no reasonable hope of internal reform of the teamster organization . . . while it is under the domination of Hoffa and his clique."[29] Nor could he resist adding that the union had not yet paid him for many services that he had rendered as a monitor. For other services, he had been compensated only after long and unconscionable delays. He became the third man to withdraw from the panel since its implementation and was replaced by a member of his own law firm, whom he had recommended.

Also going out not with a whimper but with a bang was another force that had dogged Hoffa ever since his installation as provisional president, the McClellan committee itself. Now nearing the end of its two-and-one-half-year investigation into labor improprieties, it brought back Hoffa for yet another interrogation—his fourth round and, counting each separate Hoffa appearance before the committee as a distinct entity, his thirteenth actual visit to the hearing room.

The primary objective of the senate agency this time was to show that the nation's most famous unionist had done essentially nothing to clean up the Teamsters, the federal court order notwithstanding. And the committee, secure in the knowledge that its hypothesis was correct, now pulled out all the stops.

It asked Hoffa about the two Tennessee IBT officials who were believed to have tried to quash the indictments against their constituents. It produced a witness who testified that Ohio's Teamster leader, William Presser, with the solid support of Hoffa, installed a nonunion, ex-convict brother-in-law as an official of a Cincinnati local. It brought forth another witness, ex-monitor Schmidt's attorney, Bartley C. Crum, who elaborated on the charges that Schmidt had publicly made, both recently and many months earlier, involving some $105,000 due him from the Teamsters: Hoffa, said Crum, had first tried to "starve" Schmidt out of his monitorship by refusing to pay the monies to the point where the electricity in Schmidt's home was turned off for nonpayment of bills; then, according to Crum, Hoffa had offered to pay Schmidt the six-figure amount (plus another $45,000 in new monitor's fees now due him) if he resigned from the board in favor of Crum himself. As a condition of this deal, Crum would be expected to favor the Hoffa position in his voting.

Yet another testifier, a top executive of a Detroit daily newspaper, contended that a Teamster under Hoffa's direct control was carried on the paper's full-time payroll although he did almost no work except for showing up briefly on Saturday nights, because "we want[ed] to avoid any trouble." And still a further feature of these last select committee hearing days was an allegation that Hoffa had once declared, "In the Teamsters Union every man stands up and has his vote counted, and God help him if he votes the wrong way."

Hoffa, on the witness stand, unequivocally denied all. He also categorically rejected further committee allegations that he had "betrayed" his unionists by negotiating inferior Teamster contracts in return for monetary favors from employers and that he had misused union money to finance his own personal expenses. And, in contrast to all of his earlier performances in the Senate Office Building Caucus Room, when despite moments of rage and temper he had tended to treat the senators with respect (and even to deal with chief counsel Kennedy, most of the time, with a certain cool detachment), he now stood by his statements and his actions far less politely.

He shouted, "I think you're sick," at Kennedy, accused the young attorney of taking a Hoffa quotation out of context for headline-making reasons, and threatened to sue him for "casting aspersions on my loyalty to this country" by indicating that Hoffa shared the values of the allegedly communistic secretary-treasurer of the International Longshoremen's Union, Louis Goldblatt ("I'm dealing with Goldblatt like our Secretary of State deals with Khrushchev," Hoffa yelled).[30]

The interaction between John F. Kennedy and the committee's most famous witness, never notable for its warmth, was now also far less cordial than it ever had been. When the future president, for example, inquired of Hoffa whether some $20,000 that he had invested in a business with an employer representative came from the racetrack winnings that Bert Brennan had, according to Hoffa, shared with him, the following dialogue ensued:

Senator Kennedy I have never been completely convinced, Mr. Hoffa, to be frank with you, that Mr. Brennan did win this money at the racetrack.

Mr. Hoffa Why don't you ask him?

Senator Kennedy I did, and he took the Fifth Amendment.

Mr. Hoffa Maybe he had a reason.

Senator Kennedy I think he does have a reason. You suggested that we ask Mr. Brennan. Mr. Brennan took the Fifth Amendment when he answered the question, and I have never considered that that was a satisfactory explanation of the cash you had or that these several people, business agents, who themselves had to borrow money to survive, that they loaned you $2000 in cash without any note or without any interest.

Mr. Hoffa Thank you for reviewing the testimony.

Senator Kennedy Does it suggest anything to you, Mr. Hoffa?

Mr. Hoffa It doesn't suggest anything except this fact, that you are trying again, as you have many times in this hearing, to bring a headline about or to embarrass Hoffa. That is all.

Senator Kennedy No. I am attempting to give you my reaction, as these hearings come to a close, as to where the cash might have come from.

Mr. Hoffa Then you ought to read the record.[31]

When Senator Kennedy, referring to labor reform legislation that he was currently co-sponsoring, asserted, "Mr. Hoffa, after again listening to you today, you do remain still the best argument for the passage of the bill," Hoffa snapped, "I reserve the right . . . when this bill is passed to advertise to every worker in America the individuals who voted to put the yoke around their necks and destroyed their union." (The Massachusetts senator thereupon informed him, "So there will be no mistake of it, I hope when it passes you will attempt to do that," prompting a final riposte by the Teamster, "You bet your life I will advertise."[32])

Even Chairman McClellan was not spared the Hoffa anger. When the Democrat from Arkansas, presumably misinterpreting a comment by Hoffa concerning the Tennessee Teamsters, asked the witness, "Let me inquire, Mr. Hoffa, do you approve or condone . . . the use of . . . union funds for the purpose of undertaking to fix a judge?" he was rewarded with a testy response from Hoffa, "I don't believe I am here to be ridiculed."[33] On another occasion, the union leader instructed the chairman, with no apparent deference, to "let me finish the question I've been asked."

And, away from the hearing room, Hoffa vented even more spleen on his interrogators, singling the Kennedy brothers out for special attention. In a speech made between his committee appearances, he told the Western Conference of Teamsters that the Kennedys had "probably sunk to an all-time low in attacking Teamsters before the committee on pure hearsay." He and other members of the IBT, he said, had been "harassed" out of "a desire to seek a headline—to destroy an individual." Referring to Senator Kennedy's now-announced political aspirations, he said that the American public "ought to know what type of individual [is] seeking the presidency of the United States."[34] As for the pending legislation supported by the aspirant to the White House and others, Hoffa jumped the gun on his promise to advertise: a staple of many—indeed, most—Hoffa speeches and interviews now was a charge that "the two rich Kennedy boys are trying to get a law passed that will destroy the entire American labor movement."

A few days after the fourth Hoffa round had been concluded, the select committee publicly released a new denunciation of the Teamster leader in the form of a special report to the Senate. Replete with déjà vu for the millions of people who had followed the committee's activities ever since Hoffa's first appearance before McClellan and his colleagues in August 1957, the report stressed, among its total of twenty-one charges, Hoffa's previously emphasized connections to the sinister figures Johnny Dioguardi, "Tony Ducks" Corallo, and Paul "Red" Dorfman and to the shadowy Joe Holtzman.

The first two men, the document reiterated, had helped Hoffa bring the several New York locals into the Teamsters, following which Hoffa and they had executed contracts calling for low wages and poor working conditions for the covered employees with Hoffa's full blessing. And Hoffa had done nothing at all to terminate the situation even after it had been, in the committee report's words, "brought to public light" in the Senate hearing room.

Dorfman, "the corrupt labor leader who introduced [Hoffa] to Midwest mob society," together with his stepson Allen and his wife Rose, allegedly had to date received more than $3 million in commissions and service fees for handling Teamster insurance contracts. It had been "a handsome return," the senators noted, "for a set of insurance brokers who had absolutely no experience in the field and no office space up until a few months before Hoffa successfully maneuvered the insurance business to them in early 1950 and 1951." The report estimated that the Teamsters paid $1.65 million in excess commissions and fees to the Dorfmans and to Dr. Leo Perlman, the official head of the Dorfman-controlled Union Casualty and Life Insurance Company. Even worse if possible, the senators charged, while IBT members were "literally digging into their jeans to assure comfortable living for the Dorfmans and their cronies," their benefits under the health and welfare plans were significantly curtailed.

The committee itself had done a great deal of digging, it declared: a total of six man-months had been spent by its staff in scrutinizing the linkage of Union Casualty and Life Insurance to the Central States Health and Welfare Fund and to the smaller Michigan Conference of Teamsters Health and Welfare Fund. "The evidence is clear," the report said, "that Hoffa used these two funds to pay off a long outstanding debt to the Chicago underworld."

And, lest it have been forgotten since it was first made many months earlier in the McClellan committee hearing room, the allegation that Hoffa received some or all of a $17,500 reputed payoff to end a Teamster dispute with the Detroit Institute of Laundering—through the middleman Holtzman—was also registered once more.

"In the history of this country," the report charged, "it would be hard to find a labor leader who has so shamelessly abused his members or his trust."[35]

Hoffa's immediate reaction to the press was a simple, four-worded one, "To hell with them." His amplification was no less predictable: "I'll place my record of achievements for the workers beside the record of Jack Kennedy or Bob Kennedy any time." And, returning to a now-familiar refrain, "This is another attempt to get a headline in Jack Kennedy's campaign for President at my expense."[36]

A possibly apocryphal but nonetheless widespread story has it that committee counsel Kennedy, driving back to his McLean, Virginia, home one night following a typical eighteen-hour workday, noticed the light on in Hoffa's Teamster Building office. He immediately turned his car around and went back to his own office to spend yet more time trying to get the goods on Hoffa.

Hoffa, for one, was himself quite willing to believe this account. He even, according to Edward Bennett Williams, went so far as to leave his office lights on intentionally after he did leave his third-floor suite for the night, in an effort to trick Kennedy into repeating the performance. "If this kid don't get away from this [obsession with Hoffa]," he told a reporter while the hearings were still going on, "he'll crack up. I talk to people who go to parties with him, to his home, and they say he's got one topic of conversation. Hoffa. He's got to flip."[37] The Teamster leader professed not to be concerned by the caliber of his opposition—"He's not the brightest fellow in the world," he frequently said of the "kid"—but he was fully aware of the intensity of Robert Kennedy's interest in him and of Kennedy's dry comment, "My first love is Jimmy Hoffa."

Nor was the Harvard graduate's preoccupation with Hoffa known only to a favored few. Even the *Washington Post*'s gossip columnist, Maxine Cheshire, could report about the time that Ethel Kennedy stopped for a red light near Capitol Hill and, pointing to a building in the vicinity, asked the several little Kennedy children who were passengers in her car, "What's up there?" A chorus of small voices replied, "The Teamsters Union," whereupon the wife of the committee counsel asked, "And what do they do?" "Work overtime to keep Jimmy Hoffa out of jail!" was the immediate response, prompting from Ethel an "And?" "Which is where he belongs!" shouted the children, happily.[38]

A variety of motives, some of them not entirely pure, have been imputed to Kennedy's relentless pursuit of Hoffa. To this day, many opinions attribute the phenomenon primarily to political expediency. John F. Kennedy's younger brother quite visibly had public life aspirations of his own; in the McClellan committee days, he was thought to covet particularly the Massachusetts governorship. And the presumably vulnerable Teamster president constituted, in this version, a wholly tempting target as a springboard to such a career.

A corollary has been built around the fact that Robert Kennedy was also an entirely devoted sibling. A successful exposé of Hoffa, as the latter himself so frequently contended, would greatly improve the chances of the older Kennedy's labor reform bill's being enacted, and thus produce a definite feather in the presidential candidate's cap. An investigation into such a glamorous field as labor racketeering (with special emphasis on the premier suspected racketeer) would also give the Massachusetts senator, still in 1957 not really a nationally known figure, television exposure that could perhaps be gained in no other way.

Self-respect has also been attributed: Robert Kennedy, according to this school of thought, was still smarting from his "jump off the Capitol dome" fiasco in the Cheasty case; he could offset this public embarrassment only by proving Hoffa guilty of *something, anything.* Hoffa himself, of course, had advanced his interesting Indian hand-wrestling theory as a further reason: as was noted earlier, the first time that the two men had ever met—in February 1957 at Eddie Cheyfitz's home in Chevy Chase, Maryland—he had humiliated Kennedy by beating him, twice, in this test of physical prowess. Kennedy, in turn, acknowledging his role in dethroning Beck and thus in unintentionally paving the way for a Hoffa IBT presidency, frequently joked that he now had a "debt to repay to society."

Whatever the validity of these various explanations, the reality seems to be that Kennedy primarily went after Hoffa because he came to think that in pursuing Hoffa he was maintaining the rule of law. He saw the head of the Teamsters as the leader of a gigantic conspiracy against the judicial system itself. He believed, from all of the evidence apparently quite sincerely, that the IBT—"the most powerful institution in this country aside from the United States Government," he often called it—was riddled with corruption. It would never get rid of this corruption, in his opinion, as long as Hoffa was its leader. He had no doubt that the great majority of Teamsters, including Teamster officials, were thoroughly honest. But he also believed that the union under Hoffa was frequently not run as a genuine labor union at all. Instead, as he was to write in his 1960 book, "As Mr. Hoffa operates [the Teamsters], this is a conspiracy of evil."[39]

Final statistics for the Senate Select Committee were impressive by any standard. In its two and one-half years of interrogation, it conducted over five hundred open hearings on 270 days. The testimony of its 1,525 sworn witnesses, 343 of whom took the Fifth Amendment, filled a staggering 46,150 pages of fifty-odd volumes and consumed over fourteen million words.

Its staff of more than one hundred persons, including thirty-five investigators and forty-five accountants, traveled over 2.5 million miles. Over eight thousand subpoenas were served and almost 130,000 documents were photostated. Help from not only the Federal Bureau of Investigation, but the Internal Revenue Service, the Bureau of Narcotics, and the General Accounting Office was liberally provided. State and local police departments and investigative agencies also participated. The full cost of the investigation, in 1957–1959 dollars, came to $2 million, making it the most ambitious such congressional activity in decades.

Three decades later, a tangible and significant result of all of this effort remained, in the form of a labor reform law that was enacted in September 1959. Senator John F. Kennedy's own legislation, cosponsored with his Republican McClellan committee colleague, Senator Irving M. Ives, had languished in the House after sailing through the Senate. But Kennedy had played a major role in seeing the Landrum-Griffin Act of 1959 through to passage. It constituted his only important legislation as a member of Congress, and the efforts of the bill's framers—Congressmen Phillip Landrum of Georgia and Robert Griffin of Michigan, as well as the Massachusetts senator—were undoubtedly facilitated considerably by the cumulative effect of the many widely-publicized charges related to Hoffa.

Officially named the Labor-Management Reporting and Disclosure Act, the law brought about, for the first time in the 150-year history of American labor unions, the detailed regulation of internal union affairs. Persons convicted of such serious crimes as robbery, bribery, extortion, embezzlement, aggravated assault, and grand larceny were barred from holding any union office for five years after conviction. Union members were guaranteed an ambitious and far-sweeping "Bill of Rights." The latter, among other fiats, provides for equality of membership rights in union elections, which must be held at regular intervals and either by secret ballot or at a convention of delegates chosen by secret ballot, with all candidates also being guaranteed the right to have an observer at the polls and at the ballot counting. It establishes strict standards to ensure that increases in dues and fees are responsive to the desires of the membership majority. And it mandates the filing of annual financial reports by union officers with the U.S. Secretary of Labor, to maximize the chances that union monies will be spent in the interests of the membership rather than of the officers.

The Landrum-Griffin Act also restricted union activity externally in two important ways. It closed some loopholes that had developed in existing labor law concerning secondary boycotts—union economic activity waged against one employer to get at another employer that is the actual subject of the union's interest. It also outlawed so-called "hot cargo" arrangements whereby employers would agree in a contract with their union not to handle products of or otherwise deal with another employer involved in a labor dispute. As in the case of the internal reforms, the Teamsters and the specter that the Congress had conjured up of power corrupting served as a major spur to this second facet of the new legislation.

The act was not the only visible result of the McClellan committee's mammoth efforts, moreover, Beck's inglorious career had been ended. The heads of other international unions—the Bakery and Confectionery Workers, the Textile Workers, and the Operating Engineers—had also been forced out of office. Within a year after the committee had gone out of business, over twenty individuals from the ranks of labor and management had been sentenced to prison terms. Indictments were now also pending against several of Hoffa's closer associates, including Bill Presser, who would be convicted of contempt of Congress, and Barney Baker, who would go to jail for two years for extortion. And the Teamsters had, of course, been ousted from the AFL-CIO, although the ultimate effect of this occurrence still remained to be seen.

But the committee had failed in what was obviously its major single objective: Hoffa still ran the Teamsters. He had not been toppled despite all of the charges linking him to Dioguardi, Corallo, the Dorfmans, and Holtzman, to the lucrative return on investment of the Hoffas and the Brennans as co-owners of Test Fleet, to his and Brennan's unpublicized option in Sun Valley, and to his lending of Teamster welfare fund money to the John W. Thomas department store. He remained very much in charge notwithstanding what Chairman McClellan had called the "just plain scandalous" election of some of his delegates at the 1957 IBT convention, the easy way of Frank Kierdorf with matches, and the intimidating organizational techniques of the colorful Baker.

Hoffa maintained his presidency, albeit "provisionally," despite the attempts of counsel Kennedy and others on the committee to establish his support of Joey Glimco, Glenn Smith, Bernard Adelstein, Frank Matula, Gus Zapas, and scores of other possessors of major police records, most of whom had looked on television exactly as gangsters were expected to look: jewelry bedecked, loudly dressed, and giving the impression that they might smell, as a McClellan committee visitor once said of their perfumery, "like a cross between Chanel No. 5 and musk of moose." He still held the job regardless of what he said (and most members of the committee did not believe) were Bert Brennan's racetrack winnings.

He had survived notwithstanding the boxer Embrel Davidson, the extortionist Sam Goldstein, and the suspected embezzler Ray Cohen, in the face of the "notorious hoodlums" Zigmont Snyder and John Bitonti, Paul "The Walter" Ricca, and all of the other topics on the committee's long agenda of alleged Hoffa wrongdoings.

Whether or not he belonged in jail, as the Kennedy children had supposedly chortled, whether or not he was a "very evil influence in the U.S.A.," as their father had frequently described him, Hoffa had completely weathered the onslaught of the Select Committee and its vigorous prosecutor. The committee, for all of its contentions that Hoffa had violated the law in many ways in governing his union, had proven nothing. The assumption of guilt that counsel Kennedy and many of the senators had patently imputed to the Teamster president could not remotely be equated, from the evidence presented, with the establishment of guilt itself. The required quantum of evidence certainly was not enough to hold up in any courtroom.

Hoffa still faced major, present threats from the courts. But, as John Bartlow Martin could write at the time, in the conclusion to his widely read seven-part senate investigation series in the *Saturday Evening Post*, if he could surmount these imminent other problems, "the investigation, which has made him a national figure and has given him an identity few public men possess, may someday seem to him like an almost unmitigated blessing." The committee, Martin explained, may well have strengthened Hoffa's position with both his rank and file and lesser Teamster leaders. It had helped Hoffa with the former, by creating a public image of the "persecuted little underdog who stood up to the United States Government," and with the latter, because they were stuck with him—"if he goes, many of them go."[40]

As for the lesser Teamster leaders themselves, the committee's batting average was really not much better. To the basic senatorial contention that the union was permeated with corruption, Vice-President Gibbons submitted the following specifics, none of which apparently were ever seriously questioned: of the 106 names of reputed Teamster racketeers and hoodlums that had been mentioned by the committee during its existence, 16 names could be located nowhere in the union's files; 9 other people were union members who had never been IBT officers and who, under the law, were not only entitled but usually required to be Teamster members if hired by their respective employers; 34 others no longer had any Teamster connection; and 8 others had been arrested but never convicted of a crime. Of the remaining 39 people, Gibbons noted, 26 had been convicted of misdemeanors or felonies before employment by the Teamsters or election to office. This left exactly 13 who could be said to be lawbreakers and who were still members of the Teamsters and holding office, and even some of these men had arrest records relating to disorderly conduct or traffic violations. It was hardly a bad record for a union whose membership was now not far below 2 million, the second-in-command Teamster pointed out. In fact, for an investigation as ambitious as this one was, the results constituted "a case of the mountain having labored and brought forth a mouse."[41]

The committee's chief counsel professed to see a definite silver lining in all of this. If Hoffa and his lieutenants had been forced out of office by the investigations, Kennedy often argued, the Landrum-Griffin Act most probably would never have been enacted. Hoffa and the others who still held their union offices "despite overwhelming evidence of corruption," he wrote in his best-seller, constituted "the symbol in the minds of Congress of what needed to be corrected. . . . In the long run, the legislation and the awakening of the public are what are important."[42]

But he could not possibly have been pleased. His brother would say time and time again as he ran for the presidency, "I am not happy when I see a man like Hoffa still free"—Hoffa reciprocated John F. Kennedy's sentiment by asserting, "I don't see how he can be supported by any union member"—and Robert Kennedy felt no differently. Moreover, the younger Kennedy had to live with the further fact that it was primarily he, indeed, who had ousted Beck and thus allowed Hoffa to ascend to the IBT presidency. Presumably, the ambitious attorney was also aware that as chief prosecutor he had shouldered the major responsibility for building an airtight case against his adversary, and that a more skillful performance—that of an Edward Bennett Williams, say—might have put Hoffa away.

Williams had, in fact, been Hoffa's ranking lawyer ever since his adroit handling of the Cheasty case. And on close reflection

Robert Kennedy could take consolation in the actuality that he had come up against a recognized master.

Kennedy might also have gained solace from a recognition that much of what he was trying to prove about Hoffa was fundamentally unprovable. For example, as arbitrator George W. Taylor pointed out at the time, "The exact line of demarcation between 'sweetheart' contracts and the exercise of labor statesmanship is not readily drawn."[43] Nor can a definition of an "excess commission" for an insurance broker be easily provided: the Dorfmans admitted that the commissions that they received were twice the normal rate for the industry but argued that the Teamsters only paid the standard percentage and that the rest, designed to finance the Dorfman enterprise during its early years, came from monies transferred to the latter from other operations of the parent insurance company. It is, in addition, no crime at all to be on the friendliest of terms with a mobster.

Hoffa himself, despite his moments of vulnerability, was no slouch on the witness stand, either. Poised, quick-witted, and enormously knowledgeable, the last thing that he would accept was any badgering from a chief counsel who was quite capable of such behavior (Kennedy had asked Glimco, "Morally you are kind of yellow inside, are you not?"; when Beck, after taking the Fifth Amendment on one occasion, had informed Kennedy that if he gave a truthful answer in this situation it might tend to incriminate him, the counsel had told him, "I feel the same way"; and when Momo Salvatore "Sam" Giancana, described by Kennedy in the hearings as "chief gunman for the group that succeeded the Capone mob," showed a surprising tendency to giggle as he took the Fifth Amendment, Kennedy remarked, "I thought only little girls giggled, Mr. Giancana"). Although the committee in its final report scoffed at Hoffa's testimony as "a curious and practically unfathomable mixture of ambiguity, verbosity, audacity, and mendacity,"[44] the mix was in reality a skillful mingling of stout denial, convenient forgetfulness, and patient elaboration of relatively minor details. Backed up by the taking of the Fifth by proxy, it constituted a formidable response by a man who was withstanding the most prolonged interrogation ever given anyone by a congressional committee either before or since.

For all of this, there could be no denying that Kennedy himself had made mistakes. There had been no real focus in his attack, no centerpiece such as the Dioguardi-Hoffa connection had temporarily (but only temporarily) appeared to be and around which a pervasive, ever more specific case for wrongdoing could be built. Under Kennedy's direction, the case against Hoffa was presented scatter-shot, superficially, and over a time span so large as to diminish its impact for that reason alone. It seemed to many to be nothing more than a fishing expedition, an effort to scrutinize every conceivable area of Hoffa's activities with the hope that something incriminating might emerge. It gave the impression, to the U.S. attorney general of the time among others, of being too amateurish to have any usefulness in court. It was not Kennedy's most impressive endeavor.

Not just once but twice, then—in the John Cye Cheasty trial and now in the case of the related McClellan committee—Hoffa had publicly bettered Kennedy. Even though the latter man thought that he had shown, as he said in summing up his case on national television following Hoffa's final committee appearance, that "Mr. Hoffa has made collusive deals with employers . . . betrayed the union membership . . . sold out the union membership . . . put gangsters and racketeers in important positions of power within the Teamsters . . . [and] misused union funds," Hoffa had again, in Kennedy's opinion, eluded justice. It was an untenable situation for Kennedy, who also now reminded the public that "we have fought the evil that Hoffa represents for two and a half years. It's been a hard grind all along—for the people who work on our committee and for myself. I am not going to lie down and see all that work go to waste."[45]

The Select Committee on Improper Activities in the Labor or Management Field would soon thereafter go out of existence, and its chief counsel would have to sublimate his anti-Hoffa feelings, at least for a while. But he was able neither to forget nor to forgive the unionist. As his father once said of Kennedy, "Everyone in my family forgives, except Bobby." He would get Hoffa, some day.

The Lengthening Shadow of the Law and a Stunning Triumph

7

Even as the business of the Senate Select Committee was grinding to a halt, the embattled Hoffa still faced other very real threats from the government. The latter, as expected, had lost all interest in prosecuting the Teamster chieftain on charges that Hoffa had lied in the original grand jury wiretapping investigation. And it now viewed the chances of proving Hoffa guilty of perjury in his Mc-Clellan committee testimony regarding the boxer Embrel Davidson as being sufficiently slim as to justify an elimination of this course of action, too. Two more troubles coming down the road toward Hoffa, therefore, had vanished before they had ever gotten to him. In two other arenas, however, the government was far from inactive, and the threats were consequently more meaningful for the union leader.

One of these involved an ambitious joint effort by the U.S. Departments of Justice and Labor to separate Hoffa from his presidency by toppling what the government saw as the foundation of his support. By October 1959, at least a dozen grand juries spread from New York City to Los Angeles were looking into possible illegalities committed by Teamster leaders loyal to Hoffa. More than twenty-five indictments had already been brought against major Hoffa backers in such key cities as New York, Philadelphia, Pittsburgh, Cleveland, Indianapolis, Miami, and Los Angeles. Additional ones seemed inevitable.

A few of the indictments, which were typically levied either for misuse of union funds or for extortion, hit the labor leader especially close to home, since they involved men with whom he was particularly friendly. New York's John J. O'Rourke, Philadelphia's Ray Cohen, Cleveland's William Presser, and the inimitable Midwestern organizer Barney Baker fell into this category. So did New Jersey's swaggering, intimidating gangster Anthony "Tony Pro" Provenzano, whose Local 560, with almost fourteen thousand members, was one of the largest of the international's 920 locals. Provenzano, a reputed member of the Genovese crime family, seemed so much a doer of bad deeds to the Board of Monitors that it had already ordered Hoffa to remove him from office, an order that the IBT president had steadfastly defied.

As a further part of this combined Justice and Labor project, Secretary of Labor Mitchell promptly invoked the new Landrum-Griffin Act and its provision barring anyone convicted of its many enumerated major crimes from holding union office for five years after conviction. By telegram, he ordered Hoffa to report within ten days as to what the Teamsters were doing to comply with the provision.

Hoffa, a few days thereafter, announced that he had asked every local union, through the joint council presidents, "Do you have anyone on the payroll that is wrong? Get them out," and had found only five IBT officials to be in violation of the Landrum-Griffin conviction stricture. All five were, he pointed out with some indignation, now on leaves of absence. "Please be advised," he then notified Mitchell, "that our investigation fails to disclose any person who, as of this date, is serving the international union in any capacity contrary to the provisions of [the new law]."[1] In an accompanying announcement for public consumption, he could not resist adding that the speedily dispatched wire from the labor secretary showed that Mitchell had been insincere in promising that Landrum-Griffin would not be used as a witch hunt.

More immediately ominous was a September 1959, request from the Board of Monitors to the official creator of the board, Judge Letts, that Hoffa be stripped of his presidency for having violated the judge's original clean-up order. He had misused union funds, Board Chairman O'Donoghue and the panel's rank and file representative argued (the Teamster monitor appointee refused to sign this request to Letts), by allowing some $675,000 belonging to his home Local 299 to be on deposit in three banks without drawing any interest.

The biggest of these tainted accounts was one that had already been given wide publicity by the McClellan committee in 1957: the $500,000 in the Florida National Bank of Orlando. It had served as security for a $500,000 loan to the Sun Valley, Inc. real estate development in which Hoffa and Brennan had their hidden option to buy a significant chunk of stock. Sun Valley had at this point repaid one-fifth of that loan. But the development was now in bankruptcy and in default on the balance. Hoffa had recently, at the strong suggestion of the monitors, tried to remove the local's remaining $400,000 from the Orlando bank, but the latter, in an exercise of what it believed to be its contractual rights, had refused to let him, and he was currently suing to force such a return.

Neither Hoffa's attempt at regaining the money nor the fact that the Teamsters had by this time closed the two other accounts ($50,000 in a New York bank and $125,000 in an Indianapolis one) made any difference to the monitors, however. Simply by allowing any union money to remain in banks without drawing interest following the Letts January 1958 decree, contended the two men who formed the panel's anti-Hoffa majority, Hoffa had flaunted the fiduciary standards established in the court order.

For good measure, the monitors added in their request to Judge Letts that Hoffa's option on the Sun Valley stock, which he continued to hold for almost a year after the order, was another violation. And, just in case this did not convince the jurist that Hoffa should be removed, they also argued that the subject of their appeal was defying the IBT's constitution by continuing to serve as president of Local 299: the constitution, they pointed out, explicitly called for the union's international president to "devote his entire time to the service of the international brotherhood."

Most observers thought, quite justifiably as it turned out, that the last charge would not prove to be very persuasive. Tobin had regularly taken time from his presidency to serve as labor chairman of Democratic national campaigns, and Beck had spent hours almost every day on his own community and business interests. The one weekend a month that Hoffa tended to spend in Detroit supervising the affairs of his home local hardly seemed vulnerable, particularly given the twenty-hour workdays and seven-day workweeks that he typically did devote to the service of the international. Finally, the union's constitution gave the international's executive board the power to approve or disapprove all of the president's activities, and the fifteen members of this body, essentially all of whom themselves presently held more than one union position, could hardly be expected to begrudge Hoffa his Local 299 presidency. Multiple job holding was a deeply embedded way of life among high Teamster officials and had been for years; and a man sufficiently high up in the structure could quite legally amass a very respectable income by serving as, say, president of his local union, head of his joint council, chairman of his conference, and an international vice-president. It seemed likely, then, that even if the monitors did pursue this constitutional tack in the courts, one portion of the IBT constitution would negate another.

The Sun Valley situation appeared to be fraught with more difficulty for Hoffa, particularly after a November 1959 announcement by the U.S. Supreme Court that it would not review the June circuit court decision that had strengthened the power of the monitors so appreciably. But even here the star-studded Hoffa legal staff, still headed by Edward Bennett Williams, did succeed in giving the IBT president some grounds for optimism. It delayed the ouster trial sought by the monitors by issuing so many petitions for stays, rehearings, and appeals that the docket of the Federal District Court in Washington was overwhelmed by them. And Hoffa's attorneys even, in April 1960, got Letts himself to bow out of the Sun Valley trial picture: they filed an affidavit charging him with bias against Hoffa, thereby allowing him no choice—he now told representatives of the media—but to step aside. In Letts's opinion, if any such affidavit was properly filed, a self-disqualification by the judge who was alleged to be prejudiced became automatic.

Hoffa was now spending so much time in various courtrooms that he could comment, "I'm going to be able to hang out a shingle as a lawyer myself before long." And while the ninth (or, depending on which Hoffa version is accepted, seventh) grade dropout was, of course, joking, many of his close associates believed that had circumstances been different for him he would probably have made a formidable attorney. His superb retentive powers, knowledge of details, analytical ability, and persuasiveness were envied even by his lawyers. Moreover, he possessed a genuine interest in the law, an interest that had already been whetted appreciably by his own brushes with illegality and that would only deepen as his personal legal problems grew. Despite his general eschewing of reading, he delighted in scrutinizing legal cases, which were often sent to him by lawyers and law school professors. He would frequently test the abilities of his own battery of lawyers by asking the latter numerous questions about these cases, and he sometimes astonished them with his personal insights into the subject matter. He also was never hesitant to make "suggestions"—which were invariably accepted, most often as helpful ones—by his counselors.

As for Hoffa's desire to employ so many members of the profession—at one point during the McClellan committee hearings, he was using the services of no fewer than one hundred of them—Hoffa attorney Jacob Kossman probably explained it quite accurately. In addressing Judge Letts's replacement, the seventy-nine-year-old Federal District Judge Joseph R. Jackson, Kossman said: "I don't know if Mr. Hoffa would like me to tell this or not. He is bold and fearless, but he's afraid of the court. He surrounds himself with more lawyers than I believe he should. That includes me. What he's afraid of is technically violating the law."[2]

Subsequently arguing before Jackson, in late April 1960, that there should be no Sun Valley trial, the theatrical Kossman confided, "We have come to the conclusion that [the monitors] are out to destroy Hoffa and take control of the Teamsters. . . . This is a big prize, this union, $60-million in assets, 1.6-million members, a fabulous fortune." And Kossman's distinguished colleague in the defense, David Previant of Milwaukee, declared that the "damage from a needless removal from office could be irreparable. Hoffa as chief executive officer works 20 hours a day, on everything from the lowest grievance to a major negotiation."[3] But the two men and their several fellow lawyers who also addressed the jurist spoke in vain. The man who replaced Letts quickly ruled that Hoffa did have to stand trial on the Florida-based charges. Jackson had been more swayed by the contentions of the monitors that Hoffa had not honored the fiduciary rules imposed upon him in the original judicial order than he had by any of the defense arguments.

The trial would be a civil and not a criminal one, since Hoffa had been accused not of stealing the funds, just of mishandling them. It was clear to all concerned, however, that it would be another harrowing experience for a man who, by most standards, had already had enough such experiences to last a lifetime.

The only unknown now seemed to be when the trial would be held. The Hoffa legal cadre, as expected, wasted no time following the Jackson verdict in seeking a temporary stay, and the appellate court granted this delay.

Even better from the provisional president's viewpoint, the court of appeals also ruled that the trial should not take place until it had heard other pending appeals related to the Teamster-monitor dispute. These covered a territory that was as wide as the imagination of the Hoffa legal talent. They ultimately totaled thirty-eight, to which were added nine mandamuses and three petitions for writs of certiorari to the U.S. Supreme Court by a defense force that was reluctant to forfeit any opportunity. They included a Hoffa contention that under Landrum-Griffin (which, ironically, the union had so vehemently opposed) Hoffa could not be removed from office by the court even if he were to be convicted: only the members, it was argued, could now either elect or oust their officers. Another appeal asked for an immediate presidential election. And still another one insisted that either the pro-Hoffa or anti-Hoffa forces could block any court nominee to the chairmanship of the Board of Monitors if there were "reasonable grounds" for so doing.

This last appeal, registered in July 1960, stemmed from what could be construed as both good news and bad news for Hoffa. The good news was that O'Donoghue had now, in complete frustration, resigned his position. He had lost the support of Schmidt's successor—who, indeed, had in the recent past been accusing Chairman O'Donoghue of "being obsessed with getting Hoffa." O'Donoghue had also reached the end of his tolerance for being picketed at his Washington law firm and being bothered at home by anonymous late-night telephone calls, activities that had plagued him for some time. But the bad news for Hoffa was that Judge Letts (who, even in bowing out of the Sun Valley situation, had retained overall monitorship jurisdiction) wanted to name former FBI agent Terence F. McShane to succeed O'Donoghue. The appointment of McShane, who had investigated Hoffa on behalf of the bureau and had twice testified against him in his wiretapping cases, was about as welcome to the Teamster leader as that of, say, former Michigan congressman Clare F. Hoffman or the ex-Secret Service agent John Cye Cheasty would have been.

On the other hand, there had also been another personnel change in the monitorship in the recent past, one that had preceded O'Donoghue's departure by several weeks and that was by no means coincidental with it. And Hoffa could take considerable encouragement from this change. It involved the one slot that the Hoffa forces could directly control, that of the Teamsters Union appointee on the board, and from the provisional president's viewpoint it could not have resulted in the advent of a more helpful monitor.

Wells, the original IBT monitor appointee, had long since departed, unhappy with the demands on his time that his duties were making. His successor, Daniel B. Maher, had also now resigned because of poor health. As the new man, the Teamsters had named Detroit's William E. Bufalino, the same William E. Bufalino whom the House committee investigating labor racketeering in 1953 had alleged to be the leader of a "gigantic wicked conspiracy" who had extorted, through his Teamster Local 985, millions of dollars from jukebox distributors, workers, and even the federal government itself. Bufalino's name had also come before the public four years later, when the McClellan committee had described the same local, still controlled by him, as a "leech preying on working men and women."

The colorful, aggressive new Teamsters Union selection seemed to many observers, the still-Chairman O'Donoghue included, to be bent on sabotaging the performance of the monitorship above all else. Almost from the day of his arrival in May 1960, he filibustered monitor meetings, often by eulogizing James R. Hoffa, and greatly slowed down the progress of any anti-Hoffa moves. At other times, he stalked out of these meetings in a real or imaginary fit of pique. He was frequently unavailable for private conferences with O'Donoghue or simply canceled appointments that he had made with the latter.

Bufalino also fought with the young lawyers who constituted the small, low-budget Board of Monitors staff, which was for all practical purposes the chairman's staff; at least once, when he was denied a look at some confidential mail by an O'Donoghue assistant, this actually resulted in a bandaged left hand for the monitor, who thereupon told reporters that the hand had been hurt by the staffer when they had both reached for the same mail. He refused to sign staff member expense accounts, began telephoning O'Donoghue at the latter's home very late at night (and was believed by many to have been the invisible hand behind the anonymous calls), and in general made life miserable for the chairman, who had become an anti-Hoffa minority of one in any event. He was undoubtedly the major single source of the resignation of the now highly vulnerable O'Donoghue. From the Hoffa viewpoint, he was a man well worth considering for future responsibilities.

Nor, as matters developed, did the threat of the former FBI employee McShane ever materialize. To accommodate the appeal relating to McShane's nomination as monitor chairman by Judge Letts, the Circuit Court of Appeals had already stayed this appointment. It now agreed with the Hoffa position that either party to the original Letts decree could block a nominee for the chairmanship subject only to the party's putting forth "reasonable grounds." McShane's past adversarial relations with Hoffa, the appellate court further conceded, constituted such grounds. The panel of monitors would, consequently, have to function without a chairman unless and until Judge Letts nominated someone to whose selection neither side could validly object.

Such a nomination was never made. Instead, the octogenarian justice seemed, finally, to have become disenchanted with the administrative machinery that he had once deemed a "magnificent disposition." Even before their ruling in the McShane situation, his appellate colleagues had greatly disappointed him by deciding that, because of the tenets of Landrum-Griffin, Hoffa could indeed only be removed by a democratic vote of the union membership and not by judicial order. Now his further wishes were clearly to be subservient to a Hoffa veto power. It was only a matter of time before Letts, exhausted after almost three years of involvement in the Teamster-monitor warfare and at this point totally disheartened, would abolish the board. He did so in late February 1961, announcing that the IBT could hold a special presidential and executive board election at its convenience. The union was expected to schedule a convention to conduct this election within the next few months, certainly no later than July.

Within weeks, joint councils in New York, Chicago, Detroit,

Los Angeles, St. Louis, and a half-dozen other major cities unanimously recorded themselves in favor of Hoffa and his entire slate of incumbent executive board members. For the forty-eight-year-old man who, once again, had emerged unscathed from a battle that had at one point seemed likely to end his career, election was a certainty.

But it seemed to be the Teamster chief's fate always to be dogged by *something*. Even as Letts was getting ready to issue his edict that would call off the court-appointed watchdogs, an arrest record "that's maybe as long as your arm" lengthened. In December 1960, Hoffa and two other persons were indicted by a federal grand jury on twelve counts related to his Sun Valley activities.

In promoting the Florida land development project, the indictment charged, Hoffa and the other two defendants (Henry Lower, a former Detroit Teamsters local president, and Robert E. McCarthy, Jr., a former Detroit bank manager) had engaged in mail and related fraud. They had touted the lots in the development as being "all on high, dry and rolling land," whereas many in fact were "so low and permeated with water as to make them unsuitable" for home building, and had otherwise misrepresented the real estate.

A related charge was even more damning for Hoffa, who was enormously proud of his widespread reputation for effectively servicing the members of his union. It contended that the three men had promoted the flawed land as a haven for IBT retirees, billing it as the "Teamster model city of tomorrow." Since they had charged the buyers anywhere from $150 to more than $1,000 for the lots that they had acquired for about $18 each, they had therefore, allegedly, not only realized ill-gotten gains of some magnitude but had done this at the expense of the Teamster rank and file. Eight of the twelve counts were based on use of the mails for the claimed fraud. The four others contended that the telephone and telegraph were used for the same purpose.

And, as both the McClellan committee and the monitors had done, the government also charged that $500,000 had been removed from the Local 299 treasury in Detroit and deposited in a non-interest-bearing Florida National Bank of Orlando account. The bank in turn lent money, it was once again alleged, to the Sun

Valley, Inc. land development company of which Lower was president and in which Hoffa had his concealed interest.

If convicted on all twelve parts of the new charge, Hoffa could go to jail for sixty years, five on each count. (In a distant second place, he could also be fined $12,000.) Publicly, however, he shrugged off the news of his indictment with a cavalier "It's just another lawsuit" and "We'll try the case in court." Hoffa could take care of Hoffa.

Privately, on the other hand, he was far more worried than he ever had been before when faced with a governmental onslaught, and understandably so. For the government was all set to change hands. And the U.S. Justice Department, never before exactly a staunch friend of his, would now be headed by a man who, from his viewpoint, could not have constituted a worse choice had the Marquis de Sade made the selection.

The man was Robert Francis Kennedy, the new attorney general of the United States. Hoffa might regularly describe him in such terms of opprobrium as "punk kid," "parasite living off the government," and "that little monster," but to John F. Kennedy, the just-elected Democratic successor to Republican Dwight D. Eisenhower, his younger brother was the only logical person for the job, once the President-elect's long-time supporter Governor Abraham Ribicoff of Connecticut had declined it. John F. Kennedy had joked about the nepotism involved in the selection ("I'll stick my head out that front door, and look up and down the street, and if nobody's around I'll whisper the announcement") and asked his brother, "Bobby, before we go out there to tell the press that you are to be the next Attorney General of the United States, would you mind combing your hair?" But he genuinely respected the former McClellan committee counsel's tenacity, his code of personal morality, his ability to inspire, and his tolerance for work. His brother would be up to the responsibilities of the position.

Moreover, on most matters concerning the administration of justice—the desirability of a citizen like, for example, Hoffa eluding criminal penalties—the two brothers were in total agreement. Candidate Kennedy was unhappy because the Teamster boss was still free. Robert Kennedy, appearing on "Meet the Press" the week before the Presidential election, could declare, "I think it is an extremely dangerous situation at the present time, this man who has a background of corruption and dishonesty, has misused hundreds of thousands of dollars of union funds, betrayed the union membership, sold out the membership, put gangsters and racketeers in positions of power, and still heads the Teamsters Union."[4]

What had already become a famous feud was, therefore, all set to take on a new and, for Hoffa, a far more formidable dimension. The only member of the Kennedy family who never forgave now had another chance to right a festering wrong.

He made the most of it. Almost immediately, the new head of the Justice Department set up a special unit within his domain and gave it both his complete support and much of his personal attention. For it, he hired twenty of the brightest and most ambitious young lawyers he could find, placed them under the supervision of a talented nonlawyer who enjoyed his deepest respect—the deceptively soft-spoken, iron-willed former investigator for the McClellan committee, Walter Sheridan—and made available to them all of the files of his old senate subunit. The lawyers sometimes referred to themselves as the "Terrible Twenty," but more often, in open recognition of the sensitive task with which they had been entrusted, they described their operation as the "Get Hoffa Squad." They were to complete the business concerning the head of the Teamsters that the McClellan committee had begun. It was now their responsibility to put the alleged operator of the "conspiracy of evil" behind bars.

Senator John McClellan was not entirely done with Hoffa, either. With his old select committee now defunct, he scheduled five days of late January 1961 hearings on the Teamsters Union for the Senate Permanent Subcommittee on Investigations that he continued to head. And the Senate Caucus Room, for one more time, was during two of these days the scene of testimony by James R. Hoffa.

This time, there were no television cameras, the Hoffa legal team having successfully objected to their admission, and the chief counsel's table was presided over by Jerome S. Adlerman in lieu of a more familiar Hoffa adversary. In addition, the good guys and bad guys had now, of course, been firmly established in the public's mind. Otherwise, the key ingredients were amazingly reminiscent of an earlier day—even to the point of resuming the testimony relating to New York City's gangster-controlled Teamster Local

239 at almost the exact point at which the McClellan committee questioning on this subject had, nineteen months earlier, stopped.

The alleged continuing boss of the New York local, although now he no longer had any official title in its hierarchy, was the formidable ex-convict and prior player in the Hoffa morality play, Anthony "Tony Ducks" Corallo. He appeared before the reconstituted McClellan probers as a witness, although only after a seven-month police search had located him on Long Island and he had been served with a subpoena. As an ex-officer, his presence could not itself buttress the subcommittee's basic contention that Hoffa had condoned continuing corruption in Teamster locals. But Senator McClellan did use Corallo's appearance as an opportunity to ask him—in vain, since Corallo fell back upon the Fifth Amendment—to shed light on a tape recording in which Hoffa had purportedly not shown himself in the best light.

The tape was allegedly made by the New York City police on June 30, 1959. According to McClellan, it captured a report that the Local 239 secretary-treasurer had given to Corallo following the former's visit to Hoffa in Washington. In the tape, Hoffa was quoted by the secretary-treasurer as saying that it was all right for Corallo to steal from the local as long as he didn't get caught. Hoffa also purportedly said to his visitor, in the transcription, that a jailed officer of the local (Local 239 had just such a man, its former president) had to be taken off the payroll but could certainly be paid secretly.

In his own appearance on the witness stand, Hoffa heatedly denied having said anything of the kind. He had never, he said, even set eyes on Corallo before. He called the recorded conversation "a fabrication and a lie." He said that he found it difficult to understand why the senator from Arkansas would give any weight to a garbled, often unintelligible transcription of someone's interpretation as to what he (Hoffa) had supposedly told him. He pointed out that the transcript had no fewer than nineteen deletions in it, indicating that at nineteen points whatever was said was incomprehensible to the listeners. Not only that, he argued, but the New York City police had invaded the constitutionally guaranteed right to privacy by planting their microphone in Corallo's apartment: Senator McClellan, in Hoffa's opinion, "would be the first to scream" if anybody did that to him."[5]

More calmly, Hoffa also responded to charges previously made to the subcommittee by members of Philadelphia Local 107 that they had been beaten up or laid off from work after questioning the alleged misuse of the local's money by the now-indicted Raymond Cohen, who remained its secretary-treasurer. He promised a "full report" and a "proper investigation" of these latest charges. But he had already thoroughly investigated Cohen's presumed other illegalities, he said, and had found nothing: "Mr. Cohen," he told the Senators, "denied any wrongdoing, and I believe him until proven otherwise."[6]

As for a suggestion by counsel Adlerman, who counted off eight allegedly corrupt Teamster officers still in positions of power, that he might be "afraid" of the gangsters in his union, an unequivocal answer not unlike one that he had given to counsel Kennedy more than two years earlier was both immediately forthcoming and offered without any show of emotion at all: "Hoffa isn't afraid of anybody, and that includes you. Nobody needs to try to test my guts." With perhaps the slightest bit of sarcasm, Chairman McClellan thereupon announced, "Let's put it in the record. Mr. Hoffa is not afraid, period."[7]

The two main actors in this 1961 drama, the last in which they would ever directly face each other as interrogator and interrogatee on the subject of corruption, then parted with the harsh words of the other ringing in each man's ear. Hoffa, no longer making even a pretense of courtesy to a legislator whom he was now convinced was as fully biased against him as was the new attorney general, told McClellan, "Everytime I come up here, you castigate me and the union, just so you can get a headline."[8] McClellan, not one to hold his tongue either, informed the unionist that corrupt elements "will never be put out by you, that's one thing sure and certain."[9]

The day after these neo–McClellan committee hearings were adjourned, McClellan called a press conference. Its centerpiece was a plea by the earnest Arkansan for further tightening of the labor laws to prevent malfeasance by union leaders. He would continue to speak out against labor officials whom he thought were corrupt, most especially against the man whom he held to be primarily responsible for the lawlessness within the Teamsters Union. But, unlike Robert F. Kennedy, McClellan was now just a minor irritant. He could really do no more damage to Hoffa than, through the widely publicized hearings, he had already done. The January sessions had all the earmarks of an anticlimax. Their business would never again be attempted at all by the legislative branch.

It remained to be seen just what new problems for Hoffa the Get Hoffa Squad would devise. The man after whom the squad was named had no delusions here and consistently told friends that his worst days were still ahead of him. It was a "vendetta," he would often say, "persecution, not prosecution."

He did not believe that Kennedy's pursuit of him would necessarily end badly. He had great faith in his Teamsters Bar Association and even more in his own ability to withstand a challenge. He also recognized that one longstanding habit of his might now well work in his favor: he had always conducted his business transactions only in cash—a $25,000 check that he once drew as remuneration to Edward Bennett Williams remains to this day the only known exception to this policy—and even had IBT employees cash his entire paycheck for him as soon as it was issued. This fact might also now make a successful governmental prosecution of him more difficult.

But Hoffa also now knew that he faced years of concentrated Justice Department onslaught. Outwardly, he professed complete optimism: "You know and I know that if they had found one little thing wrong on Hoffa, he would be in jail today." Inwardly, he was aware that not all of his friends were entirely reliable and that in turn for, say, a dropping of governmental charges against themselves, some of them might be persuaded to testify against him. "Hoffa trusts nobody," was another well-used Hoffa statement. "Every man has his price."

Everything is, however, relative. And, compared to his situation before the turning off of the congressional spotlight and, especially, the calling off of the monitors, the best-known unionist in America was now not badly off at all. The Sun Valley indictment was, at this point, the only cloud on his immediate horizon, and even this seemed somewhat further off than it had originally appeared to be when the twelve counts were registered back in December. Although the mail fraud trial was at first scheduled to begin in Orlando in early March, it had been postponed indefinitely after the Hoffa defense team had filed motions challenging the validity of the indictment: the grand jury was empaneled under state rules and not federal ones, Hoffa's lawyers had claimed, and thus the indictment was improper. Also contributing to the postponement was the resignation of the man whom Attorney General Kennedy had personally chosen to prosecute the case: he quit after it was revealed that his Miami law firm had paid $25,000 to a county judge in a fee-splitting scandal.

For the first time since his advent to the presidency, the controversial Teamster was, consequently, free to devote all of his energy to bona fide trade union affairs. And, more than anything else, for Hoffa, this meant directing his considerable talents toward a long-time special area of interest: widening the scope of the truck drivers' bargaining unit. The basic areawide bargaining concept involved had, as Hoffa had readily acknowledged, stemmed from the prescience of Farrell Dobbs and, of course, had first been implemented on a major regional basis by Dave Beck. But Hoffa had, as was also indicated previously, made definite progress in building upon the idea in the Midwest and South in the years preceding 1955, and in both the East and West after his installation as leader of the full union. He could now concentrate on bringing all of these developments to their logical conclusion in the form of a master freight agreement for all Teamster truck drivers in the United States.

First, however, he would solidly entrench himself in the IBT general presidency, this time with absolutely no strings at all attached, at the judicially authorized convention.

This Teamster convention, held during the first week of July 1961, at Miami Beach's plush Deauville Hotel, constituted every bit as major a triumph for Hoffa as he had hoped that it would.

The trappings of a genuine presidential contest were present. Many of the two thousand delegates wore king-sized "Re-elect Hoffa" buttons and campaign hats. An airplane carrying a streamer with the same message cruised lazily in the blue skies above the long Miami Beach coastline. Josephine Poszywak Hoffa overcame her public shyness long enough to lead a conga line of Hoffa supporters through the Deauville lobby with verve enough for a half-dozen candidates' wives. And after Hoffa was nominated—by John English, who called him "the man with the most guts in America" —there was a fifteen-minute demonstration marked by the continuous chanting of "Hoffa, Hoffa, Hoffa."

But in sharp contrast to 1957, when Hoffa's two opponents for the presidency had garnered almost 30 percent of the vote, his sole rival this time—the mild-mannered Milton J. Liss of Newark, New Jersey—received only fifteen votes out of the first one thousand cast and then withdrew, allowing the reelection of the incumbent president by acclamation. The delegates took exactly ten seconds to raise Hoffa's salary from $50,000 to $75,000—thereby giving him the highest paycheck of any labor leader in the country. And they granted overwhelming approval to scores of constitutional changes, all designed to centralize authority firmly in his hands.

Among these amendments, the already broad Teamster jurisdiction was extended to include:

all workers *including*, without limitation, *teamsters, chauffeurs, warehousemen and helpers; all who are employed on or around horses, harness, carriages, automobiles, trucks, trailers, and all other vehicles hauling, carrying or conveying freight, merchandise, or materials; automotive service and maintenance employees, warehousemen of all kinds employed in warehouse work, stockmen, shipping room employees and loaders . . . , all classes of dairy employees, inside and outside, including salesmen; brewery and soft drink workers; workers employed in ice cream plants; all* other workers employed in the manufacture, processing, sale and distribution of food, milk, dairy and other products; *all truck terminal employees; and cannery workers. (emphasis supplied)*

In reply to a delegate who said that he "would like to see office workers inserted in that particular proposed amendment," Hoffa had said: "I would say to you that if we tried to spell out everything we have in the International Union—and we gave a lot of thought to it—we would have to devote almost a Sears Roebuck catalog to it."[10]

And this was not much of an exaggeration. Beyond the categories specifically cited in the new article, the IBT already represented workers in such diverse categories as egg farmers, retail clerks, airline stewardesses, and furniture production employees, as well as office workers, policemen, tree surgeons, and many others. Only about 30 percent of the estimated 1.7 million members of the truck drivers union, in fact, now actually drove trucks. No longer a part of the AFL-CIO, the union had felt no obligation to observe anyone's jurisdictional boundaries, and a standing quip within labor circles of the time was that the "Teamsters try to organize every-thing that begins with the letter 'A'—a factory, a store, a group of secretaries . . . ." But the change did give Hoffa official and unlim-ited authorization for organizing essentially everyone outside of trucking and vaguely related occupations, allowing him now a po-tential territory of more than forty million workers.

Hoffa had repeatedly denied that he planned to "raid" AFL-CIO unions in an effort to get new members, but he had just as frequently hinted that he would actively organize the latters' juris-dictions if they failed to do so. He believed that under Meany, whom he more than once described as "that dopey, thick-headed Irishman," the federation had become lethargic and unimaginative. Someone had to do the AFL-CIO's job.

To defray the expenses of this stepped-up organizing and also to finance other activities conducted by the international president, per capita dues to union headquarters from the local unions were raised to $1 a month per member from 40 cents. This would give the parent union an estimated annual revenue increase of $12 million (to about $20 million).

And Hoffa's major goal of bringing all truck drivers under a single nationwide trucking contract was facilitated by a new require-ment that "if a majority of the affiliated Local Unions vote for area negotiations for an area contract [in trucking], all affiliated Local Unions shall be bound by such vote, must participate in such area bargaining and shall be bound by the area contract approved."

In addition, all paid officers of union locals were automatically made delegates to future Teamster conventions, a move that would thenceforth effectively bar rank-and-file members of locals from attending such conventions since most locals had regularly been allotted fewer convention seats than they had full-time officers.

The amended constitution also eliminated a clause forbidding racketeers from holding union membership, Hoffa first explaining that this elimination made sense because the ban was "more restric-tive than the most anti-labor law ever passed, the Landrum-Griffin Act [and its banning of felons from holding union office for five years]." It contained a clause allowing both the international union and locals to pay the counsel fees and all other defense expenses of officers accused of any illegalities; the only limitation here was that the international executive board or local leadership had to believe that the accusations were groundless, politically motivated, or "filed in bad faith in an attempt to embarrass or destroy the union." And it authorized the president to select a new headquarters city for his union if he deemed such a shift from Washington to be desirable. This enlargement of presidential powers was ostensibly intended to expedite organizational efficiency, but it was actually designed to make it harder for the Justice Department to prosecute Hoffa by removing the official union records from the nation's capital.

There was some opposition to Hoffa's constitutional changes. The higher dues were approved only after nearly ninety minutes of acrimonious debate and only with a provision exempting "extreme hardship cases" from the new scale. One delegate heatedly pointed out that a result of the new convention delegate provisions would be to build a "barricade" around rank-and-file Teamsters so that they could not attend future conventions. Liss sponsored an amendment that would have provided for election of the international union officers by a secret ballot referendum supervised by outside observers (it was resoundingly defeated, Hoffa's supporters arguing that the secret referendum was "based on a foreign system, the so-called Australian ballot" and that those who were not willing to get up and make their feelings public in a convention roll call were a "bunch of yellow-bellied bums"). And the change binding local unions to the results of areawide bargaining under the majority rule concept was not adopted without a certain amount of grumbling, as the following verbal exchange between a San Francisco Bay area delegate and the general president illustrates:

Delegate Painter, Local 70 It seems to me when you came out there [to California] you spoke to Local 85 and spoke to Local 70 for a whole day, and wrote letters to our wives and families and did everything in your power to get us involved in the area-wide contract, and we turned you down in Local No. 70 with one dissenting vote. Everybody in 70 wanted no part of it and now you get us here and through your machine you put—

President Hoffa [interposing] Stop that kind of a remark and expunge it from the record. Hoffa don't have no machine. This happens to be the independent delegates representing each of their memberships from their Locals. They will decide what to do—no machine.

Now strike from the record "Hoffa's machine."

Delegate Painter, Local 70 I won't strike anything from the record.

President Hoffa I will ask the Convention to expunge it from the record. . . .

A delegate [name not given] I have no discussion on this but I move you that we take a vote on the question. . . .

President Hoffa There is a motion which has been regularly moved and supported to expunge from this record any references to a Hoffa machine. . . . All those in favor please rise; now please be seated. Now, those opposed.

Let the record show it is unanimous, including Painter.[11]

But, as the above occurrence might also be said to exemplify, the Teamster leader did attempt to ensure that all of his relative handful of opponents had an opportunity to speak. Even with the vast majority of all of the delegates solidly pro-Hoffa, he was willing to take no chances that the election results would this time be successfully challenged. He had tape-recorded the nomination and election of delegates from his own Detroit Local 299 in an effort to thwart any legal protest of the 1957 variety and had encouraged other locals to follow this example. And he had issued strict orders that Landrum-Griffin's requirements for the administration of labor unions be scrupulously observed.

He was sufficiently eager to become an undisputed president that he both refused to suspend convention business on the Fourth of July and scheduled (in the process generating mock groans from the delegates) an unusual four-hour night meeting, in the interest of getting to the presidential election faster. But his primary consideration was that the election results be incapable of effective challenge, and he thus immaculately observed the rules of convention decorum.

Indeed, even Liss, whom Hoffa had telephoned when the Newark leader had failed to appear at a constitutional committee meeting to speak in favor of his secret ballot motion and assured that he would be welcome, told the convention that he had been treated with "full fairness." And Hoffa's circumspect regard for parliamentary procedure (helped by the availability of no fewer than thirty-seven Teamster lawyers to ensure his compliance) even led a Chicago delegate to say, "I don't think I have witnessed a chairman that has allowed more democracy to creep in here." For good measure, Hoffa himself proudly asserted, "I wonder if the delegates believe the chair hasn't bent over backwards to create democracy in this meeting"; the statement received enthusiastic applause.

Another, of many, delegate compliments to the presiding officer came from a Los Angeles Teamster. Speaking from his floor microphone, he informed Hoffa, "Jimmy, this is my sixth convention. I don't know of any man that has the patience of you, unless I read about him in the Bible."

In his acceptance speech, an exultant Hoffa contrasted the various AFL-CIO intramural squabbles of the time with the apparent unity of his Teamsters behind him: "While the house of labor may be divided, ours is not the wing that is crumbling and falling apart." It was the IBT's very success, he said, that was causing the union its problems: all of the forces of "wealth and privilege" were amassed against the Teamsters because they were the only union in the entire labor movement that was doing an effective job in raising real incomes and organizing the unorganized. This was true, particularly, of the accusations of gangster control registered against the union. The accusations were part of a conspiracy by the employers and their "slick, pot-bellied representatives" in Congress to discredit and destroy the union.

And, implicitly making the point that the IBT was an organization in which its members could take great pride, he invited his constituents, as he had so many times before in other speeches, to contact him at any time, day or night: "Sterling 3-0525 and Sterling 3-0670 has been there for four years. Those telephone numbers will be there the next five, and if I am not on the other end, [my office staff] will know where I am, and for the sake of a second call, you will be able to have my services around the clock as you have had in the past."[12]

For all of this unquestioned pride of the leadership in servicing the membership, and for all of the creeping into the convention of not merely the trappings but the realities of democracy, a purist might still have registered an occasional objection. Elected as the three trustees of the international union and as such entrusted with auditing the secretary-treasurer's accounts semiannually, prior to a certified public audit, were two convicts and a man under indictment. Incumbent trustees Frank Matula, already found guilty of perjury, and Ray Cohen, now still under his 1959 indictment for defrauding the union but able to fend off trial by a series of legal maneuvers, were returned to office. (Matula had actually been able to perform his 1960 duties as a trustee only because he was given a "freedom break" from the Los Angeles County jail where he was serving his perjury sentence.) William Presser, whose appealed conviction for destroying union records subpoenaed by the McClellan committee had been upheld earlier in the week, was elected as a new trustee.

In addition, Tony Provenzano, under indictment for extorting money from New Jersey trucking companies, not only sat on the all-important constitution committee but was elected as one of the thirteen international vice-presidents. The committee on arrangements included another alleged extortionist, Joey Glimco, also once suspected of murder. The former jail inhabitant Babe Triscaro was a member of the officers' reports committee, where he had something in common with at least two fellow committeemen, since Presser and Matula, too, lent their energies to this key committee.

None of these assignments would have been possible without Hoffa's approval. Each also carried the top Teamster's strong endorsement. Each was reciprocated by unbudging loyalty on the part of the man favored—Matula, for example, telling the delegates, "There is only one guy who can help you when you are in trouble; I know because I am one of the guys whom he has helped and for which I will be forever grateful."[13]

Hoffa had, furthermore, appeared to be displaying more than a little paranoia at the convention. He warned his audience that the Justice Department had dispatched "dozens" of women FBI agents to Miami Beach in an effort to unearth incriminating evidence. "These women," he asserted, "are mingling with delegates in hotel lobbies, dining rooms and bars, trying to pick them up and get them into situations where they can be forced to divulge things that are the union's private business. Don't get hooked by these Justice Department hookers."[14] Agents who were not disguised as hookers, he was convinced, could well be posing as uniformed hotel employees—bellboys, desk clerks, maids, or restaurant workers. Others, he suggested, actually had the brass to seat themselves with the delegates, and he demanded that "every single person look at the man sitting alongside of him to make sure that only delegates are on this floor."[15]

Hoffa had later displayed to the delegates a transistorized listening device which he said had been found hidden in a television set near the convention headquarters: it would not surprise him, he had declared, to learn that one of the agents, whose number he now estimated at 150, had been responsible for the "bugging."[16]

Those in attendance at the convention hall could not have known, but Hoffa was only then moving into a Kennedy-phobia that would remain with him as long as the President's brother was attorney general. Not long thereafter, he told the Jameses that FBI agents, on the younger Kennedy's orders, were following him wherever he went, tapping his telephone, and opening his mail. The agents were also, he believed, beaming electronic listening devices on him from half a mile away, aided by invisible powder that they had rubbed onto his clothes.[17] For a man whose grasp of reality tended to be total, it was not an inspiring performance.

Finally, even the most enthusiastic of Hoffa supporters in Miami Beach might privately have had second thoughts about at least one convention action that had been taken unanimously. The delegates resoundingly and without any visible objection voted to exonerate Hoffa and all other Teamster leaders on every single charge of "malfeasance, misfeasance and non-feasance" brought against them in Congress and the courts over the past four years.

The resolution absolving the leadership (and attacking the senators and judges as being part of an effort to "embarrass and harass" the Teamsters) in fact commended the officers for serving the union with a "high degree of devotion" worthy of the members' approbation." It was made after a stirring speech to the convention by chief counsel Edward Bennett Williams, who noted the fortitude with which the accused had defended their constitutional privilege against self-incrimination under the Fifth Amendment. In his address, Williams also pointed out that, after all of the McClellan committee charges had been levied, only six indictments against current major Teamster officials had resulted. He added that none of the six had resulted in court convictions, a remark that, in view of the Matula and Presser histories, led some journalists present to question his semantics.

Nobody Talks Back to Hoffa

8

Two slogans were particularly drawn upon by the trucking industry as Hoffa turned his relatively undivided attention to it in the early 1960s. "Practically everything we eat, wear, use or need comes all or part of the way by truck" was one of them. "If you got it, a truck brought it" was the other. Both, allowing for some understandable puffery, were justified, for trucking even in these years was a sector of no small dimensions. Few American industries could rival the dramatic growth that it had achieved in the previous four decades, and none of these could equal, in dollar amounts, its current importance to the economy.

Virtually nonexistent before 1914 and of little significance in our transportation system before the 1920s, trucking by the 1960s had highly impressive statistical credentials.[1] In 1961, it directly employed over seven million people and with agriculture constituted one of the two largest employers of labor in the nation's private sector. In that year, it spent $3.8 billion on new equipment, parts, and accessories and paid approximately $3 billion in special highway use taxes to various levels of the government. It also purchased 15.5 billion gallons of motor fuel so that its 11.7 million registered trucks could drive some 126.5 billion miles.

Moreover, its 15,283 common carriers (those holding themselves open for hire to the general public to transport all types of freight wherever geographically allowed to do so by the Interstate Commerce Commission) and 2,399 contract carriers (also for public hire and transporting freight on a continuing basis for individual shippers specifically contracted with) alone realized gross revenues of $7.4 billion. The revenues or value of services generated by all trucks (in addition to the for-hires, these included private carriers—those carrying only the goods of their owner's business—and "exempt" carriers, those used strictly for limited operations such as newspaper delivery or transportation wholly within municipalities and thus exempt from most ICC regulation) in that year probably exceeded three times that figure.

In achieving this 1961 performance, trucking had continued to gain against its perennial rival, railroad freight business. It now accounted for 21.75 percent of intercity ton-mile movement, as against 43.21 percent captured in the same year by the railroads. (Inland waterways, pipelines, and airways captured the rest of the market.) Only thirteen years earlier, railroads had accommodated 65.24 percent of this traffic, with trucking's share then a less menacing 10.02 percent. In terms of the even more meaningful revenue distribution among interstate for-hires, gross operating revenues of the motor carriers had risen from $2.2 billion in 1947 to their $7.4 billion total, while the trains had shown a far smaller gain in these years—from $7.1 billion to $7.9 billion.

Both the rapidity and the recency of trucking's progress appeared even more graphic when figures of a scant quarter-century earlier were considered. In 1935, when the federal government first gave the industry's growing importance tangible recognition through the passage of the Motor Carrier Act, there were fewer than 3.7 million registered trucks on the roads. Total industry revenues for that year were estimated by the Interstate Commerce Commission as being "probably no more than" $500 million.[2] And intercity truck vehicle mileage was less than one-quarter of its estimated 1960 total of 81.5 billion. While these aggregates pertain to a time of general economic depression, each is believed to represent the highest theretofore attained by motor carriers.

For the nation in this quarter-century, which saw Hoffa climb the Teamster hierarchical ladder from underpaid business agent of the bankrupt Local 299 to his present position of total supremacy, the consequences of the growth had been great. Vast industrial decentralization and the accompanying exodus of the population from the city to the suburbs had taken place because of it. Sizable economies in minimal inventory investment had been afforded many businesses by the faster and more flexible competitor of the train. Thousands of smaller, off-route communities bypassed for years by the railroads were now able to contribute collectively an important part of the national total of goods and services. The United States could prosper as it had never prospered before.

Nonetheless, trucking by no means faced guaranteed future successes as Hoffa contemplated his national agreement. Affecting it now were three increasingly ominous factors. All of them were relevant to collective bargaining.

First, the industry, always intensely competitive internally, in the 1960s was confronted by far more formidable external competition than it ever had been. The threat came primarily from the railroads, newly awakened to the potentialities of technological change after years of apparent obliviousness.

"Piggybacking," the transportation of loaded highway trailers on railroad flatcars, had grown enormously in the last few years and had now revitalized many of the rails. It possessed several advantages over long-haul trucking: greater economy in handling expenses, terminal costs, and labor productivity; increased speed, once the flatcar was moved out of the terminal; and greater safety for the freight, thus minimizing loss and damage claims. In 1955, fewer than 170,000 railroad cars were loaded in this manner. By 1960, almost 600,000 were, and even at that early point the development had already drained the profits of many once-flourishing over-the-road truckers.

Railroad competition had also become more threatening in other areas. Despite the increasingly unimpressive record of the railroads when stacked against trucks in terms of both freight-hauling revenues and total intercity ton-miles, several recent developments had enhanced the future of many railroads. There had been a pronounced trend toward railroad mergers, which inevitably decreased the huge overhead expenses of the involved companies and allowed other operating economies. Railroads were spending more money than ever before for modern, efficient rolling stock: lightweight aluminum cars with high cargo capacities; high-speed diesel locomotives; multilevel racks for transporting automobiles; and tailor-made flatcars to accommodate other specialized types of freight. And traditional railroad union work rules and practices, which had caused the perpetuation of thousands of obsolete jobs, were now slowly being modified by the unions. Part of the gains realized by the railroads from all of these developments were aggressively being offered current trucking customers.

Air freight competition could also no longer be disregarded by the trucker. The airways accounted for only 1.82 percent of revenue distribution among regulated freight carriers in 1960, but they had tripled their ton-miles in the past decade, and this trend was now accelerating. Air cargo, still consisting mainly of such lightweight, high-value items as electronic parts and jewelry, was also starting to show increased diversity.

A second growing threat to the common and contract carriers came from other trucks. Former and present customers of the for-hire carriers were increasingly envisioning sizable economies and efficiencies from transporting their own goods in their own trucks. American Telephone & Telegraph's 78,400 trucks qualified it as the nation's largest private trucker. But some thirty-eight other carriers had fleets of more than 1,000 trucks, many of these well over that figure. And the end was not in sight. In 1961, there was an estimated minimum of 57,000 nontrucking company truck fleets, up enormously in a very few years.

At least private carriage was legal, however. Of even more concern to the regulated trucker was the so-called "gray area" operator, also growing fast. The latter kind of carrier would claim to be either a private trucker or an "exempt" one. It thus could avoid the large tax burdens, rate restrictions, and safety and hour regulations of the government. Actually, however, it would act as a for-hire carrier, unfairly competing against the bona fide ones. By the 1960s, American Trucking Associations was estimating that such "bootleg" truckers were costing the regulated segment more than $7 billion a year, or an amount roughly equal to the total current revenues of the genuine for-hires.

Third and finally, as an area of worry, severe upward pressure on motor carrier prices from costs of all kinds, including labor costs, now appeared to be gaining some momentum. The industry had always been cursed by extremely low profit margins, with direct operating expenses typically absorbing over 97 cents of each revenue dollar. But the new competitive pressures were simply no longer letting the carriers raise their rates to absorb the growing expenses in payroll, taxes, plant, equipment, and insurance. Hence, operating ratios were increasingly unsatisfactory for most trucking companies and dangerously near the level of insolvency for some.

James R. Hoffa was understandably interested in all aspects of the multisectored, Teamster-organized trucking industry. Local cartage, trucking performed strictly on an intracity basis, had always received some considerable personal attention from him, as had the car hauling subdivision of trucking that had provided him with so much organizing experience in his earliest union days. Nonetheless, in more recent years he had devoted his primary efforts to the so-called "over-the-road" portion of the industry, made up of the common and contract for-hire long-distance carriers of general freight. Also known both as "intercity" and "line haul" trucking, it was the largest and, in his opinion, the most intriguing trucking segment. While his national agreement contemplated encompassing all of general truck freight, and thus the four hundred thousand truck drivers in both over-the-road and local cartage who together accounted for the largest single occupational grouping within the Teamsters, he had chosen to focus on the road drivers for several reasons.

Sheer statistics commanded his interest, for one thing. In 1961, over-the-road trucking accounted for about two-thirds of the 126.5 billion miles traveled by all trucks and by itself employed some third of a million drivers. And 90 percent of its more than seventeen thousand employers were represented by the IBT, which lacked only a few holdouts in the South among companies of any size.

In addition, Hoffa had since his first exposure to the Minneapolis Trotskyites and the pragmatic ideas of Farrell Dobbs viewed the road drivers as the key to his organizational successes elsewhere. By definition much more mobile than local cartage drivers, they could provide the needed "leapfrogging" by refusing to deliver to or pick up from unorganized workers, including the cartage workers. A favorite Hoffa expression had always been, "Once you have the road drivers, you can get local cartage, and once you get local cartage you can get all the rest."

Because of this last premise, the Detroiter had from almost the beginning gotten most of his own experience in the realm of the long-distance driver. The Strawberry Strike at the Kroger's warehouse notwithstanding, he had risen through the ranks above all as a representative of the road men. He had come to know the road sector—its technology, economics, and personalities—as well as anyone ever had. His reputation as a negotiator was built essentially on what he had done here alone.

And, presiding over an increasingly diversified labor organization that now had more members than many American states had residents, he had been forced to specialize. Even a Hoffa could not grasp all the intracacies of bakeries, brewery work, the dairy industry, and office work—let alone tree surgery, egg farming, and airline stewardessing. As one close friend of his had explained, "More than any other sector, [over-the-road truck driving] is near and dear to J. R. Hoffa's heart. If Jim knows little about warehousing and less about egg farmers, road driving is the one activity he has been able to stay both with and on top of."

He would delegate the nontrucking areas to others and even in trucking concentrate on general freight, with special emphasis on the road drivers.

Amid the rampant deregulation and fast-rising nonunion competition that today pervades the intercity trucking industry, the Teamsters Union no longer possesses enormous power. Contractual improvements gained from employers across the bargaining table have, in recent years, been miniscule enough to cause widespread dissatisfaction among IBT members. Even then, generally speaking, the union has not procured the improvements easily.

When Hoffa was the chief bargainer for the union, in sharp contrast, the IBT definitely held the upper hand. And, despite the Teamster boss's significant talents, some of this advantage simply came with the territory as it existed at the time and had existed for many years. It would have been hard in these days for any union negotiator to perform poorly. Indeed, it would not be going too far to say that almost no labor relations arena had ever historically displayed such an imbalance of power favoring the union.

Part of the explanation could be found in the basic characteristics of the employers. Even today a sector of relative pygmies, line hauling, as Hoffa pursued his goal of national coverage for it and local cartage, was an industry of small, intensely competitive carriers. The gross operating revenues of $160 million that its largest member, Consolidated Freightways, reported in 1961 barely made a dent in the $7.4 billion industry total.[3] The ten biggest carriers—beyond Consolidated, the 1961 list contained (in descending order) Ryder System, Roadway Express, Associated Transport, Pacific Intermountain Express, Interstate System, Denver-Chicago Trucking, Spector Freight System, McLean Trucking, and Cooper-Jarrett—collectively garnered under 10 percent of the industry's revenues.[4] And 13,847 of the more than 17,000 regulated carriers had (1960) gross operating revenues of less than $200,000, while an additional 2,276 grossed between $200,000 and $1 million from operations.

Despite a wave of recent mergers and consolidations, the average carrier's resources were, understandably, also anything but impressive: based on data compiled by the Interstate Commerce Commission and made available to the industry, the average management was responsible for a mere thirty-five employees, fifteen power units, twenty trailers, and an $111,500 operating property investment, even when the much larger figures for trucking's relative "giants" were taken into account. And the industry continued to be marked by exactly what had beset it from its earliest days—what one observer of it had called "a rough, brawling, extremely competitive battle royal among small units."[5]

The observer might have added that despite both the merger trend and a definite infusion in the past decade of professionally trained managerial specialists into trucking, many of the small units remained, even in the 1960s, in the hands of their founding fathers. The latter had often been motivated to go into business for themselves in the 1930s and 1940s because of the ease of entry: it required only a few dollars for a down payment on a truck (even less, if the truck was merely rented) and a strong back to haul the freight to and from the vehicle. They could survive trucking's formative years because, as one industry professional could admiringly declare, "they were rugged, tough-minded individuals, undaunted by adversity and not afraid of competition." Their continuing individualism, however, also helped explain why the cards seemed to be so heavily stacked against the employer side in the collective bargaining. The small scale of operations of the average carrier made it mandatory that the industry present a relatively united front to the union in its multiemployer bargaining if it hoped to achieve any kind of labor relations parity; the widespread individualism made this cooperation almost impossible to achieve.

But even if these two factors had not been so pervasive, the truckers would still hardly have been well equipped to exercise a strong voice in their labor relations. The basic economics of their industry also were working against them. Motor freight carriers cannot by themselves even warehouse. As soon as a truck driver work stoppage occurs, not only does the revenue completely cease, but vital customers may turn to any of the several fiercely competitive substitute forms of transportation—perhaps permanently. Few of the thousands of marginal operators in the industry in the 1960s did not believe that the loss of revenue alone might be the death blow for them: even a one-day strike in past years had forced some such carriers into bankruptcy. Not even the largest truckers, moreover, thought of themselves as being sufficiently big or competitively secure to escape extremely damaging effects from a three-week strike.

To all employers in this industry, then, the union's chief bargaining lever, the strike threat, was an even more potent tool than it was elsewhere. But, because the carriers did differ to some extent in their willingness to accept at least the short strike, the prospects for a united employer front were even further decreased, and the Teamsters had a commensurate added advantage.

As if all of this were not enough, two other factors regularly prevented the employers from getting together in their dealings with the IBT.

One of these was the huge diversity of conditions under which the intercity carriers operated. They tended to differ widely in product mix (and thus in type of shipper), degrees of regularity of their routes, kinds of equipment in operation, type of driver required, average length of haul, and, often, general financial condition. The result was that the cost impact of any given labor contract concession might not work the same hardship on one company as on another.

For example, under some of the existing contracts, special types of intercity trips such as "multiple leg runs" (those requiring the driver to pick up or drop more than one trailer and then return to the home terminal in a tour of duty) and "through runs" (where the driver would not return to the starting point within a single tour of duty) warranted special wage guarantees. Drivers fortunate enough to drive the more rumunerative of these runs could often add several of the guarantees together in a single day. Thus they could earn as much as twenty hours' pay for eight hours of work. The company with few of the runs, or none at all, could cheerfully concede the guarantees to the union in the multiemployer bargaining: not only would the concession not be onerous to it, but it would also have the beneficial result of hurting the competitor who *did* have such scheduling. The same equanimity might be shown in granting, in the areawide contract, special pay for driving heavier equipment—again, assuming that the grantor did not suffer much from the concession and particularly if other employers did.

The other factor was the ability of some companies to raise their governmentally authorized rates, and thus offset labor cost increases, more easily than could other companies. Since 1935, the Interstate Commerce Commission had tried to put the common and contract carriers operating in interstate commerce on the same basis by regulating the rates that they could charge. Companies operating exclusively intrastate had normally been subject to similar regulation by state tariff bureaus. In either case, the rates had to be reasonable, compensatory (not below costs), and not unjustly discriminatory. Traditionally the carriers had petitioned the ICC or state bureau through their respective employer associations after each round of collective bargaining, had received relatively pro forma approval to raise rates commensurate with their new obligations to the Teamsters, and had thenceforth been allowed to operate with the same profit margins as before.

Geared to protecting the carriers from what would otherwise be severe price competition and forcing them to compete strictly on service, the governmental regulation made eminent theoretical sense in this dog-eat-dog industry. In practice, however, equality under the law was not really granted the managements. Some carriers could expect to lose business immediately with their higher rates—most often to the unregulated private and exempt carriers and the illegal "gray area" ones but sometimes also to the railroads—while the revenues of others remained unaffected. Much depended on the commodities handled, the routes used, and the cities serviced. Individual carriers could always file their own lower rate schedules in an effort to reverse this customer desertion. But, given the uniformity of economic terms generally imposed on the employers within regions by the union, this hardly made income statement sense, especially with the typical employer already operating so close to the margin.

The carrier with relative elasticity of demand, then, had a choice of either resisting higher labor costs at the bargaining table or suffering in silence after the fact. But the more favored operator had no special incentive to resist demands at all, so long as these were not so unreasonable as to jeopardize either governmental higher rate approval or its own superior market position. This fact of life also helped account for the weakness of trucking's collective bargaining position.

The industry's labor relations apparatus reflected all of these varying circumstances and schisms. Although roughly 59 percent of the trucker's normal revenue in 1960 was absorbed by payroll, and unionized (or unionizable) employees accounted for over 88 percent of payroll costs, resources devoted to labor-management relations were conspicuous by their absence.

For all of the recent infusion of specialists into trucking (in sales, cargo claims, terminal design, accounting, traffic, and a variety of other functions), there were perhaps no more than fifteen full-time labor relations professionals in the entire industry. Employer industrial relations associations on the state and local levels, where they existed at all, were almost universally understaffed and underfinanced. And the American Trucking Associations, which maintained a small labor relations staff at its Washington, D.C., national headquarters, had refused to let it become directly involved in the labor problems of the industry: the ATA Industrial Relations Department was empowered to act exclusively as a "clearing-house for knowledge" and as a "coordinator" of negotiations with the Teamsters where it was requested by concerned employers to fill this role.

In over-the-road trucking, the important aspects of labor contract negotiation and administration, consistent with the growth of Hoffa's broadened scope of the bargaining units, were handled by ad hoc regionwide communities. These were composed almost exclusively of operating truckers, who had been requested to act in the interests of the industry by the regional trade associations to which they belonged. The committeemen were sometimes owners of companies and sometimes "professional" managers, but rarely lawyers, since both parties in trucking's labor relations were leery of such "outsiders." They had been either elected or "selected" by larger groups within the regional associations but either way could expect to spend considerable time away from their own duties, which related only to their own companies, and to receive no extra pay despite the long hours and tensions such assignments normally involved.

They came most frequently from the ranks of the larger carriers, the Roadways and the Pacific Intermountain Expresses, which were most likely to have become active in the trade associations in the first place. And they had accepted their assignments, generally reluctantly and "for this one time only" (although they had often returned) because they (1) had a sincere, not wholly unselfish, regard for the welfare of the industry; (2) wanted their company to have some voice in decisions that would ultimately affect it anyhow; or (3) desired professional recognition for themselves or a more prominent name for their employer.

Since the carriers they represented were consistently so diverse and since the committeeman rosters themselves might be expected to change radically from one negotiation or contract administration meeting to the next, these employer groups were rarely able to maintain unity of purpose in dealing with the IBT. The employer representatives not only began from their position of weakness but almost invariably finished in even greater disarray. "We employers still have almost no faith in each other, as parts of the same industry's management," the co-owner of a large eastern carrier could declare on the eve of the projected national agreement. "We understand each other's problems, but we have no incentive to defend each other and much incentive not to antagonize the union." Many of the committeemen also knew that they might be paying a particularly high personal price for their participation: as one of them had said, "While I'm negotiating with the union, the truckers I represent are out stealing my accounts."[6]

But the system had been, and would be, preferred to the several alternatives available to the trucking employers. Self-interest and not masochism had led the truckers, who were by no means oblivious to any of the severe drawbacks in their method of bargaining, to continue to support the labor relations status quo. That their by no means ideal machinery remained in place when the employers could have at least *tried* to increase their bargaining power by a different multiemployer system, or attempted individually (or in small groups) to negotiate with the international on their own, or even tried to strike bargains with their local Teamster leaders was attributable to the presence of a single man. And he, ironically, was not an employer at all, but a personality who both sat on and dominated the other side of the bargaining table. James R. Hoffa was very much respected by most trucking managements, sometimes to a degree that seemed to border on hero worship.

This is not to imply that the self-assured Teamster had not made enemies in the ranks of the truckers. Inveterate ones could readily be uncovered by any minimally discerning researcher. The great paradox of trucking labor relations—in view of Hoffa's demanding contracts, his natural outspokenness, and his unenviable public image—was that there were so few of them. Generally, the IBT leader who inspired such widespread popularity from his own rank and file generated equally positive sentiments from the people with whom he was officially in an adversarial relationship.

The following, entirely typical, remarks were freely offered to the author as he roamed the country in 1962 and 1963 gathering information for his Harvard Business School doctoral dissertation on Hoffa and the trucking industry.[7] In all cases, they emanated from managers who had participated in the 1960–1961 over-the-road negotiations. These same employers also (1) enjoyed excellent reputations for competency and character within the trucking industry, (2) had gotten to know Hoffa intimately, not just through this round of bargaining but in other negotiations and also in matters related to contract administration, and (3) spoke, in the author's opinion, quite frankly—their freely given opinions of other Teamsters, for example, often being not nearly as favorable as were those relating to the head of the IBT.

From the vice-president of a large carrier based in the Central States:

James R. Hoffa has many of the characteristics of the founders of our country: great personal and physical courage, boundless energy. . . . He has one of the keenest minds of anyone I've ever met. . . . He's the greatest negotiator I've ever known. He's tough, both tactically and emotionally. But he honors his contract immaculately, even to the point of placing himself in political jeopardy. He's withstood a huge personality crusade against him in the last few years better than almost any other man could have. He's affable, almost hypnotic (you have to watch out for this in negotiations) and a hard worker. . . . Has a great memory for names, faces and associations. A master psychologist, also.

The opinion of a co-owner of a medium-sized New England company:

He's an extremely intelligent man, the smartest guy I know. He's very fair in most respects, demands a fair day's work for a fair day's pay as much as any employer, and knows the overall industry better than anybody. He wants no more than any other union leader (less than many, like Walter Reuther), because of his inordinate intelligence and knowledge of the industry's problems. But sometimes he's politically not in a position to curb his demands: any labor leader must look to his constituents for his goals.

I disagree with him on some things, but I admire him tremendously and like him very much. . . . He's actually a genius.

From labor relations director of a large carrier, operating in both the Western and Central States:

Hoffa is more of a man than the general public gives him credit for being. He understands the trucking industry better than any other union official. He may ramrod his actions through, but he's been quite influential in protecting the industry. . . . He's tops—a great statesman.

And, finally, the thought of the president of a smaller, Chicago-based company:

My opinion of Hoffa is very high. . . . He has no real weaknesses, except that he's apt to fly off the handle pretty quickly. It would be almost impossible to have a better negotiator than he is. He's like an elephant with his memory—it's beyond belief. He's sharp as a tack . . . and he'll always listen to reason. He remains an ability-to-pay man. He knows just how far he can go and he won't jeopardize the goose that lays the golden egg, which is the trucking industry.

All of these men, and most of their counterparts from the dozens of other companies visited in the course of this particular research, had added that Hoffa had never been anything but honest in his dealings with them. And in these cases he had been "*too* conscientious [laughter]." Whether he was guilty of the wrong-doings charged by the government, the monitors, and the AFL-CIO, the management interviewees typically asserted that they "could not say" and until such time as he might be proven guilty, therefore, they must "reserve judgment."

This respect had made it much easier for Hoffa to implement his system of master contracts with uniform provisions.

The larger carriers, generally speaking, had always favored such an arrangement on other grounds. Its stability had worked in their favor, against the traditional cost-cutting practices of the smaller operators, with the strong union providing an effective vehicle for policing actions. In addition, many of these truckers had at least dared to hope that the broader units could strengthen the management side even more than it did the union by forcing the highly competitive and often mutually suspicious carriers into a more united front in labor negotiations. Such employers also saw this unavoidable togetherness as leading to more rational actions if tariffs later had to be raised because of increased payroll costs. To them, therefore, the high caliber of the man into whose hands most of the consolidated power on the union side had fallen constituted only one more reason for supporting his goal.

The thousands of smaller operators, who had had at least some say in their own destinies under the old local bargaining systems, had never believed that these advantages outweighed their loss of labor relations participation. Moreover, they had felt in the past that what Hoffa had really wanted in his contemplated nationwide uniformity was akin to (in the words of one small-company owner) "the U.S. Army trying to make one size of uniform for all of its men: it would do irreparable damage."

However, even these smaller companies (with a few conspicuous exceptions) now appeared to be recognizing the advantages of allowing union authority to be concentrated in the hands of a reputedly competent leader, as opposed to seeing their locals controlled by Teamsters whose abilities had varied widely and had rarely reached Hoffa's level. In coming to this conclusion, nonetheless, they were assuming that what they had been hearing about Hoffa's consideration for special local conditions would continue.

These reports about the various dispensations were fully warranted. A mere twenty master contracts governed all Teamster line haul drivers, as against over seven times that number a decade earlier, but many current departures from their provisions had been officially sanctioned by the man who now ran the Teamsters. Some of these deviations, such as the previously noted Ohio Rider, continued past practices that were more favorable to the covered *employees* than the current master contract allowances, and, although most of these would ultimately end as national uniformity made them obsolete, they understandably aroused no employer enthusiasm at all. Many other deviations, however, recognized special economic circumstances affecting particular subgeographic areas, companies, or products handled by being less costly for the carriers.

Companies operating in South Dakota, for example, to this day must labor under conditions that are unknown in most of the country. The state's widely scattered and sparse population and its general absence of centralized manufacturing activity mean that the carriers must all but literally beat the bushes for a pound of freight at times. The all-important back haul is rarely as easily obtained as it is elsewhere. In addition, secondary roads are often inadequate, and the winter weather is rigorous. Because of these obstacles, Hoffa had granted terms to the truckers for their South Dakota operations that were less expensive than those imposed by the central states agreement. Both mileage and hourly rates paid to drivers were lower and employers could use the drivers for loading and unloading, for no additional pay other than their normal guarantees.

Under the so-called "Iowa 75-Mile Rider," pertaining to trucking operations conducted wholly within that sparsely settled state, all drivers were paid on an hourly rate for runs within seventy-five miles of their home terminal. This inevitably was less costly for the employer than the alternative guarantee system.

Truckers in Nebraska, North Dakota, and other relatively unprofitable agricultural areas who could not pay the union scale could also count upon contractual relief when they had requested it from Hoffa, always assuming that they could furnish proof of their alleged inability to pay.

Riders for individual companies based specifically on financial considerations, as opposed to geographic ones, were in the 1960s most widespread in the territory that Hoffa had controlled the longest, the Central States. Not long after the conclusion of the 1961–1964 Midwestern master agreement, there were well over one hundred such riders to it. The number was also not a static one, since new riders were regularly granted by the quarterly meetings of the Joint Area Committee's Subcommittee on Change of Operations.

This latter body was normally composed of three employer and three union representatives. Its actions were subject to the approval of its parent committee, in whose deliberations Hoffa played a dominant role, as he did in its West Coast counterpart (although not elsewhere, since the existing demands on his time simply would not allow it). The riders were most often sanctioned by both unionists and employers for sound economic reasons: for the union, jobs were frequently very much at stake; in the eyes of the employers, the welfare of the industry could be affected.

At times, however, there were undoubtedly other motives for voting for relief for a requesting trucker, especially when an employer representative on the subcommittee chose to vote for the rider request of a carrier that was in direct competition with his own company. This situation might still have stemmed from a genuine desire to help over-the-road trucking under the general premise that an industry is no stronger than its weakest link. It was also known, however, to result from the fact that the employer representative (1) didn't fully understand the meaning of the rider, (2) wanted or already had a special rider himself, or (3) feared incurring Hoffa's wrath.

This last possibility could never be entirely dismissed. The involved company risked fatal consequences from it if only because of the international president's control of the awe-inspiring strike weapon. And it was therefore a rare—and foolhardy—employer representative who in subcommittee discussions disregarded a strong message from his union counterparts indicating "what Jimmy would do in this case."

Illustratively, at a typical Central States subcommittee meeting of the time, seven rider requests were approved while only one was denied. One of the successful petitioners sought to eliminate its multiple leg runs and simultaneously requested freedom from an overtime pay provision. If it could not obtain this relief, it argued, it would not only be forced out of business but a nonunion freight line would take over its customers. It provided the subcommittee with a financial statement to support its claim of adverse financial condition, and the forthcoming unanimous vote was presumably assured when a Teamster representative announced, "Jim thinks this guy has a strong case."

On the other hand, a request for both greater pickup and delivery flexibility and the elimination of all special runs was denied. No special reason for the desired concessions was presented to the subcommittee, at least in the written petition, and there was no direct reference to Hoffa in this situation at all. But the adamancy with which the three IBT representatives registered their objections to the request seemed to speak volumes to the three employers, who thereupon also voted negatively.

A third area of concessions from the Teamsters, those given on the basis of the product handled, definitely grew under Hoffa. He was willing to exclude certain types of freight from his master road contracts altogether and to cover their drivers with separate, less expensive riders, once again always subject to the test of financial necessity.

The transportation of iron, steel, and many perishable commodities, once considered to be very much an "over-the-road" operation by the union, was in Hoffa's presidency commonly covered by such contractual supplements. These types of freight are low rated and not particularly profitable, most frequently allow just one-way hauls, and result in the kind of abnormal driver and vehicle layover over which neither drivers nor the company have any control. Iron and steel carriage also demands special equipment on which no other commodity can be placed. The 1961 negotiations for the key Central States contract produced a rather lengthy addendum that was much less demanding of companies engaged predominantly in such businesses than was the master contract in several areas. It required layover pay after the twenty-fourth hour following the end of the run instead of after the fifteenth hour. In case of breakdowns or impassable highways, drivers were to receive the hourly rate after the ninth hour rather than immediately. Pickup and delivery limitations were less restrictive. Most importantly, the addendum provided that all drivers would be paid for their normal duties on a percentage of gross revenue basis, the wages to be "no less than" 23 percent of gross revenue. Most other master contracts also allowed such special relief for steel and similar commodity transportation.

Most runs of U.S. mail, likewise a low-rated commodity not readily lending itself to back hauls, had also been accorded less stringent contractual terms as Hoffa had achieved his ascendancy. Here, however, the dominant method was not the "industrywide-within-regions" type of supplement but separate riders for individual companies.

Nor, as Hoffa served notice on all parties that he wanted a single coast-to-coast contract covering not only over-the-road but also local cartage drivers in 1964, did many people expect this practice of isolating special products for less rigid contract terms to do anything but grow. As one higher-level Teamster had said of his pragmatic leader's ambitious 1964 goal, "When 'over-the-road uniformity' in its original sense is not economically practical, by taking portions of 'over-the-road' out of the traditional definition we can still have our 'over-the-road uniformity.'"

There was nothing in any of this to repel most truckers. On the contrary, most felt—as the evidence of Hoffa's various concessions to realism mounted—that they could gain the best of both worlds by supporting his widened bargaining unit program. They would have stability for their industry and individual dispensation from contractually imposed uniformity for themselves where this was genuinely warranted.

For the employer recalcitrants at the bargaining table, however, Hoffa was quite willing to take another approach. He could hardly be called a strike-happy leader. In the first four years of his Teamster presidency, only one important trucking service interruption, a four-week 1958 strike on the West Coast, had taken place; in the six years remaining to him as the chief negotiator for the union, there would be none at all. But the potential of the strike threat in an industry such as this was too obvious for him to ignore, and he used it often.

Invariably the threat was of a "selective" strike confined to a minority of the carriers. Hoffa often explained that "letting other employers operate in competition for the struck employer's business is the best way to win gains for our members because then the struck employer has to settle fast." When faced with an unexpected, if very tenuously maintained, hard line from some of the companies in the 1961 Central States negotiations, he announced, in a typical Hoffa performance, that he had "ten major companies" in mind that he would let run while the others were struck, in the event of continuing stalemate. He would not, however, name these companies. The hard-liners quickly capitulated.

Similarly, in bargaining for some 16,000 New England drivers a few months later, Hoffa again threatened "selective" strikes, announcing that he had "several" of the 1,025 involved companies in mind to be struck but again refusing to name them. He did, however, in this case throw out a few hints: "About 500" drivers would participate in this strike action at its beginning, with another 1,000 drivers quitting work "all the way to Chicago." Freight terminals used by the struck New England companies in New York, Pennsylvania, New Jersey, and Illinois would be closed down, he added. As it had in the Central States, this ploy significantly weakened what employer cohesion there had been.

For all practical purposes, Hoffa now exercised the total domination over all of his IBT negotiating teams that he had always been able to wield in the Central States, and this did not detract from his negotiating effectiveness, either. Forming a one-man united front that was solidly supported by all of his underlings, he was fully spared the internal dissension that so regularly undercut the employer efforts. In fact, well aware of his vast reservoir of rank-and-file support, he sometimes even appeared to be flaunting his hold over those who nominally helped him bargain on the union's behalf.

In the 1961 West Coast negotiations, for example, he neglected for some time to tell the 105 members of the Teamster Policy Committee, the official delegator of authority to the small bargaining team that he headed, that the talks had been transferred from San Francisco's Sir Francis Drake Hotel to the nearby Fairmont Hotel. According to a participant, "Every now and then Hoffa would have to get one of [the policy committee members] in. The union man would come into the room at the Fairmont, hat in hand, and answer Jimmy's question. Then Hoffa would say, 'O.K.—You can leave now.'" Ultimately, Hoffa did call the committee together, and according to a federal mediator in attendance at this internal Teamster meeting, he "reviewed in a very general way what had transpired. He glossed over much. And on the economic package he said, 'We're close to an economic agreement, but I'm not going to tell you guys what we've done, because you'd have it all over the street before I left this hotel.' The Policy Committee then gave him a unanimous vote of approval. This was pathetic. Nobody talks back to Hoffa."

In contrast, the three-man employer negotiating team in these negotiations was so severely constrained by *its* policy committee that one of the three people chose for a while to protest his limited freedom of action by refusing to attend the bargaining sessions at all. Later, the boycotter returned, but the heavy-handedness of the employer policy committee caused someone else to leave the room: Hoffa, who vacated the site by storming out of it after ripping up a written employer proposal and throwing it in the face of the management negotiating team chairman. He told the employers across the table that he wanted to "give the proposal back in pieces." According to one of the people who witnessed this unusual bargaining technique, "Hoffa was in no way irrational in his actions. He had thought he had a sure agreement and was just sore that the employer negotiating committee could not act freely."

The international president need not have been concerned, however. He quickly returned to negotiate a new contract that embodied virtually all of what he personally felt the industry could afford at the time. And, as always, he was aided immensely in his bargaining by the cleavages among the employers.

The split between the policy committee and the negotiating team constituted only one of these rifts. *Within* the policy committee, the representatives of the larger road carriers and those of the smaller firms displayed little cohesion. This lack of unity was based on governmental rate regulations. The operations of the larger carriers were generally interstate in nature and were thus fully subject to ICC rate supervision, but approximately five hundred over-the-road firms represented by the California Trucking Associations alone were strictly intrastate in scope and were therefore subject only to the less stringent rate regulation of the California Public Utilities Commission. Even the employer negotiation team, moreover, although united in its resentment of its overly tight mandate from the employer policy committee, was weakened appreciably by internal strains that were based on the contrasts between the companies that its three members came from: one firm, Denver-Chicago, had enjoyed relative prosperity in fiscal 1961; a second, Consolidated Freightways, had not; and the third company was far smaller and mainly interested in specialized types of freight. One leading employer could later say, in explaining the relatively rapid acquiescence to Hoffa's demands, "A minority of the carriers, including some very big and influential ones, was not in good financial shape at all and couldn't afford even a short strike." Not inconsistently, another trucker attributed the new contract to "the same old story, lack of unity among the operators."

In the 1961 New England Freight Agreement negotiations—involving companies in Massachusetts, Rhode Island, and Connecticut—Hoffa also did not hesitate either to remind his Teamsters who was in charge or to capitalize on the disunity in the employer ranks.

The union's New England Negotiating Committee numbered seventeen men—one from each of the sixteen locals in the three states, plus Hoffa. The Teamster president was believed to have said originally that his role in the negotiations would merely be that of an "observer." William J. McCarthy, the head of the largest New England trucking local (Boston) and a man who twenty-seven years later would himself become IBT president, was officially listed as chairman of the committee. And one committeeman told an interviewer: "The Committee invited Hoffa to come to these negotiations for one basic reason: to show the employers . . . that the International was 100 per cent in back of the Committee and, hence, that a strike against a firm with operations outside of, as well as within, New England, would bring about a complete shutdown of [that firm] wherever it operated."

But just before the bargaining formally opened, at Boston's Hotel Somerset in late March, Hoffa met with his sixteen teammates. He cited the expiring New England hourly wage rate of $2.41 and compared it to the new wage scale that he had just negotiated in the Central States (effective shortly in the latter area, the rate would be $2.94). The supremely self-confident IBT leader then informed his audience: "After all the helling and damning, you guys are going to have to sign a contract. . . . How can you justify having an agreement where a driver in Boston gets 50 cents an hour less than a driver [elsewhere]? Some of you guys ought to be ashamed to go out on the dock and take the members' dues. Your contracts are twenty years behind the times."[8]

From this point on, the international president fully dominated the bargaining. As had been the case elsewhere around the country, local leaders who for years had run their own provincial fiefdoms with a conspicuous lack of interference from either Tobin or Beck were now forced to recognize the realities of the Hoffa era. Most of them reluctantly concluded that resisting their activistic chief executive would be at best futile and at worst suicidal. Even disregarding Hoffa's considerable powers under the Teamster constitution (not excluding the power of imposing trusteeships on local unions more or less at will), his huge popularity with the membership, including—almost always—*their* membership, inevitably made resistance to him risky. Cooperating with him, they could at least keep their jobs and whatever duties he lacked either the time or the inclination to perform; fighting him might well mean the ending of their Teamster careers.

Not that they had to be happy about the transfer of power, which sometimes might even cause them some public embarrassment. A story told in the aftermath of this New England bargaining by both Teamsters and employers (it is presented here in the words of a management representative) illustrates how the latter circumstance could come about:

At the negotiations, Hoffa turned to [local leader X] or [local leader Y]—I forget which one but it makes no difference—in regard to a problem under discussion concerning a specialized operation. He asked, "How many men in this particular operation?" The answer was, "Five per cent of the total." Hoffa replied, "You're wrong—better think again." This time, the same man immediately answered, "You're right, Jimmy. It's fifty per cent."

Nobody talked back to Hoffa.

The carriers began in this case relatively united, for once. A respected owner, Alvin R. Holmes of the Holmes Transportation Service, Worcester, Massachusetts, headed the policy committee. He and his fellow committeemen used staff assistance provided by the American Trucking Associations. They also worked closely in planning their strategy with the full-time professional representatives of the two permanent southern New England employer associations: the Employers of Motor Carriers, representing companies headquartered in the Boston area, and the New England Motor Carriers' Council, Inc., representing the non-Boston southern New England employers. The early rapport among the three groups was deemed to be "unusually effective" by employers.

On the first day of the negotiations, however, the New England operators were surprised to find the representatives of two large and comparatively prosperous national carriers sitting at their bargaining table. These two companies had already signed the Central States agreement for their midwestern operations and now announced their intention of bargaining separately with Hoffa about the terms of their southern New England activities. Only since 1958 had their volume of New England trucking been of any consequence, and the move on their part was without precedent.

The main body of employers strenuously objected to any form of multigroup bargaining. With all of its members having much more at stake in New England than the outsiders and with most of them in considerably weaker financial condition than the latter, it contended that it had sole authority to negotiate the New England Freight Agreement. Hoffa exuded conscientiousness. The law, he said, was very clear on this point. Under it, he emphasized with just the slightest suggestion of righteous indignation, he had no choice but to negotiate with any trucker who wished to negotiate with the Teamsters. Therefore he would negotiate with the independents *ahead* of the main group, if the latter did not care to bargain with the independents.

The main group thereupon walked out of the conference room, and Hoffa proceeded to outline his proposed contractual changes to the midwesterners. He suggested that, to be both "consistent and equitable," they should grant in New England the same terms that they had already given in the Central States.

As the union's master negotiator had fully expected, it did not take long for the main group to return, apparently convinced that it was dangerous to let the independents set the pattern. Now bargaining simultaneously with the independents, the main group presented in considerable detail to Hoffa reasons why conditions in New England prevented its members from granting the Central States concessions to the IBT New England locals. Its spokesman specifically cited the relative prosperity of "most" Central States carriers (including the two visitors) as stacked against the income statement problems of so many of his own companies. He also stressed New England's comparative lack of open highways and long hauls, both normally allowing greater profitability, and the greater traffic congestion in his region, leading to higher labor costs because of nonproductive but remunerated time. Nor was New England's prevalence of what he called "outmoded and highly costly" trip rates, instead of the Central States mileage payment system, spared his attention.

This case for some concessions from the Central States key bargain was by no means without merit, as Hoffa had recognized from the inception of his own planning for these New England negotiations. He had no more intended to jeopardize the goose laying the golden egg here than he had elsewhere, and, while he was bent upon extracting a package that he considered to be the maximum one affordable by the New Englanders, there was no danger that he would push beyond this point.

The previously noted threat of "selective" strikes was enough to propel the employers to an April settlement that dealt with the New England realities. It called for wage rates to become identical to those in the Central States, not immediately but only over a five-year period. Thus, the 58-cent hourly wage rate increase was apportioned as follows:

Effective	April 11, 1961	10¢
	Oct. 11, 1961	5¢
	April 11, 1962	8¢
	Oct. 11, 1962	5¢
	April 11, 1963	10¢
	Oct. 11, 1963	5¢
	April 11, 1964	5¢
	April 11, 1965	5¢
	April 11, 1966	5¢
	Total	58¢

Hoffa granted other economic concessions, too. The lucrative trip rates were frozen at their present levels. The Central States cost-of-living wage adjustment clause that would further increase incomes as the national price level rose would not take effect in New England for two more years. And certain fringe benefits in the areas of both health and vacations would be allowed to lag behind the midwestern pattern for a while.

Some employers feared that the settlement would still drive them out of business, even though their only alternative to acceptance of this contract, suffering a strike, was an even less palatable option. As one trucker, registering the sentiments of a good many others, told the industry's weekly trade publication, "For many of us, this agreement means a slow death. But to have refused to accept it would have killed hundreds of us here and now."[9]

The employer majority, on the other hand, did not share this gloomy view. The New Englanders would have much preferred to have continued their separate bargaining with the Teamsters and fully recognized that, in the words of one owner, "we local people are paying the price of the generous concessions" of the outsiders who had joined them at the bargaining table. But they also believed that they could live with the new agreement. It had, they thought, been tailored to their own needs by a man who knew their industry as well as they did and had genuinely tried to accommodate these needs. Their ill will was reserved almost exclusively for the other truckers. Hoffa would "take care of Hoffa," as he had often boasted. But he would also, in their opinion (as in the opinion of so many employers elsewhere), take care of the companies with whom he dealt and on whose well-being he fully recognized the well-being of his drivers depended.

Hoffa probably could have implemented his areawide bargaining arrangements with their relative national standardization—by 1961, he was claiming an "85 per cent uniformity" in the terms of his twenty remaining contracts—through his popularity with the Teamsters and his respect from the employers alone. But the fact that he could give his rank and file a variety of rational arguments for his goals, and do so with great personal persuasiveness, definitely facilitated this implementation.

For internal Teamster consumption, the international president used both economic and legal reasoning.

In the economic sphere, he continually drew upon four arguments as he crisscrossed the country enlisting support for his program.

One argument was that agreements of a broader scope would

help to counteract the growing size (and, as a normal consequence, the growing resources) of the individual carriers. Smaller local unions would no longer need to deal with companies that had merged, unilaterally augmented their routes, or otherwise increased their power. The Teamsters, Hoffa often asserted without even the trace of a smile, had to meet strength with strength.

Secondly, companies could no longer justify moving from higher- to lower-wage locations, since there would be no such places. The mileage and hourly rate standardization would thus strengthen the job security of all workers and eliminate inequities of different rates of pay for different work.

Third, the pooling of pension and welfare funds allowed by the areawide mechanism would lead to more economical operation of these funds and therefore to increased benefits for the covered employees.

Fourth, the stability afforded trucking management under the broader agreements would make for a healthier industry, a situation that would necessarily benefit the workers. As Hoffa once phrased it in advancing this last argument: "We're making every company compete strictly on one level: *service*. And our bringing this about has already led to great improvements for the carriers and our members. The companies have brought in new equipment, built new terminals and introduced new operations that they never would have thought of otherwise."

Hoffa also regularly advanced two law-related reasons. He pointed out that the secondary boycott provision of Landrum-Griffin had forced the IBT into areawide (and, now, national) bargaining mechanisms. Only under the widest possible system would the union no longer have to worry about illegality here, for all strikes could then be considered "primary" ones. Hoffa had freely used this same argument long before the adoption of the new labor law, and for "Landrum-Griffin," at least insofar as the secondary boycott was concerned, one could have read "Taft-Hartley" before 1959. The only difference was that the post-1959 Hoffa used Landrum-Griffin's strictures to justify a nationwide contract, where the older law served him exclusively as a vehicle for demanding the areawide agreements.

In addition, Hoffa often informed his membership that the employers, emboldened by Landrum-Griffin and also by the anti-

Teamster Justice Department "vendetta" being waged by "the two rich Kennedy boys," were now showing more "muscle" in their labor relations. The Teamsters must, therefore, fight back—through the area and national agreements.

All of these points were made with what was apparently total conviction, by a tough-minded individualist whom Teamster word of mouth from coast to coast had already made something of a legend. The performance, consequently, was all but unbeatable. As a New York IBT leader, himself highly antagonistic toward area-wide agreements, could begrudgingly say: "I've been reelected to the presidency of this local many times without a defeat, but Hoffa could outsell me to the membership on the question of local-versus-area-or-national contract. He can outsell anybody! He's a spellbinder with the rank and file—a charmer."

Hoffa's speeches were not grammatically flawless. Even after years of experience and advice from such advisers as Gibbons, Konowe, and Steinberg, his public utterances—as his private ones—still contained occasional assertions that "Hoffa don't need nobody; Hoffa can do this job alone," "I don't have to walk around with no goddam bodyguards" and "Hoffa don't like paper work." To the end, he at times said "youse," at other times "you 'uns," when a simple "you" would have sufficed. He lacked the theatrical flair of, say, a John L. Lewis, who could both quote from Shakespeare and speak in Latin in the same address to his Mine Workers, and be rewarded by a standing ovation for his efforts. He was no Jack Kennedy or Martin Luther King.

But the Teamster chieftain was nonetheless a powerful speaker: forceful, blunt, and absolutely uninhibited. He always spoke spontaneously, never from notes of any kind. "He knew" one admirer recently recalled, "exactly what he wanted to say, and it just came from the heart." Whether railing against the Kennedys directly ("Well now, you and I know that Hoffa is nothing—just a name, just an individual. So when the Kennedys speak of destroying Hoffa, they're really speaking of destroying all of us, because we've been so successful") or reminding his membership of his inability to be intimidated by anyone ("I was brought up on the street, and nobody is going to make me squirm, wiggle, twist or turn—to hell with them"), he instinctively chose his words for maximum effectiveness. "Jimmy Hoffa speaks my language" was a statement frequently offered by Teamsters. And it was given as a reaction to Hoffa's declarations about the broadened contract no less than it was on other matters.

Therefore, it was of no consequence that some of Hoffa's detractors within the union—most of them former autonomous local leaders—asserted that none of his professed reasons constituted the true explanation for the top Teamster's steadfast espousal of wider bargaining. These critics felt that the true motivation behind Hoffa's program was an insatiable appetite for personal power. "At least Beck just stole money," as one of these detractors said. "Hoffa has usurped everybody's authority and now all the decisions in contract negotiation and administration are made solely by him." The rapidly diminishing number of people who were willing to voice such opinions, even if their theories could be proven valid, no longer mattered.

"Open End" Contract Administration

9

Workers who believe that their employer has violated their existing rights under a labor contract almost always have access to a grievance procedure. Using it, they can take their case to successively higher union and management levels and hope that somewhere along the line the involved management representative, agreeing with the union that the original employer action was inappropriate, will rescind what was done.

Should this desired outcome not take place, aggrieved employees generally can pursue the matter further. They can request that a neutral third person, to be selected jointly by the union and the management, resolve the dispute once and for all by arbitrating it on a "final and binding" basis. In almost all such situations, the arbitration provision substitutes for the labor organization's right to strike and the employer's right to lock out during the life of the agreement. Stability is thereby guaranteed to all concerned for the one- to three-year period that the contract lasts.

Spreading rapidly in the 1930s and 1940s, this system had become very widespread in United States labor relations by the 1960s. Roughly 94 percent of the nation's 125,000 labor-management contracts at the latter point had not only a grievance provision but one that called for arbitration, a figure that is not appreciably different from the approximate 97 percent statistic of today. Only two major industries, in fact, stood out for their failure to include the arbitration apparatus: construction, where the duration of the average job was (and is) deemed too brief to make the somewhat time-consuming process feasible, and trucking.

Hoffa had almost nothing good to say about arbitration. He once told an interviewer:

Even if it takes one or two hours or longer to work out a settlement among ourselves we are better off, knowing the business as we do from both sides, than to submit a grievance to some third party who attempts to please both sides and actually pleases nobody. In my opinion, the best method of settling grievances is to leave open the end for final settlement and, if we cannot mutually agree, either for the employer to lock out the union or for the union to strike the employer. If we don't come out with a completely satisfactory settlement we come out with a settlement both sides can live with and one which doesn't change the terms of the contract.[1]

He specifically attributed the sin of greed to arbitrators:

We hire a third party at $100 a day. He goes out to make a decision to please me so I will use him the next time and tries to decide halfway for the employer so he will hire him the next time too. We have had that experience and I don't think we want it again.

Many arbitrators also lacked, he felt, even the most basic communications skills. He once recounted having spent $3,000 for an arbitration, only to discover when the award was rendered that "nobody understood it, and it wasn't even on the subject we were arguing about; we finally had to settle it by ourselves."[2]

Instead of arbitration, Hoffa much preferred "open end" contract administration. Under it, all grievances would still be examined bilaterally. But no neutral could come into the picture. If the union and management could not resolve the grievance themselves, the former *would* be free to strike and the latter to lock out.

To Hoffa, the use of lower- and higher-level joint grievance committees composed solely of Teamster officials and employer representatives made sense. Even if arbitration did not have its other problems, he contended, in an industry as unique as trucking only the parties could be expected to know the real intent of the agreement. No outsider could know this, even regarding subjects that were treated at great length in the contracts, such as paid-for time and seniority, and certainly if the agreement was silent on a given topic. As he had cautioned the employers in a speech that he gave to their national association several years before he moved to Washington:

Many of the grievances that come in . . . are incidents that are not recorded in the written contract. I don't believe you can anticipate, in the contract, everything that may happen during the life of that contract. The result being that, in a matter of interpretation of some unusual situation or in the matter of a grievance which isn't actually spelled out in the contract, an awful lot of work and thought on both sides is required, in making the decision, so we . . . take care of the particular incident in a way to satisfy both sides.[3]

The award of an outsider would, the IBT leader thought, be meaningless in such a situation.

More than expertise would be guaranteed under "open end," in Hoffa's opinion. Provision for an equal number of labor and management representatives on both the lower- and the higher-level committees would make it an entirely equitable arrangement for both sides. Nor was there, to Hoffa, any danger that constant committee deadlocks would prevent any decisions at all from being rendered, at least at the higher levels, if "all cases are decided strictly on their merits." He recognized that there would be some cases of unavoidable deadlocks, where the committee was genuinely divided on the merits of a dispute. But these should be few and far between, and there were, anyway, worse things than a strike—such as arbitration.

The average employer, whose consistent attitude toward the strike was identical to that of nature toward a vacuum, quite understandably did not agree. Management's high opinion of the Teamster president notwithstanding, virtually every member of the sizable trucker community was, in fact, adamantly against "open end." It allowed, as the employers saw it, the entire labor contract to be renegotiated at many points during the latter's life, and as completely on the union's terms as the original bargaining had been. "Open end" was tantamount, as one manager phrased it, to "a football game in which one side is allowed to bring along the referee." In the opinion of the employers, it placed the motor freight carrier completely at the union's mercy in obtaining an equitable settlement of grievances.

Nonetheless, Hoffa had implemented the "open end" machinery in much of the country by the end of the 1960–1961 negotiations. Among his twenty remaining labor-management agreements, only those in northern New England and for a few widely scattered Middle Atlantic areas did not contain its basic elements. In the other contracts, while there were still some minor deviations from the Central States "open end" system that he had administered ever since his rise to broad midwestern power, the use of a third party had been either eliminated or greatly restricted.

And, despite the present departures from the Central States brand of "open end," little meaning could be read into them aside from Hoffa's tactical compromises on a temporary basis. In contrast to the Teamster president's apparent attitude toward other parts of the contracts, there was no reason for believing that he would be willing to allow any important deviations in the grievance arbitration procedure after the next round of trucking negotiations. "Universal Central States open end" was referred to at IBT headquarters as "one of Jim's 'must' demands for 1964."

Hoffa himself was predicting that after the 1964 bargaining sessions what would then be the single national contract would continue to be administered on an area basis, but that there would be only four such administrative areas. These areas would be the official conference regions, and the interpretations of the contract would then come from a master joint committee, "composed of representatives from all four conferences." Hoffa often added that he would be the union chairman of this master committee, "if the membership votes me this position."

A close examination of his preferred form of contract administration can do much to explain why, even in the face of the deeply rooted management opposition, he had given "open end" such priority. The above-cited reasons that he publicly (and, from all of the evidence, sincerely) advanced tell only part of the story.

For the trucking industry, there had been parallels between the growth of "open end" and the spread of the areawide contract itself. "Open end" also did not originate with Hoffa, having governed the first Central States agreement in 1938—three years before the Trotskyites were dislodged. (Vincent Dunne, in language that could have been spoken verbatim by Hoffa two decades later, told the 1940 IBT convention, "I think everyone here realizes that in an arbitration award it is more or less of a 50-50 proposition—you get a kick and a pat on the back."[4]) But, as in the case of the area agreement, the concept had been refined and extended by Hoffa as soon as his growing sphere of influence had permitted—to the South in the 1950s, and to the East and West in the 1958–1961 period.

The Teamster president could justify regularly attending only the higher-level joint grievance committee meetings under the Central States and Western States contracts, by far the two most important of the twenty agreements still in existence. But his influence was inevitably felt at other meetings.

In southern New England, for example, although the contract negotiated in 1961 called for the higher dispute-handling committee to meet at "established times," one year after its enactment this body had not established any meeting times and had yet to meet at all. The reason, in the words of one employer, was that "no one knew how to interpret the contract . . . Hoffa wrote it, but he didn't plan to attend our meetings."

Hoffa, accordingly, invited the involved Teamster local leaders and management representatives to his Washington office soon afterward. This meeting culminated in the IBT leader's issuance of mimeographed clause-by-clause "interpretations" of the New England Freight Agreement to his visitors. Many of these interpretations bore a marked resemblance to previous interpretations of similar Central States Agreement clauses that had been rendered, with Hoffa's direct participation, by the comparable Central States committee. The first southern New England sessions were held later in the same month and monthly thereafter.

In other contractual situations, a comment made over the telephone by the international president to one or more committee members might suffice: "If the facts are as you've stated them, the company must pay," or—and surprisingly often—"The union has no case at all here." Whether dominating a joint higher-level committee meeting in person or barking such comments as these long distance, Hoffa consistently stressed the need for objectivity in the decision-making process. Blind loyalty to fellow Teamsters just because they were Teamsters made no sense to him at all, and the union committeemen were frequently told, "If the facts are against the union, *vote* against the union. 'Open end' is good only if it's used responsibly."

Hoffa was well aware of the resentment against his preferred system on the part of the truckers. One argument used by the latter was that the union committeemen often sustained the position of the brother union business agent presenting the case to them, in complete disregard of the merits of the case. Aside from strengthening personal friendships among Teamsters, the employers frequently pointed out, this action could concretely help a union committeeman: it would gain him the indebtedness of the union agent presenting the case, and this could come in handy when the roles of the two men were reversed and the erstwhile committeeman brought a case to a committee on which the agent sat. The frequency of such voting would never be fully known, but the fact that Hoffa felt compelled to make such statements as the above indicated that it did exist.

On the other hand, Hoffa did not overlook the possibility that the other side might also, at times, vote for reasons that were less than pure. Employer representatives were regularly exhorted by him to be no less statesmanlike in *their* deliberations.

The "open end" system that the IBT president installed in the Western States in 1961 had one major official variation on the Central States theme. Five types of grievances—those pertaining to discharges, suspensions, closing of terminals, discontinuance of runs, and subcontracting—would still be reserved for an impartial third party's decision should the higher committee deadlock. There could, consequently, be no strikes in these situations. For all practical purposes, however, there was no real difference, even from the start, between the Western and Central States systems: of the first six hundred cases that came before the western higher committee (known as the Joint Western Committee), for example, exactly two stalemated and resulted in the invocation of arbitration; and these two cases were widely described both by Teamsters and employers privy to JWC deliberations as being "not very important ones."

Above all, under both the West Coast arrangement and in the Central States, the key single characteristic of "open end" was identical: James R. Hoffa dominated the deliberations of the higher joint committee in each.

Hoffa's huge influence in absentia on the Central States Change of Operations Subcommittee, actually a subsidiary of the Central States higher joint "open end" committee there, has already been illustrated. His paramountcy over the entire Central States process was no less. Nor was it, from the very beginning, any different in the West, which—since an ambitious research project of the day gave it special attention[5]—can serve as an instructive case example.

Hoffa had accepted the union's nomination to become the first union chairman of the JWC for a one-year period. Many West Coast truckers, faced with the implementation of "open end" under any circumstances, had also preferred him to any other Teamster for the job and had made this preference known to him. Once in, however, he had shown absolutely no inclination to get out. On the contrary, he seemed to have settled into his position for the long haul.

He was, in fact, allocating a relatively large share of his time to what he called "educating both parties" in the West in the intricacies of his system. And he was, toward this end, spending more time on each dispute than he had ever felt compelled to devote to cases coming to his long-established higher committee in the Central States. (This policy, for a while, necessitated that JWC meetings be held monthly, and then bimonthly, before a conversion to the midwestern quarterly scheduling was made in 1963.)

Even before the three-day JWC deliberation sessions were called to order, invariably at a leading San Francisco hotel, Hoffa's effect on both sides was always considerable. Both the union and the employers held separate sessions on the day before the first JWC session, to screen the grievances that they would actually present to the higher committee. And Hoffa's attitude concerning each case that was preliminarily slated to reach the JWC after deadlocking at the lower joint committee level was never far from anyone's thoughts at either meeting.

At the union meeting, to which all interested local business agents were invited, Hoffa was not always present because of his other duties. In that case, international office spokesmen would relay familiar kinds of Hoffa verdicts concerning agenda items that the boss felt strongly about. Regarding one dispute headed for a JWC decision, the union representatives might learn that "Jim says the contract is very clear: the employer is obligated to pay." On another, it might develop that "Jim doesn't remember the employer agreeing to this arrangement and so he doesn't think the union has a good grievance here." Or, Hoffa's opinion might be announced as more tentative: "Jimmy says if the circumstances were exactly as you've said, then there can be no argument. The contract speaks for itself and the company is at fault."

When Hoffa was in attendance, the dominance of his personal screening was fully as evident. Teamsters pressing grievances whose issues had previously been considered by the JWC were told to settle their cases before taking them to the joint committee again. Those seeking to bring cases that Hoffa felt might create an unfavorable precedent for the union were advised to withdraw them ("Here's what's wrong with this case"). And agents trying to get their disputes before the JWC by the use of such subterfuges as the insertion of a new grievance in a request for a JWC review of a lower committee decision were verbally chastised. On the other hand, agents bringing cases that Hoffa felt warranted inclusion on the agenda (even when these actions violated official JWC policy by not having been first dealt with at the lower committee level) were often given advice on their forthcoming presentations. Whether or not Hoffa had attended the meeting, his suggestions were almost always followed.

The employer screening session tended to have two objectives. Both involved the establishment of precedent.

Particularly when the employers believed that the case under consideration was a weak one for the company presenting it, or when the involved company was requesting a JWC interpretation that could affect many carriers adversely, an attempt was made to talk the company into dropping the case. Sometimes this effort succeeded. Often it did not. Companies frequently took even "weak" cases to the JWC despite the warnings of the employer group because of a mandate from the home office or, it was at least widely believed, because of a belief that the company enjoyed a good reputation with Hoffa.

A second purpose was to help the involved company representatives plan and develop strategy for what were considered "good" cases from the employer viewpoint, again with a particular eye toward the establishment of precedent. In this case, the other employers tended to ask the company representatives questions that they thought Hoffa might raise at the joint meetings. If not satisfied with the answers, the other employers most often freely offered advice on how to do better—advice that, in this stronghold of individualists, was far from always accepted.

The Joint Western Committee had an employer chairman, who officially operated with as much authority as did Union Chairman Hoffa. A visitor to the JWC hearing room would, however, have had to be shown this in writing to believe it, for the Teamster president controlled the joint sessions totally. In the opinions of many western Teamsters and employers, in fact, Hoffa had personally inherited—on an informal basis—all of the authority that had been reserved for the impartial arbitrator under the former West Coast contract administration system.

Not that the person serving as employer chairman had never tried to function independently of Hoffa. One had, once. At the very first JWC meeting, Hoffa's counterpart, a member of the Consolidated Freightways top management, took his mandate literally and challenged the union chairman's heavy-handedness. His company was immediately informed that if he did not mend his ways, it should not expect sympathetic treatment from the union committeemen when its own grievances came before the higher committee and that it therefore faced either deadlocks or losses. He resigned his chairmanship the next day, as he had been instructed to do by his superiors, and the lesson was not lost on his successors.

At the JWC meetings, it was Hoffa who almost exclusively introduced each grievance, questioned the union and company representatives in an attempt to ferret out the facts and clarify the issues, and decided when the parties should be excused. In the executive sessions held as soon as the parties had left the room, it was the union chairman, invariably, who suggested the course of action for the joint committee to take, together with a statement (often including a detailed recitation of relevent precedents) of his reasons for this.

The other union members of the JWC, typically put Hoffa's recommended course of action into the form of a motion, if the employers had not, and then voted for it. They openly disagreed with the IBT president only infrequently, and longtime observers were aware of no instance at all in which any union committeeman had gone against Hoffa's recommendations in the actual voting. (Hence, Hoffa's above-mentioned request to his agents that all cases be decided strictly on their merits would appear to have been more directed to the lower-level grievance committee voting or to other occasions in which he himself did not participate than to the Teamster JWC voting action.)

The employer committeemen, except on the rare occasions when vital industry concerns were believed to be at stake, spoke infrequently when the parties to the grievance were being questioned, and in the executive sessions argued with Hoffa only mildly and only after it had become quite apparent that his vote would favor the union's position. The extent of the employers' normal participation gave them much more in common with the union committeemen than it distinguished them from the latter, and their voting almost always favored the motion made, whether or not an employer had himself made it, so that the vast majority of all JWC decisions were made unanimously.

People who had themselves served as committeemen offered, although sometimes only privately, several reasons for this situation.

In his relations with the union committeemen, Hoffa's domination stemmed primarily from the strength of his official position. The impressive powers that the international presidency bestowed upon its holder were not to be ignored. Provided under the Teamster constitution with ample budgetary resources and patronage, Hoffa had not hesitated to use either in support of his friends. Conversely, his antagonism could serve to strip Teamster officials of their own power, now that he was in the ascendancy in the west. The Western Conference chairman, whose policies were once quite important to those who served as union committeemen, was said to have absolutely no influence at all in IBT affairs now that Hoffa, unhappy with the chairman's tepid support of a nationwide trucking contract, had asked (although not forced) him to resign. And the committeemen themselves, as elected officers of their locals, had to think about being reelected. They could rarely hope to be retained in office if their charismatic international president opposed them.

Secondly, the union delegates quite universally felt, and very likely correctly, that Hoffa knew much more about the contract than any of them: in the words of one committeeman, restating the already noted opinion of a New England employer in words that were also paraphrased by countless others, "After all, Jim *wrote* the contract." There was little point in arguing with such an expert, at least on rational grounds.

A third reason for Hoffa's unchallenged control of the union side was that, because the union committeemen were forbidden to sit on cases involving their own locals, and most often had no burning desire to engage in such "deals" with brother agents as the ones implied above, their motivation for strong argument with the international president was, at best, minimal. This last explanation, however, did not apply to questions of contract interpretation, when the decision automatically affected all locals. It also was inapplicable to the relatively infrequent other instances when the decision readily could be extended to the other locals (as, for example, in a case involving the calculation of holiday pay).

The apparent apathy of the employer committeemen was, similarly, based on pragmatic reasons.

One reason was identical to that explaining the union side's conduct: there was almost universal respect in employer ranks for Hoffa's knowledge of the contract. Although with one or two notable exceptions, the truckers on the JWC also believed that no other individual committeeman was as well qualified to decide grievances or questions of interpretation arising under the Western States Agreement.

Hoffa's familiarity with the contract was also advanced by many managers as one reason for the infrequency of deadlocks on the five subjects open to impartial outside arbitrator handling. While the employers would have preferred to see the old arbitration system retained in its entirety, they felt that any neutral's decisions on the arbitrable issues (especially on discharge and suspension disputes, by far the most common of the quintet to come before the JWC) would not differ markedly from those made by Hoffa. The companies won most of these grievances, and one employer, summing up the sentiment of the employer majority, elaborated upon this situation in the following words: "When we have a poor case, it's easier for us to give in at the JWC level than to spend a lot of time and money in losing it to an outside arbitrator. When we have a good case, we'll win it with Hoffa."

However, some employers were cynical regarding Hoffa's *motives* on the arbitrable issues. To them, the Teamster leader's decisions were not always due to his familiarity with the contract. They argued that Hoffa was probably deciding such cases even *more favorably* for the employers than an outsider would have, for it was currently in his interest to win management support for doing away with mandatory third party decision-making completely. "If Hoffa can point to a high percentage of decisions which sustain the employer position in these five types of cases," one of these truckers said, "he can claim that he is 'fairer' than any [outside arbitrator]." As later paragraphs will show, the JWC decision record did nothing to detract from this theory.

Secondly, but of at least as much importance as the first explanation for the behavior of employer committeemen at JWC meetings, was the fact that the committeemen were bound by their instructions from the companies if they had previously agreed, in the employer screening session, to accept the case. And the carriers rarely allowed the committeemen to deadlock their dispute.

Of the previously cited first six hundred JWC cases, in fact, there were only five deadlocks. These consisted of the two cases that *did* go to mandatory arbitrator handling and three others that did not involve arbitrable issues. Technically, even these latter three cases *could* have been sent on to an impartial third party, since the JWC rules (like those in the Central States) allowed this to happen if a majority of the higher committee voted to take such a course of action following a stalemate. Such voting had never occurred: the union committee members had invariably opposed it because they preferred to have the strike clause become operative. However, a strike had never been called, either: realism had prevailed and in all three cases, in the understated words of one employer committeeman, "the companies had acquiesced after the deadlock." Even the relative handful of truckers whose financial and competitive statuses might have allowed them to suffer a strike in preference to yielding on a grievance could never be sure that they would win their objectives even should the work stoppage take place.

Consequently, as a rule, the company representatives originally asked the employer committeemen to back their case independently only to the point of the vote. Under these circumstances, there was nothing to be gained by the employer committeemen if Hoffa had indicated that he would definitely sustain the union's position. Since there was also no logic in the employer committeemen speaking out if Hoffa had shown that he would support the *company,* only a small area for potential employer resistance remained: where the head of the Teamsters had not yet clearly expressed a preference for either party.

The pro-Hoffa conduct of the employer committeemen in this last situation was, however, due to a third reason. Some truckers believed that the union leader was overly proud of his knowledge of the contract, even to the point of becoming somewhat vindictive toward employers who, as their departed chairman from Consolidated Freightways, demonstrated too much initiative in committee meetings. They shared the opinion that Hoffa had not judged all cases, even aside from those involving the five arbitrable issues, on their merits. Each believed, although proof was by definition impossible to come by, that the union chairman had already penalized the few employer committeemen who had questioned his informal leadership of the JWC by voting against their companies for this reason alone when these companies had later had cases before the joint committee. (These truckers also claimed that Hoffa had shown vindictiveness toward some of his own locals in his voting. It was their contention that it was not merely a coincidence that the anti-Hoffa locals in both the California Valley of the West and in Pontiac, Michigan, in the Central States were regularly taking so few grievances to their respective higher committees: the belief of these employers was that the locals in these areas knew that Hoffa would intentionally vote against them in their grievances.)

Whether or not this allegation of vindictiveness was valid, the fact that it was fairly widespread was meaningful in explaining the employer committee's actions. Since the management committeemen, like their union counterparts, were usually considering cases that did not directly involve their own operations, most of these representatives saw little sense in going counter to Hoffa's desires with any degree of frequency if there was even the possibility of being so penalized.

Even considering Hoffa's exhortations that all cases be judged strictly on their merits, and even with the knowledge that more decisions than not on the five arbitrable issues were supporting the employer, one might logically have expected to find a high percentage of the overall JWC actions favoring the union. The strike clause, after all, allowed the Teamsters an enormous, and unique, advantage in the joint committee meetings. In addition, the decision-making process was governed by the desires of a union leader.

It is of more than passing interest, then, that approximately 60 percent of the decisions regularly sustained the employer's position. In some JWC sessions, in fact, the proportion of cases awarded to the company approached 75 percent.

No official "won and lost" record was ever kept by the parties. Nor, of course, could such a record have been easily maintained, since many types of decisions on grievances (such as those relating to reinstatement with back pay, for example) do not always allow a clear-cut "winner" or "loser." However, the accuracy of the percentages suggested above, which were arrived at by an examination of one hundred randomly selected decisions of the JWC under the 1961–1964 contract, was commonly vouched for by employer and union representatives alike.

By way of example, the joint committee heard thirty-two cases at one meeting, a three-day affair that was described by its committeemen as being "typical" for its decisions. Of the thirty-two cases, eighteen culminated in fairly clear-cut decisions for or against the company (e.g., "Company must pay"; "Discharge upheld"; "Union pay claim denied"). And, of these eighteen decisions, thirteen—or 72.2 percent—were awarded to the company.

Breaking the eighteen cases down by both their nature and their victor,

Case	Major Issue	Party Sustained
1	Runaround pay*	Company
2	Alleged improper calculation of holiday pay	Union
3	Discharge	Union
4	Discharge	Company
5	Discharge	Company
6	Seniority in job bidding preference	Union

Case	Major Issue	Party Sustained
7	Runaround pay	Union
8	Discharge	Company
9	Discharge	Company
10	Discharge	Company
11	Runaround pay	Company
12	Subcontracting	Company
13	Alleged improper calculation of vacation pay	Union
14	Calculation of mileage pay	Company
15	Leave of absence	Company
16	Runaround pay	Company
17	Runaround pay	Company
18	Runaround pay	Company

* So-called because the grievant alleges in such cases that the company dispatcher has improperly awarded the run to another driver, thus "running around" the grievant.

The dispositions of the fourteen other cases of the thirty-two considered, were as follows:

Case	Major Issue	Disposition
1	Discharge	Reinstatement with half back pay
2	Seniority in merger of three different seniority boards	Company not directly involved: union wanted an interpretation* from Hoffa
3	Holiday pay	Referred to lower joint committee, to be treated as a factual dispute rather than as one of interpretation
4	Seniority in selection of starting time	Referred to lower joint committee, to be treated as a factual dispute rather than as one of interpretation
5	Weekly guarantees (past practice) as affected by new ICC regulation	Postponed for further study after presentation by parties
6	Discharge	Case withdrawn after presentation by parties
7	Work assignment	Referred to lower joint committee, to be treated as a factual dispute rather than as one of interpretation
8	Alleged company refusal to post job opportunity	Parties were advised to settle outside JWC after their presentations

Case	Major Issue	Disposition
9	Work assignment	Referred to joint council, for involved jurisdiction of two locals
10	Alleged improper calculation of pay for work performed	Suspended while JWC determined whether lower joint committee examined the correct records
11	Runaround pay	Postponed to find out company's past practice
12	Runaround pay	Postponed to find out company's past practice
13	Alleged improper calculation of pay for work performed	Withdrawn by the parties after their presentations
14	Alleged improper calculation of pay for work performed	Neither party's position fully sustained

* A request for interpretation of contractual language in the absence of a bona fide factual controversy could go directly to the JWC, as opposed to starting at the lower joint committee level. In practice, however, some employers sought to circumvent the lower body and bring their cases directly to Hoffa by claiming that their factual disputes were interpretative ones—even though they were not.

It will be noted that nine of the thirty-two cases involved one of the five arbitrable issues, in these situations either discharge or subcontracting, and that the company position was sustained in six of them (numbers 4, 5, 8, 9, 10 and 12 in the first table), the union position was upheld only once (number 3 in the first table), and there was one "compromise" decision (number 1, second table) and one withdrawal (number 6, second table). The company's percentage of "wins" among the clear-cut verdicts was therefore 85.7. The statistic did not contradict the belief of the truckers that they might be doing at least as well on such cases as they would have done with a third party, although the evidence was, obviously, far from overwhelming.

Of the remaining eleven cases listed in the first table as having had reasonably definitive decisions, moreover, seven of them or 63.6 percent also went the employer's way.

In regard to the second table alone, two of the fourteen cases were disposed of by the JWC after Hoffa had conversed with the local union agents representing the grievants, and two after he had held private discussions with the involved management representatives. In all four instances, the desire to avoid a bad precedent by the party with whom he conferred was believed to have motivated these discussions. The withdrawals of two cases after presentation were explained by one committeeman as stemming from "a realization by one of the parties that it would lose with Hoffa and its desire, accordingly, to get a compromise outside of the JWC."

Teamsters cited the fact that the union was winning only a minority of JWC disputes as clear evidence that the cases were being decided on their merits. They admitted that the merits of many cases were more likely to support the employer's position than the union's, because of the prevalence of "political" grievances brought to the higher committee by IBT agents. And Hoffa's decisions, they argued, showed that he was exercising whatever power he had responsibly and even in a "statesmanlike" way.

The employers in the West typically agreed with this assessment and were quite free to praise Hoffa for his actions. They pointed out that their knowledge of the union president's strengths, and of his relative political security within the Teamsters, dictated their having preferred him originally as union chairman and that they were not surprised at his performance in San Francisco. They sometimes referred, however, to the reports that Hoffa was known to have decided cases of companies and locals that had incurred his wrath on grounds other than "statesmanship" in also expressing their belief that the latter quality may not have extended to every dispute.

A minority of the employers also asserted that most of the cases were of much interest only to the company and Teamsters directly involved, as indicated by Hoffa's screening only the relatively few cases that he considered to be important and by the employers' also concentrating, although less effectively, on the cases that might involve key precedents. Hence, these truckers claimed, Hoffa actually lost little by voting for the employer in the executive sessions, and he might gradually have been able to win management supporters for "open end" in the process. They contended, in effect, that Hoffa's "tactical decisions" extended to many more cases than those involving the five arbitrable issues—a theory that, if true, would explain the high *overall* employer "victory" percentage.

Challenged for proof of this theory, these truckers tended to be something less than persuasive. They pointed out, reasonably enough, that a survey confined exclusively to the "significant" cases would be the only meaningful method of appraising Hoffa's decisions. But "significance" was invariably in the eye of the beholder: what fit the definition for one employer rarely did for another.

However, there was complete unanimity among the truckers concerning one case. It was always referred to as the "miles driven only" issue, and it was deemed in all quarters as the most important single case to have come before the JWC in its first years of deliberations. It was cited by all of the theory holders as offering some grounds for hesitancy in applauding Hoffa's actions on the more important disputes.

The "miles driven only" issue stemmed from a local's request for interpretation of the "guarantee" portion of the contract's line haul single driver provisions. The language was murky at its best, and said nothing at all about pay guarantees for certain types of runs. It was inevitable that it would cause problems, and one of these problems had triggered, in March 1962, the local's plea to Hoffa that he make explicit what the original intent of the parties in negotiating it had been.

In the executive session on the case, the union chairman stated that "drivers in long line single man operations are to be paid eight (8) hours for the driving time on a particular trip, plus pay for all time spent other than driving at the hourly rate." Some of the trips in actuality consumed considerably less than eight hours. And the employer committeemen, firmly believing that the intent of the negotiators was an eight-hour guarantee for the *whole* workday and that anything more generous could be suicidal for the companies, felt sufficiently aroused to bring about the first deadlock in JWC history.

Hoffa then announced that the union would strike the companies in order of their size. But the strikes were never forthcoming: one company after another, as its strike deadline was set, chose capitulation as the lesser of two evils and accepted the new ruling.

It was left to the pragmatic Hoffa to make amends for what appears to have been a rare error in judgment on his part. Within a few months, he unilaterally modified the eight-hour stipulation to a less onerous requirement that the companies pay for six hours on trips. According to a close Hoffa adviser, his action was taken because "it was becoming too costly for some companies, and some agents also saw the sense of cutting it out. Hoffa was guided by their sentiments and reasoning."

Concerning the modification, one employer could say: "At least we can live with six hours. We couldn't have continued in business under the original ruling."

Almost no employer in the Central States, where "open end" had been so long established, shared the opinion of the West Coast trucker minority that Hoffa was using a double standard for "significant" and "less important" cases. There were, therefore, grounds for believing that the western minority would, with further experience with Hoffa, come to the same conclusion.

Otherwise, however, the similarities of higher committee contract administration in Chicago (where the Central States Joint Area Committee deliberated) and in San Francisco were even in the 1961–1964 period much greater than the differences.

The Chicago process of decision making, as indicated earlier, was identical, with Hoffa's presence being felt fully as much as it was in San Francisco. And the practical results in Chicago were quite consistent with those of the West: the employers were winning a clear majority of the cases, Central States JAC deadlocks were averaging fewer than two annually, and strikes had been all but nonexistent throughout the JAC's twenty-five-year history. Moreover, while it was admittedly more difficult to send a deadlocked case on to a neutral in the Central States than in the West (since this could be done *only* by majority vote of the JAC), the infrequency of such referrals was equally striking: there had not been a single instance in the past decade when the required majority vote had been forthcoming.

Perhaps there was a certain irony in the fact that almost all truckers were so greatly opposed to "open end," in view of the percentage of employer "victories" and given at least the Central States employers' denial that Hoffa was using a double standard in his decisions. Nonetheless, the management opposition, which marked the Central States fully as much as the West, was entirely rational under even the best of employer circumstances.

The trucker resentment, by and large, was not directed at the *products* of "open end" at all—except in a few rare instances such as the western "miles driven only" case (and the few other "significant" cases individually cited by western employers). Most employers, even those who believed that Hoffa had shown instances of personal vindictiveness in his decisions, readily admitted that the decisions themselves "usually" had been appropriate ones, and ones that an outside arbitrator might conceivably have made.

Rather, the employers indicted the *process* of decision making, and the possibilities for abuse that they saw in this process. Even the fear of a double standard, they contended, would not have existed had not the process allowed it plausibility.

Theoretically, there was still a definite place for a third party, since any deadlocked case could be referred to a neutral by majority vote. Equally theoretically, the employers could always prevent any decision that was unfavorable to them by the simple act of bringing about deadlocks through their equal committee votes. That practice diverged so greatly from theory was, of course, due to realities that were as visible as a Mack truck: Hoffa's union preferred a strike threat over voting for referral to a neutral because the threat was almost tantamount to its winning the case, and the companies were rarely willing to accept a deadlock for the same reason.

By definition, then, "open end" in the trucking industry turned the balance of power heavily in favor of the union. Because the Teamster strike weapon was anathema to the motor freight carrier, the latter was completely at the union's mercy in obtaining an equitable settlement of grievances. The labor agreement *could,* indeed, be renegotiated every time that the higher joint committee sat in session, and on the union's terms.

Moreover, at least four other doubts could be justifiably raised about the efficacy of the process in the Central States and West:

1. Because Hoffa was in such complete control of the other union committeemen and because the employer committeemen were so reluctant to speak, there was at most times not even the semblance of any "judicial" determination to "open end." Even when Hoffa listened to the stated opinions of the other committeemen, these opinions were undoubtedly often colored because of the widely held fear of antagonizing him. In either event, therefore, contract administration was based upon precedents either wholly established or crucially influenced by one man—the rule of an individual rather than that of any common consensus.

2. As a consequence of his joint committee power, Hoffa was *in a position to* reward and penalize particular carriers and Teamster agents arbitrarily, at any time. Whether or not he had actually ever done this, or would do it, was beside the point. No two cases were ever identical, and the union chairman's avowed consideration for precedent could govern his decisions only when he wanted it to. Even in a clear case of inconsistency with precedent, moreover, there was no curb on Hoffa's ability to decide any case on any basis he desired.

For example, even the politically secure Hoffa could never be guaranteed the permanent applause of his membership. As any other union leader, he always had to be attuned to the wishes of his constituents (something that, of course, he was very good at doing). While the executive sessions were officially private ones, Hoffa could not afford to antagonize large groups of rank and file Teamsters by decisions that were consistently unfavorable to them and that it was now well known that he greatly influenced. Therefore, the danger that he might—at least occasionally—feel compelled to rule in favor of the union for purely political reasons could never be entirely dismissed.

3. Hoffa's extremely busy nationwide schedule raised the possibility that he would not always be able to make decisions appropriate to the specific grievance situations, even assuming that he always desired to do this. Some representatives of both parties believed that he was increasingly overlooking circumstances peculiar to individual subregions and localized types of problems, merely because of his preoccupation with so many other regions and problems.

4. A strong case could also have been made that time pressures, both for Hoffa and the other committee members, were forcing too many cases to be decided in a single day. A daily agenda containing twenty-five cases, when the sessions followed the Central States format of being held three months apart, was not at all unusual. Thus, each case was guaranteed that it would not receive nearly the attention that an outside arbitrator would have given it—with the merits of the case consequently, at times, being overlooked in the interests of completing the business at hand in the allotted three days. The use of precedent and the consideration of lower committee minutes allowed a speedy disposition of many of the grievances,

to be sure, but these tools did not by any means fully assuage the fears.

It might have been completely true that, as Teamster supporters of "open end" were arguing, Hoffa knew the intent of the contract as an outside arbitrator could not. There was probably much accuracy in the assertion of both parties that the IBT president's knowledge of motor freight labor complexities was unmatched by that of anyone else. And Hoffa's charge that some third parties had attempted to "please both sides" and actually pleased nobody was very likely a valid one. But all of these points, and less telling ones made by those favoring "open end" (e.g., its economies in arbitrator fees and time, its "educational" value to the participants) seemed to be far outweighed by the one-sidedness of the "open end" process and the dangers inherent in it.

It was to Hoffa's credit that the employers were, by and large, satisfied with his decisions: the opportunity for his "renegotiating" the contract, intentionally or unintentionally, existed at every meeting that he attended.

Preference for the Status Quo

10

"Hoffa," said one of the most highly respected of all trucking employers in 1962, "is one of the few labor leaders who recognizes that technological change will come, and won't forestall it, though he is concerned with minimizing the displacement and ensuring that the workers share in the gains."

The statement fairly reflected the opinion of the enormous majority of the speaker's fellow managers. The Teamster president, ever the realist, had demonstrated concretely that he would not obstruct the accelerating changes pervading the industry.

The union president was well aware that many of these changes, most of which had been generated by the growing external competition that now confronted trucking, threatened either the income or the very employment of Teamster drivers. But he also recognized that cooperation from him was necessary if the industry's rapid growth trend was not to be reversed. He asked only that no more drivers than were absolutely necessary be deprived of their jobs in the process, and that those drivers remaining share in the profits resulting from the increased productivity. Otherwise, the man who was universally recognized by truckers as having, as at least one manager once said of him, "the power to say 'no' and make it stick" was eminently willing to compromise.

Four convincing examples were often cited by employers. They pertained to Hoffa's attitude toward: the minimization of "watered miles" caused by the construction of new mileage-reducing highways, trucker participation in piggybacking, sleeper cabs, and double bottoms. Each warrants attention.

1. *The Minimization of "Watered Miles"* Even though public highway construction itself could hardly be collectively bargained within the trucking industry, the great growth of highways in the 1950s and early 1960s had been very much a part of the technological change of this sector of transportation. Both over-the-road parties, while arguing in Washington and the state capitals that the trucking companies were paying an unfairly high proportion of the taxes financing the highways, had not only welcomed this growth but had lobbied for it. For the carriers, the new routes and faster delivery speeds had opened up new markets. For the Teamsters, these new markets had offered the possibility of offsetting the threat to employment that had been caused, in particular, by the railroads' piggybacking activities.

However, one major labor relations problem for the parties had also stemmed from the highway growth.

Under the contracts, mileage pay had been granted traditionally on the basis of the official American Automobile Association mileage distances. When such figures had not been available, the latest official state highway maps had been used to determine the number of miles to be paid for. And, in the comparatively few instances when the parties had had neither of these sources at their disposal, representatives of the union and employers had personally logged the number of miles on the route, with their points of origin and destination being the nearest U.S. Post Office. In the absence of new roads, these distances remained the only ones recognized for the purpose of mileage payment. Both the duplication of effort and the temptation for exaggeration involved if the individual driver was allowed to calculate the miles as these were driven were thereby avoided.

The construction of new highways, however, made many of the recognized mileages inaccurate, usually because they were now too high. Because of this fact and also because many truckers believed that the work of their drivers was considerably easier on the new roads, the industry's negotiators—in the 1955 Central States negotiations—told Hoffa that it was unfair to pay drivers on both the old and the new routes the same amounts. They requested that the companies no longer be forced to pay for the "watered" miles.

Hoffa was sympathetic. He was unwilling to decrease driver incomes by eliminating all of the "water" at one time, but he admitted to the industry negotiators that their case was a strong one. He agreed to a compromise, which was immediately accepted by the management representatives. In each of the next six years, the employers could subtract one-sixth of the excess mileage, provided that such elimination did not result in the reduction of more than one-half of each annual one-quarter-cent-per-mile pay increase granted by the contract. Moreover, this "one-sixth formula" would only apply to changes in routes made before 1955; for all subsequent changes, the actual AAA (or otherwise calculated) mileage for the new routes would be made effective immediately for pay purposes. In the 1960–1961 round of negotiations, the general mileage reduction principle was retained in the Central States and extended to most of the other contracts.

Only a labor leader who was politically secure could have carried this off, and only a statesmanlike one would have wanted to, since even with Hoffa's compromise Teamster incomes were, by definition, diminished. The truckers recognized this and were quite pleased with the unionist's response. "It's fortunate for the industry," as one top manager said in reference to what had happened here, "that Hoffa understands our problems and is willing to weigh our proposals on what's good for both management and the union."

2. *Trucker Participation in Piggybacking* The carrying of freight-loaded truck trailers on railroad flatcars, or piggybacking, has always acted completely to the detriment of over-the-road jobs, and thus to Teamster membership totals. As the practice began its rapid growth in Hoffa's early presidential years, accordingly, certain acts of violence—such as the peppering with rocks and buckshot of automobiles moving on piggyback trains—were invariably attributed (rightly or wrongly) to Teamsters on the grounds of plausible motive. On the other hand, the financial interests of individual employers had often been *advanced* by trucker participation in the piggybacking activity.

Hoffa himself, claiming that piggybacking had cost the IBT some twenty thousand drivers between 1959 and 1961 alone, made no attempt to restrain his emotions on the subject. And, in this case, he did not exempt the truckers from his tough talk: "If the trucking companies and the railroads think we're going to sit idly by while piggybacking costs us thousands and thousands of jobs," he would regularly say in these or similar words, "they'd better think again."

The harsh rhetoric aside, however, the head of the IBT attempted to reconcile the conflicting Teamster and employer viewpoints in two ways. He generally protected, through both contract negotiations and informal union-management discussions, a stable number of drivers before any piggybacking by the road carriers could be performed. And he inserted in most of the over-the-road labor agreements a clause providing, in effect, that the carriers pay a $5 fee into employee health or pension funds for each trailer that they did piggyback.

The driver protection invariably sounded more rigorous for the employers than it tended to be. Typically, a company could officially piggyback without incurring any penalty (beyond the $5 contribution) only if it did not have available at the point of origin the number of regular drivers and equipment needed to carry the freight. Should an available regular driver suffer any loss from the diversion of the freight to the railroads, the carrier had to compensate the employee for such loss. Thus, if four such Teamsters had been available to drive piggybacked freight from St. Louis to New York, for example, the carrier would now have to pay a full day's wage to each of the four drivers, plus the expense of having the railroad haul the trailer. Informally, however, the determination of neither "regular" nor "available" was drawn particularly tightly. Especially when drivers were on layoff status (although actually "available") or the company was in financial trouble, the union's definition of the two terms proved to be quite flexible and, therefore, not particularly onerous at all.

Similarly, while the $5-per-trailer contribution was itself religiously enforced, the extraction of the tariff in no way decreased the piggybacking activities of the companies. The amount went some four times further in the early 1960s than it does now. But most truckers privately considered the payment to be a "bargain" when compared to the payroll savings allowed them, especially on the longer runs. Nor was Hoffa's position that some financial sacrifice should be made by employers benefiting from piggybacking, and that the health and pension funds were the logical recipients of such money, seriously debated. On the contrary, the industry appeared to be in agreement that in this area, just as in his reaction to the "watered" miles, Hoffa had acted reasonably and, in view of trucking's competitive problems, with foresight.

3. *Sleeper Cabs* The two drivers of sleeper cabs offered their employers one enormous advantage in this era of heavy governmental trucking industry regulation. They did not have to stop en route to take the legally mandated eight-hour rest after every ten hours of driving time. With one driver behind the wheel, the other could be sleeping, back in the small metal bed-containing box on board, and the vehicle could quite legally be driven all but continuously on this basis. Because more freight-miles per day could thus be handled by the sleeper cab drivers than by the drivers of two single-man vehicles, the employers had been particularly anxious to initiate sleeper cab services.

The Teamster president was fully aware of the potential labor displacement involved here. He also recognized that the cramped quarters and constant movement of the sleepers made this kind of life one that was not popular with the majority of his drivers. Nonetheless, he was increasingly willing to allow the expansion of such two-person operations in the interests of a healthier trucking sector. In this case, in fact, he actually *encouraged* the growth, by negotiating terms that much of the industry found to be irresistible.

Each of the two drivers regularly received, under the terms of Hoffa's contracts in these years, less than a 2-cent-per-mile premium (or something under 20 percent extra) when behind the wheel, and no money at all when in the vehicle but not driving. By simple mathematical logic, this was far less costly to the employer than paying *each* of the drivers of two single-person vehicles the slightly lower rate for collectively covering the same number of miles as the single sleeper cab transversed. By the same token, however, the sleeper cab drivers also gained something in the way of additional income. They also stood to make considerably higher *annual* incomes than they might otherwise have made: the IBT-granted payment terms actually made use of the sleepers so attractive to the companies that the number of hours that these drivers could work in the course of a year was generally far more than those assigned to the operators of single-person vehicles.

Hoffa's hope was, of course, that the industry would also gain a competitive edge in its never-ending fight against railroad freight transport by passing on some of its sleeper cab savings to shippers. To some extent, this favorable reversal of fortune did happen, although—as noted earlier—the overall competition for trucking continued to be formidable.

4. *Double Bottoms* The double bottom, using a single tractor to pull two semitrailers, is of somewhat more recent vintage than the sleeper cab. It received its great impetus only in 1958, when the industry started to use it in an explicit attempt to recapture business lost to railroad piggybacking, and now, increasingly, air freight as well.

As of the early 1960s, only a few northeastern and midwestern states had allowed the double bottom to operate within their borders. Most states, fearing safety hazards and traffic slowdowns from the new type of transportation, had flatly refused to permit its introduction. Even where the double bottom had been granted an operating license, moreover, its use had commonly been restricted to superhighways, since its typical length (about 98 feet) and weight (perhaps 90,000 pounds) had not allowed it to comply with existing state length and weight laws on the regular state highways.

However, where the double bottom could be driven, it had proven itself able to offer companies significant savings in fuel, depreciation, maintenance, and interest costs. It also held out the obvious advantage of reduced labor expenses, with one driver literally pulling twice as heavy a load as was transported under the single bottom arrangement.

The union had not been oblivious to these savings. Hoffa staffers, indeed, had calculated the average overall cost reduction to the companies as being over 6 cents per trailer-mile, with the greatest single savings coming from the reduced payrolls.

Yet, as in the case of the sleeper cab, the Hoffa administration had recognized the need for the double bottom in view of the industry's competition. It had never sought to restrict the double bottom's spread, despite the threat to employment that had been involved, and its sole reaction seemed to have been to demand that part of the savings be shared with the drivers.

Under the 1961–1964 Central States contract, for example, drivers of recognized double bottom equipment were paid 11.075 cents per mile in 1962 and, after January 31, 1963, received 11.325 cents per mile—while mileage rates of 9.925 and 10.175 cents, respectively, were being paid to the drivers of four-axle single bottom units.

To minimize what Hoffa felt could be subterfuges by the companies, there was a considerably higher differential in the Central States for driving when regular highway semi-trailers were used for double bottom purposes: the mileage rate in these cases was 12.94 cents in 1962 and became 13.19 cents in early 1963. But, in an additional bow to economic realities, some Teamster contracts did not even go this far in asking for higher pay: the upstate New York agreement, for example, made no distinction between types of double bottoms being driven, calling only for an additional 2 cents in the mileage rate for *any* double bottom work.

On these bases, Hoffa was also quite willing to join the carriers in trying to convince the hesitant states that their fears about the double bottom had been unwarranted. On several occasions, states had allowed limited-period experiments with the new vehicles, but always with exacting requirements concerning driver past safety records and present physical conditions. Regularly, the Teamster leadership had cooperated with the employers in these experiments by taking drivers out of seniority so that the special rules could be met. These joint efforts of the parties had persuaded several states—among them, Massachusetts and New York—to allow more extensive permanent use of the double bottoms.

On the eve of James R. Hoffa's contemplated 1964 nationwide trucking contract most employers were not especially unhappy with their dependence upon him. If they viewed him as an autocrat (as most did), they also saw him as a benevolent autocrat, an enlightened unionist who had generally attempted to act in the best interests of trucking. And while certain terms negotiated by Hoffa (most notably, those pertaining to the "open end" system) had clearly come under heavy trucker attack, employer-offered examples of the Teamster president's "statesmanship" were far more common than the management criticisms.

Nonetheless, if offered a choice between having no union and continuing to negotiate with Hoffa, it is safe to assume that even the most enthusiastically pro-Hoffa employers would have selected the former. In that way, they could at least gain the privilege of unilateral decision making on terms of employment and thus avoid what they considered to be the few undesirable portions of Hoffa's contracts. And, while many managers had nothing but appreciation for the IBT president's role in stabilizing the industry's wages and conditions, there was also widespread embarrassment in trucker ranks that any labor leader had to be the stabilizing force for an industry.

Moreover, some employers, increasingly in these years, had more specific grounds for uneasiness concerning the future.

Some truckers who knew Hoffa well, for example, now voiced fears that he would no longer prove as willing to compromise with the industry as he had been up to that point. Even a man who was as tough both physically and emotionally as he was had his breaking point, they argued, and the severe pressures with which he had been confronted almost continuously for years now seemed to be pushing him into occasional irrationality. Often cited here was Hoffa's behavior in the negotiations leading to the most recent Central States contract.

At these 1960–1961 bargaining sessions, conducted at Chicago's Palmer House Hotel, the unexpectedly hard line initially taken by some of the carriers had triggered an equally surprising response from Hoffa. In an atypical display of bitterness, he had accused the employers of engaging in delaying tactics with the hope of causing a strike just after John F. Kennedy, no friend of Hoffa's, was installed in the White House. Kennedy would then immediately intervene and stop the strike on terms unfavorable to the Teamsters. In this "anti-Hoffa conspiracy," Hoffa charged, the fact that the two primary employer negotiators happened to be former Federal Bureau of Investigation agents could not be overlooked. (Many managers in the industry have historically had such a background, generally explained by the fact that the theft of goods in interstate commerce brings FBI agents and truckers into contact. The companies have often seen good managerial talent in the agents.)

Much worse than the complete lack of foundation for these charges, the employers contended, was their aftermath. In full view of the negotiators for both teams, the head of America's biggest union lost all of his monumental self-control for no less than thirty minutes. He broke chairs and repeatedly used the same few words of extreme vulgarity, directed at the management representatives in the room. As one witness later said of this tirade, "He quivered and shook like a man out of his mind, as he was for that length of time. It was frightening. But he ultimately regained his composure and was obviously chagrined at what had happened." Another observer of this outburst registered a widely held employer opinion: "Hoffa is not the man he was. . . . He's not as amenable to opinions contrary to his. The fuse has become shorter. . . . There are a lot of pressures on Jimmy today—particularly his legal troubles—and they're taking a toll."

This second manager and others like him felt that the new Hoffa might push national uniformity to a greater degree than many companies and even whole regions could afford, although some riders and deviations undoubtedly would be maintained. They were also quick to point out the obvious possibility that even if Hoffa did not make such demands in 1964, he might try to extract them over the length of the contract by the "open end" process.

A larger group of employers believed that the IBT president remained as responsive to the industry's needs now as ever. That group, however, voiced concern that the increasing competitive and cash flow problems of the industry might call for greater sacrifices by the drivers in 1964 than even the politically secure Hoffa, proud of the gains that he had achieved for his members, would be willing to ask these Teamsters to make.

Still a third group of truckers feared that Hoffa would not remain as Teamster chief executive at all for much longer. It predicted that his difficulties with the law would force him to resign in the relatively near future. Since no other Teamster was believed to possess either his ability or his intelligence, the conclusion here was that he would inevitably be succeeded by a less desirable union official.

These last employers also worried that Hoffa's resignation would result in a long period of chaos for the industry. They fully recognized that he rarely delegated anything of consequence in trucking labor relations and that he had groomed no one at all to succeed him. There were enough rival factions within the IBT international hierarchy to ensure a major power struggle for his job and enough ambitious local leaders still in office to make it likely that there would also be attempts to regain lost authority for the locals and joint councils. This internal warfare would patently weaken the union's bargaining strength. But it could also lead to irresponsible, politically motivated union demands being made upon the employers and to a greater use of the IBT's dreaded strike weapon.

As different as these three fears were, and as unwarranted as all may have been for at least the immediate future, they had a common thread: all warned that the continuation of an accommodating Teamster president could hardly be taken for granted.

Accordingly, the employers had had greater motivation than ever to search for ways of increasing their own bargaining strength. And, in fact, several means of achieving this end had in the recent past been advocated by managers. Some employers had urged that a system of trucking company strike insurance be implemented. Others had suggested that the compulsory arbitration of both grievances arising under existing contracts and the basic terms to be included in new contracts was the only means by which a measure of employer bargaining table equality could be realized. Still others, convinced that bargaining cohesion could never be gained for the entire industry, had argued in favor of more exclusive employer organizations to represent only carriers with similar operating problems.

None of the projects ever got off the ground. Despite their worries about the future, the truckers could no more unite as they prepared for the 1964 bargaining sessions than they ever had been able to. And that they could not, once again, said more about the man who ran the Teamsters than it did about the employers themselves.

The proposal for *strike insurance* was based on experiences in industries outside of trucking. By the early 1960s, employers who had bought such coverage from private insurance companies had been reimbursed for losses incurred by strikes in the newspaper, airline, and railroad sectors. But the concept clearly had a special appeal for motor freight, given the far greater risk of financial catastrophe in the event of work stoppages there. Trucker proponents of strike insurance argued, with obvious justification, that, if the motor carriers were guaranteed that IBT strikes would not put them out of business, their willingness to reject what they considered to be excessive union demands would be proportionately increased.

Against the logic of the proposal, however, stood two insurmountable obstacles.

First, Hoffa quickly became aware of the project and publicly expressed strong disapproval of it. He called the plans for a strike fund "a lot of baloney" and predicted that "the employers won't have the guts to adopt such insurance." He also warned the truckers that, just in case they did decide to implement the concept, the union would counter it with a huge strike fund of its own. Taking a hint that achieved in formidability what it lacked in subtlety, a large number of employers immediately asked the strike insurance advocates to drop the whole idea. They were followed, in short order, by others.

The other roadblock to strike insurance was the widespread recognition in these days that the Teamster strike threat was often a "selective" one: as the histories of the last Central States and southern New England negotiations have brought out, Hoffa was more disposed to strike only a few carriers, rather than all carriers represented in the bargaining. What was more, the few carriers were usually among the larger ones. The smaller companies saw no reason whatsoever why they should subsidize the strikes of their larger competitors. Yet it was a fact of strike insurance life that only if the majority of the truckers, large and small, contributed financially could the insurance premiums for any of them be made economically acceptable. The exodus of potential participants in the wake of Hoffa's warnings had all but guaranteed that this majority would never be realized; this second factor made such an outcome a certainty.

The plans for *compulsory arbitration* of both new contract terms and grievances arising under existing contracts fared no better.

Shortly after the conclusion of the 1960–1961 Central States negotiations, the Wisconsin Motor Carriers Association, a state affiliate of the American Trucking Associations, had officially asked its parent to "initiate legislation which will permit the Federal government to appoint impartial panels to settle labor grievances and to participate in collective bargaining between labor and management, and further that such arbitration be compulsory upon both labor and management in the trucking industry."[1]

Explaining its action, the Wisconsin group had pointed out that labor was trucking's largest item of expense, that labor "has assumed the dominant role in negotiations of contracts," and that, because of the importance of trucking, it was "in the public interest that neither labor nor management be in . . . a position to injure the general public by selfish and unwarranted actions."[2]

Viewing this request favorably, the ATA's Executive Committee announced an "endorsement of the principles" contained in it. It directed its Industrial Relations Committee and staff to propose ways of implementing these principles.

Hoffa, no supporter of arbitration in even its mildest noncompulsory and for-grievances-only form, saw red. Demonstrating no more forbearance than he had shown in the case of strike insurance, he announced that the Executive Committee's action was cause for "war" with the ATA. He telephoned the ATA's managing director and told him to call a new Executive Committee meeting to repudiate the original action. He announced that he had contacted some of the "leading" Wisconsin employers to inquire about the Wisconsin resolution, and had been told that they knew nothing about it. He also said that truckers throughout the country were against compulsory arbitration as the "first step toward fascism" in labor-management relations and predicted that, because of this opposition, "The [ATA] policy will be revoked, you wait and see. It won't happen because the industry will reject it."[3]

He was at least half right. The ATA's Industrial Relations Committee, "studying" the issue of compulsory arbitration as directed by the Executive Committee, soon made it clear that it did not favor applying such arbitration to contract negotiations. And while it did endorse the original ATA stand on the compulsory arbitration of trucking industry grievances, it did so in the knowledge that such an unprecedented system by itself would never actually be implemented.

The stand on grievance arbitration did give the employers another chance to display their hostility to the "open end" concept. They were free to admit that, were the impartial private arbitrator system still acceptable to Hoffa, the idea of governmental intervention in contract administration would have little management support. Having had years of experience with governmental economic and safety regulation, most company executives were convinced that political pressues often prevented public authorities from exercising their best judgment. Given only the choice of "open end" or the publicly appointed arbitrators, however, they preferred the latter as (in the words of more than one trucker) "the lesser of two evils"—even, in this case, in the face of Hoffa's not very subtle antagonism.

Compulsory arbitration of basic contract terms was, on the other hand, a horse of a quite different color. Most employers, exactly as Hoffa had said, had never favored it. They feared that under it the flexibility that the union chieftain had allowed companies in the form of local deviations to meet varying circumstances would be largely (or completely) abolished by the government in its understandable desire for national uniformity. They worried that such arbitration could constitute a major step toward nationalization of the trucking industry, especially since motor freight was already regulated so highly. Nor, they believed, would it even remotely mean the end of strikes, since Congress could hardly be expected to enact legislation indefinitely requiring employees to work against their will.

But most of all, the truckers opposed such arbitration on the grounds that it would lead to worse, rather than better, relations with the union in view of Hoffa's strong stand against it. The intensity of their dislike for "open end" might let them take this risk once, in the case of grievance arbitration. Here, however, there were no compelling reasons why they should further jeopardize their standing with Hoffa and, as above, several reasons why they should not.

The third course of action being considered by the employers, having *more exclusive groups of employers* bargain with Hoffa, on the other hand, seemed to have unassailable logic in back of it.

The intensity of their strike fears was not, of course, the only reason explaining the bargaining weakness of the employers. As brought out earlier, the widening bargaining units had forced an ever more heterogeneous group of employers to be represented in the single negotiations, and Hoffa had been quick to capitalize upon their diversity of operating problems.

The structural disadvantage had been plain to the companies since the earliest area contracts, but the many other reasons for supporting Hoffa's broadened bargaining had prevented the industry from attempting to offset it in any meaningful way. The current employer fears about the future had, however, been accompanied by a realization that the Teamster president's official 1964 plans envisioned even greater employer diversity (both geographically and in types of trucking operations). And several proposals for making employer groups *less* inclusive had now been advanced.

The most prominent of these proposals contemplated the formation of an organization composed strictly of the larger interstate general commodity carriers, primarily those having an average length of haul of at least five hundred miles. Its supporters were especially fearful that restrictions that were not unduly burdensome for the shorter haul intercity carriers and those engaged in local cartage but could be onerous for their companies would be applied to all carriers in 1964. Shift premiums, for example, would be far less costly to the cartage companies, which geared their operations to the needs of local retail stores and thus rarely scheduled their employees for much more than eight hours a day and five days a week, than they would to the continuously operating long-liners.

Even Hoffa himself, many of this plan's backers contended, would not now stand in the way of such specialized groupings (and separate contracts for them, despite his announced goal of the single 1964 contract). In the opinion of one of these advocates, "With his high level of intelligence, and with his bargaining becoming more visible to the government all the time, Hoffa has begun to see the danger of the open accumulation of too much power. . . . He also realizes that strong people on *both* sides can strengthen an industry."

Ironically, here it was not Hoffa—at least directly—but lack of unity among the potential member carriers themselves that doomed this effort to failure (as it did similar employer efforts on behalf of other types of carriers).

There was a crucial difference of opinion among the long-liners concerning the proposed membership complexion. Many of the firms felt that unless *all* common carriers—regardless of length of haul, type of freight, or gross revenues—were included, the nonmember carriers would be able to offer less resistance to Hoffa than ever and thus their role would be to set a high floor below which the union's subsequent demands to the long-liners could not go. Other dissenting firms believed that the creation of a group comprising just long-liners would *guarantee* that Hoffa could "divide and conquer," since it would present him with an automatic employer cleavage (long-liners versus the other groups). A rift between the ATA and the West Coast truckers prevented these two groups from combining their forces even to consider the matter further. And there were serious doubts among some employers that Hoffa would in fact favor such an exclusive organization of long-liners—and consequent fears that the head of the Teamsters would refuse to deal with the new group at all.

Given sufficient motivation for increasing their own bargaining power so that they could deal with Hoffa on more nearly equal terms, however, the truckers could have ultimately *forced* him to negotiate with their more exclusive groups and thus have obviated this last possibility. Similarly, with enough incentive, the employers could have formed, even with their own selective subgroups, a sufficiently united overall front so that Hoffa could *not* have divided and conquered them. For that matter, Hoffa's objections to both strike insurance and the compulsory arbitration at least of grievances would have made no difference, if the employers had confronted him from a position of strength rather than from their traditional weakness.

Nor was such ability to circumvent Hoffa's wishes at all unattainable by the truckers. If the latter had been so inclined, they could at any time have aligned themselves—in subarea groups—on the side of the IBT president's various local union leader opponents. Many areas still contained such people—for the most part, proud men who were suffering in silence as Hoffa's ambitious program was stripping them of their own power. They recognized that, after years of administering their provincial Teamster empires almost totally on their own, they were now being reduced to the status of not much more than dues collectors. Without any visible support for a return to bargaining decentralization from either their own rank and file *or* the employers, they could do nothing to ward off this destiny. If the employers had been willing to join forces with them, however, the combination could have exercised much constraint on the IBT chief executive's actions.

Delegation by the employers of the negotiating function to an individual who was empowered with the same authority on the employer side as Hoffa possessed on the union's was another realistic alternative had the truckers only wanted to implement it. It, too, would have achieved the result of keeping the Hoffa factor entirely within the bounds of normal labor relations.

But these avenues toward more nearly equal management bargaining strength would have necessitated a significant change in the attitude of the employers. They would have had to *prefer* to be governed, in lieu of by Hoffa, by their own representatives. And this choice was simply not one that was supported by the majority of the industry. With the sole exception of contract administration, where the desire for compulsory arbitration stemmed from employer unhappiness with the *process* and not the product of "open end" and where Hoffa was still preferred as quasi-arbitrator to any other Teamster, the employers *preferred* to be at Hoffa's mercy than at the mercy of any other authority, most particularly of each other. Moreover, this preference had been registered with a full knowledge of all of the present and potential weaknesses in the IBT leader's system.

The present drawbacks to the system were, after all, still more theoretical than real to the average trucker. If Hoffa's basic interests did not coincide with those of the industry, most operators had not personally felt the effects of this in their labor relations. If the IBT leader was vindictive, the consequences of this trait extended, at best, to a small minority of the industry. If he was overlooking localized problems under the pressure of his other duties, the results had, at least thus far, not been very grave for the typical carrier.

In addition, while the *potential* drawbacks could undo the efficacy of the whole system in rather short order, the fact remained that they related to the uncertain future and not to the present. Hoffa might prove himself to be unreasonable in his actions, opposed to asking his constituents to accept lesser contract packages than they had been accustomed to receiving, or even unable (or unwilling) to continue as head of the union for much longer. But it was also possible that *none* of these dangers for the truckers would materialize.

What the employers *had* been able to assess was a system that, however logically abhorrent it may have been, had thus far allowed them major advantages. It had satisfied their need for competitive stability, proven itself to be quite responsive to the general labor problems of the industry, and been governed by an individual whom, generally speaking, the employers both respected and trusted.

Self-interest had, in short, continued to generate their support of a powerful Hoffa and their unwillingness to narrow the bargaining strength disparity. If and when the present arrangement's weaknesses became of practical importance to them, they would have sufficient incentive to search actively for a substitute course of action. For now, the status quo was preferable.

They approached the 1964 bargaining as dependent on Hoffa as they ever had been.

Personal Diplomacy, with Significant Interruptions

11

The respite from his outside problems with which Hoffa had been provided in 1961 had allowed him to fly over a million miles in servicing his constituents. But most of this collective bargaining time had been spent in hammering out the various renegotiated trucking contracts and administering "open end." With the contracts now locked up for three years each and "open end" a going operation, his plans for these next three years featured the recruitment of new Teamsters, and he intended to emphasize what he called "personal diplomacy" in this effort. "Everybody wants to see what the devil looks like," he breezily told a reporter from the *Wall Street Journal,* "so I give them a chance to ask questions and shake the devil's hand. . . . Whenever our agents in the field tell us they need that little extra push, I'll simply hop on a plane and visit the workers myself."[1]

His hopes for new organization were ambitious. He frequently spoke in terms of "at least one million" currently unorganized future Teamsters outside of trucking. And he was well aware that his national notoriety had now made him a major drawing card: his line about the million dollars worth of free publicity that Robert Kennedy had given him had played so well that it had become a standard part of his repertoire. He had certainly become a household name, if not exactly on his own terms, and the McClellan committee had undeniably been the major reason. He almost always drew large crowds among potential recruits wherever he appeared, whether before chili con carne factory workers on the West Coast,

Michigan appliance plant employees, or an assemblage of tree surgeons in Chicago.

He also generally attracted packed houses on the many occasions on which he spoke to nonlabor groups—at the prestigious Harvard Law School Forum, where an initially hostile audience wound up giving him a standing ovation, for example, and at a variety of business executive lunches and dinners, where his candor, intelligence, and knowledge were also invariably, if begrudgingly, appreciated. After a Hoffa speech had impressed a convention of the professional journalism fraternity, Sigma Delta Chi, the editor of one of his own Teamster publications proudly pointed out that the invitations to speak throughout the country would "keep him busy full time if he saw fit to bask in the glory at the expense of the union."

Not *all* free publicity was even sarcastically welcomed by Hoffa, however. The AFL-CIO president George Meany was rewarded for his harsh words about the Teamster president by being slapped (together with twenty-four other top AFL-CIO officials) with a million dollar libel and slander suit. The normally humorless Meany had told reporters at a late 1961 AFL-CIO executive board meeting that Hoffa would remain unacceptable to him "unless he does what Saul of Tarsus did, go off in the wilderness for a year and repent," and Hoffa's sense of perspective had allowed him to enjoy *that*. But when the federation's top officer had followed this up by saying that Hoffa was still "unfit to head a trade union" and added that "I don't think that anyone in his right mind could deny that the Teamsters remain dominated by criminal and corrupt elements," and the other officials had endorsed this statement, enough was—for Hoffa—enough. The suit, which ultimately died a quiet death, called Meany a "labor sniper" and charged that he and the others had "maliciously launched a vicious, calculated and calloused attack" on the reputation of both the Teamsters and their president. "When you're old and decrepit on top of being stupid," Hoffa told reporters in reference to the sixty-seven-year-old federation leader, "you're in trouble."

The object of Meany's disaffection was actually far more sensitive than his tough exterior and general brashness might suggest. Words like Meany's hurt. So did the occasional heckling that Hoffa received in these post-McClellan committee days. An especially potent wounding came in Golden, Colorado, in the early spring of 1962: handing out organizational leaflets at the Coors Porcelain Company there, Hoffa was picketed by a hooting group of some 250 students from the nearby Colorado School of Mines. Their placards invited the father of a recent Phi Beta Kappa graduate and a current Michigan State honors student to "Go Home" and urged "Keep Golden Clean."

But the words, unsettling as they were, were nothing as compared to the sudden appearance of several tangible problems. These now more or less simultaneously piled up for Hoffa in a manner not unknown to him, and they put a definite crimp in his ambitious "personal diplomacy" recruitment plans.

In early March 1962, preliminary arguments got under way in Florida in the Sun Valley mail fraud case. The technicalities under which the Hoffa defense team had won an indefinite delay a year earlier had been successfully countered by the prosecution, and a new grand jury had indicted Hoffa in October. This time, the government's key figure, Attorney General Robert F. Kennedy, exuded optimism: "Hoffa won't be so lucky. The prosecutors have enough evidence to win a conviction."

Compounding his situation, on May 17, 1962, the forty-nine-year-old IBT boss was arrested and charged with assaulting a mild-mannered subordinate ten years his senior who had spoken back to him earlier that day. The subordinate, Samuel Baron, was field director of the Teamsters' warehouse division. In his warrant, he charged that the muscular Hoffa had knocked him down twice without provocation after cursing him in the presidential office of the union's Washington headquarters, blackening his left eye and deeply cutting the skin below his right eyebrow in the process.

As Baron later elaborated on the incident for the benefit of reporters, Hoffa had summoned him into his third-floor office to discuss a contract that the IBT head was negotiating with a major furniture company. An argument had ensued and Hoffa had suddenly advanced on Baron with his fists clenched and jaw muscles twitching. He had knocked the field director to the floor and, after the latter had risen, had shoved him down again, this time pushing him over a chair. All this had happened before some of the half-dozen other Teamster officials who were present could intervene.

"I thought," said the subordinate, " 'this man is absolutely out of his mind.' "

Hoffa for some time had known Baron to be disloyal and had strongly suspected him of leaking anti-Hoffa information to Walter Sheridan and the Get Hoffa Squad. The general president had, however, displayed his habitual inability to fire employees even here. He himself now told the press that he would have "absolutely nothing" to say about the encounter. Booked at Washington's First Precinct police station, he pleaded not guilty and was granted a jury trial. He was released on $500 bail, but if found guilty later he could face a year in jail and a $500 fine.

Then, exactly one day after his booking on the Baron charge, a Nashville grand jury indicted Hoffa for allegedly sharing in more than $1 million in illegal payments from the Detroit trucking company, Commercial Carriers, Inc. Here, he was threatened with a year in prison and a fine of $10,000 on each of two counts: conspiring with the company (as well as with his old friend, the late Owen Bert Brennan) to violate the Taft-Hartley Act provision that makes it generally illegal for employee representatives to take payments from employers, and receiving such payments.

This third problem, a remnant of the distant past, took Hoffa completely by surprise. He had heard about the indictment quite second-handedly—on his car radio while driving into downtown Chicago to give a speech to the Federation of Telephone Clerks—and in this address he levied an unusually bitter, spontaneous attack on the media, which he blamed for much of his trouble. "They live on propaganda," he told his Sherman Hotel audience, "They thrive on misery. They are sadistic minded."[2]

Of most immediate urgency, however, was the Baron assault charge, since the jury trial was scheduled to begin on June 12, and the field director, now assigned two U.S. marshals for protection, was adamantly resisting the pleas of IBT officials to withdraw his case. Not even an impassioned request from his old friend Harold Gibbons, the cause of Baron's originally coming to Washington, could get him to change his mind. And Baron remained just as impervious to a variety of more menacing pressures, including one anonymous telephone call informing him that "Hoffa wants to know what kind of coffin you want" and other telephone messages that contained nothing but heavy breathing.

But it remained, as Baron well recognized, his word against Hoffa's, since no other Teamster who was present on May 17 could be expected to corroborate Baron's story. "It would," as the field director freely acknowledged, "be absolute suicide." On the contrary, all six witnesses either told the U.S. Attorney's office that Baron was the aggressor or refused to testify at all. After delaying the trial for two months, the government—citing "serious conflicts" in the testimony—finally decided not to prosecute. And, although the well-publicized case did nothing positive for Hoffa's public relations, it clearly, from his viewpoint, could have come out far worse. He had indeed struck Baron, exactly as the plaintiff had claimed, and he was by any definition extremely fortunate in the consequences.

The same good luck did not, however, accompany Hoffa in the government's next attempt to separate him from the International Brotherhood of Teamsters. This effort involved, at the request of the Justice Department, not the Sun Valley charges but allegations that the government believed would give it an even better chance of getting Hoffa: those concerning the illegal payment of money from Commercial Carriers to the Test Fleet Corporation, the trucking company that Hoffa and Brennan had set up in their wives' maiden names. In an action that accommodated the government and displeased the Hoffa forces, the Sun Valley case was temporarily removed from the federal court docket in Tampa, where it had been scheduled to be heard. And the head of the Teamsters was instead ordered to appear in criminal court in Nashville, Tennessee, in late October 1962, to be examined regarding his Commercial Carriers activities. In the carefully orchestrated Robert F. Kennedy scenario for Hoffa, the Florida mail fraud trial would then constitute, hopefully, the frosting on the cake.

The decision by the federal judiciary to hold the trial in Nashville represented another Justice Department victory. Both the Tennessee city and Detroit were legally permissible locations—Nashville, because Test Fleet was chartered in Tennessee, and Detroit, because Commercial Carriers was based in Michigan. But the prosecution had wanted the former place. Hoffa had many friends in Detroit, far fewer in Nashville. And the major Nashville newspaper, the *Tennessean,* was edited by a friend of the attorney general, his former administrative assistant John Seigenthaler; this would more or less guarantee news coverage favorable to the Justice Department's case.

James F. Neal, a youthful graduate of the Vanderbilt University Law School in Nashville, would be the chief prosecutor for the government. He had won a bankruptcy fraud case against Hoffa associate Benjamin Dranow in Minneapolis the previous year, and had been highly recommended to Kennedy for his native intelligence and aptitude for painstaking research. He brought to the prosecution forces the further advantage of being able to speak to a Tennessee jury in Tennessee-accented tones. He was entirely convinced that Hoffa and Brennan had blatantly violated the Taft-Hartley Act by conspiring to receive hundreds of thousands of dollars from Commercial Carriers in return for labor peace and that these payoffs to Test Fleet (later renamed Hobren Corporation, after the last names of its two key figures) had continued from 1947 until 1958. They had, in other words, gone on for five years after the Wint Smith hearings in Detroit had originally taken notice of them, and for many months after the McClellan committee had accorded them full national attention. In fact, Neal had concluded, the illicit payments had finally ceased only under pressure from the Board of Monitors.

The chief prosecutor and his competent cadre of assistants, headed by another bright young criminal lawyer, Charles N. Shaffer, Jr., looked forward to proving all of this beyond a reasonable doubt in Nashville. They would operate under the overall direction of the nonlawyer Walter Sheridan, who took up residence at Nashville's Noel Hotel for the duration of the trial and who himself was in daily telephone contact with Attorney General Kennedy.

The Hoffa defense team was more seasoned than the prosecution, and certainly no less talented. It included a highly regarded Nashville native, Z. T. Osborn, Jr., who had successfully argued a landmark case on reapportionment before the U.S. Supreme Court and was now next in line for the presidency of the Nashville Bar Association. Other official members were the veteran James E. Haggerty, a past president of the Michigan Bar Association; the aggressive and effective (if highly controversial) Detroiter William E. Bufalino, who had performed so much service for Hoffa as a member of the Board of Monitors; Bufalino's predecessor as union-appointed monitor, Daniel Maher of Washington; and the flamboyant Philadelphia criminal lawyer Jacob Kossman. Many other members of the Teamster Bar Association had come to Nashville, too, although not as lawyers of record in the trial. Their services were also regularly available to the defendant away from the courtroom and generally in Hoffa's suite on the seventh floor of the nearby Andrew Jackson Hotel.

Completing the cast of major players was the presiding federal district court judge, William E. Miller. Plagued by a heart condition that forced him to limit the trial hours to four each day, the fifty-five-year-old jurist's reputation for uncompromising integrity was so widespread that Sheridan could later report that a Chicago mob plot to bribe him had never gotten off the ground because no one could be found with enough courage to approach him.[3]

Other people involved with the trial were apparently thought to be more venal than Miller, however. Even before the Nashville proceedings began, several of the government's best prospective jurors—men and women who were believed most likely to convict Hoffa—received anonymous telephone calls. The caller in all cases falsely identified himself as "Allen from the *Banner* [the *Nashville Banner,* another local newspaper]" and asked a series of questions about Hoffa and the Teamsters. This imaginative strategy, to which Hoffa was himself never linked, automatically disqualified all of those called from serving on the jury. They could no longer be considered in the eyes of the court to be objective.

Then, still prior to the final selection of the jury, an even more blatant effort was reported to Judge Miller. On the morning of October 24, 1962, James C. Tippens, an insurance company executive who had been tentatively named as a juror, told the judge that he had been contacted by a neighbor and offered $10,000 in hundred-dollar bills if he would vote against convicting Hoffa. Tippens was removed from the jury, and the neighbor—Lawrence "Red" Medlin—was booked on suspicion of attempted bribery. Once again, however, no participation by the defendant himself was ever established.

On the other hand, this time Miller was sufficiently aroused to call not only the attorneys for both sides but also Hoffa to his chambers. He conscientiously refrained from suggesting to them that either the defendant or his lawyers had had any hand in either of the two attempts to influence the jury. But he stressed to his visitors that he had never before remotely encountered such a brazen effort to undermine due process and indicated that he was now considering locking the jury up for the entire length of the trial.

Prosecutor Neal supported such a course of action. Osborn, however, was very much against it, and argued that the juror contacts were probably the work of "crackpots and do-gooders" who had independently tried to aid Hoffa. Shaffer, not one to let such a theory as the last go by unchallenged, pointed out that it was a matter of "public record" that jurors had been approached before in cases in which Hoffa had been on trial. He specifically cited the second wiretapping trial in New York, in which a juror had indeed been approached and had thereupon been excused from serving. The Shaffer statement, in turn, brought a strong protest from defense attorney Bufalino, who correctly pointed out that this New York overture had never been connected directly to Hoffa, either, and a rather testy response from Shaffer, "I say I don't have any proof to relate it to defendant Hoffa. If we did, Mr. Hoffa would be prosecuted."[4]

The meeting ended with an announcement by Judge Miller that he had decided not to lock up the jury. It was combined with a strongly worded warning that he would tolerate no further jury tampering and a disclosure by the jurist to the defense team that the FBI was now investigating the attempted bribery of Tippens.

But there *was* further evidence of jury tampering. On November 17, 1962, acting on a tip from an informant to Walter Sheridan, FBI agents observed Nashville's ranking Teamster, Ewing T. King, contacting a Tennessee state highway patrolman on a deserted road late at night. King then swapped his white Thunderbird for the drab sedan of another Teamster official and drove some eighty miles in it to the home of the patrolman, James Paschal, whose wife Betty happened to be one of the jurors. Several days later, with the courtroom having been emptied of all spectators, Neal revealed these facts to Miller and asked for removal of juror Paschal on the grounds of "compelling, suspicious circumstances indicating an improper approach."[5] The judge, agreeing fully, promptly complied.

King, taken into custody, took the Fifth Amendment when questioned. Patrolman Paschal told the court only that King had offered to get him a promotion. When asked by Miller if he hadn't found it strange that a complete stranger had offered to do such a good deed for him, he had replied, simply, "I don't know."

And yet another juror was excused from further service on December 21. The same informant who had triggered the Paschal investigation by tipping off Sheridan had also told the head of the Get Hoffa Squad that Hoffa had confided to him (the informant) that he had "the colored male juror in my hip pocket." Hoffa had explained, said the informant, that a black Local 299 business agent, Larry Campbell, had come to Nashville from Detroit prior to the trial and seen to this item of business: Campbell's uncle, Thomas Ewing Parks, lived in Greater Nashville and knew the single black male on the jury, a retired railroad worker named Gratin Fields.

Sheridan and his assistants immediately investigated the story by tracing the telephone calls that Campbell had made to Hoffa over the past few months, a project that was made much easier for them by the fact that Campbell had apparently disregarded instructions to use pay telephones. They learned that Fields's son, Carl, had indeed been offered $5,000, with another $5,000 to go to his father if the father voted to acquit Hoffa. The bribe money had been channeled through Parks.

There was no evidence that the senior Fields had himself in any way acted improperly. But the circumstances seemed sufficiently striking that prosecutor Neal, possibly harboring the thought that the case might now be threatening the Guinness world record for number of attempted jury tamperings in the course of a single trial, decided to ask Judge Miller to remove yet another juror from the jury box.

Neal made his request, once again, in closed session. But this time there was a variation on the theme. He produced a sworn affidavit from the informant that affirmed and elaborated upon the alleged statement by Hoffa that the latter had the black juror in his hip pocket. The informant, who clearly had assumed no little risk in signing his real name to the document, had been willing to do so only with the promise that his identity would be kept confidential: even the notary public who witnessed the signing in Sheridan's hotel room had not actually seen the signature, and the affidavit was submitted to the judge in a sealed envelope, which Miller was then asked to reseal without showing it to the defense.

The judge quickly complied with both of these prosecution

requests. Over the heated objections of the Hoffa attorneys that there was no meaningful evidence of jury tampering at all, he resealed what he had read and directed that Fields be replaced on the jury by an alternate. The whole case, he told both parties, contained the "most amazing set of circumstances" that he had ever seen.

He was referring just to the extracurricular interest in the jurors. But the trial, now almost nine weeks old, had been marked by two other circumstances that, if not exactly amazing, at least could also qualify as being highly unusual.

One of these had been the December 5, 1962, appearance in the courtroom of a former mental patient with an air pistol. The man, a young itinerant dishwasher named Warren Swanson whose father was serving a life sentence for murder in Nebraska, showed himself to be a chip off the old block by walking, almost unnoticed, up to Hoffa and firing several pellets at him. He later claimed that a voice "from a higher power" had told him to "kill Jimmy Hoffa" as he had sat reading the Bible in a Cincinnati hotel room some months earlier. He had found himself compelled, he said, to carry out this instruction.

Fortunately for both Hoffa and Swanson, the pellets did Hoffa little harm, merely bouncing off the defendant's face and arms. But they understandably enraged the Teamster president and, with the personal fearlessness that even his worst enemies never doubted, the 5'5½" Hoffa sprang at his assailant, landed a right uppercut squarely on his jaw, and knocked him to the floor. Others then took over the treatment of Swanson—Hoffa's near-at-hand assistant Chuckie O'Brien by jumping on the assailant and kicking him on the head several times until Hoffa yelled "Stop!" and courtroom marshals by handcuffing Swanson and taking him away. Swanson required fourteen stitches in his scalp.

Had the weapon been almost anything but the air pistol—for example, the German Luger that it resembled—Hoffa might well have been killed, and he undoubtedly recognized this. (O'Brien, in fact, at first thought that Hoffa had been murdered.) But the union leader shrugged the incident off with his typical coolness. Swanson, he told reporters, was just "some jerk with a pellet gun." And, sounding as though he encountered such potential assailants as Swanson on a regular basis, he explained when asked why he had sprung at the gun wielder, "You always run away from a man with a knife, and toward a man with a gun." (Years later, however, he attributed a more sinister characteristic to the event than he did at the time: after pointing out that "everyone was searched that went in and out of the courtroom," he asked, "How the hell did he get in with a gun? . . . I'm sure the marshal didn't overlook *him*. And he walked in with a gun, after everybody'd been searched! Like Martin Luther King. You're suspicious but you can't prove it.")[6]

The defense, recognizing opportunity when it knocked, immediately moved for a mistrial. "What happened in this courtroom," attorney Maher informed the court, "is the inevitable result of the hostility evidenced against the defendant by the Government in the past five years. Prior to the trial we said we couldn't get a fair trial . . . because of the flood of publicity brought against the defendant by the Government and the Attorney General of the United States."[7] Judge Miller was unmoved.

Actually, defense motions for either a trial delay or a mistrial were at this point old hat to the judge. He had denied them all, but the frequency of such requests, as well as the sheer volume of other objections by the Hoffa team, had constituted the second more unusual aspect of the Nashville proceedings. Osborn had tried to win dismissal of the original jury panel on the grounds that it systematically excluded females, blacks, and workers; Miller had refused to entertain this challenge on the ground that the defense had produced no evidence to support its contention. Maher had moved for a mistrial after the Justice Department's Shaffer had cited alleged Hoffa violations of Taft-Hartley that occurred in 1947 because the legislation did not go into effect until 1948; he was overruled. The defense had tried to get the case abrogated by arguing that the government was actually accusing Hoffa of accepting a bribe, and thus of having committed a felony, rather than sticking to the official charge of conspiracy, which carried with it the less serious penalties of a misdemeanor; Miller ruled that this argument was frivolous. Hoffa's attorneys objected in vain that their telephone lines had been unconstitutionally tapped by government agents, they objected to the testimony of a variety of witnesses for the prosecution, and they objected to the showing of checks and other documents that purportedly let Test Fleet profits flow into Hoffa's pockets. Bufalino objected, Haggerty objected, and Kossman objected—often and, at times, both so vehemently and so simultaneously that the judge finally announced that each legal team had to designate a single attorney to handle the objections and not "have two or three lawyers jumping up at the same time."

Hoffa registered his own objections, with the outspokenness that never seemed to desert him for long, to the reporters who surrounded him when the court was not in session. The Justice Department, he asserted, was indeed monitoring the telephone lines: "Our phones are tapped and our hotel rooms are bugged. [We] make remarks just to see, and the Government attorneys [know] next morning what [we've] said. We're building a new . . . office building in Detroit, and they come to me and say the whole place is wired and bugged. I say, 'Hell, whaddya expect? Go on and finish the building.' " The FBI agents were "all stool pigeons. A bunch of rats and stool pigeons."[8]

He still espoused his invisible powder theory, too: "You are walking on a picket line and an FBI agent comes up and rubs this white chemical on you and you're wired from then on. They can pick up everything you say until you have the suit cleaned." And the FBI was not above using other devious methods as well: "They go to the school and investigate my kid. He's a good kid, if I do say so. They go around to his friends and say, 'How many suits of clothes has Jim Hoffa got? How much money does he carry around in his pocket?' They gave orders to every airline office in the country—when Hoffa makes a reservation, call the nearest FBI office and give the time he takes off and the time he arrives. You wouldn't believe some of the creepy stuff they are pulling."[9]

On the afternoon of December 21, the long-lasting case was finally handed over to the jury for deliberation. For seventeen tense hours over the next two days, the six men and six women (Fields had been replaced by a female alternate) tried to reach a verdict. Seven jurors reportedly favored acquittal but could sway no others to their position. Three times the jurors came back and told Judge Miller that they seemed to be deadlocked; each time he sent them back to their locked room to try again. They finally reported that they were "hopelessly" deadlocked. And, with the greatest reluctance, the judge thereupon did what he had so steadfastly refused to do on so many prior occasions: he declared a mistrial. "There comes a time," he said, "when if the members of the jury cannot agree, they cannot agree, and that is it."

But Miller was hardly willing to let it go at that. He also announced that, because of the "shameful" attempts that had been made to "corrupt our jury system," he was taking three alternative steps. He was convening a new federal grand jury to make a full investigation of all the jury tampering evidence and to return indictments where probable cause might exist for them. He was requesting the U.S. Attorney's office to present all relevant information that it had in its possession to this new jury. And he was directing that the entire records of the two closed court sessions that had resulted in the dismissals of jurors Paschal and Fields be unsealed and made public; the only exception to this would be "certain documents read only by the Court at the second session which because of their strictly confidential nature cannot be released at the present time."

For the defendant, the outcome was cause for both elation and concern. In the situation immediately at hand, Hoffa was obviously emerging with a victory. For the fourth time in little more than five years, starting with his acquittal on the Cheasty bribery charges, he was leaving a trial in federal court as a free man. Although he told the press that he was "naturally disappointed" with the hung jury, his mood was one of huge relief as he cheerfully wished "everybody connected with the trial a Merry Christmas" and headed for victory celebrations back in Detroit. He fully shared the proud sentiments of his attorney Bufalino that "in 1962, Santa Claus has simply refused to put Jimmy Hoffa in Bobby Kennedy's stocking."

But now, just as patently, a new trouble was coming down the road for the controversial union leader, in the form of a potential jury-tampering charge. And where the worst-case scenario for him in the just-concluded Nashville trial would have sent him to prison for two years, jury tampering—exactly like bribery—was a felony, and he was now threatened with, should he be found guilty, at least five years behind bars. And this on top of whatever liability he might face in the Sun Valley mail fraud case, which had now been revived by the Justice Department and awaited only the setting of a trial date. It was also fully understood that Attorney General Kennedy was readying even more challenges to present to the Teamsters Bar Association: a federal grand jury was currently combing the investments of the Central States, Southeast, and Southwest Areas Pension Fund in an effort to unearth Hoffa wrongdoing; and it was well known that the Hoffa family's past tax returns were being studied with almost religious fervor for the same reason.

Back in Detroit, Hoffa's initial jubilation left him. He told a television interviewer that Judge Miller had been prejudiced against him. As for the prosecution, Neal was "one of the most vicious prosecutors who ever handled a criminal case for the Justice Department." It was a "disgrace," in his opinion, "for anyone to make a statement that this jury was tampered with."[10] In his case, he was firmy convinced, the government was much more interested in persecution than it was in law enforcement.

His testiness was understandable: he was well aware of the seriousness of his position and the fact that the prospects of his ultimately going to jail had never before been so large. He knew, and told intimates, that his worst days were in front of him.

Nonetheless, for the first time in several months, since the original scheduling of his Nashville trial, Hoffa was now free, temporarily, to devote more than pro forma attention to his role as labor leader. And he made the most of the opportunity.

Back on the hustings in a resumption of his postponed "personal diplomacy," he once again seemed to be a man in perpetual motion as he met with groups of potential new Teamsters from coast to coast. His off-the-cuff speeches varied and were typically tailored with considerable skill to his specific audiences, but they could be counted on to contain at least one rhetorical question: "Do you think if Hoffa really did all the things that Bobby Kennedy says he did he'd be standing here with you today?" It was standard fare, too, for a Hoffa address now to include words like "vendetta," "spoiled brat" and "trumped-up charges."

He also accepted a large variety of other speaking invitations and displayed on these occasions the same conspicuous bluntness that had always marked his public addresses. He told an audience of Michigan building trades unionists that proposed legislation in Congress to regulate the organization of labor unions was "garbage" and that the sponsors of the proposal were "bums." He informed a Mine, Mill, and Smelter Workers convention that Attorney General Kennedy had "conspired to create a Gestapo" to try to break down the largest union in the United States. He announced, on the NBC television program "David Brinkley's Journal," that "there are more con men in Washington than there ever was in a carnival"; that Senator McClellan was a "faker. Flat, right out, a faker"; and that as Teamster president he contributed a lot of his own money to the union because it "pays dividends. Let's be honest about it. I expect to get elected."

And for more than two months, from February to late April 1963, he made the Warwick Hotel in Philadelphia his primary base of operations, in an effort to stop a group of dissident Teamsters in that city from bolting to the AFL-CIO.

The Philadelphia rebels had warranted such personal attention from Hoffa for several reasons. First, unlike the relatively few other IBT dissidents since his 1957 ascent to the presidency—cab drivers in Chicago and San Diego and milk, soft drink, and cab drivers in Cincinnati, for example—these Teamsters were all over-the-road drivers and thus represented not only the heart of the union but also Hoffa's strongest base of support: a successful effort by them might encourage other road drivers to attempt (very possibly with AFL-CIO encouragement) the same kind of rebellion, with obvious ominous ramifications for both the union and its president. Second, the local involved—Local 107—was, with some eleven thousand members, the fourth largest within the Teamsters. Third, while the rebels had originally based their arguments on both the corruption and the dictatorial ways of their local's leader, the now-indicted Raymond Cohen, they had subsequently altered their attack to make Hoffa their primary target; the latter's personal prestige was therefore very definitely on the line. Finally, even though they had been both underfinanced and not especially well organized, the dissidents had almost won a National Labor Relations Board election in November on the issue of the local's remaining with the Teamsters or switching to the AFL-CIO: they had received the surprisingly high total of 3,274 votes, with the pro-IBT forces getting 3,870 votes. The NLRB had set aside the election after the rebels had given it evidence of Teamster-generated violence prior to the balloting. In this second election the challengers definitely had momentum going for them.

To help him ward off the threat, Hoffa imported almost one hundred Teamster leaders from other cities and closely supervised them as they, separately and in small groups, tried to approach all of the Local 107 drivers with a pro-Teamster sales pitch. He issued a variety of well-publicized personal statements from the Warwick, condemning the dissident leaders as "a small group of men, who are willing to sacrifice the security of [the union's members] in order to satisfy their own selfish ends."[11] Several special telephone lines installed in his hotel suite carried recorded messages; many of these were in Hoffa's voice and contained both an incentive (the promise of higher wages and benefits in future road driver contracts) and a threat (an announcement that anyone who went over to the AFL-CIO would lose pension benefits). He was pulling out all the stops.

The effort paid off. In the second election, the Teamsters won big, getting 4,893 votes to a relatively meager 2,550 for the dissidents. And the greatly relieved Hoffa, who immediately told reporters that he was willing to "let bygones be bygones" as far as the Local 107 supporters of the bolt were concerned, wound up with even more of a victory than the sheer statistics would indicate: the ham-fisted Cohen, who had theretofore run his Philadelphia fiefdom without interference from Hoffa (while giving the Teamster president wholehearted support nationally), now had no choice but to give total obeisance in all ways. One of the last of the old-time IBT local autonomists, he recognized the realities of his having been forced to turn to Hoffa for rescue and would no longer oppose the nationwide trucking contract.

Then, on May 9, 1963, the grand jury that Judge Miller had convened in late December to look into the jury-tampering matter presented Hoffa with another indictment. He was charged with having "unlawfully, willfully and knowingly" attempted, with six coconspirators, to influence members of the Nashville jury. Named as Hoffa's codefendants were Ewing T. King, the Nashville Teamster leader who had driven to the home of juror Betty Paschal; Nashville merchant Lawrence W. "Red" Medlin, the man who had allegedly tried to bribe juror James C. Tippens; Detroit Teamster business agent Larry Campbell and Campbell's uncle, Thomas E. Parks of Nashville, the two reputed approachers of Gratin Fields; a close Hoffa friend and the handler of considerable IBT insurance money, Chicago insurance broker Allen Dorfman; and Nicholas J. Tweel of Huntington, West Virginia, and New York, the owner of a company handling cigarettes for vending machines.

The indictment contained five counts. The first of these

charged that Hoffa and the six other named men had conspired to influence the jury. Each of the other counts alleged a specific instance of jury tampering. If convicted on all five, Hoffa could be sentenced to twenty-five years in prison and fined $25,000.

Hoffa denied all wrongdoing. He pointed out that he had never even met three of his six codefendants (Medlin, Parks, and Tweel) and wouldn't know them if he saw them. In a message that—however heartfelt—was now becoming entirely predictable, he attributed his new difficulty to an attempt by Attorney General Kennedy to "smirch the union in his war against me." He surrendered to authorities in Philadelphia and after signing papers on the coffee table at the home of a U.S. Commissioner there was released on $10,000 bail.

Several people who observed Hoffa at this point noted that he seemed to be relatively cheerful all things considered, and it was no false impression. In the more than four months since Judge Miller had terminated the Nashville trial with the announcement that he was convening a new grand jury, the labor leader had had time to reflect further on his vulnerability to a jury-tampering charge, and he was now convinced, as were his lawyers, that it was not really that great. Whatever his codefendants might be ultimately proven to have done—and both King and Medlin, having been caught more or less red-handed, appeared to be in a particularly unenviable position—any evidence that could be produced against himself would have to be construed by a jury as being highly tenuous. He had never personally made contact with any jurors, nor did the May 9 indictment so much as hint that he had. He was charged only with "aiding, abetting, counseling, commanding, inducing" the tampering.

He would again be represented by solid legal talent, too: Osborn, Haggerty, and Bufalino, once more, with the aggressive and outspoken Jacques M. Schiffer, a New York attorney whom Hoffa had known for years, now also slated to play a starring role. Nor did his own track record do anything but give him cause for optimism: since his convictions in the 1940s on the two relatively minor charges related to his labor leadership, he had been found guilty of absolutely nothing despite being tried twice for illegal wiretapping and once each for bribery and accepting illegal employer payments. He was heartened by the thought that the respective juries may have concluded in each case that the Justice Department action against him had not constituted fair play. He was well aware, in addition, that he had personally shown himself to be no pushover in his courtroom appearances. Now, with so much experience behind him, he would presumably be even more effective in his testimony. With a variety of motions expected from both the defense and the prosecution, months would probably go by before the Tennessee retrial would actually be held, but he would be ready for it when it came.

Hoffa was not, however, ready for another action of a convened grand jury. It was announced less than four weeks after the jury-tampering indictment, and this time it threatened him with the not insignificant total of 140 years in jail, as well as $37,000 in fines. It came about, ironically, as an offshoot of the government's investigation of Hoffa's Sun Valley role, the alleged set of illegalities that had been shelved in favor of the Test Fleet case because the Justice Department had thought that the latter would more easily result in a Hoffa conviction.

On June 4, 1963, a federal grand jury in Chicago indicted the IBT president and seven other persons on charges of having fraudulently obtained $20 million in fourteen loans for themselves and others from the $200 million Central States, Southeast, and Southwest Areas Teamsters Pension Fund. Named with Hoffa was the latter's old associate Benjamin Dranow, who was now in jail for the bankruptcy fraud that James F. Neal had proven him guilty of committing. Also indicted were an accountant, a lawyer, and three real estate operators and builders.

Only eight years earlier there had been no such pension fund at all. Hoffa, whose truck driver constituents were on the average relatively young as compared to workers in other industries, had ignored the subject rather consistently even while unionized workers in automobiles, steel, and many other sectors were gaining meaningful negotiated retirement incomes in the decade after World War II. By 1955, the omission was becoming rather glaring, however, and the Central States and Southern contract that he bargained that year called for the trucking employers to pay $2 weekly per worker into a newly created fund for pensions. The arrangement was designed to be self-administered jointly by the Teamsters and the employers. (Other Teamster contracts, not negotiated by Hoffa himself, also implemented pension plans in the mid-1950s, but these tended to remain outside of Hoffa's authority. The second largest plan, that of the Western States, was entirely administered by the Prudential Insurance Company, for example.)

In the years since 1955, the weekly employer payment had steadily increased: to $3 in 1958, $4 in 1960, $5 in 1961, and $6 in 1963. And since the number of workers covered by the Central States, Southeast, and Southwest Areas Pension Fund had more than doubled—to over 200,000 by 1963—some $5 million each month was now automatically going into the fund treasury, with very few legal strictures as to how the monies could be invested. The only major governmental requirement was that there had to be a board of trustees to administer the pension fund, and this board could not contain more union representatives that it did management representatives.

Hoffa had insisted to the employers from the start on three stipulations. The board, in the first place, had to be a large one, with at least six appointees from each side. The number of employer trustees, secondly, had to be matched by the number of union ones. And the Teamster leader was adamant that a simple majority vote suffice for board decisions. He had anticipated opposition from the employers on this combination of three points, since with it— assuming only that he could win one employer over to his viewpoint on a given vote—he could control the board just as fully as he did any other combined group of Teamsters and employers.

He had indeed been met with such resistance, and at a fateful March 1955 pension meeting he had surmounted it. According to Ralph and Estelle James, he belligerently informed the management representatives as he made his way out of the room then that unless he got his way, "representing the union, we will file a grievance against every carrier, every one, and we will take you out on strike. God damn it, until you do agree to draw up the proper kind of trust that we can live under. I can tell you that much, and I will, God damn it. Take that home, and see how you like it." The employers did not like it. And they did not have to go home to envision vividly all that Hoffa was threatening. As the same authors have pointed out, "the tremendous latent force inherent in the open-end grievance procedure; the image of selective shutdowns, dictated by Hoffa over hastily manufactured grievances, came immediately to mind."[12] Once again, Hoffa quickly got his way.

For a year or so after this conquest, the Teamster leader had let a variety of favored midwestern and southern banks invest the employer pension contributions for him. But by 1957 he had come to appreciate that there was no need to abdicate a more active role in the handling of these many millions of dollars and many advantages in not so doing. From that time on he had personally made almost all of the CSPF's important investment decisions.

He had not been a timid portfolio manager. Other institutional pension funds of the era tended to put most of their money into high-grade common stocks, corporate bonds, and governmental securities. Hoffa's investments heavily favored speculative, leisure-oriented real estate. Many hotels in booming Las Vegas—Caesar's Palace, the Circus Circus, the Sands, the Dunes, the Stardust, and the Desert Inn, among others—were indebted either exclusively or primarily to Central States Pension Fund loans for their establishment. The same could be said for Miami's Castaways Motel, Reno's Harold's Club casino, and two major high-flying projects in Cleveland, the huge Eastgate Coliseum recreation complex and the Cleveland Raceways.

The key figure in the CSPF readily explained his proclivity for this kind of investment. With the labor force getting ever more liberalized vacation and holiday benefits all over the United States, there was time to enjoy life as there had never been before. Hoffa believed instinctively that loans for leisure-time ventures were only logical in view of this graphic fact. They would pay dividends many times over.

It had not, however, been so easy for Hoffa to explain two other circumstances that often attended the loans.

In the first place, many of the recipients were something less than model citizens. Ohio's William Presser was a major beneficiary of the Eastgate Coliseum loan, for example, and a variety of people whose names were linked to midwestern organized crime received financing for the Las Vegas activities. Hoffa made it clear that business was business and that, anyway, some of these people (like the hugely successful Las Vegas hotelier Morris Dalitz, a former bootlegger whom Hoffa had known since his early days in Detroit, and Presser) were close friends. He made no apologies.

It was also frequently commented that CSPF loans tended to burden the borrowers with relatively low interest rates ($6^1/_2$ percent, for example, when the going rate imposed by other lenders might be several points above that percentage). Here, Hoffa often pointed out that the Teamsters' primary goal in forging the loan policy was "to reward friends and to make new ones" and that extracting the maximum possible return on investment would accomplish nothing to achieve these ends. Recognizing that rumors of illicit payoffs would inevitably result, he nonetheless let it go at that. Such rumors could never be corroborated, and a bad press in such directions as this seemed now to be his unavoidable lot. He was proud of the fact that the Central States Pension Fund was flourishing, had grown significantly each year, and was anything but cheap in the retirement dollars that it paid out. As he often asked rhetorically, "What other large industry pays a pension of close to $200 every month?"

In the June 4, 1963, Chicago federal grand jury indictment, Hoffa was accused of "fraud, deceit, misrepresentation" and of "overreaching" as one of the now sixteen trustees (eight of them appointed by the employers and the others by the Teamsters) of the fund. Specifically, he was charged with having knowingly familiarized himself with fraudulent loan applications prior to their filing with the fund and then having talked his fifteen fellow trustees, none of whom was indicted, into approving these loans. All of the defendants, it was alleged, had taken cash, stock options, and stock as "finders fees" and had collectively siphoned off roughly $1 million worth of the fraudulent loans into their own pockets.

From the $1 million allegedly diverted in this way, Hoffa stood accused of having taken $100,000 to "extricate" himself "from personal involvement" in the Sun Valley situation, and the Sun Valley case was now consequently dropped as a separate one for him because aspects of it were "necessarily embodied" in this Chicago indictment. But the twenty-eight counts contained in the June 4 grand jury action hardly confined their allegations of Hoffa wrongdoing to the Florida retirement project. The man who both ran the Teamsters and controlled the decisions of the pension fund trustees had also, it was contended, falsely told these trustees that $2 million in borrowed funds were to be used for construction of a North Miami hospital. In point of fact, "a substantial portion" of the hospital construction funds had already been diverted. And Hoffa had allegedly made similar false and misleading statements to his fellow trustees to get them to approve loans for a variety of other projects, involving hotels and shopping centers in Florida, Alabama, Louisiana, Missouri, New Jersey, and California.

Aside from the sheer enormity of the charges and the fact that he was from all accounts genuinely surprised by their issuance, Hoffa was particularly bothered by two aspects here.

For one, coming on top of his need to prepare for his jury-tampering trial, the new indictment guaranteed that he would in the months ahead again be preoccupied with his legal problems even while conducting Teamster-trucker labor relations. As in the case of the first cloud now hanging over him, the trial for fraud was undoubtedly some months away. There was simply too much at stake, however, for him to approach it with anything less than maximum readiness. In this case, as was not true of the jury-tampering matter, moreover, Hoffa did not initially even comprehend exactly what he was being charged with: as one of his lawyers announced, apparently quite sincerely, on the day of the Chicago grand jury action, "He doesn't understand it. He's absolutely at a loss." This inability on the part of the normally knowledgeable Hoffa would by definition compound his preparation problem.

But even more unsettling to a union leader who prided himself on servicing his membership was the implication that he had abused his position of trust as the de facto dominant figure in the administration of the mammoth pension fund. The $200 million in the fund had come from contributions by the employers, consistent with their contractual obligation to the Teamsters, and was intended solely to benefit IBT retirees. Anything that milked the fund therefore took money out of the pockets of Hoffa's own constituents, the same ones who had for so long been cheering for their leader because he delivered.

They would undoubtedly continue to cheer, at least for a while. Hoffa, who immediately denied any wrongdoing and pointed out that he was "just one of the sixteen trustees," had still only been accused, after all, and not convicted. In addition, the government's past failures in Hoffa-connected trials were fully recognized. Most

Teamsters continued to see their president as the innocent victim of Justice Department persecution. Nonetheless, a reputation that had been proudly and painstakingly erected on a foundation of bread-and-butter membership gratitude now, for the first time ever, faced a potential blemishing. And Hoffa, ever the realist, was well aware of this circumstance.

As he summoned his seventy-five-man national bargaining committee to Washington in early November 1963 to outline the demands that the Teamsters would serve on the truckers in the national contract bargaining that was scheduled to begin in December, Hoffa consequently had much on his mind. The Tennessee trial would begin in Nashville on January 6; it had already been postponed several times while the courts considered—and rejected—Hoffa requests to dismiss the indictment on a variety of grounds. The case had now also been marked by the recent disbarment of the eminent Hoffa lawyer Z. T. Osborn of Nashville, on the shocking and ironic grounds that he had tried to bribe a prospective juror for the upcoming trial (Osborn told the court that his overture was made entirely on his own: his feelings toward Hoffa, he said, had gradually changed from that of a lawyer to that of a friend, and his friend was being "persecuted" and "abused" by the government). The Chicago trial, tentatively and depending upon what happened in Tennessee, would open on February 3, 1964.

Moreover, several of Hoffa's closest associates had been convicted in the recent past of crimes. Ohio's William Presser had been found guilty of contempt of Congress. New Jersey's Anthony Provenzano had been sentenced to seven years in prison for extortion. Barney Baker was appealing the two years that he had been awarded for taking illegal monies from an employer. Frank Collins, the Detroit Local 299 secretary-treasurer and former "Strawberry Boy," had been convicted of perjury and sentenced to a three-year jail term. Collins had for years been as much of a Hoffa intimate as any person, but all of them were longtime friends and loyal allies. Their problems hit the IBT president close to home.

And there was always the chance that the court problems of the foremost Teamster himself would inspire some kind of dump-Hoffa movement. This latter action might, for example, presumably be triggered by some of the erstwhile local IBT autonomists whose power Hoffa had usurped.

This last possibility was a remote one at the moment. The head of the Teamsters was now regularly claiming that "there are really no anti-Hoffa locals left today." In his words, "The members are almost solidly in our camp. And the local leader has learned that he loses nothing under the master contract system. He actually gains: he gets greater economic strength on his side, better contracts, and less trouble with fewer people." But vestiges of fervent opposition to Hoffa did remain within Teamster trucking locals in at least several cities. In New York, one ranking IBT official was ominously telling visitors, "Everything boils down to how you enforce the contract." In Chicago, Hoffa had never been able to win over one local—Independent Local 705 which, with approximately twenty thousand members, was as large as any within the Teamsters. In San Francisco, much bitterness against Hoffa for allegedly trying to "sell out" superior local conditions in the interests of regional standardization in 1961 remained. In Los Angeles, the union president's popularity had suffered for the same reason. These locations remained the conspicuous exceptions to Hoffa's successes and posed no real threat as matters stood. A Hoffa conviction would, however, do much to give an oust-Hoffa drive some momentum.

A growing fear among the sixteen thousand over-the-road and local cartage employers with whom the IBT president would be negotiating had been that Hoffa, in the face of all of these factors, might feel compelled to recement his popularity with the membership by going after an unusually costly wage and fringe benefit package. And when the demands were outlined at the early November Teamster bargaining meeting in Washington, this fear appeared to have been amply justified. Hoffa, who only weeks earlier had informed the employers that "we won't hit you too hard" and that a "uniform" national agreement would be the main Teamster consideration, now made demands that exceeded even the worst dreams of many truckers. He requested a staggering $600 million over a three-year period—"$900,000 a day," as he bluntly restated the figure—and he immediately conceded that it would be impossible for the companies to meet this cost without raising their rates.

The employers hoped that the demands, which represented by

some large distance the most costly that Hoffa had ever made upon them, would be whittled down appreciably during the actual bargaining sessions in December and January. They assumed that he still placed his primary value on national standardization and a single national agreement. And most of them fully recognized that the IBT boss had regularly shown himself to them over the years to be an entirely reasonable bargainer, governed above all by ability-to-pay considerations. But, with so many strains now converging upon Hoffa and tales of his verbal abusiveness and temper becoming increasingly widespread, they could no longer be sure of anything.

Certainly, Hoffa's reaction to the events of November 22, 1963, allayed no one's fears.

When he heard the news of John F. Kennedy's assassination, Speaker John W. McCormack of the U.S. House of Representatives asked, "My God, what are we coming to?" In the Senate, the chaplain said, "We gaze at a vacant place against the sky, as the President of the Republic goes down like a giant cedar." An eighty-four-year-old Texan declared, "I've never had anything hit me so in my life." More than a thousand people from all over London boarded buses or tube trains, drove, or walked to the American Embassy in Grosvenor Square ("They had to do something," a BBC analyst explained). And, in Moscow, the wife of Soviet Premier Nikita Khrushchev quickly burst into tears. Overpowering grief typically followed shock as people learned of the fatal shooting in Dallas. As never either before or since, the world was bound together in mourning.

Hoffa was in Miami Beach discussing the national trucking agreement with officials of the Southern Conference of Teamsters when the news came in to the Teamsters Building. Harold Gibbons was also out of the headquarters, enjoying a leisurely lunch with Edward Bennett Williams at Duke Ziebert's celebrity-studded restaurant two miles away. Larry Steinberg, in charge of operations in the absence of his two superiors, broke down and wept when he was told (by telephone) of the tragedy. He immediately ordered the American flag lowered to half-mast—before, in fact, the flag of the U.S. Senate across the street was so altered. And, closing the offices, he sent all of the employees in the building home. Gibbons soon thereafter returned from his midday break, supported the Steinberg actions in their entireties, and joined with his longtime friend to compose a statement of condolence that would be issued on behalf of the Teamsters. Gibbons then telephoned Hoffa in Florida to inform him of what had been done and to read him the proposed statement.

Hoffa's response was not sympathetic. He flew into a towering rage and announced, as he had upon the occasion of Frank X. Martel's death almost a decade earlier in Detroit, "I'm no hypocrite." Expressing his own wishes for the slain president ("I hope the worms eat his eyes out"), he asked Gibbons to tell him who gave the instructions to close the building ("Which one of you thinks he's the General President?"). Under no conditions, he said—punctuating his declaration with a heavy dosage of profanity—would he authorize the expression of condolence. He then hung up, but to emphasize his sentiments he shortly thereafter telephoned both Gibbons and Steinberg and administered his verbal blasts again. He also asked a secretary who participated in one of these telephone calls why she was "crying instead of rejoicing."

For Gibbons, who in recent weeks had been the object of considerable oral abuse from his increasingly testy roommate, it was the last straw. He told Hoffa that he could "get himself a new boy" when he returned to Washington and tendered his resignation from the executive assistantship on the spot. He later told reporters that he "stuck with the little guy" despite his treatment by Hoffa because "the guy has been through a lot of trouble without deserving it." But enough, he now announced, was enough. Not long afterwards, Steinberg also asked to be relieved of his duties with the international union, as did three other key Hoffa aides who had worked on Gibbons's former staff in St. Louis: both of the Keathleys and Kavner.[13]

Subsequently, Hoffa was widely quoted as having asserted that, with the events in Dallas, "Bobby Kennedy is just another lawyer now." However, he shortly after this stated that *this* remark on his part had been misconstrued: he had merely sought to convey the thought that the attorney general would now be one of ten cabinet members and no longer have any special personal relationship with the nation's chief executive. As to what he actually had said on November 22, on the other hand, he had no regrets at all:

for the rest of his life, he would often declare that he would do the same thing again if confronted with the same circumstances.

On November 25, the date of the funeral and a National Day of Mourning, most Teamster locals were closed for business. They included the St. Louis units controlled by Gibbons and the Steinberg Teamster affiliates in Toledo. But Local 299 in Detroit, the Excalibur in the Hoffa personal closet, and other Michigan locals in close geographic proximity to it were conspicuously open from morning to evening. No one could accuse Hoffa of insincerity.

In 1964, the President's Commission on the Assassination of President John F. Kennedy, headed by Chief Justice Earl Warren and including some of the nation's foremost public servants and attorneys, concluded that there was no more to the killing of America's thirty-fifth chief executive than had originally met the eye. Lee Harvey Oswald—the unstable gunman who had been arrested on November 22 and charged with the crime—had acted alone, the Warren Commission found. In its mind, there was no "persuasive evidence" to support arguments for a conspiracy, the plethora of rumors that continued to suggest the latter notwithstanding.

Fifteen years later, however, a Select Committee on Assassinations appointed by the U.S. House of Representatives contradicted the 1964 conclusions. It relied heavily on the findings of an acoustical examination of the assassination site. This indicated the presence of a second gunman, and the select committee consequently offered as its opinion that Kennedy was "probably assassinated as the result of a conspiracy."

As to the kingpins in this conspiracy, the committee suggested that three men had the motive, the means, and the opportunity to carry out the murder, although it considered the possibility that any one of them was actually involved to have been remote. One was Carlos Marcello, reputedly the most powerful Mafia chieftain not only in his home state of Louisiana but throughout the entire Gulf Coast area. He had been singled out by Robert F. Kennedy in the Attorney General's massive campaign against the mob; with the elimination of the source of his power—his brother—the younger Kennedy would no longer be a meaningful threat. And two birds could be killed with one stone since a new president would presumably not be as committed to pursuing the Mafia as was JFK. (In fact, in August 1962, Marcello had reportedly explained to an acquaintance why President Kennedy, and not Attorney General Kennedy, would be killed with this rationale: "You know what they say in Sicily: if you want to kill a dog, you don't cut off the tail, you cut off the head.") Moreover, Marcello had publicly threatened to arrange the president's murder, according to some testimony.

Florida's Santos Trafficante, also known as one of the country's major Mafiosi and another prime Robert Kennedy target, was a second possibility in the committee's scheme of things. He had told an FBI informer in 1962 that "Kennedy's not going to make it to the [1964] election; he's going to be hit."

Still a third member of the conspiracy, the House panel indicated, might have been—although the committee pointed out that he might also *not* have been—the late leader of the International Brotherhood of Teamsters, James Riddle Hoffa.

Several considerations had led the members of Congress to this highly qualified last conclusion.

In the first place, there was the testimony of a Louisiana Teamster official, Edward Grady Partin, to both the FBI and to the House Assassinations Committee itself. Partin had quoted Hoffa as having told him in the late summer of 1962, "I've got to do something about that son of a bitch Bobby Kennedy. He's got to go," and as having talked about killing the president's brother on other occasions as well. And, as others, Partin found it quite credible that such a plot might have been transformed into one aimed at the attorney general's superior. Hoffa, after all, clearly detested the president as much as he did the attorney general; he would, Partin once said, "fly off [when] the name [of the president] was even mentioned. . . . I think he would have died himself if he knew he could have gotten them [both] killed."[14]

By themselves, these Partin allegations would presumably have carried no weight at all with the committee. Talk, as has been observed by many evaluators of it, is cheap. Even accepting as givens Hoffa's intense hatred of the two Kennedys and the reports of others besides Partin that Hoffa had talked about having Robert Kennedy murdered,[15] a linkage of the Teamster president to the November 22, 1963, assassination could exist only in the wildest of imaginations. But two other Partin-related considerations combined with these first to give the committee reason to keep Hoffa's name in its live file.

For one thing, if Partin was to be believed, Hoffa had discussed with the Louisiana Teamster a specific plan for disposing of Robert Kennedy. And it was remarkably similar to the one actually used in the John F. Kennedy killing. Hoffa had proposed "the possible use of a lone gunman equipped with a rifle with a telescopic sight . . . an assassin without any identifiable connection to the Teamster organization or Hoffa himself." He had noted the "advisability of having the assassination committed somewhere in the South," where segregationist zealots could be blamed. And he had commented on "the potential desirability of having Robert Kennedy shot while riding in a convertible."[16] Secondly, when Partin had informed the FBI of this plot, the governmental agency had administered a polygraph test to him, and he had passed it to the agency's complete satisfaction.

In addition to the Partin testimony, there were clear connections between Oswald's killer, Jack Ruby, and the Teamsters. In 1939 and 1940, Ruby had been second-in-command of Chicago Local 20467 of the Scrap Iron and Junk Handlers Union. A mob-controlled labor organization that was notorious for its shakedowns and physical intimidations even in the city of Al Capone, the local became a Teamster affiliate in 1939, immediately after the unsolved murder of its founder. Its new leader, and Ruby's immediate superior, was the mobster Paul "Red" Dorfman, who, it may be recalled, later served on the Sponsors Committee for the 1956 "Jimmie Hoffa Testimonial Dinner" in Detroit. As was also noted earlier, Dorfman was to be officially connected to Hoffa in at least one other way: his insurance company was the recipient in the early 1950s of so much Central States Health and Welfare Fund monies that a congressional investigatory committee in 1953 questioned him and his stepson Allen about possible illegal payoffs to Hoffa here and recommended that he and Allen be cited for contempt when the two Dorfmans consistently refused to answer these questions. (Paul and Allen also each took the Fifth Amendment when asked essentially the same questions a few years later by the McClellan committee.) Allen had, of course, been named as a Hoffa coconspirator in the May 9, 1963, jury-tampering indictment in Tennessee.

Both Dorfmans, indeed, could also quite accurately be described as two of Hoffa's closest personal friends from the 1950s on. The deceptively soft-spoken, red-haired father was a constant enough companion of the Teamster president that Robert Kennedy could observe, at the peak of the McClellan committee hearings, "Paul Dorfman and Jimmy Hoffa are now as one." And both the father and his lean, athletic son were often in attendance at IBT conventions and other meetings. In addition, the Dorfmans were partners with Hoffa in a variety of business investments, including an oil company, a girls' camp, and several real estate ventures.

Dorfman père was not, moreover, the only Ruby-Hoffa linkage. FBI records established that, in the month preceding the John F. Kennedy assassination, Ruby had engaged in several long-distance telephone conversations with close Hoffa associates.

At least two of these conversations were with the gargantuan Robert "Barney" Baker—the Teamster "organizer" who had done so much to enliven the McClellan committee hearings five years earlier. Baker had phoned Ruby collect (in response, Baker later said, to a message from Ruby asking him to do this) and talked to him for seven minutes on November 7, 1963. And Ruby had placed a fourteen-minute call to Baker on the following day. Between late October and November 22, 1963, Ruby also placed a twelve-minute call to Irwin S. Weiner, the primary Teamster Union bondsman, and a four-minute one to Murray W. "Dusty" Miller, the head of the Southern Conference of Teamsters.

Baker told the House Assassinations Committee in 1978 that Ruby had sought his help regarding a labor problem: the owner of a competing nightclub was being allowed to run amateur burlesque shows by the American Guild of Variety Artists, but the union wouldn't let Ruby's nightclub do this. Weiner testified, also in 1978, that Ruby had asked him to write a bond in connection with a lawsuit against that competitor. Miller offered the committee the same basic union-related explanation for the telephone call that he had received.

The House panel nonetheless found these testimonies to be less than convincing. There were considerable evasions and inconsistencies on the part of the witnesses. It also seemed odd that a small-time nightclub owner like Ruby would come to such Teamster heavy hitters as Baker and Miller (who were also, apparently, strangers to him) with such a minor problem as this stripper-related one or that he would know their private unlisted telephone numbers. Nor did the panel find any indication that Ruby was in fact planning the lawsuit that Weiner described. The congressmen could not, therefore, dismiss the possibility that Ruby and the Teamsters had transacted a different kind of business than the one described by Baker, Miller, and Weiner. Unlikely as it might have been, some kind of conspiracy could have been forged between Ruby and Hoffa, presumably through intermediaries, to silence the man who had himself silenced John F. Kennedy.

In addition, it is quite possible that Ruby and Hoffa did know each other. They certainly had many mutual acquaintances, including a wide variety of New Orleans, Dallas, Chicago, and Florida mobsters. And Hoffa's son, James P. Hoffa, once told an interviewer, "I think my dad knew Jack Ruby, but from what I understand, he [Ruby] was the kind of guy everybody knew. So what?"[17]

Finally, Hoffa could count both Marcello and Trafficante among his many friends. Marcello had had business dealings with the IBT leader in Louisiana, where his widespread influence extended into the Teamsters. And when Hoffa was subsequently faced with imprisonment, according to FBI files, Marcello apparently had $1 million placed at his disposal by organized crime for purposes of bribing judges and others who could stave off this jailing. ("In taking on this large and risky responsibility," one John F. Kennedy assassination student has asked, "was Marcello paying back Hoffa for whatever services Hoffa had rendered to him in the . . . assassination?"[18])

Trafficante, too, had described himself as a friend of Hoffa. Immediately before the Floridian had made his 1962 statement to the FBI informer that John F. Kennedy was "going to be hit," he had, in fact, told the same informer: "Have you seen how his brother is hitting Hoffa, a man who is not a millionaire, a friend of the blue collars? He doesn't know that this kind of encounter is very delicate. . . . It is not right what they are doing to Hoffa. . . . Hoffa is a hardworking man and does not deserve it. Mark my word, this man Kennedy is in trouble, and he will get what is coming to him."[19]

Putting all of these facts and theories together, one ingredient is still lacking to show that Hoffa had any hand at all in the November 22, 1963, killing: hard evidence.

The Hoffa-as-part-of-a-conspiracy conjectures, which began to be widely disseminated in John F. Kennedy Assassination publications and documentaries once the House committee had introduced Hoffa's name, and which perhaps reached their fullest flowering in the torrent of "Mafia Murder" explanations surrounding the twenty-fifth anniversary of the killing in 1988,[20] make for intriguing reading and conversation. They lack anything that remotely provides proof, however. Even if one accepts the highly controversial conspiracy theory *and* attributes to the head of the Teamsters not only motives but expressed desires and clear personnel linkages, this still hardly justifies a conclusion of Hoffa complicity. As with anything else, the burden remains on those alleging wrongdoing to build a case so cogent that it must be accepted by an open mind. To date, such a case has simply not been erected, although it seems certain now that the speculation concerning Hoffa's involvement will be a permanent part of the Hoffa legacy.

What has been established is that the Warren Commission, surprisingly in hindsight, apparently never investigated any of these possible Hoffa connections to the occurrences in Texas. (A single, early 1964 memorandum of the commission did specify the Teamsters Union as the first of six groups that might have desired the president's death,[21] but there was no meaningful follow-up at all to this.) Yet, the FBI did begin, independently, to explore at least the Ruby-Barney Baker relationship as early as December 1963. And, from the very beginning, Hoffa was understandably sensitive to the fact that he was not above suspicion.

He could hardly deny his connection either to Baker or to the other key players. But he could avoid compounding any potential problems that he might have in this area, and in at least one set of circumstances he aggressively did so. In the mid-1960s, Lee Harvey Oswald's widow, Marina, came to the University of Michigan in Ann Arbor to take a variety of special courses. At the time, the Michigan student body also contained, at the Law School, James P. Hoffa. And, defying all laws of probability, the widow of the unstable gunman proceeded to meet and date at least two Law School

With Josephine at the 1961 Teamster convention in Miami Beach. (Crancer Collection)

Swearing-in ceremony at Miami Beach, 1961. (Crancer Collection)

The first lady of the Teamsters and her husband, immediately following Hoffa's 1961 presidential acceptance speech. (Crancer Collection)

(below) Deep sea fishing in Florida, approximately 1963. (Crancer Collection)

(above right) At the U.S. courthouse in Chicago, immediately after his conviction for conspiracy and mail and wire fraud, 1964. (AP/Wide World Photos)

(below right) A rented plane conveys birthday greetings to Lewisburg's best known resident, 1969. (AP/Wide World Photos)

(above) A considerably grayer Hoffa leaves the Lewisburg Penitentiary after four years, nine months, and sixteen days, 1971. (AP/Wide World Photos)

(above right) Testifying about parole procedures at a U.S. House of Representatives Judiciary Subcommittee hearing, 1972. (AP/Wide World Photos)

(below right) Hoffa supporters picketing the IBT Building in Washington, 1973. (Crancer Collection)

(above) Leaving U.S. District Court in Washington after receiving Judge Pratt's unfavorable ruling regarding the constitutionality of his parole restriction, 1974. (AP/Wide World Photos)

(below) Hoffa's dark green 1974 Pontiac Grand Ville hardtop, just after Bloomfield Township, Michigan, police had opened its trunk in a search for the missing Teamster's body, 1975. (AP/Wide World Photos)

students who were friendly with the younger Hoffa. The latter, strongly encouraged by his father, went to great lengths to avoid being seen anywhere with the famous special student. The Teamster president had enough troubles already; there was no sense in tempting fate to burden him with one more.

Chattanooga, Chicago, and the End of an Era

12

Outwardly, Hoffa showed little signs of concern in the face of all of his problems, now augmented by the resignation of his top aides in the wake of the Kennedy assassination, as he opened the formal trucking negotiations at Chicago's Edgewater Beach Hotel in mid-December 1963.

Barely suppressing a smile, he informed the employer bargaining team at the first meeting of the parties, "I'm happy to see you're so well organized this year and I hope you don't fall apart at the seams." He steadfastly denied to reporters that there was any "palace rift" involving Gibbons, Steinberg, or anyone else: the union, he insisted, was as "strong and united" as ever, and rumors of dissension "don't mean a thing." He predicted that the six Teamster locals—four of them in greater New York City, and one each in Chicago and San Francisco—that had now officially rejected the national bargaining concept would yet approve it. He publicly confirmed the fact that he was asking for about $600 million annually, or for a package increase of 30 cents hourly—divided equally between wages and benefits—and announced that he fully expected to get all of it.

But Hoffa's actions, as the bargaining proceeded, spoke more loudly than his words. He seemed to be far more considerate of both his personal assistants and elected Teamster officials than he had been in past weeks: his easily aroused irascibility with them was now almost nonexistent, and he displayed a willingness not only to accept but to solicit advice from subordinates that was very much removed from the normal Hoffa *modus operandi*. He also soon gave clear signals to the employers inside the bargaining room that he would in fact be willing to settle for a good deal less than the official $600 million package, quite possibly for concessions that would cost only half that amount.

Nor, amid so many legal and political problems, did he any longer appear to have his heart set on achieving national uniformity of contractual terms for the four hundred thousand road and cartage drivers. He needed all the friends he could get at this point, and there was no need to ask for problems by pushing either recalcitrant Teamsters or employers beyond their points of toleration. Winning the 100 percent uniformity of wages, fringes, and conditions that he had claimed as a 1964 goal for so long could wait; he would be satisfied with enacting the first national contract in the history of the once totally decentralized trucking industry.

Hoffa did, however, insist on speed in the negotiations. He did not want the bargaining hanging over his jury tampering trial, which, having been postponed for one final time, would now definitely start in Chattanooga, Tennessee, on January 20, 1964. He set a strike deadline for six nationwide companies for midnight, January 15, and assumed that the threat would have its usual traumatic effect.

The contract was agreed to by the truckers less than an hour before the deadline. It was forty-seven pages long, "the most complicated one ever worked out between a union and employers" in Hoffa's opinion, and it would cost the industry by union estimate some $300 million in the course of its thirty-eight months. Industry spokesmen thought that $400 million was a more realistic figure and agreed fully with the union president that trucking rates would have to be raised appreciably to absorb the added costs. Hoffa pronounced the document "a great contract," and no less an authority than the *New York Times* called it "a personal triumph for the union's president. . . . The [national] agreement will tighten Mr. Hoffa's grip on the union and will increase his power in dealing with the industry."[1]

But the national pact was also noteworthy for what it did not do. Even in the area of wages, no further progress was made toward national uniformity beyond what had been achieved in the 1960–1961 round of negotiations: drivers in New York, Los

Angeles, and Detroit—to cite only three examples—would contractually continue to earn wage rates that exceeded the national scale, and it was fully expected that political realities would generate a number of additions to the list through various local supplements. Working conditions, while now relatively uniform coast to coast, would continue to be left up to local negotiation almost entirely. And "open end" would remain essentially untouched from its present parameters, Hoffa's original 1964 plans for a single centralized administration by himself of this novel system notwithstanding.

On the other side of the ledger, when this new basic agreement expired on March 31, 1967, the nation's best-known labor leader would for the first time have the power to call a nationwide trucking strike. And the very thought of such an occurrence was already setting off an avalanche of dire predictions.

The worries of old Hoffa enemy Senator John L. McClellan, written in anticipation of the common expiration date, were typical. His opinion, verbalized in an article that he wrote for the *Reader's Digest,* was that

the International Brotherhood of Teamsters . . . is now powerful enough by itself to put a stranglehold on our nation's economy. The Teamsters control the trucking industry. . . . If they called a nationwide strike, you could not get ambulances to take sick people to the hospital, nor hearses to carry the dead. Farmers could not get produce to urban areas; food manufacturers could not send in canned goods. Milk would not be delivered. Market shelves would soon be swept clean. City dwellers would literally face starvation.

Hoffa is reported to have said that he would not call such a strike. But I believe that the American people, instead of relying on the mere word of the head of the Teamsters union, would prefer to be protected by law. Hoffa admits that he has the power and can use it if he wishes. No one else in our society can wield such force. Industry cannot; our laws prevent it. The government itself, under the Constitution, has no power to prohibit commerce. Hoffa does. . . . And such power constitutes a threat to the security and well-being of our country.[2]

Hoffa had indeed said many times that he would not call such a strike. But, beyond the Teamster president's professions of intent, there were convincing reasons why he could not do what the senator and so many other people feared.

First, the nationwide contract did not cover either the drivers of perishable single-produce freight (the milk and most of the farm products alluded to) or the nonfreight drivers (the ambulance and hearse workers cited by the senator). These employees continued to be governed by a variety of contracts, many of them confined to individual metropolitan areas and with widely different expiration dates.

Second, the presence of alternative transportation (railroads, nonunion trucking, airlines, and barges) meant that no Teamster strike could place a "stranglehold" on the economy. While a nationwide over-the-road and cartage strike would clearly present a major inconvenience to the public, "stranglehold" was simply a word that went too far.

Third, there was the very practical reason that, as IBT Research Director Abraham Weiss could observe, "the Teamsters already have a bad enough press and much government opposition . . . the public reaction to any large-scale Teamster strike would be too drastic." There was, in the opinion of many Teamsters, an excellent chance that restrictive legislation would be immediately forthcoming should Hoffa ever attempt a nationwide road and cartage strike. In Hoffa's own opinion, this prospect alone made a general strike unthinkable: "Only an idiot who couldn't recognize the consequences would call such a strike," he would often say, "And I'm no idiot."

Finally, the Teamster general president favored the selective, limited strike to the large-scale strike under any conditions. His frequently offered rationale for the former kind of strike—that the struck employer, with his competitors allowed to operate in this dog-eat-dog industry, had no choice but to settle fast—made eminent sense. And the selective strike threats that Hoffa had actually made several times in the course of recent over-the-road negotiations lent further credence to a belief that he was sincere in this preference.

By the same token, words like McClellan's, even if stripped of all of their hyperbole, bore witness to just how far Hoffa had come since he had sat quietly at the feet of Farrell Dobbs a quarter-century earlier. The old master from Minneapolis had to be proud, his later rupture with Hoffa notwithstanding, as he watched his pupil climax his long-embraced dream. Even in its incompleteness, the 1964 contract did represent a stunning triumph for the union's president. And there was no reason why Hoffa could not achieve the rest of his national objectives in the years immediately ahead, assuming only that he could avoid court conviction.

Chattanooga had been designated as the site of the jury-tampering hearings at almost the last minute. Three weeks before the scheduled January 20, 1964, start of the trial in Nashville, Federal District Judge Frank W. Wilson had agreed with the attorneys for Hoffa and his codefendants that their clients could not get a fair trial in Nashville because of the widespread publicity there concerning not only the first trial but now also the effort of prominent Nashville lawyer Osborn to influence the new jury. He had, accordingly, ordered the case transferred to its new location some 140 miles southeast of Nashville, although the trial date would remain as it was.

Judge Wilson, a tall, soft-spoken forty-seven-year-old Tennessean with a reputation for painstaking research and judicial scholarship, made another major decision on the trial's opening day. He decreed that this time the jury would be locked up from start to finish, even though—with at least forty prosecution witnesses and possibly as many people testifying for the defense—the proceedings were expected to last a minimum of a month. The twelve jurors, once chosen, would be under the constant surveillance of seventeen federal marshals. They would spend their nights at a hotel and be allowed to see or talk by telephone only with members of their immediate families.

The judge had anticipated a negative reaction from the defense attorneys to these security measures, and he got it. Lawyers for the defendants vigorously objected that such precautions would prejudice the cases of their clients. They also argued that there should be some proof that the measures were necessary before they were imposed. Wilson overruled them.

Nor was the Hoffa legal staff happy with the complexion of the jury that was finally, after five days of examination and challenges by both sides, seated. The defense attorneys conveyed to Wilson their opinion that the twelve-member panel contained too few blacks (one), too few union members (also one), too few blue-collar workers, and too many college-educated people among its eight men and four women to fairly represent a cross section of the community. Even worse from the defense standpoint, a large majority of the two hundred Chattanooga residents who made up the original body from which the twelve jurors were selected seemed genuinely to want to serve on this particular jury—an ominous sign to at least one Hoffa lawyer, who offered his opinion that keen interest in serving on any jury was more often than not displayed by those who favored conviction.

The trial began uneventfully enough, with possibly its biggest surprise over the first two weeks being the fact that the name of the most famous defendant was almost never directly mentioned in the testimony. Instead, the parade of witnesses put on the stand by the two chief prosecutors—Nashville trial alumnus Neal and now a second native Tennessean, noted trial attorney John J. Hooker, Sr.—testified about the alleged activities of Hoffa's five codefendants.[3]

Nashville policeman James T. Walker led off. He told the court that defendant Thomas Ewing Parks had come to his home not long after the start of the Nashville trial, asked him if he knew his (Walker's) neighbor Gratin Fields, and inquired as to whether Fields might need money to pay off some debts. Parks, he said, had also informed him that "the big boy" (not further identified) needed "one other person on the jury to hang the jury."

Fields's son Carl then testified that Parks had offered him $5,000 for himself and $5,000 for his father if his father voted for an acquittal. After pocketing five $20 bills that Parks had placed near him, he had had second thoughts and telephoned Parks that he couldn't talk to his father about the trial at all. Parks, apparently a good sport about the whole thing, had told Carl to keep the money anyhow.

Testimony was also introduced in an effort to show that Chicago insurance broker Dorfman and West Virginia businessman Tweel tried to pay Dallas Hall, a Nashville nightclub operator, to get in touch with jurors. A member of Nashville Teamster leader Ewing King's local stated under oath that King had offered to get sergeant's stripes for the Tennessee state trooper, James Paschal, whose wife was on the conspiracy trial jury. Evidence was produced in a prosecution attempt to connect Detroit Local 299 business agent Larry Campbell to the jury fixing.

But anything that might meaningfully link Hoffa himself to

the tampering effort was conspicuous by its absence. After two weeks, the IBT general president had yet to be remotely involved in what prosecutor Neal was calling "a solid chain of evidence." The labor leader's repeated professions of innocence to the media people who surrounded him as he walked the block from his Patten Hotel suite to the gleaming Chattanooga federal courthouse were consequently, as the days went on, becoming more and more convincing. And the jaunty optimism as to the trial's outcome that Hoffa had exuded for months now seemed to be entirely sincere.

In fact, the energetic Teamster's primary worry appeared to be that the sedentary courtroom conditions forced upon him during the long trial would cause him to get out of shape physically. To obviate this possibility, he soon arranged to have regular workouts with barbells at the local YMCA (where he often crossed paths with Neal, whose fear of getting flabby rivaled his own).

Then, after the noon recess on February 4, the prosecution unleashed a thunderbolt. It put on the stand a surprise witness, Edward Grady Partin, secretary-treasurer and business agent of Teamster Local 5 in Baton Rouge, Louisiana and a personal acquaintance of Hoffa's. He was the same man whose reports to the government that Hoffa had talked about having Robert Kennedy murdered would later help generate the Select House Committee on Assassinations' highly qualified conclusion that the Teamster president might have had a hand in the murder of John F. Kennedy. Far more ominously for Hoffa at this point, Partin had been in and out of Nashville during the entire length of the 1962 Test Fleet trial. He had been freely accepted in the Hoffa camp and had at times even acted as guard at the door of Hoffa's hotel suite. He had been privy, he now informed the court, to jury plot talk involving not only Hoffa's associates but Hoffa himself. And he was ready to provide as many specifics on these discussions as the court was willing to request of him.

Hoffa was visibly shaken by this abrupt turn of events. People sitting near him when the business agent walked into the courtroom heard him say, "My God, it's Partin." The color drained from his face. Chewing on the end of his ballpoint pen, he then glowered intently at the tough Louisianan whom he had known since 1957 and who had until that very moment enjoyed his complete confidence. The "deep, strange, penetrating expression of intense hatred" that Robert Kennedy thought that he and his brother had received during the McClellan committee hearings was a look of love when compared to what was now directed toward the witness stand in this dramatic Chattanooga confrontation.

Partin, who had anticipated such a reaction, shrugged it off. And, in a southern drawl that was surprisingly soft given his tall, muscular appearance, the thirty-nine-year-old minor Teamster official proceeded with his testimony.

It was tantalizing enough, even from the start. Before going to Nashville, he informed the more than one hundred people in the hushed courtroom, he had contacted Department of Justice lawyer Frank Grimsley, who had given him Walter Sheridan's telephone number in Nashville and told him to get in touch with Sheridan if he discovered any evidence of tampering. He had arrived in Nashville on the first day of the trial, and that night, in the Andrew Jackson Hotel coffee shop, had met Tweel. Once the social amenities had been attended to, Tweel had informed Partin that Hoffa's close friend Dorfman had called him (Tweel) and told him that it would be a "personal favor" to Dorfman if Tweel "would come to Nashville and help him set up a method for getting to the jury."

The witness could get no further at this point. Several Hoffa attorneys successively leaped to their feet ("like pistons," in the words of one observer) to demand a mistrial or, at the very least, the suppression of further testimony by Partin. The role of the Louisiana Teamster in Nashville, they contended, was illegal because he had been planted as an undercover agent by the U.S. government and had consequently improperly intruded on Hoffa's rights: any reports leading to the current trial that he might have given the government were therefore, as one member of the large Hoffa stable of lawyers phrased it, "clearly the fruit of a poisonous tree."

With the jury excused from the courtroom, defense attorney Schiffer also offered Judge Wilson a second reason for ruling out Partin as a witness. Partin had been indicted in Louisiana in July 1962 on twenty-six counts involving stealing money from his local union and making false entries in its books, and Schiffer suggested that the Teamster's price for cooperating was that the indictment would be dismissed. Partin retorted that he had neither asked anything nor been promised anything.

Judge Wilson took the defense request under advisement overnight and the next morning announced that the Baton Rouge Teamster could testify. He found, he said, that the government had not placed Partin in the midst of the defense. Partin had, on the contrary, been "knowingly and voluntarily placed there by one of the defendants."

The tale that Partin told in his three and one-half hours of testimony on February 5 was repeatedly interrupted by defense objections and mistrial motions—an awesome 168 of them by one count. At times, in a manner reminiscent of not only the day before but also the Nashville trial, two or three of the nine attorneys for the defendants jumped up simultaneously. But when the surprise witness was done for the day, there was no question that he had done Hoffa and his codefendants incalculable damage.

Partin now testified that on the night of October 22, 1962, when he had met Tweel and learned of Dorfman's interest in jury tampering, he had also been invited by Hoffa himself to come into the bedroom in the three-room Hoffa suite at the Andrew Jackson Hotel. "Mr. Hoffa told me to stick around for a few days, that there might be some people he wanted me to talk to," Partin stated, "He said that they were going to get to one juror and try to get to a few scattered jurors and take their chances."[4]

The next day, Partin said, he was getting ready to leave Nashville temporarily, and "Mr. Hoffa [again] called me into the bedroom and told me when I came back he might want me to pass something for him and he put his hand behind his back and hit his back pocket." Hoffa further asserted, according to Partin, that he would pay $15,000, $20,000—whatever it takes to get to the jury."[5]

The prosecution's trump card also left no doubt in anyone's mind as to who had been the informant who had tipped off Walter Sheridan at least twice in Nashville. On November 7, Partin said, he had commented to Hoffa that the trial did not appear to be going very well for the defense, and had thereupon been told by Hoffa, "Don't worry too much because I have the colored male juryman in my hip pocket. One of my colored business agents—Campbell—came in and took care of it." Partin also testified that, some two weeks earlier in Nashville, Ewing King had told him that he knew a highway patrolman whose wife was on the jury: King was going to try to get the patrolman to talk to his wife "to see if he could sway her toward Mr. Hoffa." And even here, the Louisianan directly implicated Hoffa by quoting the latter as saying, "King keeps telling me he can get to the patrolman, but he doesn't get to him. He keeps fumbling around."[6]

As harmful as this presentation was to the defense, it had not been planned by the Justice Department without a major misgiving: Partin, as Hoffa attorney Schiffer had pointed out in the previous day's private session with Judge Wilson, was himself not exactly saintly.

In addition to the 1962 indictment for misuse of union funds and falsification of records that Schiffer had not let pass unrecognized, the man from Baton Rouge had over the past twenty years been convicted of breaking and entering, received a bad conduct discharge from the U.S. Marines, and been indicted for rape, forgery, and first-degree manslaughter. When he had contacted the Justice Department's Grimsley, indeed, he had done so from a Baton Rouge prison cell that was serving as his home away from home in the aftermath of an ultimately dismissed kidnapping charge that had been lodged against him. The FBI, not believing him to be trustworthy, had not wanted to work with him (although Sheridan had not shared such suspicion and had drawn heavily on his services).

One of the few entirely predictable happenings of this trial was that the defense would pounce upon this unsavory record in the cross-examination to raise doubts about Partin's credibility.

Partin's story to the Justice Department as to why he was contacting it in the first place, some three weeks before the Nashville trial was to start, moreover, was also open to some questioning on grounds of believability. He had done so, he said, in words that would, of course, be probed long after the trial, because Hoffa had asked him to help assassinate Robert F. Kennedy.

He had actually not been happy with his general president for some time before this request was made of him at the IBT Building in Washington, Partin had told Grimsley and Sheridan. Hoffa had become too much of a power-hungry dictator for his tastes. But he had been willing to suffer in silence until the overture to join in the murder had been made to him. Now, he had no choice, he had declared: breaking and entering was one thing; the killing of the attorney general of the United States was something else again. He would be less than a man if, without any request for a favor for himself, he did not tell the authorities everything that he knew.

And even if this account—which Partin had professed to be the unvarnished truth and on which he had passed a lie detector test administered to him (at Sheridan's orders) by the FBI—did not strike the jury as being sufficiently farfetched as to detract considerably from the Baton Rouge Teamster's credibility, there was a related problem. The assassination talk, irrelevant as it might be construed anyhow to a jury-tampering trial, might also be interpreted as inflammatory and prejudicial to Hoffa's rights. The defense could be confidently expected to probe Partin's motives for entering the scene and thus to try to delve into this Robert Kennedy matter. But the prosecution recognized that the topic had to be treated with extreme delicacy or it could backfire.

For all of this, the prosecution forces believed strongly that when Partin left the stand at the close of court on February 5, a conviction of their primary target was well within reach. Nor were they alone in their opinion. One of Hoffa's lawyers came up to Sheridan in the hallway and said, "I have seen some great coups in my time but that was the greatest coup I have ever seen."[7] And the general president himself not only unleashed an avalanche of profanity at an assistant outside the courtroom but was reported to have picked up a heavy desk chair in the defense room and hurled it several yards.

The expected counterattack on Partin began the next day. Hoffa's legal counsel, Chattanooga trial lawyer Harry Berke, asked questions about the various offenses that the witness had been charged with—not all of which Partin claimed to remember ("If I knew I would tell you," he finally told Berke, "I'm not ashamed of my past. I have lived it down"). He got Partin to admit that in his earlier years he had been forced to steal milk and food to stay alive and that he had received a bad conduct discharge from the Marine Corps. He also informed the court that charges were still pending against Partin not only for stealing money from his local union and making false entries in its books but for manslaughter and leaving the scene of an automobile accident in which there had been a fatality. Certain of Berke's questions ("Weren't you charged with the rape of a colored girl in Mississippi in 1948?") brought him a stern rebuke from Judge Wilson on the grounds that they tended to "degrade" Partin with "unwarranted charges" (Berke replied that he was merely trying to test Partin's memory), but the trial lawyer clearly was of the belief that this was a small enough price to pay for raising them.

Over the next month, the defense, both in cross-examination of Partin himself and through the production of a host of witnesses of its own, continued to give the government's witness considerable negative attention. He was described (by, among others, a Baton Rouge psychiatrist who had treated him in 1960) as neurotic. He was depicted as a narcotics addict who owned a kit containing needles and a syringe. He was characterized as a woman chaser. A dozen witnesses told the court that they would not believe what Partin said even under oath, and one of these, the Teamster's former secretary in Baton Rouge, termed him "a professional liar." Near the end of the trial, testifying in his own defense, the artful Hoffa himself described a late 1962 conversation that he had held with Partin in words certainly not calculated to help the latter: "I just couldn't envision what this man was talking about, and I finally asked him whether or not he was physically ill and whether he should have some type of treatment because he was nervous, upset, almost incoherent, talking about the 28 counts [sic] that he had ranging all the way from kidnapping to manslaughter."[8] And, through it all, the prosecution seemed now to be as optimistic as to what the jury would decide as Hoffa had originally been. "The government does not contend that Mr. Partin has led a perfect life," Justice Department attorney Neal declared, "The government does contend that he is telling the truth."

The government's uneasiness concerning what Partin might say about the alleged Robert Kennedy assassination plot vanished far more quickly. In a closed session with the parties from which the jury was excluded, Judge Wilson disappointed the defense by ruling that talk of the plot was not germane to the current trial and consequently was not to be explored in any detail. The jury subsequently learned only that Partin had originally talked with Grimsley about "an assassination plot . . . not involving President John F. Kennedy" and that he had thereupon been given and passed a lie detector test on his version of this plot. The defense team could find absolutely no Justice Department vulnerability in this.

Most of the Hoffa lawyers were convinced, however, that getting a mistrial declared for *some* reason constituted their only hope after Partin's February 5 testimony. And, with the stakes at this point so high, they pushed for such an outcome, on several different grounds, no less fervently than they had in Nashville—and with even less success.

They repeatedly charged that the government was carrying out illegal surveillance in Chattanooga of the defendants and their lawyers. One such contention was accompanied by an affidavit from Hoffa's professional wiretapper friend, Bernard Spindel, that he had eavesdropped on coded conversations between FBI agents. The charges invariably received a statement from Judge Wilson that he would hold a hearing on this matter only after the jury-tampering case had gone to the jury. (Such a hearing was held by the judge. In it, the government steadfastly denied all illegal surveillance, and Spindel took the Fifth Amendment at one point. Wilson ruled that the surveillance complaints were "utterly without merit" and dismissed them.)

The defense also claimed that the $900 that the government had paid to date to Partin was a witness fee in violation of federal law. The prosecution successfully argued that the money was only for Partin's expenses and therefore legal (even though it was paid in disbursements of $300 per month to Partin's estranged wife and constituted exactly the amount that he owed her under their separation agreement).

And three defense lawyers vociferously accused Wilson of showing bias against the defense. Jacques M. Schiffer contended, in the course of a series of outbursts, that the district judge was allowing a "drumhead court-martial" and had indicated "time and time again to the jury that the defense counsel are charlatans, that we're tricksters, that we're trying to fool the jury." Harvey Silets (whose last name Neal regularly mispronounced, to Silets's obvious discomfort) said that Wilson had displayed "prejudice against the defense." And Berke, following a reprimand from the judge for having "willfully disregarded the court's instructions," argued that he had been thereby "unfairly chastised in the presence of the jury." Wilson, after refraining from replying to any of these accusations, finally responded, "This court has absolutely no bias and prejudice against any of the defendants. The attorneys have made it difficult for the court throughout the trial."

On March 4, 1964, after deliberating for five hours and forty minutes, the Chattanooga jury found James R. Hoffa guilty on two counts of trying to fix the jury in his 1962 Nashville conspiracy trial. If he received the maximum penalty on each count when sentence was pronounced in a few days, he could go to jail for ten years.

Three of Hoffa's codefendants—the two Teamsters, Ewing King and Larry Campbell, and Campbell's uncle, Thomas Ewing Parks—were also found guilty of obstructing justice. Allen Dorfman and Nicholas Tweel were acquitted.

Hoffa received the announcement of the jury foreman impassively, but at least one interested party could not restrain his emotions. Walter Sheridan raced out of the courtroom upon hearing the news and placed the telephone call that, in one form or another, Robert Kennedy had been awaiting for seven years. Sheridan's first words to his superior were, "We made it!" A jubilant Kennedy responded to the man whose input had been so vital to the conviction, "Nice work."[9]

Outside the courtroom, his two crestfallen children and Barbara's husband, Robert, at his side (Josephine was convalescing with a heart ailment in Miami, and Hoffa would join her there immediately after the sentencing), the general president had much to say to the spectators and media representatives who surrounded him. He would, of course, appeal. The whole trial was a "farce of American justice" and "a railroad job." He pitied those who "don't have the money to pay for an appeal." The jury had been intimidated by being "locked up" in a hotel and allowed to speak to no one unless they were accompanied by federal marshals. As for his leadership of the world's largest union, he was hardly ready to be counted out: "You can rest assured of one thing. The entire membership of the Teamsters Union is behind Hoffa in his fight. The wages, working conditions, health, the welfare and the pensions, the things we have got for them. This is what they want, and this is why they are all behind Hoffa in this."[10]

Only time would tell how accurate the IBT chief executive was in these last words. The general reaction was that no one would try to oust him at present, not until his appeal was decided, but this was by no means a certainty: Hoffa was, for the first time ever in his long career, now considered by many of his enemies to be vulnerable.

On March 12, Judge Wilson, before announcing Hoffa's sentence, delivered an eloquent statement to the celebrity who stood and faced him:

Mr. Hoffa, it is the opinion of the court that the verdict of the jury in this case is clearly supported by the evidence. It is the opinion of the court that those matters of which you stand convicted, that you did knowingly and that you did corruptly, after the trial judge had reported to you his information with regard to an alleged attempt to bribe a juror.

Now, it is difficult for the court to imagine under those circumstances a more willful violation of the law. Most defendants that stand before this court for sentencing—and certainly sentencing is the most distressing duty that this court ever has to perform—most defendants that stand before this court for sentencing have either violated the property rights of other individuals or have violated the personal rights of other individuals.

You stand here convicted of seeking to corrupt the administration of justice itself. You stand here convicted of having tampered, really, with the very soul of this nation. You stand here convicted of having struck at the very foundation upon which everything else in this nation depends, the very basis of civilization itself, and that is the administration of justice, because without a fair, proper and a lawful administration of justice, nothing else would be possible in this country, the administration of labor unions, the administration of business, the carrying on of occupations, the carrying on of recreation, the administration of health services, everything that we call civilization depends ultimately upon the proper administration of justice itself.

Now, if a conviction of such an offense were to go unpunished and this type of conduct and this type of offense permitted to pass without action by the court, it would surely destroy this country more quickly and more surely than any combination of any foreign foes that we could ever possibly have.

Having said this, the judge sentenced Hoffa to eight years in prison and a $10,000 fine. King, Campbell, and Parks got three years apiece. And Hoffa lawyer Schiffer, who was cited for contempt of court (he had, according to Wilson, tried to prevent justice and "degrade and debase" respect for the court during the trial), was given a sixty-day jail sentence.

Hoffa, who had told Wilson in his presentencing statement that when the "evidence is sifted calmly and coolly" it would prove his innocence, would be eligible under the terms of his sentence for a parole after approximately thirty months. He icily now responded, when asked if he had any questions regarding the sentence, "I understand the sentence perfectly and I will take my appeals." Free on $75,000 bail, he left immediately for Florida with two items of no small urgency, in addition to the filing of the appeals, on his agenda: the rallying of sufficient support from the Teamster rank and file as to thwart any danger of a revolt within the union (his claim of having the "entire membership" behind him notwithstanding, he was quite unsure as to how his constituents would now react) and preparation for his trial on charges of fraudulently using union pension funds. The new trial would start in Chicago on April 27.

His first move was designed to shore up his membership support. Within days of the sentencing, all officers and members of the union received a two-page letter from their general president assuring them that "nothing has changed." He was just beginning to fight, he asserted, and would do so not so much for himself as for his union, for the Chattanooga jury "did not return a verdict against Jimmy Hoffa, private citizen: it returned a verdict against Jimmy Hoffa, president of the Teamsters Union." "Until that day when the Teamsters Union lays down its arms and reaches into your pockets to pay for the price of peace," he continued, "the president of this international union, whether he be Hoffa or someone else in the future, will occupy a precarious place in society, indeed."[11]

He expressed in this letter confidence that his conviction would be reversed, by the Supreme Court if it were necessary to go that far in the appellate process, because "the best legal minds in the country are certain that the record [in Chattanooga] is filled with error." He and his attorneys would reveal "the police state and vendetta methods of the Justice Department" so that "this foul conspiracy to jail a labor leader will be reversed." In the meantime, he would be as accessible to the membership as he always had been: "Whenever possible, I will be in the field talking with you . . . finding out what your problems are. . . . The open-door policy in

Washington headquarters will continue." He asked in turn for "your continuing support . . . in our efforts to secure a better way of life for you and your family" and reminded the readers that "we have come quite a way down that road thus far."[12]

A few days later, the general president was able to announce something more tangible. The fifteen-member general executive board of the union, holding its regular quarterly meeting in Hollywood, Florida, unanimously passed two resolutions. One of them expressed "continuing faith" in and "continuing support" for James R. Hoffa, as well as the opinion that the Justice Department had "trampled on" Hoffa's "constitutional rights and civil liberties." The other authorized rank-and-file IBT members to set up committees through which voluntary contributions to pay their president's legal bills could be made.

On the surface, the second resolution, which was proposed by staunch Hoffa friend and northern New Jersey Teamster leader Anthony Provenzano (presently appealing his extortion conviction), was unnecessary. Months earlier, the executive board had authorized Hoffa to pay his sizable legal bills, said to have exceeded $600,000 since 1961, from the international union treasury. And the constitutional amendment adopted at the 1961 IBT convention had seemingly made even *that* move superfluous by sanctioning defense expenses for union officers then. In fact, however, there was a very solid reason for Provenzano's action: the union's respected general counsel, Edward Bennett Williams, had just warned Hoffa that he considered it illegal under the Landrum-Griffin Act for the Teamsters to spend any union monies on either the upcoming Chicago trial or the Chattanooga appeals process.

Relations between Williams and Hoffa had been strained for some time. Hoffa had wanted the lawyer who had done so well for him in the Cheasty bribery case to represent him in his subsequent court appearances. Williams had refused: personally defending a man accused of selling out the union members was, he thought, inconsistent with his mandate as Teamster general counsel. Hoffa had asked Williams for his resignation; Williams had threatened to take the issue to the executive board, where he possibly had as many friends as Hoffa. Lately the dispute was merely simmering, a "Mexican standoff" in the words of one IBT insider.

But Williams was not the only person holding the view that

paying Hoffa's defense fees with union funds was illegal. Lawyers for the U.S. Department of Labor also did. And, in April 1964, twelve dissident Philadelphia Teamsters announced that they would sue every executive board member not only to end the practice but to recover the payments that had already been made. Their attorney also advised the members of the board that they could be held personally responsible for reimbursing the union if the courts ruled the payments to be unlawful and, prodded by this threat, two board members immediately asked IBT secretary-treasurer English to make no more payments until the issue could be clarified.

It did not take long for English, a board member himself, to comply. He suspended the payments, ironically, on the exact date that the Chicago trial began. And Hoffa consequently faced what would most likely be his most expensive and longest court case— estimates were that it might last for four months—with a definite cash flow problem.

Not that the politically astute general president could publicly admit that he had suffered a defeat even in this situation. He encouraged his lieutenants to state that the decision to stop the disbursements was entirely his own. He also announced that he would not even, for the time being, tap the voluntary contributions sent to him by the rank and file in the wake of the March Provenzano-sponsored executive board resolution. These latter contributions, which ranged from $1 to $100, had been somewhat disappointing. They nonetheless still totaled over $50,000 and could have been helpful to a man strapped for funds, but Hoffa emphasized that he would not "touch a penny" until the Internal Revenue Service had ruled on whether or not they were taxable. Instead, he said, he would dispose of some of his own stocks, bonds, and real estate to pay his present and upcoming legal bills.

Only elder statesman James Haggerty of Michigan, from the long list of lawyers who had defended James R. Hoffa in prior court proceedings, was with the Teamster leader as the pension fraud trial opened in Chicago on April 27. The other attorneys were either unavailable or, in at least as many cases, had fallen out of favor with their former client.

With the conspicuous exception of Williams in far earlier days, Hoffa had generally not been happy with the performance of any of his criminal lawyers for long. His original confidence in his Chattanooga legal staff notwithstanding, his treatment of his attorneys there had been marked by angry outbursts during the court recesses and scathing dressings down back at the hotel at night. He tended to exercise a layman's cynicism about the profession anyway, believing that many lawyers were motivated by greed and that they therefore prolonged the proceedings so as to increase their incomes. In Chattanooga, his worst suspicions as to what all the money was financing had, he thought, been confirmed: in his free moments, he had read the variety of often obscure legal cases that various law professors and others had sent him and then, when he had questioned his legal staff about these cases, had frequently drawn blank stares from his audiences in the process; an attorney who failed the test was often informed, "You son of a bitch. You're not doing your homework!"

He had sometimes, too, whispered in anger to counsels whose performance before the Chattanooga judge and jury did not come up to his own high standards, "Sit down!" or "Cut it out!" On several occasions, when the whispers were insufficiently audible to achieve the desired result, he had handed the offending lawyers notes expressing the same command in written form. He would be represented now by only two other lawyers in addition to Haggerty, both experienced Chicagoans: Maurice Walsh and Daniel Ahearn.

In other details, though, history would tend to repeat itself. The federal judge, strong-willed Richard B. Austin, overruled defense objections and announced that the jury would be locked up at the Great Lakes Naval Training Center and closely guarded for the length of the trial, with each juror being permitted a single visit from a family member each week and only one telephone call daily. As in Chattanooga, the defense table would have little space to spare, with Hoffa's seven codefendants here being represented by six lawyers of their own. As in Nashville, the prosecution would rely to some large extent on facts that the McClellan committee had initially turned up. As in the jury-tampering trial, the government would try to convict Hoffa by linking him to the illegalities committed by other defendants: in this case, too, it had insufficient evidence to connect him to the alleged crime by a more direct route.

The key man in the linkage attempt was Benjamin Dranow,

the Hoffa friend who was currently serving federal terms not only for the bankruptcy fraud that James Neal had successfully prosecuted him on but also mail fraud, income tax evasion, and bail jumping. Over the years, the McClellan committee had alleged, his path and Hoffa's had crossed frequently under highly questionable circumstances. Dranow had, for example, owned the John W. Thomas department store in Minneapolis when Hoffa had reportedly been instrumental in getting it a $1 million Central States Pension Fund Teamster loan despite the fact that the store was near bankruptcy. According to Robert F. Kennedy, Hoffa and Dranow had once spent $350,000 of Teamster monies to purchase twenty-six thousand Teamsters Union jackets to be given free of charge to rank-and-file IBT members in Detroit; Dranow had allegedly received a commission of some $17,000 on the transaction.[13] And now Dranow stood accused of having helped Hoffa bail himself out of Sun Valley, the Teamster-promoted Florida retirement community, in the wake of its financial collapse in 1958. The former Minnesota retailer, the government contended, had located people who wanted to borrow from the Central States Pension Fund, charged the latter high finders' fees for the $20 million in loans that Hoffa would ultimately engineer, and then diverted some $1 million of the fee money to the Sun Valley creditors. All of the other defendants were accused of having in some way participated in this venture, which the Justice Department viewed as a labyrinthine exchange of checks to conceal an improper use of union funds.

At the core of the government's case against Hoffa was the argument that he had used "misrepresentation, deceit and artifice" in obtaining loans from the pension fund, with the goal of extricating himself from the Sun Valley project in which he had a 45 percent secret interest. And most of the 114 witnesses whom the prosecution put on the stand during the ten weeks of its presentation (which was also highlighted by the introduction of a mammoth twenty thousand documents) tried, in one way or another, to establish this as fact.

One witness on whose testimony regarding both Dranow and Hoffa the government placed especially high hopes was Bal Harbour, Florida, real estate investor Stanton D. Sanson. He told the court that after he had applied for a $2.5 million apartment house mortgage loan from the Teamsters in 1958, he had been contacted by Dranow, who had put him in telephone touch with Hoffa. Hoffa had assured Sanson that if he would take over Sun Valley, he would get not only the apartment house loan but sufficient funds to turn the Sun Valley project around. But Sanson had wanted no part of the retirement community and pulled out of all dealings with both men, he testified, after Dranow had asked him for a 10 percent commission, payable in cash, on the apartment house loan.

Another witness was potentially even more damaging to Hoffa. Real estate investor Vaughn P. Connelly of Miami asserted that Dranow and Calvin Kovens, another defendant in this Chicago trial, got him a $3.3 million loan from the pension fund and then demanded that he pay them a $300,000 finders' fee, "under the table" and in cash. When Connelly was tardy in coming up with some of this fee, he said, Dranow told him that he was hopeful that no physical harm would come to him, but that "these boys play rough" and that "Mr. Hoffa is raising hell [about not getting the money]." Connelly said that he subsequently gave Dranow $100,000 in cash for the "boss," who was not further identified but was hardly a mystery.

Yet another key prosecution witness was Frederick Lowe, the son of the now-deceased former president of the Sun Valley land development company, Henry Lower. Although Hoffa had denied having any ownership in Sun Valley to the McClellan committee and stated to the select committeemen that he had only an option to buy into the venture, Lowe identified a document (that he said he had found in a cookbook in his father's home) that, the government claimed, proved that 45 percent of the development was in actuality being held in trust for Hoffa. The paper was, indeed, signed by "J. R. Hoffa." Some time later in the trial, an FBI handwriting expert testified that the signature was Hoffa's.

But Hoffa, who had entered this trial expecting the worst, was unexpectedly heartened as the parade of governmental witnesses continued, by the cynicism of Judge Austin himself regarding the prosecution's efforts. On several occasions, the outspoken jurist indicated that he was something less than overwhelmed by the prosecution's performance. The government was simply not proving its case, he said. Austin described the federal evidence as being both contradictory and confusing, and once bluntly stated that the Justice Department's case was "full of holes." On July 9, he dismissed not only seven out of the twenty-eight counts in the original indictment but all of the charges against one of the defendants (Herbert R. Burris, a New York attorney whose accountant father remained on trial) because of insufficient evidence.

By the same token, however, Judge Austin rejected a series of motions now made by a newly optimistic defense that the twenty-one other charges also be dismissed. He could not agree with the defense position that the entire governmental case was based on "inference drawn from conjecture and without foundation" and, after two days of hearing these motions, ordered the attorneys for the defendants to start calling their witnesses immediately.

Austin also dashed defense hopes by refusing to admit evidence that Haggerty, Walsh, and Ahearn had counted on to bolster the Hoffa position. The attorneys had planned to show the jury that the Central States Pension Fund was in solid financial shape, had been growing each year, and was paying its beneficiaries more than it ever had. The judge decided not to let them because, as he tersely declared, with the trucking industry employers "putting $58 million a year into this thing, it's bound to grow," and this growth had nothing to do with the case anyhow, in his opinion.

Dranow was not impressive on the stand. His prison pallor and generally unkempt appearance vividly symbolized how far he had descended from his halcyon days as a financial wheeler and dealer. They also bore mute testimony to the fact that he was even now a jailhouse resident. And he tended to rant and rave as a witness, once announcing that he was being intimidated by the presence of governmental agents in the courtroom. Although his basic message—that he was innocent of everything—was at all times consistent, much of his other testimony was not. He seemed confused, preoccupied and ill at ease. At several points, he punctuated his answers with long silences while he swallowed pills, an action that the prosecution warned the judge was designed to let him collapse so that he could not be cross-examined ("as he did at his trial in Minneapolis").

Hoffa, on the other hand, registered his typical facile performance. He stressed to the court what he had originally emphasized when indicted more than thirteen months earlier: he was only one of the sixteen pension fund trustees, with no more or less authority than any one of his fifteen colleagues. He insisted that he had always acted in good faith in performing his duties as trustee. He firmly denied that he had ever used his position as IBT president to induce the other trustees to approve loans to his fellow defendants or anyone else. He had had neither anything to do with the alleged kickbacks from the loan recipients nor any knowledge about these kickbacks and nothing whatsoever to do with the preparation of loan applications for his codefendants, he said.

As for the "J. R. Hoffa" signature on the document that Lowe had found in the cookbook in his father's home, it was not his signature, the testimony of the FBI handwriting expert notwithstanding. He always used the fuller "James R. Hoffa" in signing legal documents. When prosecutor William O. Bittman thereupon produced a copy of an apartment lease agreement between Hoffa and codefendant Kovens and got Hoffa to acknowledge that the "J. R. Hoffa" on *it* was indeed his own signature, the general president insisted that it was not a legal document.

In his five-and-one-half-hour closing argument, Bittman portrayed Hoffa as a man who had "betrayed his responsibility" to the Teamsters Union. He did have the 45 percent secret interest in Sun Valley, the thirty-two-year-old Assistant District Attorney contended, and to recover the $400,000 of Teamster monies that he had placed in a Florida bank as security for Sun Valley, he violated his fiduciary obligation to protect the pension fund by fraudulently obtaining loan approvals for his coconspirators. Bittman pointed out that of the 114 governmental witnesses, not one had been convicted of a crime, whereas Dranow was now in prison for four of them, and he suggested to the jury that deciding whose position was more credible was hardly a difficult assignment. And Dranow, he asserted, had been in complete cahoots with Hoffa and the other defendants: the seven men on trial made, in fact, "Jesse James and his gang look like purse snatchers."

On the humid afternoon of July 26, 1964, after seventeen and one-half hours of deliberation and 441 ballots, the eight men and four women who had been sequestered since late April convicted Hoffa on one count of conspiracy and three counts of mail and wire fraud. Hoffa was acquitted on the seventeen remaining counts. Each of his six codefendants was found guilty on the conspiracy count and at least one other count, with Dranow being convicted on a total of four counts.

The general president would not learn his exact penalty this time for three weeks, but he now could be sentenced to jail for the next twenty-eight years. If he received the maximum punishment for each of the four Chicago counts, his obligation would total twenty years on top of the eight years that he had been awarded in Chattanooga. He also faced $13,000 in fines, making his new potential 1964 fine total $23,000—clearly the least of his worries.

Appeals would be made as soon as possible, just as in the case of his jury-tampering conviction. And Hoffa's legal team, which was taken by surprise by his guilty verdict, was guardedly optimistic that the Chicago decision would ultimately be overturned. But for the Teamster chieftain to escape jail at this point, not one but two convictions would of course have to be reversed, and privately Hoffa recognized that the odds were against him in this regard.

He could still almost definitely stay on as Teamster president pending the appellate process, which might drag on for as much as two years. Not one of his fourteen colleagues on the IBT executive board had the individual clout to dislodge him, and his internal influence remained such that almost no one was willing to try. A conspicuous exception was Vice-President John B. Backhus of Philadelphia, who was now publicly calling for his resignation because "he's done too much damage to the union's reputation," but Backhus, while undoubtedly reflecting the private views of many other executive board members, seemed to be standing alone. Even if the board did muster the ten votes that would be needed to oust the twice-convicted chief executive, moreover, Hoffa could still under the union's constitution appeal the action to the next Teamster convention, which would not be held until 1966.

There was essentially nothing beyond this single comforting consideration, however, to cheer Hoffa up now. In fact, the realistic unionist recognized that it was entirely possible that new charges would be filed against him by the Justice Department. The Get Hoffa Squad had still only tentatively gotten Hoffa, and it would presumably continue to pull out all the stops that it could until its quarry was actually behind bars. Attorney General Kennedy was said to be seriously thinking of bringing him to trial again on the old charge of accepting illegal payments from Commercial Carriers,

Inc. that had led to the hung jury in Nashville. Rumors were circulating that a federal grand jury in New Orleans would soon be indicting him for allegedly trying to bribe an official of the National Labor Relations Board. It was known that the Internal Revenue Service was continuing to go over his old federal tax returns with a fine-tooth comb. And he now might need money more than ever: 452 Philadelphia-area Teamster rank and filers, on the heels of the Chicago conviction, had filed suit to recover all of the hundreds of thousands of dollars already paid from the Teamster treasury to defend Hoffa and other IBT officials. In a career marked by personal problems, Hoffa had never before had to contend simultaneously with as many.

At least Judge Austin's exact sentence for Hoffa, when it was announced on August 17, was far from the maximum that could have been meted out by the jurist. The head of the IBT received five years in prison on each of the four counts, as well as a $10,000 fine, but Austin mandated that the four terms would run concurrently. Hoffa would also be eligible for probation at the discretion of the federal parole authorities and consequently could, leaving aside his appealed eight-year jury-tampering penalty, be out of jail in perhaps as little as two years.

There was no doubt in the judge's mind, however, that prison was the right place for America's best-known labor leader. In a sentencing statement that was less elaborate than the one made by Judge Wilson five months earlier in Chattanooga but no less graphic, Austin asserted, "This court is one that believes that the sound of the clanging jailhouse door has a salutary effect on the defendant and the community. This may be an old fashioned idea, but it is one that I hold."

On Friday evening, October 22, 1965, a lavish $100-a-plate testimonial dinner was held in the ballroom of New York City's Americana Hotel. The sixteen hundred guests, most of whom arrived in time to attend a preliminary smorgasbord reception and partake of an open bar, had a choice of rolled filet of salmon or prime ribs of beef (thick cut) as their entree, and could conclude the meal with baked Alaska and petit fours. They also received a copy of an ornate printed program, whose gold-lettered cover announced the name of the person who was being honored by the affair: James R. Hoffa.

The speakers were anything but sparing in their praise of the general president. Cecil B. Moore, president of the National Association for the Advancement of Colored People's Philadelphia chapter, after lauding Hoffa for what he had done to help blacks in that city, said of the honoree, "He's just about like Jesus Christ who died on the Cross. Bobby Kennedy was on one side, some informers from the teamsters on the other." Dinner chairman Thomas E. Flynn, director of the Eastern Conference of Teamsters, made a similar analogy: "He's been crucified. His troubles are nothing but a vendetta from top to bottom." New York Teamster leader John J. O'Rourke, intending also to pay a high compliment, told the enthusiastic crowd that the IBT had grown enormously "because General President James Hoffa is somewhat of a business agent."[14] Tony Provenzano extolled the virtues of his friend. And a delighted Hoffa, for whom the thirteen-piece band played "Hey, Look Me Over" as he walked to his seat at the head table, received both a lengthy standing ovation and the $150,000 proceeds of the dinner (some of the guests had received complimentary tickets).

O'Rourke, in presenting his union president with the money, had announced that Hoffa could use it as he wished, "perhaps as a gift to some charitable institution."[15] There was little question, however, as to where the money would actually go. If, in happier times less than ten years earlier, the proceeds of another Hoffa testimonial dinner had helped to build the James R. Hoffa Children's Home of Jerusalem, this time charity would begin at home. The $150,000 would go to Hoffa himself, to finance his mounting legal expenses.

The union had, in fact, in recent weeks scheduled several such dinners to help its president out. A Detroit dinner was canceled after its sponsors decided that they could not, under the Taft-Hartley Act, take money from employers with whom the Teamsters had labor contracts, but Hoffa subscription dinners were planned for Chicago, San Francisco, and two or three other large cities. The several hundreds of thousands of dollars that were contemplated would go a long way toward getting Hoffa out of the bind in which the continuing unavailability of the IBT treasury to his legal defense projects had placed him. He was currently, he freely said, paying for his ongoing appeals by the not altogether satisfactory method of personally borrowing the money.

So far, these appeals had not been going well for him. Three requests for a new jury-tampering trial had been quickly denied by the courts. One of these had been based partly on the testimony of bellhops that they had seen "a lot of drinking going on" among the jurors in Chattanooga. A second new trial request had featured a Hoffa charge that the government had planted a spy in the offices of one of his lawyers. A third contended not only that the government had provided prostitutes for some of the Chattanooga jurors but that Judge Wilson had told one of these prostitutes that he was going to "get" Hoffa (Wilson, in a bristling, ten-page statement, had denied the hooker's affidavit as a "complete and total fabrication and fraud"). And recently, in a unanimous decision, the U.S. Sixth Circuit Court of Appeals had affirmed the jury-tampering sentence: the three appellate judges here, announcing their opinion, had flatly stated that they had found no errors affecting Hoffa's "substantial rights."

The U.S. Supreme Court now remained the Teamster president's sole realistic hope for reversing this first of his two convictions. If the High Court declined to review the Sixth Circuit Court action, as was expected, only the quite unlikely granting to Hoffa of a rehearing on grounds more convincing to the judiciary than the ones already offered would keep him out of jail. Meanwhile, the appeal in his fraud case remained pending at the circuit court of appeals level.

His notoriety was not proving to be good for Teamster business, either. There had been some recruitment of new members, about twenty-five thousand of them over the past year. But the international was at this point spending almost $3 million annually on organizing, and in the light of this hefty investment the payoff was not especially impressive. Some of the lack of success, certainly, could be attributed to the handbills and other communications from target employers, reminding their workers that Hoffa "faces thirteen years behind prison walls" and asking, "Do you want to put your fate in the hands of people like this?"

Worst of all for Hoffa, he was already being written off within the union by many IBT officials. The executive board had officially (and sincerely) pledged that he could keep his presidency until such time as all of his appeals were exhausted. But this process was now expected to terminate reasonably soon in imprisonment for Hoffa, and behind-the-scenes jockeying for his job had become embarrassingly visible. Western Conference leader Einar Mohn was openly campaigning for the presidency "should Jim be unavailable," and supporters of Vice-President Harold Gibbons were aggressively trying to advance the prospects of their man, on the same not-so-subtle basis.

The paeans of praise at the Americana Hotel notwithstanding, Hoffa was clearly a man on the rocks. He would continue to occupy such a precarious position unless his convictions—both of them—were reversed, and no new ones were forthcoming.

He got some sort of reprieve on January 31, 1966, however, when the Supreme Court unexpectedly did agree to review his jury-tampering conviction. It would be only a limited review, confined strictly to determining whether or not Edward Partin's testimony should have been admitted in evidence, and would not delve into any of the twenty other points that the general president and his lawyers had requested the justices to ponder. But it nonetheless gave the Hoffa camp new hope. If the High Court could be swayed to the Hoffa position that the presence of the governmentally-paid-and-placed informer Partin violated Hoffa's Fourth Amendment protection against unreasonable search and seizure, and/or Fifth Amendment privilege against self-incrimination, and/or Sixth Amendment guarantee to the right to counsel, Hoffa could be home free.

And, at the very least, Hoffa was now virtually guaranteed something that prior to January 31 he was not really entitled to expect at all: reelection to the IBT presidency at the union's upcoming convention at Miami Beach in July. It would presumably take at least until the fall for the Court case to be decided.

He would certainly run for reelection, he immediately told reporters, and—in language clearly meant to abort any Mohn or Gibbons boomlets—he said that he did not "expect any opposition." He also hinted broadly that he would ask the convention to change the union's bylaws so that he could personally name an acting president should he be jailed.

That he would get whatever he requested of the Miami delegates was a foregone conclusion. He had derived considerable pride, during the dark days in both Nashville and Chattanooga, when truck drivers had pulled up to him as he walked down the street and yelled, "Hi, Jimmy. We're with you all the way" from the cabs of their vehicles. There had been many such occasions, and he had taken the frequency as a solid barometer of his popularity just as he did now when big tractor-trailers pulled up in front of the marble palace in Washington and their drivers, invariably without an appointment, asked the receptionist if they could personally convey their best wishes to the general president; when he was in town, he always made himself available. All of his troubles notwithstanding, he continued to receive enthusiastic support from his Teamsters. In 1966, no less than in previous years, the hold that he exercised over his immense union was all but total. When he was almost anyplace within the domain of the 1.6-million-member labor organization, he was among rabid partisans.

Equally notable was the almost total absence of membership *anti*-Hoffa sentiment, a continuing source of satisfaction to the IBT president. A Midwestern building and construction trades labor leader who over his long career met literally thousands of Hoffa's constituents recently observed, "I never heard a rank and file Teamster say anything bad about Jimmy," and these words could be restated by many other disinterested viewers.

Other leaders might find it awkward to discuss, even obliquely, their legal problems. Hoffa was so politically secure that he could flaunt his, as he did in Detroit, to the thunderous applause of his membership, a week after the Supreme Court announcement: "I hope you never experience the turmoil, the torture that goes with an indictment . . . [or the] long, anxious hours that go with a trial. . . . I have lived that road with my family for nine long years [but] I would not surrender. We will continue the fight, continue the struggle . . . no matter how bad it becomes."[16]

He decided not even to wait for the July 4 opening of the convention to endorse the person who would succeed him if he vacated the presidency. On May 3, he announced that his preference for the new office of general vice-president, the mechanism through which his hand-picked successor would ascend to the top job, was an old friend: Frank E. Fitzsimmons, Detroit Local 299 vice-president and (since 1961, when Hoffa elevated him to an international vice-presidency upon Owen Bert Brennan's death) one of the thirteen international vice-presidents as well.

He could have made a more popular choice. A bland and plodding if affable lieutenant, Fitzsimmons had for years been regarded by those who saw him in action either in Detroit or at executive board meetings as a man who held his jobs solely because of his close relationship to Hoffa. When in Hoffa's presence, he was seen as very much of a gofer, an "errand boy for Jimmy" (as many observers described him). His most significant contributions to a meeting were typically the pouring of coffee and the distribution of sandwiches to those in attendance. He would quite probably have won a contest for "least respected of all executive board members" hands down if such a competition had been conducted.

When operating on his own, Fitzsimmons was even less impressive. A prominent Detroit newspaperman remembers him as "unbelievably stupid. . . . My strongest memories of him are of his smoking non-union Camel cigarettes hidden in an alligator skin case, and my interviewing him in his office one morning at about 11 A.M., when he ate bon-bons in my face and poured himself a glass of whiskey without offering me anything. I don't think I got one page's worth of usable notes from the whole interview." As a speaker, Hoffa's heir apparent was also, almost invariably, a complete bust: he could, as a member of his union once said of him, "empty a hall in nothing flat," and he tended to be described in such less than flattering terms as "tangle-tongued."

But Fitzsimmons offered Hoffa something that more than compensated for his weaknesses: total, unquestioning loyalty. With the exception only of Tony Provenzano, there was probably no one else on the executive board of whom this could be said at this point. Even Gibbons, as of November 22, 1963, could no longer be counted upon to support the general president in all situations. Many of the eleven other board members would disavow Hoffa's fully centralized and highly personalized system of governance in a second if they could, in favor of what they saw as a better alternative for themselves. But there was no better alternative: considerations of Hoffa's huge popularity with their own constituents and the inability of any single board member except Hoffa to command much allegiance from his board colleagues would have made such a disavowal of the general president foolhardy, as all of the executive board members fully recognized.

With Fitzsimmons, it was a different story. The devoted Fitz could be relied upon to keep the presidential seat warm for his fellow Detroiter should Hoffa go to jail. Even better, his compliant personality might actually allow Hoffa to run the Teamsters himself from prison through a messenger system. Such an absentee management would not be unprecedented, either, as Hoffa well recognized: Joey Fay of the Operating Engineers continued to lead his union unofficially after he went to Sing Sing for extortion in 1947; and, as the Jameses could report in their 1965 book, Fay was "one of Hoffa's idols . . . Hoffa enjoys pointing out that Fay continued to make crucial decisions from prison, and clearly conceives of this as a possibility for himself, as well."[17] Fitzsimmons would carry out a Hoffa command to award an employer economic relief or pour more union funds into the organization of agricultural processing workers every bit as faithfully as he had implemented the coffee and sandwich orders.

Hoffa did not publicly admit that he harbored these thoughts, of course. On the contrary, he insisted to the media people who pressed him hard on this plan for a caretaker administration that Fitzsimmons would not be a "fill-in" at all: "When the general vice president becomes president, he becomes president in fact." But the words fooled absolutely no one—least of all Gibbons and Mohn. Both of the latter vice-presidents quickly recognized reality and shelved their initial intentions of challenging Fitzsimmons at the convention for the general vice-presidency. Both would have beaten the Local 299 vice-persident handily in a race pitting their delegate support against that of Hoffa's gofer. But neither of them, nor anyone else, could expect remotely to prevent Hoffa himself from getting everything that he wanted—Fitzsimmons as the Number Two Teamster included—at Miami Beach.

"The most amazing fact about the whole convention," was, indeed, as *Time* magazine's correspondent at the Florida July 1966 gathering put it, "that Jimmy Hoffa continued, despite everything, to exert his iron hold on the Teamsters."[18] From the Fourth of July opening session moment that Vice-President Murray Miller introduced him as "the greatest Yankee Doodle of them all," to the banging of the closing gavel four days later, Hoffa dominated the two thousand delegates as completely as he had, in this same city, in 1961.

Testimonials to his hold on his audience abounded. He was not likened to Jesus this time, but one speaker described him as the most important American since George Washington. Secretary-treasurer John English received almost deafening foot-stomping applause when he said of Hoffa, "He says he's not guilty and I say he's not guilty and the executive board says he's not guilty. Come what may, we don't care. The hell with everybody!" Sales of a recorded song called "Hoffa's Blues" in the lobby outside the convention hall were brisk. And a sandwich named "The Jimmy Hoffa," consisting of roast beef, mustard, sauerkraut, chopped olives, and swiss cheese was also in considerable demand (although here it is possible, of course, that people simply preferred the ingredients in this offering to those in the relatively few other sandwich alternatives and that they might even have devoured "The Edward Grady Partin" if it were on the menu and sufficiently attractive).

The feistiness that had always been so much a part of Hoffa's appeal to the membership was no less in evidence this time, either. "To hell with our enemies," he shouted in a keynote address that attacked, in particular, "stupid reporters" who were writing "filth, lies and garbage" about the union. Looking directly into the press section beside his rostrum, he thundered, "You are overpaid for the filth you write about labor. You shouldn't have the right to cover a labor convention." The delegates started to chant, "Throw them out."

The IBT chief executive was rewarded by more than a chant when he elaborated on these opinions about the fourth estate. He got a standing ovation when he asserted that the members of the Teamsters Union, and not journalists, were the only ones qualified to judge "whether or not I am a fit person to run this international union." Whatever private thoughts may have been harbored, the official verdict in Hoffa's favor was unanimous.

And, speaking even more loudly than the words, were dozens of convention actions that gave the fiery Teamster leader absolutely everything that he had wanted. The most highly paid labor leader in the United States received a $25,000 raise, to $100,000 a year. He got, with exactly one delegate being recorded as opposed to the move, convention approval for the legal defense of union officials, most obviously Hoffa himself (assuming that the pending suit being brought by the Philadelphia rank and filers was satisfactorily resolved). An amendment raising minimum monthly membership dues from $5 to $6 was overwhelmingly approved. Hoffa received comprehensive new authority to establish local union contract terms. He would henceforth be allowed to determine the format for negotiations and to name whomever he wanted to the union bargaining teams. And, to the surprise of no one, Frank E. Fitzsimmons was unanimously elected to the new position which placed him first in the line of succession.

No union president had ever been granted quite as much by a duly constituted convention. If this was Hoffa's last hurrah, he was at least going out in style.

On October 4, 1966, by a two-to-one vote, the U.S. Circuit Court of Appeals in Chicago upheld the Teamster president's fraud and conspiracy conviction. It also sustained the convictions of Hoffa's codefendants in the case.

Writing the majority opinion, Judge F. Ryan Duffy rejected two defense contentions, that (1) adverse publicity and "public clashes" between Hoffa and Robert F. Kennedy (now Senator Robert F. Kennedy, Democrat of New York) had prevented Hoffa from getting a fair trial, and (2) the pension fund had lost no money at all on the loans involved.

"Whenever any person of prominence is charged with a crime," the judge declared rather matter-of-factly, "the story usually will receive wide distribution through various news media. . . . The fact that a juror may have read newspaper accounts or heard comments on radio and television relative to a criminal charge is alone not sufficient ground for excusing a prospective juror." As for the no-loss-on-the-loans claim, "Due to the long-term nature of the loans and fact that subsequent loans were made to refinance earlier loans, it was impossible to ascertain with certainty whether or not a loss occurred. In any event, it is well established that actual loss isn't an essential element of the crime."

The minority of one was not happy with his two colleagues. In his dissent, Judge Luther M. Swygert stated that "a number of trial errors independently require reversal of convictions of all defendants." In Swygert's opinion, the prosecution's case "sustained neither a single scheme to defraud the Teamsters pension fund as charged in the indictment, nor a single overall conspiracy to violate the mail fraud statute as alleged. There was a fatal variance between the charges and the proof. . . . Much irrelevant prejudicial evidence was submitted to the jury." In fact, said Swygert, a study of the record convinced him that the prosecution had intentionally charged "a sprawling, amorphous scheme and conspiracy, in order to allow the presentation of a mass of immaterial, prejudicial evidence."

Within a month, an appeal of the appellate court verdict was filed with the U.S. Supreme Court, which had recently heard oral arguments in the jury-tampering case. The new appeal was based on two grounds. One, essentially, was the reasoning articulated by Judge Swygert in his dissenting opinion. The other one, which did not lack for imagination, was a defense contention that the Justice Department had improperly juggled the scheduling of Hoffa's fraud and conspiracy trial so that it took place a mere six weeks after the Teamster president had been convicted for jury tampering. The goal on the prosecution's part in taking this latter action, the defense argued, was to bias the Chicago jurors against Hoffa and make them more amenable to convicting him a second time. And this was particularly unfair to the defendant, in the eyes of Hoffa's lawyers, because the alleged pension fund incidents took place long before, and not after, the jury-tampering activities. Therefore, if the Court were to overturn the jury-tampering conviction, it must necessarily reverse the fraud and conspiracy conviction.

The jury-tampering oral arguments that were presented to the Supreme Court on behalf of Hoffa by Joseph A. Fanelli, another member of the seemingly limitless stable of Hoffa attorneys, were heard by only seven of the nine justices. Justice Byron R. White had disqualified himself because he had been Robert Kennedy's deputy attorney general in 1962; Justice Abe Fortas had bowed out because his former law firm had once represented several Virginia Teamsters in a suit against Hoffa. The remaining judges, like all other people who sat in the filled courtroom on October 13, listened to a dramatic presentation by Fanelli that focused exclusively, as the Court had earlier directed, on the issue of whether or not Edward Grady

Partin's role as an informer had violated Hoffa's constitutional rights to privacy and counsel and against self-incrimination.

To Fanelli, who began by pointing out that "the opening scene, starting in late 1962, finds Partin in a Baton Rouge jail facing charges of kidnapping, manslaughter, embezzlement and forgery," there was no question that Partin's role had done so. The government, the attorney said with some passion, had planted Partin in Hoffa's Nashville camp as a paid agent, a "spy." In return for providing reports on the IBT leader on an almost daily basis to the Get Hoffa Squad, Partin had been treated so leniently by the government that in the four years that had now elapsed since he first volunteered to spy on Hoffa, not one of the serious charges pending in 1962 had been pressed. Hoffa was constitutionally entitled to protection from such treatment, and the fact that he did not receive this protection made a travesty of the process of justice.

With equal fervor, Assistant Attorney General Fred M. Vinson, Jr., asserted to the justices that the government had throughout merely taken "reasonable steps" to protect the integrity of the Nashville jury. Partin, he declared, had been specifically instructed not to relay any defense plans that he might learn. Moreover, he argued, it had been Hoffa himself who had originally invited Partin to come to Nashville.

But many who left the High Court building following the summations of both sides, including Walter Sheridan and other members of the Get Hoffa Squad, were by no means convinced at this point that the Justice Department's position would be sustained when the seven judges rendered their decision.

Nor did those who had been present in the courtroom to hear the oral arguments by any means stand alone. Hoffa now had not one but three hopes of reversing the Nashville conviction: if a majority of the justices found that even one of the three constitutional rights alleged by his lawyers to have been violated by Partin's intrusion had been actually infringed upon, the head of the Teamsters would yet one more time emerge from an indictment unscathed. In recognition of this fact, indeed, a new consensus seemed to be emerging among Hoffa watchers, especially Hoffa watchers who were also members of the bar: as former federal prosecutor Robert M. Cipes crisply put it in an article published in the *Atlantic Monthly* in November 1966, "When the appeal is discussed in legal circles, the usual question is not whether Hoffa will win, but how he will win."[19] Within the Teamsters Union, too, a heavy majority of both rank-and-file members and officers was convinced that Hoffa's long run of luck would continue and that the case would be dismissed.

The Supreme Court's announcement, on December 12, that it was affirming the jury-tampering conviction and eight-year prison sentence, consequently took many people by surprise. Four justices—Potter Stewart, Hugo L. Black, William J. Brennan, Jr., and John M. Harlan—joined in the majority opinion, written by Stewart. It held that Partin had entered the Hoffa hotel suite on Hoffa's invitation and that Hoffa had relied upon "misplaced confidence that Partin would not reveal his wrongdoing." There was nothing in the Constitution protecting people against such "misplaced confidence," the opinion added. Nor, it said, was the legal employment of informers anything new: "Courts have countenanced the use of informers from time immemorial." Two other justices, William O. Douglas and Tom C. Clark, asserted that the Court lacked jurisdiction to hear the Hoffa appeal in the first place, making a total of six Court members who were opposed to reversing the Chattanooga conviction.

Only Chief Justice Earl Warren dissented. Fourteen years earlier, as Governor of California welcoming the Teamsters to their international convention in Los Angeles, he had been positively effusive in his praise of the IBT. The union was, he had declared then, "not only something great of itself, but splendidly representative of the entire labor movement."[20] Now, while he presumably did not still harbor the same thoughts about the Teamsters, he sided with the present head of the organization in an opinion that made up in vigor what it lacked in colleague support:

Here the government reaches into the jailhouse to employ a man who was himself facing indictments far more serious (and later including one for perjury) than the one confronting the man against whom he offered to inform. It employed him not for the purpose of testifying to something that had already happened, but, rather, for the purpose of infiltration, to see if crimes would in the future be committed. The government in its zeal even assisted him in gaining a position from which he could be a witness to the confidential relationship of attorney and client engaged in the preparation of a criminal defense. . . . I cannot agree that what happened in this case is in keeping with the standards of justice in our federal system.

Hoffa still would not go to jail immediately. Technical appeals would delay the event for several weeks and possibly months— enough time, almost certainly, for him to participate in the national trucking contract negotiations that were scheduled to begin on January 17. Some of his more rabid supporters even dared to hope that the conviction would still be set aside on the grounds that the government had used illegal wiretapping and eavesdropping devices to gather evidence in the case: attorney William E. Bufalino, in the name of the "Friends of James R. Hoffa Committee," immediately announced that a $100,000 reward awaited anyone who came forward with proof that this had happened, and the publisher of New Hampshire's *Manchester Union-Leader* newspaper (perhaps not entirely coincidentally, the recipient of a $2 million loan from the Central States Pension Fund eighteen months earlier) offered another $100,000. Others thought that the fertile collective imagination of the Teamsters Bar Association might find other ways of gaining for Hoffa yet one more day in court, possibly through a rehearing of the key argument that Partin's testimony should never have been admitted in the case: they took heart from Justice Warren's words.

But such optimism in the Hoffa camp was as uncommon as it was unrealistic. Far more typical now was the opinion of a Detroit Local 299 truck driver who, explaining why he had joined some two thousand of his colleagues in staging a surprise sympathy "holiday" to protest the High Court decision, pointed out that the contract let him take a day off for a funeral—and that this was a funeral, to honor a man who was "dying." It was widely acknowledged, even—privately—by Hoffa himself, that a long string had finally come to an end.

The prosecutorial methods that had nailed the head of the Teamsters after so many years may have been, as the editors of the *New York Times* (quoting Warren with approval) believed that they were, "offensive to the fair administration of justice."[21] The Supreme Court's decision may have overlooked what Justice Douglas in another case had called "the need to make as sure as it is humanly possible that one after whom the mob and public passions are in full pursuit is treated fairly," as the editors of the *Nation* were quite convinced that it had.[22] And Victor S. Navasky may well be correct in arguing that there was something fundamentally improper about the creation of the Get Hoffa Squad in the first place: "There comes a point," he has contended, "at which the disproportionate allocation of men, money and time moves from a matter of quantity to a matter of quality, from prosecution to persecution."[23] Hoffa had, of course, frequently offered the same opinion, if less articulately.

But a jury of his peers had found Hoffa guilty, and the appellate process had now been essentially exhausted. Even before any final judicial verdict was rendered in the pension fund case, the only real unknown after December 12, 1966, was the exact date on which the jailhouse door would clang behind America's most powerful labor leader.

It was, nonetheless, business as usual as the triennial national trucking negotiations opened in mid-January, in the ballroom of the Washington Hilton Hotel. One supremely self-confident figure thoroughly dominated both sides of the bargaining table. As a newsman who was present summarized the situation,

Mr. Hoffa told employer and union officials where they would sit and how the session would proceed. He read an 86-page document of master contract proposals, identifying the specific problem each was designed to overcome. He chastised the operators for supposed shortcomings in treatment of employees, calling each of the employers by their first names as they stood to respond to his questions (they called him "Mr. Hoffa" and "Mr. Chairman," usually with a "sir"). He further told them how future bargaining sessions would be conducted. Power was clearly talking and the employers knew it.[24]

At one point, according to another report, Hoffa snapped at the chief negotiator for the major employer group, "You are so wrong it's almost impossible to believe your statement."[25] At many junctures, he made it clear that he would accept no back talk. He had already personally communicated with every employer of any size, he said, and what he was proposing—increases of about 5 percent in each of the three years—was eminently affordable by the companies (after being allowed to raise their rates by the Interstate Commerce Commission) and fair to both sides. He would never consider a national strike, only selective ones against individual, unnamed companies. But he insisted that all of the employer groups be represented at the table: the fact that the major employer association wanted to exclude the others because the latter groups were seen as friendlier to him and thus usable by him in a "divide and conquer" strategy meant nothing to him. Everyone had come to Washington to negotiate a new national contract ("my life's work," Hoffa called it once), and only if all companies that had signed the 1964 agreement were parties to this new one could such a result be effected. It was a performance that was both familiar and impressive.

The employer representation issue was resolved after a one-week deadlock. It was agreed that an "observer" representing the carriers outside the major group could sit in on the negotiations, thereby allowing Hoffa both the leverage and the national coverage that he had demanded. The "observer" was obligated to "speak through" the major group, and the latter could consequently also claim a victory of sorts, but it was generally concluded that, one more time, Hoffa had gotten his way.

On the other hand, the general president also received a rare rebuff in these negotiations. The major industry group, now tempted to take its chances bargaining with the genial and low-powered Fitzsimmons rather than continue across the table from the increasingly abusive Hoffa, refused to join the union in a petition to the Justice Department to delay Hoffa's imprisonment until the negotiations were over. The refusal was conveyed at an early bargaining session. Many people who were present felt that it made the head Teamster thenceforth even more testy and insulting than he had been: at one point, the level of invective was such that the management negotiators walked out and did not return to the table for several days. But others attributed Hoffa's snappishness strictly to the imminence of his jailing, with or without a short postponement.

The $200,000 reward aggregatively offered by the "Friends of James R. Hoffa Committee" and the *Manchester Union-Leader* did produce one result. Benjamin David (Bud) Nichols, a Tennessee specialist in electronic gadgetry, came forward and swore in an affidavit that he had been paid $1,684 by the Get Hoffa Squad's Walter Sheridan to eavesdrop during the Chattanooga trial not only on Hoffa and his lawyers but also on the jury members. At Sheridan's instructions, he had, he said, placed four microphone "bugs" and tapped six telephone lines in the Patten Hotel rooms of the Teamster president and his attorneys. He also claimed that he had inserted tiny transmitters under the hotel room mattresses of the sequestered jurors.

In mid-February, Hoffa's lawyers, hoping for the best, sent the Nichols affidavit and a variety of supplemental materials charging illegal governmental spying to the Supreme Court. Sheridan denied everything, asserting that he had never so much as met Nichols. Solicitor General Thurgood Marshall, on behalf of the prosecution, wrote the Court in a separate memorandum that a thorough, recent review of the Hoffa case by the Justice Department had turned up no support whatsoever for the Nichols story.

On February 27, the Court responded to the spying charge by refusing, without comment, to reconsider its December decision. Consistent with its normal practice in such situations, it immediately mailed this finding to the district court judge who had originally rendered judgment in the case, Frank W. Wilson of Chattanooga. Wilson would now determine the exact schedule for Hoffa's jailing.

While the Tennessee jurist was weighing these logistics, Hoffa had an unexpected visitor: the hot-headed and very tough leader of the Teamsters in Puerto Rico, Frank Chavez, whose hatred for both John F. Kennedy and Robert F. Kennedy was legendary. Chavez, in early 1964, had written a letter to the grieving younger brother of the slain president that was notable for its lack of subtlety:

Sir:

This is for your information.

The undersigned is going to solicit from the membership of our union that each one donate whatever they can afford to maintain, clean, beautify and supply with flowers the grave of Lee Harvey Oswald.

You can rest assured contributions will be unanimous.

Sincerely,

Frank Chavez

Teamsters Local 901[26]

And in the fall of 1964 he had come to New York City with the intention of killing the now-U.S. Senatorial candidate Robert Kennedy because of Kennedy's treatment of Hoffa. He had been talked out of his homicidal plan on that occasion at the last minute by friends.

On March 1, 1967, however, Chavez resumed his effort and arrived at the Teamsters Building in Washington with his two permanent bodyguards, all three men armed with pistols. This second time, Hoffa himself aborted the Chavez project—according to an informed report, by pleading with the Puerto Rican to "give me that goddamn gun . . . the last thing we need is another investigation."[27] Chavez, who was so intimidating to many merchants that they never even asked him to pay his bills, did surrender the weapon to his superior and returned to Puerto Rico. A few months later, he was shot to death by one of the two bodyguards under circumstances that have never been satisfactorily explained. (Hoffa's immediate reaction to this murder was very different from his response to the John F. Kennedy assassination: within minutes of hearing the news, he relayed a message to a key aide to "go to Puerto Rico and take care of the Chavez family.") It is a further interesting footnote to history that Chavez, the avowed admirer of Lee Harvey Oswald, also knew Jack Ruby, the man who killed Oswald ostensibly because of his intense admiration for John F. Kennedy.

Hoffa's attorneys made two last attempts to stave off their client's imprisonment. They asked Judge Wilson to extend bail while they filed additional motions on Hoffa's behalf. The judge refused, pointing out that if he acceded to this request, Hoffa could stay free almost indefinitely, since the motions could be filed more or less forever. The lawyers also made the same request of Wilson that Hoffa had asked the trucking companies to join him in making to the Justice Department, that the labor leader not have to go to jail until the national negotiations were concluded. Wilson replied in the negative here, too: he acknowledged that Hoffa had "large responsibilities," but the greatest of the defendant's responsibilities, said the man who had found that Hoffa had "tampered, really, with the very soul of this nation," was his responsibility "unto the orderly process of justice."

Hoffa, Judge Wilson thereupon announced, would have to surrender to a U.S. marshal on March 7 at 9 A.M., to be taken directly at that point to a federal prison.

No. 33-298 NE

13

At 8:51 A.M. on Tuesday, March 7, 1967—appropriately, a gloomy and drizzly day—Jimmy Hoffa got out of a black Lincoln Continental in front of the U.S. Courthouse in Washington, D.C., to be taken into custody.

The small, informal farewell dinners that he and Josephine had hosted each night over the past week for old friends—the Allen Dorfmans, the Frank Fitzsimmonses, and others to whom the Hoffas felt particularly close—were now over. And so was a brief period of intense personal anguish. "The last couple of weeks before [Hoffa] went to jail were hellish," says a Teamster staffer who was with him constantly during this time. "He was on the verge of a nervous breakdown. He would lie on the floor and yell, 'I'm not gonna go!'" (The staffer, who thinks that he too almost had a breakdown because of the imminency of his boss's imprisonment, went home after Hoffa arrived at the Courthouse and stayed in bed for two weeks.)

At 8:20 A.M. on March 7, the doorman at Hoffa's apartment house had telephoned up to the building's most famous resident with a warning and a suggestion. The warning was that a swarm of reporters was awaiting Hoffa in the lobby; the suggestion was that the Teamster leader avoid meeting these interviewers by leaving through a back entrance. But Hoffa had spurned this advice with thanks: "No; they have an assignment to complete, the same as me." And, holding the hand of his four-year-old granddaughter, he had tearfully walked to the main elevator and downstairs to the interrogation.

Similarly, he had turned down a like recommendation of Chuckie O'Brien and attorney Morris Shenker, who had then accompanied him to the federal building (he had wanted to spare his wife and children the ordeal and had convinced them not to come). They had urged that he avoid the expected large crowd of media people there by going around to the back door. And Hoffa had again, with characteristic fearlessness, declined: "I never ran away from anybody and I'll be damned if I'm gonna start now. Drive this son of a bitch right up to the front door."

Instead, shoulders slumping under his tan raincoat, he now told the assemblage of microphone and camera holders that had pressed in on him as soon as he had left the automobile: "I know you all have a job to do . . . for which I hope you're getting paid union wages, which I doubt if most of you are. You fellows with the mikes, get up here." And, standing in the cold rain, he offered an impromptu farewell statement: "This is a very unhappy day in my life . . . the Government has wire-tapped, room-bugged, surveilled and done everything unconstitutional it could do. . . . They have temporarily been able to do so. . . . I hope to be back."

His voice quivering a bit, he directed the rest of his remarks to his own members:

This will never be a weak union . . . remember this: None of the courts, none of the legislators understand your problems . . . only you, who work for a living . . . understand that.

I hope and trust that those who have been a part of this conspiracy will realize it's not just Hoffa they are doing this to. If they can do this to Hoffa they can do this to any citizen. . . .

I urge everyone to beware of the Constitutional rights they are losing. . . . That's all I have to say, gentlemen.[1]

He then, accompanied by four lawyers, entered the granite-faced building—the same one that he had been taken to a decade earlier by FBI agents on the John Cye Cheasty bribery charge—and shook hands with U.S. Marshal Luke C. Moore. Moore led the attorneys and Hoffa, now officially in custody, into the marshal's office to work out the final details for the incarceration.

Two hours later, the massive steel garage door at the back of the building opened and a dark blue Pontiac pulled out. It bore a glum-looking Hoffa in the back seat between two marshals—his raincoat on his lap hiding the handcuffs on his wrists and his legs firmly chained to the floor ("As if, for Christ's sake, I was John Dillinger or somebody," Hoffa said later. "I don't know where the hell they thought I was gonna run to").[2] The leader of the Teamsters leaned forward in the vehicle and spat vehemently against a closed window at Clark R. Mollenhoff, now the Washington correspondent for the *Des Moines Register and Tribune,* the same man who a decade earlier had convinced Bobby Kennedy that the Teamsters Union was a quarry well worth pursuing and thus the person who had started the long progression of events that had led to this day. (Mollenhoff, a 1958 Pulitzer Prize winner, is alleged by another former Hoffa aide to have told the latter in the mid-1960s, "If it weren't for Jimmy, I'd be out of a job.") And the Pontiac, as the lead car in a caravan of several government vehicles carrying marshals, began its 192-mile drive to the federal prison in Lewisburg, Pennsylvania, where Hoffa would serve his prison term.

Ironically, this entire humiliation for Hoffa—the shackling and chaining and the caravan, which he likened to a "capture scene from *Bonnie and Clyde*"—could have been avoided. As the IBT president was informed by the authorities only when it was too late, he could quite legally have exercised an option of reporting directly to Lewisburg on his own. Instead, as his son has observed with no attempt to hide his bitterness, "he became a media event."

In his first hours at the 943-acre complex of Italian Renaissance buildings known as the Lewisburg Penitentiary, Hoffa was photographed, fingerprinted, issued a regulation blue denim prison uniform, and assigned the prison number 33-298 NE. Also in complete keeping with prison custom, he was told by the admissions office of the behavior expected of him: "You will keep your person clean and neat and your bunk made each day. . . . You will get along with your fellow inmates and respond willingly and courteously to any directions that may be given to you by staff members. . . . You will conduct yourself at all times as a person who sincerely wishes to take his place in the free community as a morally responsible person." Following this, he was stripped, run through a delousing shower, and placed in isolation behind an iron door for twenty-four hours.

Hoffa's orientation schedule at the federal institution also contained meetings with psychologists, the prison chaplain, the chief correctional officer, and a variety of other staff specialists. And he took a battery of intelligence and general aptitude tests calling for such feats as fitting blocks together and placing pegs in holes, challenges that presumably gave him no trouble.

Lewisburg, a thirty-five-year-old "medium security" prison, was by no means the least desirable place to which No. 33-298 NE could have been sent. Its inmates ate at four-man tables in a relatively cheerful dining room. They could greet their visitors in a comfortable area decorated with paintings done by fellow prisoners while sitting on brightly painted chairs and at attractive modern tables. After completing their daily job assignments (for which they could earn as much as $70 monthly), they could partake of a wide choice of activities that included, in addition to television viewing (with movies on weekends as well), baseball, volleyball, tennis, weightlifting, leathercraft, painting, and academic classes. Or they could pursue a literary interest by drawing from the ample offerings of the large Lewisburg library or follow a more civic-minded path by participating in the prison chapter of the Junior Chamber of Commerce.

By other standards, too, the Lewisburg administration could be judged as progressive. It coordinated a growing number of rehabilitation programs, including one that allowed as many as thirty prisoners at a time to work in the small central Pennsylvania college town of Lewisburg. Each cell had radio earphones. The guards walked around completely unarmed.

On the other hand, Lewisburg was both crowded and dangerous. Constructed early in the Depression to hold 1,050 prisoners, it at this point bulged with just under 2,000 people of all kinds—double lifers, gunmen, safecrackers, forgers, arsonists—and space for any purpose was at a premium. Homosexuality was widespread, as were rapes, by both gangs and individuals. "No one has the foolhardiness to intercede in the rapes," Hoffa quickly observed, "because then they, too, would be punished for fighting. So you just sit there or lay on your bunk. Pretty soon the screams are over."

The food, sometimes maggot infested, was frequently inedible. Heroin and hashish, as well as most other kinds of drugs, were easily available, often brought in by the guards and sold to the inmates by them. Weapons were even more accessible, with the metal bunks that were furnished the prisoners providing all that was needed to fashion knives. ("And," as Hoffa was subsequently to say, "you'd sure as hell better have a knife to protect yourself if you're in your twenties because you're a prime target for rape.") Four prisoners were "shanked"—killed with a knife—during Hoffa's time there. There were two doctors, neither available after 4 P.M., for the entire prison population.

Hoffa's cell, too, was not one to cause envy. Seven and one-half feet in width and about ten feet long, it contained a cot, toilet facilities, a wooden chair, and a clothing locker that was two feet by one foot, leaving the energetic labor leader not much more than nine square feet in which to move around. One of a dozen such living quarters that fronted on a long corridor opening into a court-yard, the corridor windows made it relatively light and airy, and it was actually for this reason one of the prison's more sought-after cells. But to Hoffa, residing in it was tantamount to "being buried alive."

Nothing about Lewisburg, indeed, appealed to Hoffa. He saw his new address as a place marked by "bad guards, bad food, and bad everything" and was to say of the fifty-eight months that he spent there, "I can tell you this on a stack of Bibles: prisons are archaic, brutal, unregenerative, overcrowded hell holes where the inmates are treated like animals with absolutely not one humane thought given to what they are going to do once they are released. You're an animal in a cage and you're treated like one."[3] To old associate Larry Steinberg, he confided, "I'd have been better off if I'd killed somebody." One of his favorite expressions became, "Prison is hell on earth, only hell couldn't be this bad."

Little indignities were constantly inflicted on the man who for most of his adult life had known none at all. For most of his time at Lewisburg, he had to wear shoes that did not fit and pants that were both too long and too large. A bright light immediately out-side the door of his cell often kept him awake for hours, and when he finally did manage to fall asleep, he could count on being reawak-ened by a guard shining a flashlight in his face. He ultimately wore a special eyeshade to keep the light out. In the winter, snow from the corridor windows regularly blew into his place of confinement. Prison officials frequently brought their friends to the Hoffa cell simply to look at him, "as you'd look at a caged lion," as he put it. His basic job assignment, unstuffing old mattresses and then restuffing them, for forty hours each week, caused not only his hands but his nose (from the lint) to bleed on many occasions. Consistent with prison policy, his anus was invariably inspected for drugs before he was allowed to return from the visiting room.

Most of all, he missed his family. Despite his workaholic habits, he had always prided himself on being a family man first "and everything else second," and he surrounded himself in jail with photographs of Josephine, Barbara, Jim, his granddaughter Barbara Jo Crancer, and Jim's two boys, David and Geoffrey, both of whom he would have to wait to meet since they were born while he was in prison.

He was particularly concerned about his frail wife, who was taking his confinement very badly, and invariably concluded his letters to Barbara—living in St. Louis—with a request to "keep in touch with your mother." In the case of his lawyer son, the same desire was made known in person, since Jim came to Lewisburg weekly from Detroit not in the role of an immediate family member (who, under prison rules, could visit no more than three hours a month) but as an attorney (whose visits, so long as pending litigation was the only topic discussed, were basically unlimited).

For eminently practical reasons, Hoffa now officially designated Chuckie O'Brien as his "foster son." If family members could only see prisoners for three hours a month, no other nonlawyers could visit at all and No. 33-298 NE wanted as much liaison with the union that he still headed as he could get. O'Brien if a "family member" could help as a courier, relaying messages to the international headquarters. He could drive Josephine to Lewisburg once a month and perform other personal services for the man who had raised him. After three decades, accordingly, Sylvia Pigano's son was finally accorded an official status within the Hoffa family. The rules of prison visitation simply made it unwise not to make such a move.

Just before he went to prison, Hoffa had told his family, "I want you to forget about me." But nothing now gave him more happiness than Josephine's visits or those of his children, although his pleasure was patently tinged with no small amount of shame. He would not allow his daughter to bring Barbara Jo, even though small children were permitted, and on the relative few occasions when the family visits were not made known to him in advance he became very upset because he couldn't look his best.

For a man whose superabundance of energy had filled twenty-hour workdays, sometimes seven days a week, and taken him all over the country without the need for any justification to others, the loss of freedom was also especially jarring. "His frustration was not on the physical side: he could handle that," his son has observed. "It was on the mental side, at being caged up like a bird." But physically, too, the confinement had to be traumatic for Hoffa, who had rarely been able to sit still for more than a few minutes at a time and whose nervous vitality had regularly found an outlet in push-ups and other calisthenics, as well as in sheer work.

For all of this, Hoffa soon accepted his fate philosophically, buoyed by an ever-present belief that he would eventually return as Teamster leader. Officially he was still the general president, although his $100,000 annual salary had ceased when he went behind bars (replaced, for the duration of his prison stay, by a $48,000 annual living allowance for Josephine). With the time off for good behavior that he fully assumed he would receive, he felt that he would be back in time to accept reelection in person at the IBT's next convention in 1971.

Meanwhile, Fitzsimmons would hold down the fort. Fitz's many detractors might dismiss the general vice-president as an intellectual midget and a "peanut butter sandwich." But it was comforting to know that many months after the Hoffa incarceration Fitzsimmons remained so deferential that the nine-foot Hoffa mahogany desk in the Washington headquarters building continued to bear Hoffa's gold name plate, the Hoffa "Illegitimi non Carborundum" plaque, and Hoffa family photographs.

Hoffa's handpicked successor had implemented "suggestions" relayed to him by O'Brien and the various Teamster lawyers who had visited Lewisburg very well, too. True, Fitzsimmons had received much of the credit for the big package that had ultimately been extracted from the trucking companies in the 1967 national bargaining (at least 70 cents per hour over the three years, with a potential of 78 cents if inflation continued). But Hoffa had called many of Fitz's negotiation signals from jail, and Fitzsimmons was also conscientiously following Hoffa's orders regarding the awarding of Central States Pension Fund loans and other major matters.

The visitors to Lewisburg, indeed, regularly reported Hoffa as being "very cheerful" and "making the most out of his prison life" and the Lewisburg warden, Noah L. Aldrich, deemed him a model prisoner: "He is a very strong character . . . and has an excellent mental attitude. He gives us most courteous treatment, and we give him the same."[4] He appears to have asked for no special favors, something that his celebrity status might have impelled him to do, and he seems to have won for himself considerable respect from both his fellow inmates and the guards. His rapport with the latter was, indeed, such that more than once when he heard the guards complaining about working conditions, he offered to unionize them.

Hoffa was also quite popular with the other prisoners, and for good reason. Ever the labor leader, he formed and headed a committee that brought prisoner gripes directly to the attention of the warden (although, except in the case of a temporary improvement in the quality of the food and a permanent upgrading of the law library offerings, this mechanism apparently achieved little). He was the source of many jobs within the Teamsters Union and elsewhere for parolees, whose being paroled often depended on their having a job waiting for them: his son and other visitors rarely left the visiting room without a mandate to call some ranking member of the IBT hierarchy and "get this guy a job." He also helped less sophisticated prisoners prepare the legal briefs that might pave the way for their eventual release from Lewisburg. Each year, he sent one of his former Teamster assistants a considerable sum of money to buy Christmas cards to be sent to the families of his fellow prisoners. Once, when he learned that the dog of an inmate's child had died, he sent the child money for a replacement.

By every report, he seemed, in fact, to get along well with all segments of the heterogeneous Lewisburg convict population. Black Muslims, whose belligerence intimidated many other inmates (and with whom the completely unprejudiced Hoffa initially ran some definite risks by his free use of the word "nigger"), developed a high regard for him; he, in turn, was quite favorably impressed not only by their stress on physical conditioning but by their devotion to their religion. Morton Sobell, the World War II spy whose eighteen years in prison overlapped with Hoffa's first two years, was a fan of his; Sobell delighted in telling the story of how the IBT president on one occasion saw him scrutinizing a snapshot that had been taken of Sobell and his wife and asked, "What do you have there, Morty, blueprints?" Hoffa's four-man complaint committee included a former army major and a Puerto Rican, as well as a black. His friends included both highly literate white-collar inmates and illiterates.

To fill the many hours available to him each day after completion of his work in the prison mattress factory, Hoffa regularly worked out in the penitentiary gymnasium and took fast walks around a track in the prison yard. He also, as noted earlier, embarked on an ambitious reading program under the long-distance supervision of his daughter Barbara.

Hoffa had always been a conscientious peruser of newspapers, particularly the *New York Times,* the *Wall Street Journal,* and the Washington dailies. But with this exception, he had never made reading even a minor hobby. For years, the built-in bookshelves in his Detroit office had contained only a set of unused labor reference books and a 1912 congressional report on industrial relations, and his Washington office had been equally barren of reading material not directly related to his job. It was widely rumored that in his adulthood he had finished only a single book, Robert F. Kennedy's *The Enemy Within.* And Larry Steinberg claims that the Teamster president didn't even read *it,* but rather asked Steinberg to summarize Kennedy's chapters for him.

Now, he devoured the books that Barbara selected for him (each time sending not only a copy to her father but a second copy for permanent inclusion in the prison library): biographies of John L. Lewis, whom Hoffa had always greatly admired, and Eugene V. Debs, the Indiana-born socialist head of the American Railway Union, who had been jailed when he attacked America's entry into World War I because he considered it to be a wholly capitalistic war; a book by Drew Pearson about Washington, D.C.; books about John F. Kennedy; the latest Peter Drucker; *Future Shock; Hoover's F.B.I.; The New Centurions; The Greening of America; The Rise and Fall of the Third Reich.* All, at his request, were in the nonfiction category, and most were written about some aspect of America, by American authors. He wasn't much interested unless he could see some practical applicability.

His self-imposed regimen of exercise, combined with the involuntary dieting necessitated by the unattractiveness of the prison food, resulted in an even more practical benefit for the Teamster president. The mild diabetes that he had suffered in recent years and that had required him to visit a doctor every two weeks, with as little publicity as possible since he did not want this condition widely known, in short order vanished. With some bitterness, he later observed that the prison authorities had done him a favor in this area, "the only favor I can think of," because they had confiscated his diabetes pills and torn up an explanatory letter from his Washington, D.C., physician upon his admission to Lewisburg, forcing the chronically health-conscious Hoffa to become even more so. Nor was there any reappearance in prison of the bleeding ulcer that had required a brief hospitalization and the transfusion of eight pints of blood in early 1966 and had constituted Hoffa's only other known health problem. He was to emerge from prison, in his daughter's opinion, "trim, hard and tough. Prison might actually have saved his life physically."

No. 33-298 NE also cultivated three other interests, if minimally. After decades of conscientiously avoiding the practice of any religion, he apparently attended Lewisburg's Catholic chapel with some reasonable frequency, possibly in deference to Josephine's wishes. He became sufficiently interested in Hoffa family history to inform his son on more than one occasion that "there's a lot of Hoffas buried around here. You should go and check it out," although the busy young attorney—for whom the weekly airplane round trip from Detroit to Lewisburg (the last leg, from Williamsport, Pennsylvania, by automobile) was adventure enough—did not avail himself of this invitation. And he listened to the phonograph records that inmates were allowed to receive in addition to their books; Barbara sent him mostly classical music.

In prison, too, the nation's best-known labor leader found time to collaborate with journalist Donald I. Rogers in what was to be the first of two autobiographies, *The Trials of Jimmy Hoffa*. The book, published by the Henry Regnery Company in 1970, contains some valuable information, particularly about its subject's early years. But it presents a biased (if understandably so) view of Hoffa as a put-upon victim of a governmental vendetta. And it frequently puts language in Hoffa's mouth that even with the most willing suspension of disbelief no one who knew the Teamster boss can accept as genuine: Hoffa used words like "perforce," "dialectics" and "Herculean" about as often as he did "isoniazid" and "amethopterin."

There was also, of course, always the daily news—Hoffa's abiding avocation, which at times brought the imprisoned Teamster information that he found of more than passing interest. One such occasion took place some fifteen months after his incarceration, when he learned that his old adversary Robert F. Kennedy had been assassinated in Los Angeles while celebrating his California Democratic presidential primary victory over Eugene McCarthy.

Hoffa would later report his reaction to this June 1968 news as having been one of relative indifference: "I can't honestly say that I felt bad about it. Our vendetta had been too long and too strong. Over the years I'd come to hate him and yet when he got it I felt nothing."[5] It is more than possible, however, that the man who had reacted with such extreme rage to the Gibbons-Steinberg condolence efforts of November 22, 1963, felt somewhat more negative sentiments in this case: in one of his two autobiographies, Hoffa asserts of R.F.K., "Don't think I was the only one who hated him. I want it known that a hell of a lot of people felt the same way I did about him." Hoffa then goes on to quote with approval an article appearing one day after Kennedy's death in which the New York Senator is described with words like "demagogue," "greedy rich kid," "rude, arrogant and pushy" and also to cite Dwight D. Eisenhower's contemporary finding that Kennedy was "shallow, vain and untrustworthy." "If you think I pass these along with satisfaction," says Kennedy's best-known target here, "you're right."[6] (Not one to forgive and forget where Kennedy was concerned, Hoffa to the end in fact referred to Kennedy as a "creep" and a "vicious bastard who was out to get me at all costs.")

But other news from the outside world was not as welcome. Increasingly, as Hoffa languished in prison with his court appeals still pending but no particular grounds for optimism on them for at least the near future, Fitzsimmons was showing signs of wanting to keep the job to which he had been assigned only a care-taker's role.

It was now Fitz who was getting the $100,000 salary and almost unlimited expenses, after all, and not Hoffa. It was now Fitz-simmons who received the deference around the Teamsters marble palace, the White House dinner invitations, and the newspaper headlines. Hoffa no longer had a jet airplane at his disposal and institutional powers of the purse and patronage unrivaled by any other labor leader, but his replacement did. For the personally se-lected Hoffa stand-in, it was a lot better than pouring coffee and being the butt of Hoffa's abuse. Fitz was starting to make it known that he had decided that he liked the lifestyle and did not want to give it up.

The process of revelation was a slow one. Eight months after Hoffa went to prison, the *International Teamster,* always an accurate barometer of Teamster leadership positions, mentioned Hoffa's name no less than thirty-four times in its thirty-two pages and also included five Hoffa family member photographs: two each of the general president and Josephine, and one of the Hoffa children. For at least two years after March 1967, almost every *Teamster* issue, moreover, could be counted upon to offer at least one unabashedly pro-Hoffa feature ("Hoffa Nation's First Political Prisoner in Two Generations," "Hoffa Named One of 10 Greatest Living American Labor Leaders," "Eastern Conference Trade Divisions Reaffirm Support for Hoffa"). And considerable publicity was still being given by the publication to the "James R. Hoffa Scholarships," awarded annually to eight especially meritorious college-attending children of Teamsters "as a living tribute to the dedicated leadership of General President James R. Hoffa."

Furthermore, for months, Fitzsimmons continued to insist to James P. Hoffa and other Hoffa loyalists that he and the Teamster lawyers were doing everything that they could to expedite Hoffa's appeals in the fraud case and reopen the jury-tampering one. "Don't do anything, you'll only rock the boat," he told them after the Nixon administration took office in January 1969, "I'm taking care of it with [Attorney General John N.] Mitchell." More than once, he pulled out the keys to the general president's office and said to the son of his old friend, "I don't want these: Jimmy can have them." Publicly, there was no question where Fitz stood regarding the man who had put him where he was: "Jimmy Hoffa is my friend," he announced time and time again, to the reporters who regularly questioned him on the topic and at Teamster meetings around the country, "and if he is available in 1971, he will have my wholehearted support, as he always has had."

But as early as July 1967, the pudgy general vice-president started to telegraph his signals. He told a union executive board meeting in that month that unlike Hoffa, he neither could nor wanted to make all of the decisions, big and small, for the IBT. He intended to restore decentralization to the regional and local officials. It was proper, he said, to channel local problems through lower-level Teamsters. The vice-presidents, also, would henceforth have the authority over matters in their respective regions that they had lacked in recent years. But in return for such treatment, Fitzsimmons emotionally asserted, he expected loyalty. He had heard rumors that he was being bad-mouthed, he said, and even stories that the vice-presidents would soon try to replace him as acting Teamster chief executive. If anyone had any criticisms, he wanted to hear them now. The only comments forthcoming from the members of his audience were entirely complimentary to him.

Fitzsimmons was starting to make rather major personnel changes around the headquarters building, too. Konowe and Steinberg, both of whom had sublimated their feelings about November 22, 1963, and returned to pinch-hit for Hoffa in Hoffa's last preimprisonment months, were informed that they would no longer be welcomed in such a role when Fitzsimmons was away from Washington. Fitzsimmons's favorites—Ohio's "Big Bill" Presser, Murray W. "Dusty" Miller of the Southern Conference, and Eastern Conference director Thomas E. Flynn—received substantially enlarged duties. New presidential assistants who had never worked for Hoffa were now regular denizens of the general president's office.

And Fitz was striking out on his own in other ways. He joined scores of civil rights and liberal leaders in marching in the spring 1968 funeral procession for Dr. Martin Luther King, Jr., something that the politically conservative Hoffa (although he both knew and admired King) could never have brought himself to do. In July 1968, Fitzsimmons met with old Hoffa rival Walter Reuther of the United Automobile Workers to design a new labor federation. It would ultimately be named the Alliance for Labor Action and constitute a potential competitor to the AFL-CIO.

Perhaps none of this really meant anything. The administrator of the nation's largest union clearly had to make a myriad of decisions every day, and it could hardly be expected that every one of them would duplicate what Hoffa himself would have done. But Hoffa, as he was increasingly telling his visitors at Lewisburg as the weeks and months went on, was no longer as confident as he had been that he had picked the right man to keep his presidential seat warm.

On the other hand, another old Hoffa friend was fully living up to expectations during the general president's early prison tenure. Anthony Provenzano, the New Jersey Teamster leader and reputed Genovese family captain, had preceded Hoffa to Lewisburg by ten months, having been incarcerated there in May 1966 to begin a four-year term for extortion. He had immediately used his connections and resources to generate a number of special jail privileges for himself, and he was now happy to do the same for his old mentor. "Tony Pro" gave Hoffa a seat at his own four-man dining table, an arrangement that frequently brought with it the availability of somewhat higher-quality food than that offered to the rest of the inmates. He saw to it that the IBT president's privacy was not unduly invaded by the other prisoners when Hoffa worked out in the gymnasium and prison yard. And he and his associates shielded Hoffa from the violence, homosexual and otherwise, that was always a threat at Lewisburg. A few years earlier, at a banquet honoring Hoffa, Tony had proposed a toast, "May he and his family live as long as they want and never want as long as they live." Now he could help implement some of that vow himself.

Hoffa, in turn, probably saved Provenzano's life. When the New Jersey extortionist was suddenly ravaged by a stomach problem and quickly wasted away to not much more than ninety-five pounds, the prison authorities unaccountably refused to grant his wish to get treatment at a hospital outside the prison. Hoffa intervened and threatened the warden and his staff with both adverse publicity and a lawsuit should Provenzano not be allowed such aid. Within hours, Provenzano was transported to a local medical center, where he underwent surgery.

But a rupture ultimately took place between the two friends.

Now looking forward to his golden years, the fully recovered Provenzano asked Hoffa to use the clout that the latter still had with the Central States Pension Fund to amend the fund's bylaws. Provenzano hoped that he could, through such a process, get a Teamster pension even though his current prison term would prevent him from holding union office. (Under the strictures of the Landrum–Griffin Act, an extortion conviction, as noted earlier, automatically disqualifies a person from serving as a union officer for five years, but the legislation is silent on both jury tampering and fraud.)

Hoffa, whose court experience involving the Central States machinery had generated for him a philosophy of once burned, twice shy, adamantly refused, reportedly asserting that "it's because of people like you that I got into trouble in the first place." A heated shouting match, accompanied by some physical jostling between the two men, ensued. And Provenzano—once, with Fitzsimmons, Hoffa's most dependable source of support at Teamster executive board meetings and a man whose admiration for the IBT president was absolutely unquestioned by anyone—was from then on a vehement Hoffa enemy.

Hoffa may have gone, but he was hardly—as far as countless Teamsters were concerned—forgotten. Even as he spent his fourth Christmas in jail in 1970, many thousands of cards conveying holiday greetings to him from members and their families arrived at Lewisburg (in accordance with prison regulations, he was allowed to receive only correspondence that contained no written personal messages).

The "Free Jimmy Hoffa" movements that had sprung up around the country ever since his jailing also seemed to be at least as numerous as ever, and some of these locally sponsored efforts were quite ambitious in their thrust: a large contingent of Teamster wives from Newark, New Jersey, had, for example, recently returned from a trip to Washington, D.C., where it had demonstrated for Hoffa's release from a "political" imprisonment. In a few more weeks, on Valentine's Day, Hoffa could expect a private plane bearing a banner that announced "Birthday Greetings Jimmy Hoffa" to fly over the prison: such an event, financed by an IBT local in Massachusetts, had taken place each year since his first behind-bars birthday in 1968; on all three occasions, there had been considerable national publicity.

Non-Teamsters remembered him, too. The White House had just been presented with a petition sponsored by a wide variety of non-IBT labor groups as well as by the Teamsters. The document bore 250,000 signatures from people in all walks of life and called upon President Richard M. Nixon to grant executive clemency to Hoffa and commute his sentence.

As far as the prison authorities were concerned, however, the subject of all of this attention continued to be just another inmate. On the one occasion to date that he had been allowed out of Lewisburg—in mid-1969, when he had gone to Chicago for a hearing on his contention that his conspiracy and fraud conviction had been obtained through illegal wiretapping—he had hardly received special treatment. He had been handcuffed once more and housed in a room with several other convicts at the DuPage County prison. Even the single small luxury allowed him on this trip—a steak dinner at one of his favorite restaurants, Berman's Chop House in Detroit, on the automobile route that he and his two federal marshal escorts traveled to Chicago—was marred. The marshals received severe disciplinary penalties for taking him to this modest restaurant instead of directly to the Wayne County jail, where a bunk in a ward with nine other prisoners awaited him and where he did go immediately after the meal.

Nor had the Chicago hearing itself produced the desired results. District Court Judge Austin, ruling that the wiretap material used in the pension fund trial was irrelevant to the evidence on which the Teamster president was convicted, had denied Hoffa's request for a new trial. Austin had also turned down a request that the five-year sentence that he had originally meted out to Hoffa be allowed to run concurrently with the eight-year jury-tampering sentence. Hoffa would, the judge decreed, have to serve his time for conspiracy and fraud after he had paid his debt to society for what he had done in Tennessee.

Even a thirteen-year sentence, however, might not prevent the general president from emerging from Lewisburg before the upcoming Teamster convention in July 1971, as Hoffa fully recognized. He had actually been eligible for parole on the jury-tampering conviction in October 1969, having served more than one-third of his first sentence at that time. And while the U.S. Board of Parole had rejected his request then, it had told him to reapply in March 1971. By the latter month, he would have served almost one-third of his combined thirteen-year sentence, and it was just possible that the Board might see fit to free him.

Hoffa's release in March would be even more likely, some of his friends believed, if pressures could be exerted on influential officials. And, as the date for the Board's hearing in the matter of James R. Hoffa approached, various reports that such influence was being attempted surfaced. Justice Department officials announced that unidentified "intermediaries" had tried to get Hoffa to advance them $1 million. The intermediaries would then use the money to try to persuade Senator John L. McClellan to intrude on Hoffa's behalf with the Parole Board. (The Senator said only that he had received a "mysterious suggestion" to this effect and that he had immediately spurned it.) There were also widespread rumors that major potential financial contributors to Nixon's upcoming 1972 reelection campaign were attempting to influence the White House to release Hoffa.

The efforts, whatever their specifics, failed. On March 31, 1971, the Parole Board, notwithstanding Hoffa's record as a "model" prisoner and the fact that Josephine Hoffa had recently suffered a severe heart attack and several small strokes and lay hospitalized in San Francisco, once again denied Hoffa's parole. It gave no reason, although many observers believed that a January 1971 Supreme Court reaffirmation of Judge Austin's sentence had been influential in the board's action. Hoffa would not get another chance at parole until June 1972.

He was now, however, allowed a small consolation. He could leave Lewisburg to visit his ailing wife in California and was permitted, moreover, to travel this time on his own recognizance, unaccompanied by marshals. The Bureau of Prisons granted him this furlough, one of fewer than one hundred such arrangements that it authorized in 1971, strictly for a family emergency, and technically no union business of any kind was to be discussed. But while the highlights of Hoffa's five April days in San Francisco were his frequent visiting of Josephine at the University of California Medical Center and a reunion with his eight-year-old granddaughter Barbara Jo (as well as with the other Crancers), he did conduct considerable

Teamster business. In fact, as his daughter would recall, "he called everyone and held meetings all the time" in his spacious suite on the nineteenth floor of the San Francisco Hilton. His extensive guest list included not only old Teamster associates Harold Gibbons and Robert Holmes but the Southern Conference's "Dusty" Miller and IBT vice-president Joseph Diviney. A man who had been constantly on Hoffa's mind for more than four years also came to the Hilton: Frank E. Fitzsimmons.

The general president did not seem to his visitors to have changed very much. One IBT official told an interviewer, "He's the same Hoffa: it's refreshing to see him." Another said, "At dinner in the hotel he was telling everybody the score on everything. He was still giving orders to the lawyers, arguing with them just like he always did. . . . I couldn't detect any change, the same bouncy guy and just as sure he's right on everything as when he went away."[7]

But there *was* a difference. Beneath the veneer of self-confidence, Hoffa was genuinely unsure as to what he should do regarding the Teamster convention that would begin in Miami Beach in three months. He wanted to be president as much as ever and was aware that he could theoretically be reelected from his prison cell (a petition backing him for another five years was, in fact, already being circulated throughout New England, and it pointedly included the words "wherever he may hang his hat"). He had no doubts, either, that the membership overwhelmingly preferred him as IBT leader to anyone else—and, specifically, to the unimpressive Fitz. He still, at fifty-eight, considered himself to be a relative stripling, and his superb physical shape certainly had to be reckoned as all to the good. If he had to wait until mid-1972 to resume running the union on a day-to-day basis, so be it.

On the other hand, he was greatly worried about Josephine, whose condition had improved since his arrival in San Francisco but whose health was generally described by her doctors as being very poor. He was convinced that he had been denied his parole solely because he had continued to hold union office. He believed, accordingly, that if he resigned from his several Teamster positions (not only the international union and Local 299 presidencies but his lesser jobs as head of the Central Conference of Teamsters, Joint Council 43 in Detroit, and the Michigan Conference of Teamsters), he could gain his freedom within a matter of a few months on the basis of "significant and new information." And while this course of action would by definition deprive him in the short run of his union leadership, he thought that he would definitely be able to get it back at the latest by 1976, when the next international convention would be held. Maybe earlier, if something could be worked out with the ever-pragmatic Nixon.

Broaching the subject to his San Francisco Hilton guests in what was for him a rare request for counsel, Hoffa received mixed advice and returned to Lewisburg on April 12 still undecided. He had not made up his mind even by mid-May and at that time requested, and received, an extension until the beginning of June from an increasingly impatient Teamsters executive board, which could not make its own plans for the July convention without knowing Hoffa's. Finally, on June 3, he dispatched his son to an executive board meeting in Washington with a letter stating that he would not be a candidate for the general presidency "because of my present legal difficulties" and endorsing Fitzsimmons for the slot. Seventeen days later, he officially resigned from all five of his union positions by taking out a piece of paper, writing "I agree not to be in organized labor as a [sic] officer" on it, and sending it to his old walnut-paneled office in Washington.

The Miami Beach convention almost aggressively minimized mentioning the man who had dominated prior IBT conventions for so long. The most that Fitzsimmons could bring himself to say of his old friend was that "Jimmy Hoffa is Jimmy Hoffa. I am Frank Fitzsimmons." And while one speaker did bring many of the twenty-one hundred delegates to their feet by asserting that Hoffa was "a political prisoner" and that he would have "been paroled last April if his name had not been Jimmy Hoffa," the speaker was not a Teamster at all but the new president of the United Automobile Workers, Leonard Woodcock. An official Teamster history summarizing union highlights since the 1966 convention cited Hoffa by name exactly once, in brief reference to the establishment of the Hoffa Scholarships.

The ex-president did get something tangible from the delegates: the lump sum of $1.7 million, before taxes, in lieu of the annual pension of $75,000 to which he was now entitled. And two other Hoffas would also be receiving incomes from the IBT: James P. would henceforth get a retaining fee of $30,000 to serve as a counsel for the union, and Josephine would continue to receive her $48,000, now as director of the women's political action section of the Teamsters.

Ironically, however, this latter inflow of funds to the Hoffa family coffers turned out to have done the man at Lewisburg a major disservice. The Parole Board, as Hoffa had expected, granted him an August hearing on the basis of the "significant and new information" provided by the resigning of his union offices. But it quickly also, now for the third time, denied Hoffa his parole, and, while the board again refused to explain its action, it is known that the employment arrangements with the two members of his immediate family were viewed as evidence that Hoffa had really not severed his connections with the IBT after all. To James P. Hoffa, who had written the board that his father intended to be "a teacher, lecturer or educator" if paroled, the denial was completely "arbitrary and unfair." Just like Leonard Woodcock, he felt that parole was being withheld strictly because the requestor "was named Hoffa."

On his very first day as general president—June 21, one day after Hoffa's official resignation was accepted—Fitzsimmons had received an honor that his predecessor had never been remotely accorded: The president of the United States had gone to a Miami Beach meeting of the IBT executive board to congratulate Fitz on his elevation and to pledge complete cooperation with him.

In paying this visit, Richard Nixon had not needed to go particularly out of his way. He was in the vicinity, anyhow, at his Key Biscayne compound, and even counting his twenty-minute speech to the IBT leaders at Miami Beach's Playboy Plaza Hotel, the entire project consumed less than one hour. But the very fact that the nation's chief executive had been willing to schedule the trip, particularly given the status of the Teamsters Union as the most notable pariah of the labor movement for almost fifteen years, showed how much Nixon valued his existing friendship with Fitzsimmons and hoped to strengthen it. No one doubted that Fitz was, as Nixon called him in his rather fulsome address, "my kind of labor leader." Almost no one doubted that Fitz's appeal was based on the considerable help that the head of America's richest and biggest union could lend to Nixon in the latter's 1972 presidential reelection campaign.

Nixon could, however, do something for Fitzsimmons, too. The pressures on the former caretaker that had been exerted ever since 1967 by Hoffa's legion of supporters to get their man released from prison were now becoming almost intolerable. At every turn, Fitz was being badgered not only by his own constituents but by Hoffa friends and family members to get Hoffa out of jail, and Fitzsimmons's explanation to them that he was doing everything that he could was appearing increasingly lame. The best of both worlds for the latter, now, would be a Hoffa who was: (1) a free man, and (2) no longer any kind of threat to Fitzsimmons within the Teamster hierarchy. Nixon could, with one sweep of his pen, satisfy both requirements.

The Post-Prison Years

14

Early on the afternoon of December 23, 1971, Robert Crancer received the telephone call that he had been anxiously awaiting for several hours in his Lewisburg, Pennsylvania motel room. It was from the warden at the federal penitentiary, and it informed Hoffa's son-in-law that Lewisburg's most famous temporary resident was now ready to be released.

The commutation by President Nixon had been signed late that morning, in response to a petition on Hoffa's behalf that had been filed by attorney Morris Shenker only one week earlier. In giving the former Teamster president his freedom so soon thereafter, Nixon had acted especially quickly. Normally, the need to get input from the sentencing judge, the original prosecutors, and others might be expected to take as much as two months. In this case, Nixon had done without such help. Only the recommendations of Attorney General John N. Mitchell and the U.S. pardons attorney had preceded the president's own.

Now, all that remained was for Hoffa to sign a "Conditions of Parole" form in the warden's office, and, with Crancer looking on, he prepared to do so. The document contained the customary language: the parolee would not use drugs, possess firearms, drink to excess, or violate any law. It also stipulated that Hoffa would reside in Detroit and regularly report there until March 1973 to a federal probation officer. Hoffa then asked the warden to "call Washington and find out if there are any other restrictions on the parole," and the warden, after honoring this request, advised him that there were "no restrictions except the ones you see here." Hoffa announced that he "could live with these" and, almost casually, affixed his name. With his son-in-law, he then departed, through three sets of electronically controlled gates and to the cheers and good luck wishes of scores of Lewisburg inmates who witnessed his final moments at the prison after four years, nine months, and sixteen days.

Harold Gibbons had engaged a private plane, which waited for Hoffa and Crancer at the Williamsport Airport to convey all three men to St. Louis. Hoffa would spend the Christmas holidays with his family in the nearby suburb of Glendale, as a houseguest of his daughter and son-in-law. The plane would first stop in Detroit, where James P. Hoffa would be picked up (and where in another part of the city labor leaders were all set to toast Hoffa's release from Lewisburg with champagne, in a party that would last for several hours).

Josephine was already in Glendale. Only hours before her husband gained his freedom, she had—very possibly from the excitement of anticipation—suffered yet another in her seemingly endless series of small seizures. But a cardiovascular specialist had come to her bedroom at the Crancer residence, and her condition had improved so rapidly that she had actually gone out to a neighborhood beauty parlor. She told Barbara, "I'm going to look nice when your father comes home." Barbara Jo would also be present to share in her grandfather's Christmas celebration, and the former IBT president was particularly eager to reveal to the eight-year-old his surprise gift for her: a riding horse named Black Gold, which Hoffa had purchased while in prison. It would be a holiday such as the former bearer of penitentiary number 33-298 NE had not known for years.

Hoffa was himself, however, also in for a surprise. Among the questions fired at him by the host of media people who met him when he got off the plane in St. Louis was one that came, he would always claim thereafter, completely out of the blue: "Jimmy, what do you think about the restriction that you can't engage in any union business?" Asking for a clarification, the parolee was informed that the wire services were reporting that the commutation had been granted on condition that Hoffa not engage "either directly or indirectly in the management of any labor organization prior to March

6, 1980," the date on which his original thirteen-year sentence would have ended. If he were to violate this condition, just like any other, he would have to return to jail to serve out the full sentence.

Hoffa was bitter upon learning the news. He wanted nothing more than to resume his old job—when the plane from Williamsport had stopped in Detroit, a *Detroit News* reporter had asked him, "Jimmy, do you want to be president of the Teamsters again?" and he had answered, "Jack, do you like to breathe?"—and now he would have to wait years. "I never would have accepted the commutation if I'd only known," he adamantly insisted to intimates. "What the hell, I'd have been out without any restrictions in 1974."

In the months immediately after his St. Louis trip, however, he publicly denied harboring any hard feelings. On the American Broadcasting Company's "Issues and Answers," he announced not only that he didn't believe that his release had involved political considerations but that "President Nixon is the best qualified man at the present moment for the presidency of the U.S. in my personal opinion." Fitzsimmons, he insisted to reporters, was still his friend and relations between the two men were "good."

In point of fact, Hoffa did not seem to hold anything personal against Nixon. But Fitzsimmons was something else again. Hoffa believed his successor to have engineered the restriction on conducting union business, and he now privately expressed the opinion that "there has never been a rat like this rat Fitz." He was also increasingly inclined to make statements such as "Fitzsimmons doesn't know his ass from first base about running the union."

Still and all, the conditions of his parole could have been worse, and Hoffa knew it. Such activities as mediating a strike involving trucking companies and Teamsters in Puerto Rico were out—both parties had asked him to serve in such a role within weeks of his release, and the Justice Department had almost immediately refused him permission—and he obviously could not run for union office as matters stood. But, as probation and parole officers soon interpreted the strictures of his parole, he could not only attend union social affairs almost at will but even, within limits, show up at meetings of his old springboard Local 299. He could be as friendly as ever with individual Teamsters. He could freely offer his opinions on national issues, including those that directly related to his old union (for example, Nixon's current price and wage restraint program, which Hoffa soon after his release told reporters was "not bothering the Teamsters").

He was also essentially at liberty to travel far from Detroit, and for substantial chunks of time. Specific Department of Justice authorization had to be granted in each case, but this was almost always readily conferred, and even the stipulation against conducting union business seemed to be given a certain amount of poetic license at times. Right after his release, the former general president was allowed to join the ailing Josephine for ninety days at the couple's Miami Beach condominium (in Blair House, a building erected a decade earlier with Central States Pension Fund loans) and managed during this period not only to speak at an IBT leadership institute but also to show up twice at the hotel in which the AFL-CIO Executive Council was holding its midwinter meeting. (George Meany studiously ignored his presence on the latter occasions, but he was warmly welcomed by many of the other labor leaders, several of whom commented on how well he looked.) Granted a detour, in turn, from Florida to attend the Washington-area funeral of Teamster Secretary-Treasurer Thomas Flynn in March 1972, he convened some of his supporters in an anteroom at the funeral parlor to make known his views as to who should succeed Flynn. He then engaged in a heated argument with Fitzsimmons over the matter.

He would do anything short of jeopardizing his parole to pave the way for his ultimate return to power. But he did not have a one-track mind about his situation. And much of Hoffa's attention these days was also devoted to a cause that was quite unrelated to unionism and about which the Lewisburg alumnus also harbored strong opinions. He became an active, if improbable, advocate of prison reform and willingly shared his opinions on the subject with the world. Almost no Hoffa interviewer, no matter what the original line of questioning, departed without having heard a lengthy narration about just how bad life in the penitentiary was. Hoffa appearances on "Face the Nation," "Firing Line," and other widely watched television shows almost exclusively focused on this single issue. Old friends could count on a scathing first-hand indictment of the confinement system by a man who had so recently emerged from it. Special judiciary subcommittees of both the U.S. Senate and House of Representatives listened to Hoffa, whom they had invited to testify before them once his degree of feeling had become known, as he expounded on the topic.

Prisons, in Hoffa's view, were turning out "nothing but trouble." Young people who came out of the violence-prone, drug-infested, homosexual rape–prone institutions left either "embittered or enthused about how much they think they can make as criminals." Everyone suffered from the overcrowding. The guards, from his experiences, were worse than incompetent: "You [might] come back and find some guard sitting on your bunk reading your personal mail or making remarks about pictures of your family or something. There's nothing you can do." So-called experts in penology were anything but knowledgeable: "They've never been there. Let 'em go spend 90 days."[1]

He had no end of suggestions, most of them well-worn ones: segregation of prisoners by age and offense, no imprisonment at all for first offenders in most situations, higher salaries and improved training for guards, adequately stocked libraries and better recreational facilities, substantially less crowding, and the training of inmates in skills that would be marketable on the outside. He also advanced a more imaginative idea of his own: a parole commission for each prison to decide when inmates should be released, with an inmate elected by other prisoners serving as adviser to it (on the premise that no one would be better qualified to evaluate other inmates than such a person). The realistic Hoffa was well aware that nothing would in the short run come of any of these proposals. Making them, however, might help pave the way for their longer-run implementation. His efforts also allowed a chronically restless man who now had plenty of time on his hands to vent frustrations that had been building for years.

In September 1972, it was revealed that Hoffa had tried to help another kind of prisoner, although in this case the attempt was rather quickly aborted. Apparently at the initiative of Harold Gibbons, an outspoken critic of the Vietnamese War and a man who had already brought back peace feelers from North Vietnam to the White House, the former IBT president tried himself to go to Hanoi to negotiate the release of American prisoners of war.

For Hoffa, there were three attractive aspects to this last project. He could again use the bargaining skills that he had once honed to perfection but that he was otherwise these days not permitted to use at all in any other way. He could in this case, if his talents succeeded, achieve a very tangible result, and in a short time frame. And, of greatest appeal, his serving Nixon, who was under considerable pressure to bring the POWs home, in such a manner might well induce the nation's chief executive to waive the parole restriction on union business. Hoffa and Gibbons met with the president's special assistant for national security affairs, Henry A. Kissinger, who was reported to have offered no resistance to the idea. Attorney General Richard G. Kleindienst was also believed to have favored the plan, although he officially denied this. Secretary of State William P. Rogers, however, was vehemently opposed. And Rogers's position combined with a generally negative public reaction, once the matter had become known, to end both the POW effort and Hoffa's hopes for an imminent parole amendment.

The parolee's best chance of having the union business restriction set aside now lay back with the courts. If he could get his jury-tampering conviction overturned, he and his lawyers believed, he would immediately become a "free agent": there could be no parole constraints if there was no conviction, and in having already served almost all of his five-year pension fraud sentence, he had satisfied his obligation to society in his other case.

The striking down of the jury-tampering conviction, however, at this point hinged on a rather shallow reed: a thirty-one-page alleged recantation statement made by none other than Edward Grady Partin. The Baton Route Teamster's own difficulties with the law had by no means yet been resolved, and he was therefore quite vulnerable to suggestions as to how he might end them. He had been informed by agents of his fellow Louisianan Carlos Marcello, the powerful gangster who was thought to have tried to keep Hoffa out of jail in the first place by putting money for bribing judges and others at Hoffa's disposal, that his best course of action here might be to sign an affidavit stating that he had perjured himself in Chattanooga. In gratitude, Marcello would then intervene on Partin's behalf with the forces of law.

Inspired by this news, Partin had given some kind of statement to the Marcello agents. But he had not been willing to sign the document that incorporated this statement, and he later announced that he had really admitted "nothing" to the affidavit-seekers. "Sure, I said some words," he had declared, "and they wrote them down. But . . . I just told them what they wanted to hear."[2] Predictably, the U.S. Court of Appeals for the Sixth Circuit was less than overwhelmed by the Partin document when it received it as the foundation of Hoffa's fifth jury-tampering appeal. And in January 1973, it announced that it would not grant a rehearing. An appeal of *this* court action had immediately thereafter been filed with the Supreme Court by Hoffa's lawyers. But it was similarly being accorded little chance of prevailing.

On the other hand, the Hoffa legal team was at this point considering the use of an imaginative argument that its members and their client, increasingly, were convinced might let Hoffa regain control of the Teamsters. If the courts could be convinced that the ban on union business imposed by Nixon in his 1971 commutation order was illegal, Hoffa would automatically be free to become an officer in his old Local 299 and then to run for the IBT presidency in 1976. No president, after all, had ever before imposed such a condition—one that obviously was not in the original sentence—on a person whom he had released from jail. And the condition, quite aside from any absence of precedent, might be construed as being illegal on other grounds. For one thing, it could be argued that Nixon's action ran counter to the Constitution's separation of powers, since only the judiciary can impose punishment. For another, the condition might be said to have violated Hoffa's right to earn his livelihood, guaranteed under the Fifth Amendment. The parolee's First Amendment guarantee of free association was also arguably being taken away.

By mid-1973, Hoffa was highly optimistic that this latter line of argument would be fruitful. Having submitted the concept to three different law firms for analysis and then asked a fourth group of attorneys to evaluate the findings of the first three, he had concluded that there was "about an 85% chance in court" of getting the restriction removed.[3] He was firmly determined to pursue the novel strategy, and he had begun to shop around for the best possible constitutional lawyer to present the case to the judiciary.

Meanwhile, Hoffa's superabundance of energy would hardly let him be idle on other fronts. He accepted his son's offer of space at Jim's downtown Detroit law office, which the younger Hoffa had opened in 1967 on the top floor of the city's ancient Guardian Building. There, he spent many hours daily communicating with

Teamsters and others all over the country as he planned ahead for the day when he would once again be general president.

After his parole period ended in March 1973, he was completely free to go anywhere and do anything that did not involve the "management of any labor organization," and he became once again the peripatetic Hoffa of old. He gave several speeches monthly, selecting his engagements from the literally hundreds of requests to lecture that arrived at the Guardian Building in the same period of time and generally favoring college groups and charitable organizations. Although he probably could have gotten up to $10,000 a date for his services, he never charged either of the latter kinds of audiences anything except his expenses and frequently absorbed even these costs himself. When he addressed industrial organizations—the Michigan Automobile Dealers Association, for example—he tended to ask that his honoraria be given to charity (often, to a children's charity).

He also devoted a great deal of attention to the National Association for Justice, founded in 1972 by former convict C. Edward Lawrenson and pledged, as he was, to prison reform. Not only did he publicize the NAJ in many of his speeches and the television and radio talk show appearances that he now frequently made, but he dug deeply into his own pockets to help finance NAJ expenses. In return for such support, the organization's leadership offered him the directorship of the Association's Crisis Control Center, designed to mediate prison disputes and quell inmate riots—if need be, on the shortest of notice. Accepting the position, he flew around the country exercising his outstanding negotiating skills. He was instrumental in improving conditions for prisoners in Lucasville, Ohio, and thus in thwarting what was shaping up as a major prisoner protest there. He almost single-handedly averted riots in both Baltimore and Rockville, Maryland, resolved a Washington, D.C. strike, and cooled off an explosive situation in Lorton, Virginia. Once again, he refused to accept any money for his efforts.

A visible platform such as the directorship clearly could only help him in his attempt to regain his Teamster general presidency, but he seemed genuinely to take great satisfaction in his NAJ projects and much pleasure in the few strides that prison reform made in these years. A District of Columbia Office of Personnel policy revision that allowed the employment of former inmates on any job for which they qualified, except positions related to the crime for which they were convicted, gave him considerable gratification. An April 1974 U.S. Supreme Court decision that restricted the arbitrary opening by prison guards of personal mail sent to inmates did likewise.

He told friends that he fully intended to keep his Crisis Control Center directorship even after he resumed union leadership. In turn, the National Association for Justice was delighted to have him. Once, when Lawrenson was asked by a reporter why his organization allowed such a controversial figure as Hoffa to hold such an important post, he answered, "You wouldn't be asking me any questions if we didn't have such a controversial figure."

"What stands out about him," says a former law partner of the younger Hoffa who came to know the firm's celebrity guest well in these days,

was his generosity. And his honesty. He had integrity to spare. He did what he said he would.

I had a friend whose dad made a product, but didn't know how to market it, and [the father] was teetering on the brink of financial disaster. He was about to lose his farm, his bar and restaurant, and his hotel. . . . I paid the father a visit, evaluated the situation and told the father that [the business] couldn't go and that he should get rid of it. . . . The son became indignant, said that I had insulted his dad's ability . . . he wouldn't hear of it.

I came back to Detroit. Hoffa breezed in and saw that I was disturbed. He asked me, "What's the problem?" I said, "Nothing, Jimmy." He persisted. I told him the whole story, and then Hoffa said, "This is a good guy?" I told him, "Helluva good guy." Hoffa made two phone calls, and a market now opened up for my friend's dad in both Washington, D.C. and Detroit. He could now sell all he could produce. . . . Soon the father could sell the business at a very large profit, and he insisted on giving Hoffa a handsome fee. Hoffa gave it to charity.

As for Hoffa's keeping his word, this attorney fondly remembers the former labor leader's accepting one Michigan speaking invitation (for the Scrap Dealers Association) at the behest of the attorney and then, in the press of his scores of other obligations, forgetting all about it: "Two days before the speech he went down to Florida, to spend some length of time there. I phoned him and he flew back the next day. He prided himself, as he always said, on honoring his commitments. And he wouldn't even accept money for the plane fare."

His rapport with the Teamster rank and file continued to be remarkable. On a typical day, as many as forty letters from members were deposited in the large Hoffa mailbox at Lake Orion, where he and Josephine now lived much of the time. When he walked down the streets of Detroit, he could count on being enthusiastically greeted by significant numbers of his former constituents and often being, despite his uneasiness with close physical contact, hugged and kissed by them. (In the words of one observer of this adulation, "He was like the Messiah." "We'd walk from the Guardian Building down Woodward Avenue over to Grand Circus Park and back. It was literally impossible to go more than a few feet without people crossing the street and coming over to greet him.") On many occasions, cab drivers would thank him profusely "for what you did for my family" and refuse to accept his money, often causing him to force compensation well in excess of what the meter had called for upon them.

Hundreds of drivers made special detours to the Hoffa lakefront cottage just to "say hello to Jimmy." Thousands of "Bring Back Jimmy Hoffa" bumper stickers sprouted on trucks from coast to coast. In 1974, a random poll conducted by the truck driver magazine *Overdrive* revealed that a staggering 83 percent of the respondents would vote for Hoffa as Teamster international president if they were given the chance; for the rest of his life, he would regularly cite this result, with enormous pride.

The former general president was well aware, however, that he could take nothing for granted in his quest to regain his office. Hundreds of thousands of new Teamsters had joined the union since he had gone to prison, and they had for the most part done well economically under Fitzsimmons. Hoffa was, to many of them, nothing more than the name of a past president—no different than, say, Beck. And the man who had tended in his pre-Lewisburg days to express disdain for public relations was at this juncture, accordingly, quite convinced of its importance to him.

In this regard, Hoffa welcomed an overture from the actor Robert Conrad, former star of the television series "The Wild Wild West," who was planning a movie version of Hoffa's life. Hoffa met at length with Conrad, who subsequently announced that he had acquired the rights to produce the movie and to play the Hoffa role. Conrad added in making this statement that it was his aim "and it's also Hoffa's aim . . . not to make this a whitewash but a hard-hitting biography that will tell it as it is."[4] But it was obvious that Conrad, an ex-Teamster in Hoffa's Central States Conference himself, enjoyed Hoffa's confidence that the movie would do the latter no harm at all with his electorate.

Conrad's project never became a reality. But another endeavor that the undeclared campaigner viewed as also being potentially helpful to him did. Hoffa decided to work closely with veteran professional writer Oscar Fraley in putting together the second of his two autobiographies, *Hoffa: The Real Story*. The short book, all of whose future earnings were assigned in advance to the National Association for Justice, was scheduled for publication in February 1976, four months before the union's convention. Hoffa anticipated that it would lend a major boost to his presidential candidacy, which he assumed would by then have been legalized by a lifting of his commutation condition. "We'll have a hell of a last chapter," he told Fraley, "if things break as quick as I expect."[5]

Hoffa: The Real Story was published ahead of schedule and posthumously, six weeks after its protagonist's mid–1975 disappearance, and Hoffa's hypothesis about its potential influence can never, therefore, be evaluated. But no publication has ever painted a darker picture of the man whom Hoffa had chosen as his successor. Fitzsimmons,

a guy I took off a 3-C Highway Company truck and hand-carried all the way from shop steward to general vice-president . . . forgot who made him when he got Washingtonitis. . . . He knew damned well that when I stood for reelection, he didn't have the chance of an ice cube in hell. So he was the man who had conditions attached to my commutation.[6]

Fitz, according to Hoffa, "would have done almost anything to keep the Teamsters' presidency. And he did." The author specifically charged Fitzsimmons with

. . . political influence peddling and conspiring with . . . Nixon's "Watergate staff" to prevent me from regaining my office.

. . . selling out to mobsters and letting known racketeers into the Teamsters.

. . . *blackjacking union officials into line by giving $7 million in annual organizing funds only to people who promise to support him.*

. . . *sending Hoffa supporters among the Teamster officials to "Siberia" so they couldn't influence delegates to the 1976 convention.*

. . . *awarding a $1.3 million Teamster "public-relations" program in 1973 to two men with criminal records.*

. . . *permitting underworld establishment of a union insurance scheme which in one year was a ripoff to the tune of $1,185,000 in the New York area alone and in which his own son, Don, participated on a national level.*

. . . *making vast loans from the billion-dollar Teamster pension fund to known mobsters.*

. . . *winning Teamster support by giving regional union officials powers that belong to the International executive board.*

. . . *stripping my wife and my son of union posts as a further means of undermining my influence.*[7]

Much of this sweeping indictment was elaborated upon either briefly or not at all. But to Hoffa, himself the alleged doer of so many unsubstantiated similar deeds in the McClellan committee days, it did not much seem to matter. His basic message—that Fitzsimmons was unfit to continue as IBT head—was one whose justification was to him self-evident. He intended to have everyone know that he was "back, very much back" and that he would be the general president again "come hell or high water." He was "not a guy who believes in limited warfare," he wrote, "so the rats better start jumping the ship."[8]

Fraley developed a deep admiration for him in the course of their taping sessions, most of them at the Blair House condominium in Miami Beach. He was impressed, as so many others had been, by Hoffa's retentive memory, his mental alacrity, and his personal charm. In the book's epilogue, the professional journalist says of his coauthor,

There was about him a magnetic quality and he talked of the power struggle ahead with an almost joyful anticipation. Combat had, after all, been his way of life. And his faith never wavered that "my guys," the nation's [truck drivers] who are the backbone of the Teamsters, would stand behind him in a showdown.

*You had to believe him. As one old-line trucking company owner told me:
"To the Teamsters, Jimmy was God. They knew he was always fighting
for them, physically if necessary. And I'll tell you another thing. His word
was as good as gold; a handshake was better than a bale of legal papers
drawn up by a battery of lawyers."*

*[Hoffa] laughed when I told him that, a deep rumble coming out of the
broad chest like the sound of a subway train. "You see? They all knew I
was the boss."*[9]

The negative portrayal of Fitzsimmons in the book symbolized
a no-holds-barred public attitude toward the incumbent Teamster
president that had actually been publicly displayed by Hoffa since
early 1974. In February of that year, the former IBT leader informed
the audience of his home city's widely watched television program,
"A.M. Detroit," "Fitzsimmons is crazy. He goes to a shrink twice
a week and he's running a union for more than two million Teamsters?" and thenceforth he freely repeated this claim to interviewers.
Hoffa also now delighted in asserting to the press not only that
much of Fitz's time was being spent unconscionably far afield from
union business, on various golf courses throughout the nation, but
also that golf was a game for "fat old men." It did not take Fraley's
posthumous publication, either, to break the news that Hoffa considered Fitzsimmons to be a "liar" and a "double-crosser": Hoffa
had been liberally saying it to media people for more than eighteen
months prior to his disappearance.

What seemed to convert the man on parole from a vehement
private critic of Fitzsimmons to a no less impassioned public antagonist had been Hoffa's new awareness of an affidavit that the U.S.
attorney general had signed on October 15, 1973. In it, Mitchell
declared that no one in the Justice Department, himself very definitely included, nor President Nixon had initiated or suggested the
inclusion of the no-union business parole restriction. In the document, the attorney general also said that the first time that Fitzsimmons had ever talked to him about getting Hoffa out of jail was in
June 1971—more than two years after Fitzsimmons had started telling James P. Hoffa and others that he "was taking care of it with
Mitchell." One year earlier, Fitzsimmons had fired Edward Bennett
Williams as Teamster general counsel and given his lucrative on-
retainer job to former White House lawyer Charles W. Colson.

And Hoffa was now convinced, "putting two and two together," that Fitzsimmons had done this to pay off Colson for getting the parole restriction added. He was at this point absolutely certain that his original belief in Fitzsimmons's active hand in creating the restriction had been justified.

The once-tractable Fitz was by no means taking this onslaught on him by his old boss docilely, however. Even before Hoffa began his public attack, he had made moves that were every bit as hard-hitting as Hoffa's would be and no more subtle. In February 1973, IBT officials who might have been tempted to attend a testimonial dinner for Jimmy and Josephine Hoffa (on the occasion of the ex-president's sixtieth birthday) at the Latin Casino in Cherry Hill, New Jersey, were advised not to come: only one international vice-president, Harold Gibbons, subsequently accepted an invitation, and lesser officials under Fitzsimmons's patronage were also conspicuous by their absence there. Three months later, Gibbons was forced by Fitzsimmons to relinquish his post as St. Louis Teamster Local 688 secretary-treasurer, a move that automatically also cost him his presidency of IBT Joint Council 13 in his home location.

Then, while addressing the Western Conference of Teamsters in San Francisco in September, Fitzsimmons announced that when Hoffa had come to that city twenty-nine months earlier to visit Josephine, he had in fact discussed union business, the conditions of this special prison furlough notwithstanding. The Teamster general president did not explain exactly what had motivated him to make such a disclosure. Anyone who thought that this portion of the speech came strictly under the heading of small talk, however, would probably have made a contribution to the family of the Unknown Soldier had Fitz solicited it.

Equally lacking in mystery was a resounding endorsement of Nixon by Fitzsimmons, made in November. The President had already been badly embarrassed by Watergate disclosures, and most other labor leaders were now demanding either his resignation or his impeachment. To Fitz, nonetheless, Nixon was "the most influential President this country has ever had and I'm sure that he will end his term in the glory that he deserves."[10]

Not too much remained to be done, Fitzsimmons thought, to ensure a Hoffa-free Teamsters Union until 1980. But the IBT head did act on one remaining bit of unfinished business not long after

Hoffa's aggressive public campaign against him began: in the spring of 1974, he fired Josephine Hoffa as director of the union's women's political action auxiliary, thereby depriving her of her $48,000 annual income, and terminated James P. Hoffa's $30,000 annual lawyer's retaining fee. He could live with the aspersions that Hoffa had cast on his golf playing, although not happily, but words like "crazy" and "liar" went beyond the range of his tolerance.

Fitzsimmons was not the only visible Hoffa enemy these days. Anthony "Tony Pro" Provenzano, the once-close Hoffa friend who had aborted the relationship in Lewisburg when the still-head of the Teamsters had refused to help him get unearned credits toward an IBT pension, had been released from jail in late 1970. He had gone to live in Hallandale, Florida, not far from the Miami Beach condominium where the Hoffas wintered. He was becoming increasingly embittered that his extortion conviction disqualified him for the money, while Hoffa's jury tampering and fraud convictions did not. Not one to accept defeat gracefully, he had resumed his effort after Hoffa's parole on the premise that the former president still had clout with the Central States Pension Fund administrators, and on several occasions Tony had tried to contact his old friend by telephone. His attempts were in vain: Hoffa had refused to take the calls.

In Florida in 1972, the enraged Provenzano had given Joe Konowe, whom he had encountered on the street, a message for the man whose special assistant Konowe had once been: "Tell Hoffa I'm gonna snatch his granddaughter and put her eyes out." Hoffa had been visibly shaken when he got the news and said to Konowe, "Joe, I'd talk to him, but he's a crazy son of a bitch."

In 1973 and 1974, Hoffa apparently did talk to Provenzano, but about a different topic. According to a former New York City Teamster official, Daniel Sullivan, in a version corroborated by others, Hoffa met several times with Tony Pro to solicit support in his fight with Fitzsimmons. The passage of time had not changed the New Jerseyite a bit: in the course of these conversations, he again threatened physical violence, now (according to Sullivan) by "pulling out Hoffa's guts" and by kidnapping his grandchildren. Hoffa could not afford to take these threats lightly: at least two of Provenzano's political opponents within his Local 560 were believed to have been murdered. Others who had spoken out against him had been physically assaulted. Tony was known within Teamster circles as "a real bad guy" and two of the more frequently used descriptive words about him were "intimidating" and "scary." Even his conversational style tended to be formidable: in the mid-1970s, journalists still talked about a press conference that he had called years earlier at Local 560 headquarters; in it, he had denounced the then-Attorney General Robert F. Kennedy in language that was so filthy that the newspaper reporters could not locate a single direct quotation that they could share with their readers, and the television tape had been unusable. According to a Hoffa intimate, Provenzano was one of the few people on earth—and possibly the only one—whom Hoffa himself feared.

Hoffa's family thought that he should be wary of other people, too. In his relentless attempt to dislodge Fitzsimmons, the former Lewisburg inmate was antagonizing a variety of men whose records proved them to be fully capable of physical violence, not excluding murder. Hoffa's amiable successor was at this point perceived by the latter as a man after their own hearts as they pursued their various criminal interests administering IBT local unions in New York, New Jersey, Chicago, and Detroit and influencing Central States Pension Fund loans. Fitzsimmons left them alone. They had no desire at all to go back to dealing with the stronger-willed and less predictable Hoffa, their past friendships with him notwithstanding.

The former head of the Teamsters still adamantly refused to have a bodyguard, however, either in Florida or at Lake Orion, where he and Josephine in these years spent the bulk of their time. "You get a bodyguard, you get careless," he would often say, sometimes adding that "a lot of people *with* bodyguards have been killed." He assured his children, who were particularly concerned about their parents living alone at the isolated lakefront country cottage, that "no one will bother us out here, because it's on a dead-end road." Above all, he naively believed, despite the threats of Provenzano and the potential of the other mobsters to kill him, that no one would really want to do away with him: as he told one of the many journalists who interviewed him at Orion, "I don't cheat nobody. I don't lie about nobody. I don't frame nobody. I don't talk bad about people. If I do, I tell 'em. So what the hell's people gonna try to kill *me* for?"[11] He had come a long distance from the days when he thought that he would die a violent death.

Death, on the other hand, held no fear for him: he told intimates, "I've had a full life and done everything I wanted to do. I could die tomorrow with no regrets." He asserted to his son-in-law, "Bob, I've been fortunate. I was just a farm boy from Brazil, Indiana, and I became president of the world's greatest union. I've been able to smell the roses. How many other people can say that?"

Not that he by any means struck visitors as harboring a death wish as he delighted in the company of his children and grandchildren at the two Hoffa locations. When at Lake Orion, he could particularly enjoy his two little grandsons, since they lived less than an hour away. He frequently came by his son's greater Detroit house and took David and Geoffrey, in a move that was much appreciated by his daughter-in-law, to the cottage for entire weekends. He installed a merry-go-round, a teeter-totter, and a collection of swings and slides there for the two boys and often went out with them to look for frogs and to catch minnows. He became an expert in repairing toys at his workbench and was probably one of the few grandfathers in the Lake Orion region whose grandsons regularly sat with him on his rider as he rid his three acres of their excess grass. Nothing gave him more pleasure than these latter occasions, which were rivaled only by the visits of the St. Louis branch of the family both to the lake in the summer and to the Florida condominium in the winter. On both properties, he was the proud paterfamilias, making up for lost time.

He also took pride in keeping himself as physically fit in these years as he had ever been. The banquets that supplemented many of his speaking engagements were always a threat, but workouts with two fifty-pound dumbbells and a hundred-pound barbell, every night when he was home and twice a week in any event, helped ward off their effects. So did a daily series of 150 stretches with ropes attached to a doorknob and swimming and tree-chopping at Lake Orion. At sixty-one, he had the body of a far younger man—not like, say, Frank Fitzsimmons—and he intended to keep it that way.

He was proud, too, of his continuing reputation for candor and now seemed almost to flaunt it in his speeches and interviews. Arriving at a Belleville, Illinois, meeting of retired Teamsters and seeing a heavy representation of late-model Cadillacs and Buicks among the cars outside the building, he told his audience, "The reason why unions have gotten so soft these days is right out there in the parking lot. We've fought long and hard, but in the process we've lost something that's very important. You've gotten so soft and your bellies are so full that you have no interest in helping the Teamsters out by going out and carrying picket signs. Until you get skinny again and there aren't wrinkles in your bellies, labor will continue to deteriorate." He sat down to great applause.

He frequently charged that "a lot of the politicians in Washington, they couldn't make a buck doing anything else. They can't spell rat backwards; they can't run their own personal lives at all. But they go all over the place shooting off their mouths about how to govern the country and how to deal with the Russians." Nobody, he was wont to say quite openly now, ever even heard of the Kennedy family before the McClellan committee was created: "They were absolute unknowns. The old man was a goddam bootlegger. Just a bootlegger." And while many judges "start out okay, they often become sons of bitches and abuse their power. They see too much misbehavior in front of them and they start to think that the only way to handle people like this is to send them to jail, out of sight. They get very cynical about law-breakers in general. They think of them as sub-human. They get to look down on people. But try getting them to quit the bench. They hold on for dear life so as to get their retirement benefits some day."

In his effort to convince the courts that President Nixon's ban on his conducting union business was unconstitutional, Hoffa had, by early 1974, completed his shopping around for a constitutional lawyer. He had selected for the job of suing both the president and the attorney general of the United States, the necessary avenue for reversing the Nixon stipulation, the highly regarded and articulate Leonard B. Boudin.

In one sense, Boudin was an unlikely choice. He had primarily built his reputation on defending such well-known liberal luminaries of the 1960s and early 1970s as Daniel Ellsberg and Benjamin Spock. Hoffa's political views, such as they were, tended to be much more conservative: "Give a bum a dollar every day and the first time you miss paying him, he'll say, 'Okay, where's my dollar, you cheap SOB?' Everybody wants to take today; nobody wants to give." Hoffa favored neither gun control nor enforced school busing: in the former case, it was the shooters who should be stopped, not the guns; in the latter, the right of Americans to send their children to schools in their own neighborhoods was basic. And the Hoffa prescription for both drug pushers and rapists was a notably uncomplicated one: "Line them up against the wall and shoot the bastards."

But each man genuinely respected the other. Hoffa above all esteemed Boudin's will to fight: "Too many of these people are subservient to the judges. 'Yes, Your Honor; no, Your Honor. Don't upset the judge. This is only one case,' the lawyer thinks. 'I gotta come before him another day' "[12] Boudin, like Hoffa, was his own man.

Boudin, in turn, accepted the case because he agreed with Hoffa that it was unique constitutionally ("A President shouldn't be running the labor movement") and also because he liked Hoffa personally. "He was a great trade-union leader," he told an interviewer, "and maybe will be one again. . . . He's a relatively relaxed client; tough, confident. He has confidence in his lawyers and in himself for having chosen them."[13] Nor was Boudin unimpressed by Hoffa's grasp of the relevant constitutional issues: the school dropout had devoted days to studying the law literature that might pertain to his situation, and he consistently surprised Boudin by his sophistication on this score.

On June 5, 1974, the case was heard by Judge John H. Pratt of the U.S. District Court in Washington. Boudin, with some passion, stressed his belief that Nixon's restriction was unconstitutional for four reasons: an absence of any inherent power in the Presidency to establish punishment, a violation of the double-jeopardy clause (since the ban on Hoffa's union activities until 1980 was actually an additional penalty), an infringement on the First Amendment's guarantee of freedom of association, and a violation of the Fifth Amendment's guarantee of the right to earn a livelihood. He also charged that the ban resulted from an illegal conspiracy between Fitzsimmons, Nixon, Colson, and former White House counsel John W. Dean, who had a few days earlier testified in a deposition that he had originated the restriction. In return for the condition, Boudin suggested, Nixon got both a political endorsement and financial contributions in 1972 from the International Brotherhood of Teamsters.

Asking Pratt to dismiss the plaintiff's plea, Assistant U.S. Attorney Michael A. Katz matter-of-factly argued that the judge was confronted in the case with only one question: whether the restriction imposed by Nixon was legal. Whatever motives may have been in back of the condition were absolutely, in Katz's opinion, irrelevant. And, to him, the condition was a valid one, lawfully imposed and properly accepted.

Pratt's decision, issued on July 19, went against Hoffa. Nixon, the jurist ruled, acted fully within his pardoning power in commuting Hoffa's prison sentence in late 1971 with the union activity restriction. Even if the alleged Fitzsimmons-Nixon-Colson-Dean conspiracy could be proven, he said, the White House action could not be invalidated "for the same reason [that] one cannot attack the validity of an act of Congress on the grounds that the Congressmen who voted in favor of it did so for improper motives." What was more, Pratt held, the crimes for which Hoffa had been convicted were directly related to his union activities: Nixon was consequently justified in imposing the ban because "the public . . . has a strong interest in the integrity of union activities inasmuch as unions exert great influence on the economic life of the nation and on the welfare of individual members of unions."

Hoffa had expected better. He had come to his downtown Detroit office to await Pratt's announcement, which would be relayed to him by Boudin by telephone, and in anticipation of a victory celebration he had scheduled a press conference there. When he got the bad news from his attorney, in full view of the many media people who had jammed the premises, his face turned ashen. He then, in a flash of the well-known Hoffa temper, lashed out long-distance at Boudin, in whom he had placed so much faith.

Less than a minute after this conversation was concluded, he took a second telephone call, from Josephine, at Lake Orion. In a very different league from Boudin's communication, it expressed a mild complaint that the workmen who were then expanding the cottage accommodations were being noisier than they should have been. And Hoffa's response to this was very much at variance with his prior reaction: "Now, Jo, don't worry about it," he said softly to his wife. "In a few days we'll have a beautiful new addition to the house." To the newspeople who did not know Hoffa, the change of pace was remarkable, particularly given the circumstances. To those who did, however, it was entirely in character, on two counts. First, his displays of temper rarely lasted long, and having unleashed his thunderbolt at his constitutional lawyer, he was almost instantaneously able to compose himself. Secondly, he was unfailingly solicitous of his frail wife and always, in the words of one Hoffa friend, "unbelievably nice to her."

The former general president, no novice at using the appellate process, would quickly appeal the Pratt decision. And he still, once the shock of July 19 had worn off, expected to win his case: Boudin and his other attorneys remained optimistic that his position was a strong one and that the judges at the next level, the Circuit Court of Appeals for the District of Columbia, would find it more persuasive than the stand taken by the attorney general's office. Other constitutional scholars, some of them by no means favorably disposed toward Hoffa himself, agreed, and this fact also encouraged him.

But final arguments would not be heard by the appellate court until early 1975, and a decision would presumably not be rendered by it until much later that year. Such a timetable ruled out his running for the presidency of his old Detroit Local 299 in January, a step that he had originally planned so as to position himself to return as general president at the July 1976 Teamster national convention. He had expected to win the Detroit post handily despite a bitter power struggle between his supporters in the local and those of Frank Fitzsimmons that had become embarrassingly public even before he emerged from prison.

The fighting had not been confined to mere words, either. In 1970, the local's president, old Hoffa friend and loyalist David E. Johnson, was brutally assaulted. Subsequently, shotgun blasts shattered two of Johnson's office windows, and in 1974, a mysterious explosion destroyed his forty-five-foot cabin cruiser. A trustee of the local had lost an eye to another shotgun blast, the local's secretary-treasurer had had his barn burned to the ground, and a bomb had exploded outside the home of yet another Local 299 official. Johnson had announced that he would retire at the end of 1974 and support Hoffa as his successor. But with the latter no longer available for the job, he abandoned his original plans and, refusing to be intimidated, ran for reelection in order to thwart the presidential chances of the Local 299 vice-president—Fitzsimmons's son, Richard. The two factions ultimately agreed on a compromise that resulted in both Johnson and Fitzsimmons being reelected to their present positions without opposition. The situation remained tense, however.

The world of violence was never very far from Jimmy Hoffa, of course, but in the spring and early summer of 1975, his son feared that it might be coming even closer. "Dad was pushing so hard to get back in office," the younger Hoffa recalls; "I was increasingly afraid that the mob would do something about it."

There had been three visits in a short time frame to Lake Orion and one trip to the Guardian Building law offices by Anthony Giacalone, an alleged kingpin in the Detroit Mafia, and his younger brother Vito. Friendly with Provenzano and believed to be related to him, their avowed purpose in coming to the cottage was to set up a "peace meeting" between Tony Pro and Hoffa, with whom in years past they had also had a close relationship.

Hoffa had, in fact, helped Anthony Giacalone get a half-million-dollar loan from the Central States Pension Fund a decade earlier, and the elder brother was widely believed to have been the principal contact for some years between the Detroit mob and the Teamster leader. (Nor had Hoffa ever remotely tried to hide his association with Giacalone in these years: once, when a reporter had observed the two men walking together in Miami Beach and subsequently asked Hoffa, "What were you doing with Tony Giacalone?" he had been given as an answer, "All I know is that Tony is a great guy and he's a friend of mine.") But Hoffa's son had viewed the "peace meeting" overture as only a pretext. He was convinced that Tony Giacalone, who at one time was known to hand out business cards listing himself as president of an "exterminating company"[14] and was thought to be capable of the extermination of humans as well as animal and insect life, was "setting Dad up" for a hit. And, while the senior Hoffa had concluded each of the meetings with the Giacalones by adamantly refusing to meet with Provenzano (who, he told the brothers, was a "bum"), this hardly ended the young attorney's fears. The son knew that his father, too, was becoming increasingly uneasy each time that the

Giacalones arrived in their big new tan-topped green Cadillac Fleet-wood: "I could tell by the look in his eyes when he was with them."

He finally forced upon his father, for future self-protection, his own pistol. It was an act of desperation, not so much because the senior Hoffa had never owned an armed weapon before and re-quired much persuasion ("He was," says his son, "a fist guy, not a gun guy") but because, as a convicted felon, the former IBT leader was forbidden by law to carry such an instrument.

July 30, 1975, and Its Aftermath

15

Normally the soundest of sleepers, James P. Hoffa was awake at the Traverse City, Michigan, summer home of his in-laws almost the entire night of July 30, 1975. He had an uncomfortable feeling that something was very wrong, and he was unable, as he tossed fitfully in the light of a brilliant full moon, to rid himself of his anxiety.

He was quite sure that the difficulty related directly to his father, so much the object of his concern in recent weeks, but he was at a loss as to further specifics. Tony Giacalone had paid yet another visit to Lake Orion a few days earlier, and this might or might not be relevant. Tony still maintained his allegiance to James R. Hoffa's sworn enemy, Tony Provenzano, and now he might have another reason to harm the elder Hoffa: on the very day after the latter had talked to a Pontiac, Michigan, grand jury, Giacalone had been indicted by the same jury on fraud and income tax evasion charges. From leaked information, Hoffa had not said anything against Tony in his testimony, but who knew what the mercurial Provenzano friend might now be thinking? Similarly, another violent incident in the crowded series of happenings within Local 299 that now extended back five years had taken place on July 10: Richard Fitzsimmons's shiny new union-owned Lincoln Continental was dynamited as the Local 299 vice-president sat in Nemo's Bar, not far from his office. This might possibly also have presaged a problem for the elder Hoffa, although the line to the former IBT head here was somewhat more tenuous.

And both Hoffas believed at this point that what they viewed as the "flawed" parole arrangement would soon be rescinded—possibly within days. They had learned that a memo recently prepared by Justice Department lawyers for the use of Attorney General Edward Levi had concluded that the restrictions were unconstitutional and therefore should be eliminated. President Gerald R. Ford, approaching the end of his first year in office, was also considered as a potentially positive factor: a fellow resident of Michigan, his relations with the former IBT president had never been unfriendly, and he was presumably far removed from the Nixon-Fitzsimmons agreement. The elder Hoffa had only the previous week told *Detroit Free Press* reporter Ralph Orr, whom he greatly respected, that he hoped that Orr would personally cover the story of the rescission, and upon learning that Orr planned to be on vacation for the following two weeks and would have to turn the assignment over to a fellow journalist should the news break then, had said, "Just so it ain't no kid, Ralph. I don't want no kid." What would be good news for James R. Hoffa would not, of course, be received with equal happiness by others.

Morning proved the young attorney justified in his fears. At 7 A.M., Josephine Hoffa, who had refrained from contacting her son for several hours only with great difficulty, reached him by telephone. She was calling from the Hoffa lakefront home to tell him that his father, due back at Lake Orion from a luncheon appointment by 4 P.M. the previous day, had not been heard from in all this time. Jim had to ask her to repeat some of the information: her conversation was so frantic as to be, for a while, almost unintelligible.

Josephine's hysteria would have been understandable under any conditions, given Hoffa's turbulent professional world. For the wife of a man who was in addition so dutiful toward her that he invariably kept her fully informed of his whereabouts, and when away rarely let more than a few hours pass without telephoning, the absence of communication was highly ominous. Within minutes, the son had chartered a plane and was on his way to his parents' home.

Barbara Hoffa Crancer, like her brother, already had much on her mind before receiving, at 7:30 A.M., the same tearful message from her mother. Robert Crancer had recently been in a serious automobile accident and was in a St. Louis hospital for plastic surgery on his nose. This had necessitated Barbara's postponing a visit to Michigan for herself and Barbara Jo. The visit, in turn, had originally been scheduled to coincide with a cataract operation that had been planned for Josephine in early August—the mother's second such eye surgery.

As she closed her eyes in her airplane seat en route to Detroit on July 31, the daughter had a vision of her father, whom she was already sure was dead. He was slumped over, wearing a dark-colored, short-sleeved polo shirt. It has mystified her ever since that, while she could not possibly have known this fact prior to her arrival at Lake Orion, the clothing was exactly what Hoffa was wearing when he disappeared.

Josephine Hoffa did not wait long after 4 P.M. on Wednesday, July 30, had come and gone without word from her spouse to take action. By early evening, she had summoned close friends Louis Linteau and Cindy Green, the operators of a Pontiac, Michigan, airport limousine service in which Hoffa was believed to have an ownership interest, and they decided to spend the night with the distraught woman. Linteau and Hoffa went back a long way: more than two decades earlier, after Linteau had pleaded guilty of conspiring to receive gratuities from employers as an officer of Pontiac Teamster Local 614 and had gone to jail for this, Hoffa had seen to it that he continued to receive his union salary.

Josephine told her two guests that her husband had left the house at about 1 P.M. on that afternoon to meet "somebody" in the parking lot of the stylish Machus Red Fox restaurant in Bloomfield Township, some fifteen miles northwest of Detroit and approximately twenty miles from the cottage. At about 2:30 P.M., he had telephoned her to ask, "Where the hell is Tony Giacalone? I'm being stood up." It was the last contact that she had had, or ever would have, with her spouse.

Linteau provided Josephine with slightly more recent information. He had received a telephone call from an enraged Hoffa at about 3:30 on the same afternoon. Hoffa had told him, too, that he had been "stood up" but had not elaborated.

The Federal Bureau of Investigation could not enter the case for a while. Federal kidnapping legislation requires a twenty-four hour wait before the presumption that the victim has been taken across state lines takes effect and, of course, the bureau would have to be offered a convincing showing that there had been a kidnapping at all to be able to involve itself on this basis. Other statutes—those involving extortion, for example—might also allow it jurisdiction, but these, too, would have to await future developments.

On the other hand, the five-man Bloomfield Township Police Department could come in as soon as it was notified of the disappearance, at 8 A.M. on July 31 by Linteau, and its investigators took action within the hour. They forced open the trunk of Hoffa's unlocked dark green 1974 Pontiac Grand Ville hardtop, which was now standing almost alone in the Machus Red Fox lot, to make sure that there was no body in the trunk. They also questioned Red Fox employees and various other possible witnesses, in vain since no one had seen anything. They did, however, learn (from an afternoon telephone call triggered by the now fast-spreading news) that two men had seen Hoffa in the restaurant parking lot on the previous day: he seemed to be waiting for someone, and the two men had stopped to chat with him briefly and to shake his hand. The local police chose, however, not to speak with Anthony Giacalone for the moment: With somebody like that, you "just don't go talk," the Bloomfield Township's chief investigator had explained. "You wait until the right time."[1]

James P. Hoffa spent most of his first afternoon at Orion on the telephone, calling people whom he thought might be able to shed some light on the disappearance. But he drew a blank. He emerged from the lakefront house in the early evening to tell the large group of reporters that had gathered outside that he and his family could offer no news and that there would, accordingly, be no press conference. The Hoffas, he said, were just waiting and hoping.

In fact, however, he was attempting to do more than this. With Giacalone so obviously a key suspect in the July 30 chain of events, the younger Hoffa had arranged to meet the alleged Mafioso the next day, at an intersection not far away from Bloomfield Township. He hardly expected to take good news away from this meeting. But he did anticipate finding out something.

He waited at the intersection, on August 1, for forty-five minutes before concluding that "Tony Jack" (as Giacalone was widely known) had replicated his performance of July 30 by now standing *him* up.

Giacalone was not the only person whom Hoffa's son immediately suspected of having had a hand in the disappearance. Chuckie O'Brien, in his opinion, might also know something that he would not be willing to divulge, the forty-one-year-old foster son's once-close ties to the vanished labor leader notwithstanding.

The beer-bellied O'Brien had drawn steadily away from Hoffa in the postprison years—by some reports, because his foster father had refused to help him become president of Local 299, by others because Hoffa had not been willing to pay O'Brien's considerable gambling and other debts after advancing him some $50,000 that O'Brien still had not repaid. The straight-laced Hoffa had also opposed his foster son's recent second marriage to a divorced former beauty queen with three children.

Always friendly with Giacalone (as, of course, Hoffa himself had been), O'Brien was these days all the closer with the man he called "Uncle Tony" and, to the Hoffas, he now seemed capable of doing almost anything that Tony asked so long as he could personally benefit from it. He appeared additionally to have gone very much over to the Frank Fitzsimmons camp: he had survived Fitz's purge of both Josephine and James P. Hoffa from the Teamster payroll and was now a $45,000-a-year IBT organizer, scheduled to be reassigned soon to the anti-Hoffa Southern Conference of Teamsters main office, a choice assignment. He was openly saying that the Hoffas were "ungrateful" and was in turn believed by the Hoffa family to be not only very much of an ingrate himself but also a turncoat. He combined in a single person, in the words of one Hoffa relative, the qualities of "a pathological liar, a mooch, and an opportunist."

James P. Hoffa was convinced that his once-admired surrogate big brother was suffering from a guilty conscience: just three days before the disappearance, the attorney had learned from a client that O'Brien had been surprised by Jim's visit to the union hall (to give a legal seminar) and "turned white and just took off without saying a word when he saw you here." This behavior of Chuckie's had defied explanation at the time, since relations between the two men were still, if cool, not overtly antagonistic. Now, it seemed to the lawyer to have made total sense.

According to Hoffa's son, O'Brien had told "conflicting stories" when he telephoned the family on July 31 to convey his concern about the disappearance. And, although O'Brien's offer to guard Jim's wife, Ginger, and their two boys at the son's home while Hoffa stayed with his mother and sister at the lake had been accepted, the lawyer had subsequently had second thoughts. "Jimmy called me about 3:30 in the morning [of August 1] and said he wanted me to come right over to the cottage," the Teamster organizer later told friends. "At first, I told him no, that his wife and kids were secure in bed asleep, and I wasn't going to leave them. But he wanted me to, so I got one of the [union business] agents . . . to come over and stay with them and I went out there. I didn't like what he was saying that night. I didn't like the way his conversation was going. So I said, 'Look, Jimmy, you're tired. Go to sleep.' "[2]

Far from going to sleep, the younger Hoffa (soon joined by his sister) had kept insisting adamantly that O'Brien take a lie detector test to "resolve the doubts that we have about you." Just as firmly, O'Brien had declined, declaring that he would have to check with his lawyer first. Following a heated verbal exchange, O'Brien had departed. During the next several days, he seemed to drop completely out of sight.

En route to the Bloomfield Township restaurant on July 30, Hoffa had stopped at the Airport Service Lines, Inc. office of Linteau and Green to talk to Linteau. His old friend having just left for lunch, Hoffa was forced to settle instead for small talk with employee Elmer Reeves, in the course of which he informed Reeves of the names of the men whom he was on his way to meet.

Reeves was initially unable to remember any of the names when pressed to do so by police investigators. But under hypnosis, which he was then administered by a psychologist hired by the Hoffa family, he had no trouble at all. One of the three men, Anthony Giacalone, was no longer in doubt by anyone as a suspect (all the more so now that Hoffa's office calendar had revealed a July 30 notation, "TG—2 P.M.—Red Fox"). A second was a close Giacalone associate and Detroit area labor consultant, ex-convict

Leonard Schultz. The third was Anthony Provenzano, of northern New Jersey and Florida.

Tony Jack and Tony Pro, presumably the major players in this drama, each had a formidable alibi. Giacalone was widely observed on the early afternoon of July 30 getting a rubdown, a sauna bath, and a haircut at Detroit's suburban Southfield Athletic Club, owned by Schultz's sons. A friend of his told police that he also spent the rest of the afternoon at an office building attached to the club. When finally contacted by reporters, Tony Jack snappishly denied that he had scheduled any meeting with Hoffa and shortly thereafter flew south, reportedly to the Miami area.

Tony Provenzano was also seemingly in solid shape. A number of people claimed to have seen him playing cards at the Union, New Jersey, office of his old Teamster Local 560. And he, too, angrily told members of the media that his hands were entirely clean. "Jimmy was, or is, my friend," he blurted to the journalists who besieged him a few days later at his expensive winter house in Hallandale, Florida. "I don't know where Jimmy went. I'm as shocked as anyone by his disappearance, and if I can do anything to help find [him], I will." He then urged his visitors to leave, telling them, "You're embarrassing me in front of everyone in the neighborhood. You guys out on the lawn make me look like a mobster. I'm not. I'm just a truck driver." They did leave, but before one member of the press corps departed, the tough ex-convict noticed that he was sweating and laughingly remarked, "Hey, you think you weren't gonna get out of here alive or something?"[3]

The FBI entered the investigation on August 3. Its director, Clarence M. Kelley, announced that it was doing so because, during the previous twenty-four hours, "extortionate communications" had been received in connection with the disappearance. Under the federal extortion statutes, the agency was therefore assuming investigative jurisdiction, although very few of its investigators thought that Hoffa was still alive, and many of them freely spoke about him in the past tense. Most of the bureau's almost three hundred agents in the greater Detroit area were assigned to the case, and several of these immediately moved into the Lake Orion cottage with their telephones, radio equipment, sleeping bags, and cots. The new house guests overcrowded the residence's single bathroom, and they gave Barbara, in particular, "a strange, although comforting, feeling: they were the former enemy, after all."

Anyone with meaningful knowledge of Hoffa's whereabouts, as was widely publicized, now stood to gain some $275,000 by coming forth and sharing it with the authorities. Local 299 had almost immediately upon learning of the July 30 happening offered a $25,000 reward for such information, and this had been followed by an announcement by the Hoffa children that they would add $200,000 to the fund and by a pledge by *Overdrive* Magazine that it would put in $50,00 of its own. The hope was that the money, combined with governmental promises of complete confidentiality to all tipsters, would operate as a powerful motivator.

Such, in fact, was the case. Telephoned reports flooded the law enforcement agents, as well as various television and radio stations and newspapers not only in Michigan but throughout the country. One caller announced that Hoffa was sailing around Lake Michigan on a 141-foot yacht. Another said that while sleeping he had received a message that the missing man was in a South American jail. A woman claimed to have seen Hoffa's body on a small lake near Somerset, Michigan. A man who called himself "Morning Star" told a Los Angeles TV station that Hoffa was in nearby Glendale, California. The Chicago office of the FBI was informed that the labor leader was buried under the floor of a Midwestern truck garage. An eight-year-old "Secret Witness" program sponsored by the *Detroit News* received a record total of 120 tips on Hoffa, some 20 of them from people claiming to have extrasensory perception. The Michigan state police, who had also now joined the search, were told to look on the grounds of the Franklin Cider Mill, not far from the Red Fox restaurant.

There was no paucity of communications to the James P. Hoffa law firm, either. Several people claiming to be psychics telephoned the attorney son or his partner, Murray Chodak, that they had seen the missing man while in a trance. A truck driver regretted to say that while driving along the banks of Ohio's Maumee River he had observed Hoffa in a burning house trailer. Several people called the Guardian Building to announce that they themselves were holding the labor leader prisoner and would be happy to exchange him in return for the reward money. One man tried to raise the ante to $500,000 in a call that he made from California: even as he was telling the two law partners (conversing with him on two telephones) that he could produce Hoffa if they could produce the half-million, he was arrested by the FBI, which had been alerted to the call and had traced it. (The West Coast extortionist's last audible words had been, "I can't talk to you now. I'm on the telephone.")

All of the stories that seemed remotely credible were investigated, and none of them checked out. By mid-August, the FBI alone was sufficiently nettled by the number of false tips that had come to it that it publicly warned that it was a violation of federal law knowingly to furnish the bureau with false information about a case under investigation. Privately, even at this early date, many investigators believed that Hoffa's body would never be found. They shared the opinion of former Los Angeles crime figure Mickey Cohen, whom the Hoffa family had independently asked to look into the matter by questioning some of his underworld friends, that there was a good chance that no one would ever know what had happened.

For a brief while, there had been optimism. Chuckie O'Brien's sudden dropping out of sight following his August 1 early morning verbal altercation with James and Barbara Hoffa had combined with other factors to make him a prime suspect within a matter of hours. Witnesses placed him in the Machus Red Fox Restaurant parking lot at 7 A.M. on July 31, the morning after the Hoffa disappearance. Although he had originally claimed to have been at the Southfield Athletic Club at the time of the disappearance, club records gave no evidence that the Teamster organizer had been there at all that day. And a maroon 1975 Mercury that O'Brien had admitted driving on the afternoon of July 30 was found by FBI examiners to contain stains on its seat that appeared to be blood. When the foster son resurfaced in Detroit on August 6—from, as it turned out, Memphis and then Washington, where he had apparently been ordered to go back to Michigan by Fitzsimmons—it looked as though the investigators had their key man.

But during intensive interrogation of him by federal and local authorities, O'Brien was able to weaken all of this potentially incriminating evidence. He had never really been missing at all, as the FBI well knew, he said: he had gone to an August 2 suburban Detroit wedding at which three FBI agents were also in attendance, then traveled to Memphis to spend time with his new bride, and finally paid a business visit to his boss, Fitzsimmons, at the IBT Washington headquarters. He often stood in the Red Fox parking lot early in the morning: it was very close to the red farm house in which he was living these days, and having no car of his own, he frequently went to the restaurant to await a ride to work from a friend, Robert Holmes, Jr., who was also on the Teamster payroll. July 31 was therefore hardly unique in this regard. In addition, he had been initially confused in recounting his whereabouts on the early afternoon of July 30 and later recalled that he was actually driving a car at the time: a maroon 1975 Mercury owned by his friend Joey Giacalone, the son of his Uncle Tony.

He had, he said, found that he would need an automobile that day only after he had come to work and so had called Joey and prevailed on him to drive the Mercury over to the Teamster Detroit office complex. He had then driven Joey back to the latter's office and gone on in the car to the home of Robert Holmes, Sr. (the old Strawberry Boy, now the head of Teamster Joint Council 43) to deliver a twenty-pound coho salmon. The fish, a gift to Holmes from another Teamster official, was packed in ice inside a plastic bag in a box, but it had started to leak fish blood in the car on the way over to the Holmes house. Mrs. Holmes had taken the fish off his hands and chatted with him for so long that it was too late for him to meet Anthony Giacalone at the Southfield Athletic Club, as he had originally planned to do. Instead, he went to a car wash and had some of the fish blood washed off. He then returned the car to Joey's office. Joey Giacalone and the Holmeses would, he knew, be happy to furnish the investigators with further particulars should these be desired.

O'Brien would continue to be suspected of having had some hand in the disappearance by many people, most particularly by James P. Hoffa. But he would never again come as close to being the star performer in the Hoffa mystery as he was prior to his giving this chronology. What had for a short while seemed so obvious would now be insufficient to indict him. Everything that could be definitively used against him—his embarrassing retraction concerning the Southfield club, his flaunted ties to the Giacalones, his unseemly near vanishing during the critical five days prior to August 6, and even a denial by the manager of the car wash that anyone had brought a 1975 maroon Mercury in to his establishment on the day in question—added up to nothing more than a very superficial case. (Within a week, the forty-five-year-old car wash supervisor was dead, apparently of natural causes, in another interesting but once again unusable O'Brien-related happening.)

In late August, with promising leads conspicuous by their absence, the FBI and the U.S. attorney in Detroit decided to issue subpoenas for grand jury appearances to anyone who might know anything about the events of July 30. The hope was that the threat of contempt citations, possible under such machinery, would induce testimony that might be possible in no other way. And on September 2, 1975—the same day that the eighty-five-year-old Viola Hoffa was buried without knowing that her son had disappeared but after a month of having asked for him daily in vain—a duly constituted jury heard from the first of some seventy witnesses scheduled over the next few weeks, Joey Giacalone.

Many of those who testified in these closed sessions cooperated fully. Martin and Irene Woehl, next-door neighbors of the Hoffas at Lake Orion, said that Hoffa appeared to be quite relaxed as he worked on his grounds on the morning of July 30. Elmer Reeves, no longer requiring the services of a hypnotist to jog his memory, told all that he knew about Hoffa's conversation with him. Ernest Lawicki, a truck driver who regularly delivered food to the Machus Red Fox restaurant, testified at some length that he saw nothing unusual at the restaurant when he stopped there early on July 31. Stanley Gould, one of several lawyers assisting Leonard Boudin in the effort to rescind Hoffa's union business restriction, revealed that for a few embarrassing moments on July 31 *he* had been thought to be Hoffa's kidnapper: when he had telephoned Lake Orion and given Cynthia Green a message for Hoffa's son, his words had been sufficiently garbled that until the son phoned Gould back for clarification, it looked as though Gould was holding the elder Hoffa captive.

But such witnesses as these, while models of loquaciousness, were clearly of limited usefulness to the grand jury. And witnesses who might have had much more to tell seemed almost universally determined to keep the information to themselves.

Chuckie O'Brien, wearing a size fifty sports jacket, refused to answer a variety of questions in his appearance. (James P. Hoffa later told reporters that it was "appalling" when a "man like this

who claims to be a foster son withholds such needed information.")
Tony Provenzano pointedly informed the journalists who pressed
upon him in the hallway outside the courtroom that this was his
first trip to Detroit since Barbara Hoffa's wedding to Robert
Crancer twelve years earlier, but he had nothing much else to say
to anyone: although his lawyer, William Bufalino, announced to
the waiting reporters that Tony Pro had answered every question
asked of him inside the jury room, it was clear that in his ten
minutes on the stand Tony had also been less than enlightening.
And Tony Giacalone, worried that the publicity linking him to the
Hoffa disappearance would hurt his prospects for a fair trial in his
upcoming mail fraud and tax evasion case, was told by his attorney
to plead the Fifth Amendment. A few months earlier, Giacalone
had swung at a newspaper photographer who had approached him
with his cameras snapping when Tony Jack had come to this same
courthouse for his indictment, and his appearance this time accordingly attracted a record number of cameramen, but he had nothing
at all to communicate now, and he entered and left the building
staring stonily ahead.

Some of the witnesses appeared unwilling to leave anything to
chance. Lawyers were not allowed to accompany their clients into
the hearing room, but there was no restriction on conferences with
counsel in the hallway outside, and several people who testified
seemed to be almost in perpetual motion during their time on the
stand. Joey Giacalone left the room twenty-one times to converse
with his attorney, leading to speculation that he was a heavy user of
the constitutional amendment against self-incrimination. Suspected
Detroit mobsters Raffaele Quasarano and Peter Vitale, two more
men who were once friendly with Hoffa and had now gone over
to Fitzsimmons, between them had a slightly higher average: the
two partners in a garbage disposal plant that was believed to have
been the last resting place of several gangland murder victims, Quasarano and Vitale talked to their lawyer in the hallway twelve and
thirty-one times respectively. (The lawyer, putting the best face on
the situation, explained to reporters standing near him, "These men
are not sophisticated individuals. They don't speak the English language fluently. We wanted to make sure they understood each question in its proper context before answering it so their answers would
best help the grand jury."[4])

Other witnesses, not content with merely reacting to questions, themselves went on the offensive. Anthony J. Zerilli, the reputed chieftain of the Detroit Mafia, angrily threatened to sue anyone who described him as a Mafioso: "I am not now, nor never have been," he announced, "a member of organized crime or an organized-crime conspiracy. I serve notice on all persons that from now on I intend to challenge all such accusations in a court of law."[5] Zerilli said that he knew absolutely nothing about the disappearance. At least one courtroom visitor contended that James P. Hoffa, who no differently than O'Brien had earlier refused to take a lie detector test, should be given more rigorous scrutiny as a possible suspect. Another witness wanted the jury to know that a prior witness who had cast aspersions on him was himself a "liar" and a "prostitute."

Still others who testified—various Teamsters, Southfield Athletic Club employees, an attorney with offices in the building contiguous to the club, friends of Chuckie O'Brien—were so unshakably precise in the facts that they offered to support the Giacalone, Provenzano, and O'Brien July 30 stories that not a few observers suspected that their testimonies had been coached.

As the grand jury investigation proceeded, without producing any meaningful results at all despite the large quantity and considerable variety of its witnesses, an unexpected development took place. William B. Gallinaro, the chief investigator for the U.S. Senate's Permanent Subcommittee on Investigations, was approached by Harry Hall (alias Harry Haller, alias Hary Helfgot), an informant who brought "greetings" from a group of Mafiosi and claimed to be speaking on their behalf. The crime bosses, Hall said, felt that they were being treated unfairly by the FBI and Michigan state police in their respective Hoffa investigations because they were in fact innocent of any wrongdoing. The mobsters had learned, according to Hall, that Hoffa had been executed not by Mafia people but by lower-level Teamsters, and they were consequently getting publicity that they neither deserved nor wanted. To take the heat off themselves for the "hit," they wanted the investigators to find Hoffa's body. And, as it happened, they knew exactly where the latter was, since another informant who had helped in the burial had told them, and they now wanted to share this information with Gallinaro and his senate associates.

Gallinaro, an experienced Mafia investigator, was intrigued. He had known Hall, a former convict with ties to both the Mafia and the Teamsters, for two years and had found him to be a generally reliable source. He was further impressed by the fact that Hall asked for no money for his efforts. After further negotiations, during which Gallinaro guaranteed complete anonymity to the Mafiosi, he and a colleague, F. Keith Adkinson, met Hall in a Los Angeles restaurant as Hall had instructed them to do. There the senate employees received a map containing information as to the purported burial site from the ex-convict. An elated senator Henry M. Jackson, chairman of the Senate Permanent Investigations Subcommittee and a candidate for the U.S. presidency, thereupon publicly acknowledged the receipt of the information and announced that the "first big break in the case" had taken place. He added that, while he could not reveal where his staffers had obtained the map, he could say that organized crime was "definitely involved" in the procurement.

The map could have been clearer. It contained no street names at all and ignored most other details, allowing considerable room for confusion. Those who scrupulously followed its vaguely worded commandment to go "left" from the Machus Red Fox restaurant for nine and one-quarter miles and then proceed another six and a half miles could, for example, still wind up some distance apart from each other. Even a further message from Hall to Gallinaro and Adkinson that the site of the Hoffa body would be marked by no means eliminated the room for misinterpretation as to how to get to this site. Ultimately, however, the senate investigators concluded that the burial area was within a twenty-nine-acre site a half-dozen miles west of Pontiac, Michigan, in Waterford Township. They, accordingly, went there—to be joined not only by a sizable corps of Michigan state policemen but also by many private citizens, who hoped to gain the $275,000 reward money by being the first to discover the body. Their intensive digging of holes in the rattlesnake-infested tract also attracted hundreds of curious local residents, who created what one newspaperman called "a picnic-like atmosphere, many of [the neighbors] bringing along beer and soft drinks."[6]

But several days of searching in the relatively small area brought no more success than the grand jury investigation had produced. Not a trace of a burial site was found—to the apparent consternation of Hall, who at this point relayed a communication to Gallinaro and Adkinson that the mobsters were upset by the inability of the investigators to follow simple instructions. Soon, the rented backhoes, garden tools, and other implements that had been used in the search became, for the Waterford Township tract, history. Gallinaro, now in some disgrace, continued to maintain that he had great faith in Hall, but he was increasingly unhappy with the informant's failure to furnish any more specifics at all. After a few more days, he and Adkinson asked for and received permission to return to their Washington offices. What had begun with such promise was now ending as an apparent hoax.

If the Senate Permanent Investigations Subcommittee was in fact victimized, it did not stand alone. No less sophisticated an organization than CBS News was, shortly after the Waterford Township wild goose chase, parted from $10,000 of its money by an imaginative escaped convict who claimed that he knew where Hoffa's body could be found. The convict, Clarence N. Medlin, said that he had known the former IBT leader five years earlier when both men were at Lewisburg. And Medlin indeed had. But the rest of a story that he had just told an impressionable Greensboro, North Carolina, freelance writer and college journalism instructor named Patrick O'Keefe had been concocted out of whole cloth. Hoffa's remains, Medlin told O'Keefe, lay surrounded by concrete on the ocean floor two and one-half miles off Key West, Florida. Hoffa had, he said, been shot to death while on a fishing trip to Key West. Medlin had decided to reveal this to the public, through a journalist, because of his deep friendship with Hoffa.

O'Keefe, excited, immediately contacted *Harpers Magazine*, for whom he had done previous work, and was advanced $700 by the publication to bring himself and Medlin to New York for further discussions. But the involved *Harpers* editor, Lewis Lapham, apparently did not believe Medlin's story when it was presented to him in face-to-face discussion and sent the convict and O'Keefe over to CBS. The network reacted more favorably: Medlin was interviewed that same night on videotape, by Morley Safer of "60 Minutes," and received $1,000 for his Hoffa comments. The next day, O'Keefe was hired as a CBS consultant and given $9,000 more for his agreement to lead a network news team to the body: CBS assumed that the money would soon find its way into Medlin's pockets, but it wanted, it later announced, to avoid making any kind of direct payment to a newsmaker such as the convict.

The network was quite correct in its assumption: Medlin took the money. He also, during an overnight stopover at Tampa with O'Keefe, while the two men were presumably en route to Key West, vanished. He was arrested five days later in New Orleans even as a CBS news team was exploring the ocean waters off Key West for a third successive day. On the previous day, he had visited the news offices of the *New Orleans Times-Picayune*, represented himself as having been Hoffa's former bodyguard, and asked, without success, to be paid for the "true story" of Hoffa's disappearance.

The visit proved to be his undoing. Watching the CBS Evening News that night, a *Times-Picayune* reporter recognized Medlin (now wanted for his Tampa vanishing act) as the same person who had come to the paper earlier in the day. The reporter alerted the FBI, which blocked off New Orleans exit points and then began its successful manhunt.

On December 4, 1975, a genuine break in the frustrating case seemed at long last to have occurred. On that date, Robert C. Ozer, chief of the U.S. Organized Crime Strike Force in Detroit, revealed that the government had unearthed two witnesses to the Hoffa "abduction and murder." One of the witnesses, Ozer said, had seen Hoffa in a car at the time of the crime, accompanied by three men, but this witness did not know the identities of the men. The other witness had done more: he had already named the three men, who had now been subpoenaed to testify before the Detroit grand jury and were, in fact, currently in the city. They would appear in the jury room the very next day.

The three, all from New Jersey, were known to law enforcement authorities in that state as close associates of Anthony Provenzano, and all were members of Tony Pro's Teamsters Local 560. Salvatore "Sally Bugs" Briguglio, a forty-seven-year-old business agent in the local, was described by those familiar with his professional life as a "right-hand man" for Provenzano and a "soldier" in the Vito Genovese Mafia family. He was believed to have participated in a variety of "hits" on Tony's behalf and was known, his short, slender build and eyeglasses notwithstanding, to be on regular call as Provenzano's prime muscleman. Gabriel Briguglio, nine years younger than his brother and, at five feet, two inches, five inches shorter, was reputed to specialize in loanshark operations: he had been a colleague of Armand "Cookie" Faugno, a loanshark who had disappeared in December 1972 and whose body was believed to lie in Brother Muscato's Dump beneath the Pulaski Skyway in Jersey City. The third member of the trio, thirty-eight-year-old Thomas Andretta, had recently served two years in prison for his role in a counterfeiting conspiracy; he had also been found guilty of threatening the life of a used-car salesman who had been either unable or unwilling to pay more than $35,000 for a 1967 loan of $5,000.

All three men appeared briefly before the grand jury on December 5 and, to no one's surprise, refused to answer any questions. When one of them was later asked bluntly by a reporter if he had killed Hoffa, he intriguingly responded, "No comment."

The three suspects also refused to be included in a police lineup at the nearby Oakland County Jail the next day, but Ozer quickly obtained a court order that mandated such participation from them. When the two witnesses—camouflaged among decoy witnesses for their own protection—were shown the lineup, one apparently had no trouble in identifying Salvatore Briguglio as one of the men who had driven off with Hoffa on July 30. But she had been unable to identify the others, and even her one apparent success was greatly diminished by her admission that she had seen Sally Bugs's picture in the paper in connection with the Hoffa abduction on the previous day. The other witness reportedly was unable to identify any of the three Provenzano associates.

The prosecution, however, had a trump card to play in this case. One month earlier, a convicted murderer who was hoping to lighten his sentence had provided federal investigators with a fascinating statement. The murderer, a former Local 560 truck driver named Ralph Picardo, claimed that a few days after Hoffa's disappearance, he had been visited at the New Jersey State Penitentiary in Trenton by Thomas Andretta, Andretta's brother Stephen (also a New Jersey Teamster), and a union accountant. Stephen Andretta, Picardo said, had told him that the Provenzano group had been involved in the Hoffa event. Andretta had further stated, according to Picardo, that Hoffa's body had been stuffed into a fifty-five-gallon oil drum at a Detroit terminal owned by the Gateway Transportation Company and then carted across the country on a Gateway truck to a garbage dump in Hudson County, New Jersey. And, Picardo reported, Andretta had also told him that he himself was not present in Detroit on July 30 because by staying behind in New Jersey, he could "provide an alibi for Tony Pro."

Picardo, who had been in prison since May 1975, when he was found guilty of firing five bullets into the head of an associate, was obviously not a model of integrity. But, in the government's opinion, certain facts warranted giving his story some credence. Prison records showed that he had been visited at Trenton by the Andrettas and the Teamster accountant exactly when he claimed to have been. Tony Pro had prominently placed the name of Stephen Andretta among those who could vouch that he was playing cards in New Jersey on the afternoon of July 30. And, most importantly, Picardo had recently furnished authorities with other charges concerning the Provenzano wrongdoing, and these charges upon investigation had checked out almost in their entireties. Stephen Andretta's name, accordingly, had been added to the list of those to be called before the Detroit grand jury.

In the case of Thomas Andretta's brother, however, the authorities were unwilling to accept a Fifth Amendment plea. Instead, Stephen Andretta was given an unwanted immunity from prosecution for anything that he might say and on this basis was prevented from using his constitutional right to silence as an excuse for not answering grand jury questions. If he refused to answer now, he could be jailed for contempt of court.

He nonetheless chose not to talk when he appeared before the Detroit jury on December 11. When asked by Ozer where he was on July 30, 1975, he replied that he would first have to speak to his attorney, William Bufalino. He had already been told that Bufalino could not represent him because the attorney was now representing the other three suspects (his brother and the two Briguglios) against whom Andretta would be asked to testify, and Bufalino was in any event unavailable because he had suffered a heart attack and was in intensive care. Andretta, however, stuck to his demand, was handcuffed, and led away to jail. Maintaining his silence, he was sentenced to nine weeks in Michigan's Milan Prison for contempt.

The court finally allowed a recovered Bufalino to include Stephen Andretta among his clients, and Andretta thereupon agreed to testify—in a manner of speaking. During his eleven early 1976 days on the witness stand, he eclipsed the walking performances of Joey Giacalone, Raffaele Quasarano, and Peter Vitale by leaving the room a total of 1,117 times to consult with the attorney.[7] He steadfastly denied that he had discussed anything about Hoffa with Picardo and insisted that on the afternoon that Hoffa disappeared he had been playing a card game called Greek rummy at the Local 560 union hall with Provenzano, the Briguglios, and his brother. When he came back to New Jersey, his testimony completed, he was handed the keys to a new union-leased car, and that night he was the guest of honor at a Local 560 party.[8]

More than a decade and one-half after James R. Hoffa vanished, one of the most famous missing persons cases in American history is officially, according to the Federal Bureau of Investigation, still open. A Detroit FBI agent continues to be assigned to it on a full-time basis, and he can now draw from the contents of a dozen crowded file cabinets for his information. The Department of Justice agency nonetheless believes, as it has believed for years, that no one will probably ever be brought to trial. The Hoffa file is, as one bureau agent could recently put it, "for all practical purposes, dead as a doornail."

For the FBI to have to hold this conclusion is nothing if not frustrating, since almost from the beginning the bureau was convinced, as were most of Hoffa's friends and associates, that there was no question as to who had caused the labor leader's death and why. In the years since 1975, it has subjected Ralph Picardo's story to the closest of scrutiny and not found it, in its major details, wanting. Moreover, in the long period since the disappearance, other informers, whose identities to this day remain closely guarded bureau secrets, have also come forward and independently confirmed various portions of the convict's tale. Prosecutor Robert Ozer himself today feels that indictments should have been sought by the government, because the chance of these resulting in conviction would certainly be no less than in most Mafia-related cases. But he stands almost alone: for all of their confidence that they know what happened on July 30, 1975, most investigators are equally convinced that they lack the quantum of evidence necessary to convince a jury.

The bureau is of the opinion that Tony Provenzano and his New Jersey colleagues indeed killed Hoffa, most probably with Chuckie O'Brien as an unwitting dupe and Tony Giacalone as a conscious expeditor, and out of motives that were fully known on the date of the crime. As his son feared, Hoffa could no longer be counted on by the mob—more specifically, by the Vito Genovese Mafia family in which Provenzano was a reported capo—to allow it to have its way in its administration of its Teamster locals and its infiltration into the Central States Pension Fund, while Fitzsimmons could be. The violence-prone Provenzano also had his further, more personal reason involving Hoffa's refusal to help him get his pension.

In the version of the disappearance that has been generally accepted by FBI officials, Tony Pro's mobster superior, Russell Bufalino, decided that Hoffa should be done away with, and he gave the man who had harbored his grudge against Hoffa since their days in Lewisburg the contract. Provenzano's Detroit relative, Giacalone, was then asked to invite Hoffa to a "bury the hatchet" meeting with Provenzano at the Machus Red Fox. When the former general president arrived at the restaurant, neither Giacalone nor Provenzano was there, but others were: Thomas Andretta and the two Briguglios, who had flown from New Jersey to Cleveland that morning on a private jet and then switched to another small plane and landed it at a small, secluded greater Detroit airport. O'Brien met the three men at the latter location and drove them to the Bloomfield Township restaurant, most likely without accurate knowledge of their mission.

In the Machus Red Fox parking lot, O'Brien picked up another passenger: Hoffa. The latter was waiting there in accordance with Giacalone's instructions, to be driven ostensibly to meet both Giacalone and Provenzano at a nearby home owned by a Detroit industrialist (the red farmhouse that was serving as O'Brien's temporary residence in this period). It is highly unlikely that Hoffa, uneasy with both Tony Pro and Tony Jack, would have entered a car sent by one or both of them and containing passengers such as the Briguglios and Andretta unless someone whom he trusted (O'Brien, despite the recent differences between the two men) was driving it. With O'Brien welcoming him, it was a different matter, and Hoffa got in—and was killed in the vehicle, probably by strangulation, after being knocked unconscious.

In this FBI version, the Briguglios and Andretta then flew back to New Jersey, again by way of Cleveland where they changed back to the private jet. Other Provenzano associates—quite possibly led by Frank Sheeran of Pennsylvania, who had for years also been close to Hoffa—proceeded to dispose of the body, perhaps by depositing it in an incinerator owned by Quasarano and Vitale, or perhaps by sending it across the country in the fifty-five-gallon oil drum described by Picardo and then placing it in Brother Muscato's Dump in Jersey City.

The last location, it may be recalled, was believed to contain the body of loanshark Armand "Cookie" Faugno, who had also apparently fallen into disfavor with Provenzano. And, in fact, the rat-infested sixty-acre landfill was also thought by many investigators to have served as the final resting place for at least one other man who had incurred Tony Pro's wrath through the years: Anthony Castellito, a union competitor who vanished in 1961 in Ulster County, New York, and whose body was similarly never found. But intensive searching of the location at various points over the years has failed to produce any of the bodies, and, although some mobster leaks to the FBI still vouch for Brother Muscato's as the chosen ground for all three victims, this appears to be the one major ingredient in the Hoffa chronology on which bureau personnel remain to this day divided.

The FBI's widely shared viewpoint that Hoffa's death was a planned mob killing has, however, been disputed by at least one respected criminologist. Vincent Piersante, former chief of the Organized Crime Task Force in the Michigan attorney general's office and the chief investigator on behalf of the state in the Hoffa case, is firmly convinced that the murder of Hoffa would have been

the single most counter-productive act that organized crime could have committed at that time. And they're not that stupid. The mob realized that something like this would be absolutely devastating to it. . . . And it was. . . . All kinds of anti-crime strike forces were reactivated in its wake, instead of being the casualties of Ford Administration budgetary cutbacks. . . . All kinds of mobsters went to jail who probably wouldn't have gone otherwise. . . .

Hoffa's disappearance did a lot of good for law enforcement. If Jimmy ever wanted to get a measure of revenge against the mob for refusing to back him [in his fight with Fitzsimmons], he certainly got it in his death.

In Piersante's opinion, Hoffa both wanted and very much needed mob support in his 1975 efforts to return as IBT president. Whatever popularity he continued to have among the Teamster rank and file, the only presidential votes that would be cast at the 1976 convention were those of the local union officers and business agents who were now indebted to Fitzsimmons and consequently had no choice but to give Fitz their backing. Hoffa might have had some outside chance if his old allies in organized crime could be persuaded to grant him their allegiance once again. "The mob could give him both financial and physical backing, and it had political clout, too. That was his motivation: overturn the parole restriction and get the mob to use its clout with the local unions so that he could be reelected." But "Fitz was not the emperor that Jimmy was and the mob preferred Fitz, one reason being that it got its hooks into the pension fund under Fitzsimmons even more deeply than it ever had under Hoffa. Jimmy was not a complete tool of the mob, as some people thought . . . our [wiretap] tapes showed the trouble that the mob guys often had getting his permission to do things."

Nor, Piersante thinks, could Hoffa use a threat to put mobsters in jail by revealing things about them to the government if they did not now support him: "Most specifics that he knew that might hurt them either also involved himself, so he couldn't say those things, or were beyond the statute of limitations."

Piersante's scenario as to the events of July 30 runs this way:

The mob sent some insultingly low-level messengers to the Machus Red Fox to tell Hoffa in effect, "Jimmy, you're through; retire—you've got enough money," and Jimmy, who was always a volatile guy, just blew up. He was, even at 62 years of age, in great shape, and he had great anger. He attacked [the Briguglios and Andretta]. They hit back. There was a fight. . . . And either they killed him in the fight or he just had a heart attack. But nobody had planned to kill him. . . . There would have been no reason to. . . . In 1975, he was not the threat to come back as president that he thought he was. . . .

Right after he died, the hoods had to make a phone call, and in it they were told, "For God's sake, get rid of the body somehow!"

The Michigan criminologist, who with some justification feels that he knows the "mind of the mob" after more than four decades of firsthand observation, supports his unplanned killing theory with one last point:

Usually, in a gangland murder, we know within hours why it was done and who did it. They want it known. Even when there's a disappearance, the information is easy to get. Here, there was complete silence from the mob for weeks. This was absolutely extraordinary. I can't recall it ever happening before, in fact. The mobsters were all in a state of shock.

The Piersante school of thought, if definitely a minority one, has other adherents besides Piersante. But a third and last explanation of Hoffa's death appears to be the exclusive property of a single person. It would consequently warrant no attention at all were it not for two facts: (1) the espouser of this third hypothesis is a Hoffa family member, and (2) the chief culprit in it is none other than Richard M. Nixon.

Nixon, the family member alleges, was "scared to death" that Hoffa would return to power, and for a very understandable reason: the former U.S. chief executive had had a sizeable sum of money—possibly as much as $6 million—placed in his name in a Swiss bank by Fitzsimmons and the Teamsters as remuneration for his approval of the Hoffa parole restriction. And such a transaction, while it might be heavily camouflaged, could never be guaranteed total concealment. Hoffa, with his keen powers of observation and inquiring mind, would be sure to find out about the deal and expose it when he got back to his old job. He must, therefore, not be allowed to come back. Hoffa's parole restriction, even if it were not overturned in the courts, would ensure such a desired outcome only until 1980. The murder of Hoffa would make his nonparticipation permanent. With so much at stake, Nixon ultimately commissioned the latter action.

Asked for proof of this blockbuster theory, the family member is not convincing. Nixon and Fitzsimmons were "close friends" who met on a social basis both at Nixon's Key West home and his San Clemente one. They also golfed together at Southern California's La Costa Country Club, some twenty minutes from San Clemente and the location of Fitz's West Coast home. A Dallas newspaper alleged that Nixon got the Swiss bank payoff from the

IBT. "There was just too much going on between Fitzsimmons, Charles Colson and Richard Nixon and it all centered around [Hoffa]." "When a decision is made to kill a man like [Hoffa], there has to be an awful lot at stake, and for Nixon in this situation there definitely was." The family member fully recognizes the problems in persuading others, and is used to being received with incredulity. A person who was far closer to Hoffa than most people will, however, take a deeply harbored belief in Nixon's guilt to the grave.

Some key figures in the Hoffa case's cast of characters have already departed, taking whatever inside knowledge concerning the disappearance that they might have had with them.

Salvatore Briguglio, indicted in 1976 for the 1961 murder of Provenzano rival Anthony Castellito and scheduled to stand trial soon, was riddled with six bullets fired by two unidentified men as he stood outside a restaurant in New York City's Little Italy on March 21, 1978. Law enforcement authorities were unanimous, for a change, in concluding that he was killed to keep him from talking about the Castellito crime and very possibly also about July 30, 1975. One month earlier, he had ruefully confided to an interviewer, "I've got no regrets, except for getting involved in this whole mess with the government. If they want you, you're theirs. . . . I have no aspirations any more; I've gone as far as I can go in this union. There's nothing left."[9]

Frank Fitzsimmons died the death of a heavy cigarette smoker, of lung cancer, in 1981. Although he clearly had much to gain by Hoffa's removal from the scene, and notwithstanding the fact that he was on the best of terms with Provenzano and Giacalone (as well as O'Brien) at the time of the disappearance, no known investigation has ever tied him to the event in any meaningful way. In the opinion of one insider, Fitz's devout Catholicism alone would have prevented him from participation. In the opinion of another, for all of Fitzsimmons's weaknesses, he was incapable of endorsing any crime of violence: cheating at golf, by widespread allegation, was second nature to Hoffa's pudgy successor; murder was something that he would not have sanctioned even in his wildest dreams. This is not, however, to say that Fitz did not have advance, and even total, knowledge of the July 30 plans. Many people who knew him well believe that he did.

Anthony Provenzano died in December 1988 of a heart attack in a hospital near a California prison where he was serving twenty years for labor racketeering. For the past two years, poor health had prevented him from performing his prison job assignment as a janitor. He had been eligible for parole in 1985, but at that time had waived consideration: on his release from the California prison, he would have had to serve twenty-five years to life in New York for the Castellito murder, for which he had been convicted following the gunning down of Sally Bugs in 1978. (Testimony at Tony's murder trial showed some interesting parallels with the Hoffa disappearance as the FBI understood the latter. Provenzano was shown to have paid mob enforcer Harold Konigsberg $15,000 and offered the elder Briguglio brother a business agent's job with his local in return for their killing the union boss's competitor. Kongisberg, Briguglio, and two other men then enticed Castellito to an Ulster County, New York, summer home, hit him with a lead truncheon, and strangled him with piano wire. Provenzano had, for a while, an airtight alibi: he was marrying his second wife when Castellito disappeared. And Castellito's body, like Hoffa's, was never found.) On the eve of his seventies and knowing that his days were numbered, Provenzano chose to spend his sunset years in California. To the end, he resisted governmental pressure to talk about Hoffa.

The Provenzano and Salvatore Briguglio Castellito murder indictments were triggered by the fallout from the Hoffa case. And, as the mob had feared, other indictments and jailings were the further result of a reemphasis by the FBI and other agencies on the links between unions and organized crime in response to a post-July 1975 public outcry for it. The reemphasis hardly spared many other alleged principals in the Hoffa disappearance. These men were all the more tempting as targets because of an understandable governmental belief that *their* non-Hoffa legal problems might generate revelations from them about Hoffa in return for lighter sentences.

No such revelations were forthcoming. Gabriel Briguglio imparted nothing of value to mitigate a seven-year sentence for racketeering and extortion. Thomas Andretta, the recipient of twenty years for racketeering, and his brother Stephen, who got the same number of years for racketeering and extortion, steadfastly maintained their silences. Anthony Giacalone, who was sentenced to ten years for tax evasion, was equally unhelpful to the authorities. So was Tony Jack's brother, Vito, who served a short prison term for a firearms felony. Chuckie O'Brien, convicted of several relatively minor crimes and behind bars for ten months in 1979 after a labor law violation, had nothing significant to say. Nor did Frank Sheeran, Russell Bufalino, or anyone else. All, in holding their tongues, quite possibly took a lesson from the fate of Salvatore Briguglio. Some of them conceivably, the opinion of the overwhelming majority of Hoffa case investigators notwithstanding, know nothing that would help break the case. Whatever the actuality, it now appears clear that only the unlikely occurrence of some kind of deathbed confession will at this late date solve one of the great mysteries of modern times.

Should this revelation ever take place, Josephine Hoffa will, however, not be available to be informed of it. She died in her son's arms in 1980, at sixty-two years of age, five years after the disappearance and five years after she had told her children, "I'm not going to be around much longer."

Less than three weeks after her husband vanished, she collapsed at her home and was taken to a Detroit hospital, physically and emotionally exhausted. She soon recovered sufficiently to return to the cottage, but she seemed from that point on to have lost the desire to do much of anything except sit silently for hours in front of the small Catholic shrine that had been one of James R. Hoffa's last presents to her. Well-meaning friends and relatives who tried to entice her out of her shell with a variety of social invitations were firmly, if politely, rebuffed by a woman who for years had loved parties and dancing. She had no desire for personal vengeance, but she knew that justice ultimately would be rendered by God concerning her husband's disappearance. She would leave matters in His hands.

Never much of an eater, Josephine ate only the barest essentials after her husband went and she steadily lost weight. By 1980, from a normal poundage of 112 she had fallen to a skeletal 84 pounds. At the time of her death, she had a malignant tumor in the sinus cavity behind her nose that was pressing on her spinal column. She possibly also had a brain tumor. On her final night, a patient in a Detroit hospital while her children were making plans to move her to Boston's famed Lahey Clinic, her health was further debilitated by a series of heart attacks that resulted in her being transferred to the hospital's intensive care unit. In the opinion of both her son and her daughter, however, the real cause of her death is not carried on her medical certificate: she died of a "broken heart." The last words that Josephine probably ever heard were from her daughter: "Mother, if you want to go, go and be with Dad."

Hoffa Evaluated

16

Eddie Cheyfitz, whose untimely death of a heart attack in May 1959 deprived Hoffa of one of the closest confidants he ever had, once observed of his old boss, "He's a man who never knows when to stop. He'll keep going until he gets to the 102nd floor. And then, because he won't realize that he's at the top, he'll step off and that will be the end of him."

There was certainly that aspect to James R. Hoffa. And Cheyfitz's statement was remarkably prescient in explaining the feisty labor leader's ultimate downfall. But there were many other key ingredients too, and they were not by any means all consonant with each other.

Hoffa had the deepest of feelings for his family, but he spent by far the majority of his many waking hours in the service of his union. He was an instinctive cynic who claimed to see his belief that "every man has his price" constantly justified by events, but he regularly, if naively, placed considerable faith in business and labor union associates whom he often barely knew at all. He prided himself on his candor and was naturally outspoken, but he tended at the same time to express himself tersely and warily. In his personal life, his code of behavior was irreproachable; in his professional life, it was twice found to have been criminal, and, to his considerable discredit, he willingly—even proudly—associated with some of the seamier members of the American underworld. No labor leader has ever been more popular with his own rank and file, primarily because of the economic and employment conditions gains that he was able to produce for them, but the employers with whom he dealt and who necessarily financed these gains remained to the end his equally ardent supporters. He was both intellectually curious and an anti-intellectual. In addition to being documentably kind, generous, and thoughtful, he was capable of being ruthless, self-centered, and temperamental. He worried little, if at all, and was almost completely fearless, but he was at the same time a driven man.

Of all of these attributes, Hoffa's connection to lawbreaking and lawbreakers is understandably associated first and foremost with his name. The linkage was the most widely publicized facet to Hoffa's life, and it captured the public imagination, particularly because of the enormous power that he wielded. It was also, of course, thoroughly proven to have existed, if not as abundantly as many of Hoffa's detractors always insisted, at least far more amply than his supporters typically admitted.

There is nowadays almost a unidimensional quality of this portrayal of Hoffa. The well-tailored saleswoman in a Missouri second-hand bookstore who not long ago informed the author when he inquired of her whether she had the valuable 1965 book, *Hoffa and the Teamsters,* "If we have it, it would probably be under 'Crime,' " was conceivably echoing the opinion of millions. Nor did the respected *New York Times* do anything but reinforce the situation when, in a front-page 1989 article, it reported that a powerful Mexican labor leader "is sometimes compared to Jimmy Hoffa and Al Capone. But most people here say the accusations that he sells jobs in the oil industry, skims profits for his own use and has been responsible for murdering opponents are merely the inventions of jealous politicians and rivals."[1] And most of the seemingly endless if generally tasteless Hoffa jokes that appear to circulate as widely today as they did in the immediate aftermath of the disappearance also focus on the Hoffa-as-mobster motif: "Question: Who was the last person ever to see Jimmy Hoffa? Answer: Jacques Cousteau." Hoffa, so to speak, sleeps with the fishes.

It is a matter of record that Hoffa was found guilty by a jury of his peers on two counts of knowingly and corruptly trying to fix a jury. It is no less a statement of fact that he was also convicted on one count of conspiracy and three counts of mail and wire fraud in connection with the Central States Pension Fund. Although he had at his disposal more legal talent than most people have ever been able to draw upon, both verdicts were sustained by higher courts in the elongated appellate processes that followed. And no amount of rationalization related to Edward Grady Partin's role or background, to allegedly illegal surveillance engaged in by the government, to claimed judicial bias against Hoffa in Chattanooga, to defense contentions that irrelevant prejudicial evidence was submitted to the jury in Chicago, or to anything else, can remotely alter these actualities. Nor can any talk of a governmental "vendetta" do so, however much Robert Kennedy's allocation of so many of his resources to the mission of putting Hoffa behind bars may help to explain the latter's fate.

It is also incontrovertible that, for all of the unsubstantiated charges of Hoffa-mobster affiliations that dogged the labor leader throughout his career, many such relationships clearly did exist. They tended to be based entirely on pragmatism, in the same way that Hoffa's selection of liberal intellectuals to assist him in his Washington office could be said to have been, and by themselves these relationships were not, of course, illegal in the slightest. At the very least, however, they could be said to have been morally reprehensible; at the most, they always posed the risk of siphoning off Teamster resources for purposes that were never intended.

To give Hoffa his complete due, he was accused of much more wrongdoing in his mob liaisons than he warranted. The McClellan committee charged, for example, that his collusive channeling of health and welfare insurance monies to the Union Casualty and Life Insurance Company, although it was not low bidder, cost the union some $1,650,000 in excess commissions and fees paid to the family of Hoffa's close friend, ranking Chicago gangster Paul Dorfman, as owner of the involved agency. But as objective and scholarly an observer as Sam Romer, upon conscientiously studying all of the relevant committee documents here, concluded that while there was certainly favoritism in the awarding of the business to Union Casualty, "it is less certain that the union members, who were the fund beneficiaries, suffered from this transaction." Romer was particularly impressed by the fact that the McClellan committee staff did not challenge two major sets of statistics presented to it by Union Casualty's successor company. One was a claim that, while the expenses-related percentage of premiums that Union Casualty initially proposed to retain was a high 17.5 percent, actual experience over an eight-year period reduced this to an average 7.6 percent. The other was an insistence that, while commissions to the Dorfman agency were twice the normal rate, these commissions were charged to the fund at the standard rate, with the company itself paying the rest from profits earned elsewhere.[2] (As noted earlier, the Dorfmans themselves also made this second claim in appearing before the McClellan committee.)

As another example, the well-publicized Hoffa purchase for his union of the northern Indiana home of the infamous Al Capone henchman Paul "The Waiter" Ricca, in retrospect seems to have been just the opposite of a sellout. Even with the acknowledgment that the $150,000 that Hoffa spent went a lot further in 1955 than it does now, getting a five-acre greater Chicago lakefront estate that came complete with tennis courts, a swimming pool, and a house with sleeping facilities for twenty people for that price was, if anything, a steal.

Nor, it must be recognized, did the Central States Pension Fund do anything but flourish, the unsavory character of so many of its loan recipients notwithstanding. Its assets virtually doubled in Hoffa's last four preprison years (to $400 million), there were relatively few loan defaults, and CSPF pensions compared favorably to those received by essentially all other American workers. Hoffa's lawyers were, it will be recalled, sufficiently proud of its performance that they tried, unsuccessfully, to introduce this aspect as evidence in his Chicago trial.

But there is nothing speculative about Hoffa's attempts to place thirty thousand New York City taxicab drivers under the leadership of the convicted labor extortionist and indicted acid thrower Johnny Dio, or his conspiring with Dio to establish a group of bogus locals in an ostensible effort to gain for himself control of New York City Teamster activities. Or about Hoffa's hiring of the armed robbers Herman and Frank Kierdorf as Teamster business agents, and his employment of the underworld enforcer and strong-arm man Barney Baker as his own personal performer of special assignments. It is fact, not conjecture, that both Paul Dorfman and his equally mob-related son, Allen, were two of the closest friends Hoffa ever had and that the labor leader's circle of genuine intimates also included the major league gangster Tony Provenzano. Hoffa did sponsor and strongly endorse for key Teamster leadership positions such ex-convicts as Babe Triscaro, Frank Matula, and William Presser. And his associations with Detroit mobsters were both longstanding and freely acknowledged.

Undoubtedly, some of these criminal connections—the original linkage in 1941 to the underworld in Detroit, certainly, and very possibly also the ties to Dio—were voluntarily established by Hoffa. They were viewed by him as sound business moves. In other situations, such as in both Chicago and northern New Jersey, the Teamster leader inherited locals that were already controlled by organized crime, and he may have believed that he had no choice but to allow the status quo. Robert Kennedy, for all of the "conspiracy of evil" that he placed Hoffa in charge of, himself felt that the latter no longer had the luxury of getting rid of the mobsters even if he wanted to do so ("He wouldn't live," Kennedy once remarked in predicting the consequences of such a Hoffa effort).

To recognize that Hoffa's deeply embedded sense of realism dictated his embracing of his gangster clientele, however, no more excuses what he did than does an appreciation that the IBT chieftain apparently did not view himself as a captive of the mob at all. He was quite willing, certainly, to go against underworld wishes at times. The wiretap tapes of Michigan criminologist Vincent Piersante and Hoffa's turndown of Provenzano's pension request both testify to this. So, above all, does the clear-cut preference of organized crime for the more pliable Fitzsimmons to Hoffa as the general president once Fitz had taken over that office and exhibited his laissez-faire predilections. Yet such considerations change nothing: an assessment of James R. Hoffa's life must place his connection to some of America's more blatant law violators prominently in its equation, as it must Hoffa's own two convictions.

But it is no less mandatory in evaluating these sixty-two years to inspect Hoffa's role as head of the largest, strongest, wealthiest, and most strategically located union that the nation has ever known. He was, after all, more than anything else a labor leader. If it is fair to judge him on criminological grounds, it is as justifiable to measure him on labor relations ones, in the performance of his chosen profession. And here a very different and vastly superior Hoffa must by any objective standard be said to have existed.

It is no exaggeration to say that no major union leader has ever enjoyed the combination of popularity with his own rank and file and respect from the employers with whom he dealt than did the school dropout from Brazil, Indiana. John L. Lewis of the Mine Workers got as much, if no greater, adulation, but the coal mine operators were not nearly as positive about Lewis as the people who ran the trucking companies were about Hoffa. Walter Reuther was greatly admired and appreciated by his Automobile Worker constituents for such pioneering breakthroughs in collective bargaining as supplemental unemployment benefits and profit-sharing. But Reuther's aloofness and unconcealed sense of self-importance prevented any real popularity with the membership, and his cheering section among employers was almost nonexistent. No one else comes to mind at all.

Popularity is not often easily explained. In Hoffa's case, an accessibility to the membership that extended to the inclusion of his office telephone numbers in many of his speeches and a willingness to spend two-thirds of his mammoth workweeks out in the field certainly helped. So did a background that was, in marked contrast to the histories of many labor leaders, not an easy one, combined with Hoffa's determination not to let his electorate forget this: he was "brought up on the street," as he often reminded his audiences, and the reminder got him mileage in what remained a union of tough-minded individualists.

His oratorical skills in general served him well, too. Not many leaders could make such entirely personalized attacks as those emanating from Robert Kennedy and intended solely for him appear to be the laying down of the gauntlet for all Teamsters. Hoffa could, and regularly did. ("We all know that Hoffa is nothing. Hoffa by himself is just a name. Hoffa by himself is just an individual. When Hoffa is attacked, this whole union is threatened. The government wants to destroy us because we've been so successful.")

Some of his personal living habits conceivably also, to some extent, aided his standing with the membership. The frugal Hoffa life-style—the unimposing Detroit residence and modest Lake Orion cottage, the almost aggressively unpretentious wardrobe, the inexpensive and personally driven automobile, the utter absence of show on any dimension—got considerable publicity in Teamster publications and allowed further identification of his rank and file with him. And the eschewal of liquor and smoking, the almost

Victorian approach to sexual improprieties, and the visibility of a loving and clean-cut family presumably only added to the appeal.

But none of these factors would have meant very much, of course, without a demonstrably superior collective bargaining performance. And Hoffa's immense popularity without question stemmed primarily from the extremely favorable contracts that he was able to execute ever since 1940, when he replaced Farrell Dobbs as negotiating chairman of the Central States Drivers Council. The mileage and hourly wage rate gains that he first achieved in the Central States were dramatic, unprecedented, and well publicized. They were soon paralleled by huge progress in such other contractual fields as job security and fringe benefits and then, as his bargaining scope widened, by economic and noneconomic improvements in other geographic areas and ultimately on a national basis.

The bread-and-butter gratitude of Hoffa's membership for this proven performance accounted considerably for the fact that his legal problems decreased his standing with the rank and file not at all. He was living proof of the validity of the theory that he had once propounded to Johnny Dio: a leader who treated his constituents right wouldn't have to worry. Some members undoubtedly believed Hoffa's assertion that "all of this hocus-pocus about racketeers is a smoke screen to carry you back to the days when they could drop you in the scrap heap." Others surely held to the view that everybody had a little bit of the cheater in them and that Hoffa was being scapegoated for being such a successful labor leader. Still others, quite probably, thought that what their leader did on his own time was his own business. It did not much matter which rationale was embraced. Hoffa delivered, and that was the only criterion that counted.

What was so impressive about the delivery was in no way reflected in either Hoffa's contracts or his popularity, however. By themselves, the gains attest to no particular sense of leadership responsibility. And it is a matter of record that other labor leaders who have extracted significant improvements for the members have often done so only to the severe detriment of the industry: the concessions have far exceeded any long-term employer ability to pay and have flown in the face of competitive realities. In Hoffa's case, the industry—by many standards, America's most important single industry—was protected, too. The Teamster leader, in the opinion of the overwhelming employer majority, remained to the end an ability-to-pay adherent. He understood the trucking sector as well as any trucking company executive, knew exactly how far he could go at the bargaining table, and would go no further. His ability to exhibit this degree of accommodation was made much easier by his high level of political security within his international. It was also facilitated by his union's great institutional security within the industry. In view of the unparalleled amount of bargaining power that always supported his actions, he demonstrated a remarkable sense of statesmanship nonetheless.

By the readily acknowledged if sometimes embarrassed admission of the trucking companies, Hoffa represented all of their labor cost interests better than these historically close-to-the-margin, mistrustful, highly individualistic, and zealously competitive operators could ever have done themselves. He was responsive to the need for offering economic relief to employers who could not have survived without it and freely granted dispensations based on geographic handicaps, the handling of relatively unprofitable products and services, and other pressing reasons. Ever the realist, he recognized that such innovations as sleeper cabs, double bottoms, and trucker participation in piggybacking were inevitable if the industry's rapid growth trend was to continue, and he was willing to allow these technological introductions, even though many threatened either the income or the very employment of Teamster drivers. He merely asked that the displacement be minimized and that the workers share in whatever productivity gains might result.

Even Hoffa's grievance decisions under the controversial "open end" procedure, for all of the dangers inherent in the latter and its unpopularity with the employers because of these dangers, gave evidence of generally being statesmanlike. At the very least, the decisions consistently satisfied the majority of the industry. And "open end" was very probably a far more efficient means of area-wide labor standard supervision than any that the mutually suspicious employers would have been either willing or able to create on their own.

The overall performance was so impressive that the managers almost without exception preferred to be at Hoffa's mercy than at the mercy of any other authority—most particularly, of each other.

He may have been a dictator, but he was an enlightened and benevolent one. He infused a once-chaotic industry with a great deal of stability and allowed it to prosper. Trucking was undoubtedly better off for there having been a Hoffa.

As a labor leader, then, Jimmy Hoffa must necessarily be given the highest of grades. As Warren Bennis has pointed out, vision is the commodity of leaders and power—or the capacity to translate intention into reality and sustain it—is their currency, and the man who ran the Teamsters amply possessed both of these prerequisites.

Hoffa knew exactly what he wanted to achieve in trucking. His goal was a nationwide contract that combined maximum membership gains with the greatest possible economic well-being for the industry. And to a very large extent, in the face of both a strong tradition of local government within his union and the abiding opposition of many employers to either areawide or national bargaining, he was able to make the vision a reality. The trucking contract that he negotiated in January 1964 and that covered most of the nation's four hundred thousand road and cartage drivers, dramatically symbolized the culmination of a project that he had embarked upon twenty-four years earlier. That there was not, even when he went to prison three years later, either a total uniformity of working conditions from coast to coast or the elimination of all area wage and benefit differentials should in no way detract from the magnificence of his accomplishment.

If the Teamster truck drivers and the trucking industry were both the beneficiaries of Hoffa's career, on the other hand, it would be difficult to erect a case that the labor movement also gained. On the contrary, organized labor undoubtedly suffered and continues to suffer from the connection in the minds of millions of the criminalized Hoffa to unionism. Hoffa's far more laudable but infinitely less newsworthy industrial relations contributions are no more relevant to this connection than is the fact that most people would today be hard pressed to provide accurate information on exactly what the Teamster leader did wrong. An imperfect understanding that he was the crime-prone leader of a crime-ridden Teamsters Union is Hoffa's sole legacy to most people, and the longevity of this understanding is one more, and not insignificant, cross that today's problem-beset labor movement has to bear.

An evaluation of the controversial union chieftain, then, depends very much on the criteria applied. Proust may have been overly generous in estimating that "there are a thousand selves in each of us," but there were demonstrably several fully formed ones within James Riddle Hoffa. That his substantial darker side is far better remembered than are his many entirely admirable accomplishments for his unionists, his industry, his family, and others hardly negates the latter. Despite his reputation, he was no more a study in black or white than anyone else: as with all of us, shades of gray apply. He was stronger willed, more hard charging, more powerful, and more notorious than most people. But he was, in his many strengths and his many weaknesses, no less human.

Notes

Chapter 1

1. James R. Hoffa, as told to Donald I. Rogers, *The Trials of Jimmy Hoffa* (Chicago: Henry Regnery Company, 1970), p. 5.

2. Ibid., pp. 6–7.

3. James R. Hoffa, as told to Oscar Fraley, *Hoffa: The Real Story* (New York: Stein and Day, 1975), p. 29.

4. Teamsters Joint Council 13, St. Louis, Missouri, *The Name Is Hoffa* (April, 1956), p. 17.

5. Rogers, *Trials,* p. 27.

6. Fraley, *Hoffa,* p. 29.

7. Jim Clay, *Hoffa! Ten Angels Swearing* (Beaverdam, Va.: Beaverdam Books, 1965), p. 53.

8. Fraley, *Hoffa,* p. 31.

9. Clay, *Hoffa!,* p. 59.

10. Robert D. Leiter, *The Teamsters Union* (New York: Bookman Associates, 1957), p. 19.

11. John Cummings, "The Chicago Teamsters' Strike—A Study in Industrial Democracy," *Journal of Political Economy* (September, 1905): 568.

12. Clay, *Hoffa!,* p. 67.

13. John Bartlow Martin, *Jimmy Hoffa's Hot* (Greenwich, Conn.: Fawcett Publications, 1959), p. 29.

14. *The Name Is Hoffa,* pp. 19–20.

15. *Newsweek,* February 25, 1957, p. 40.

16. Ibid.

17. Paul Jacobs, "The World of Jimmy Hoffa—II," *Reporter,* February 7, 1957, p. 14.

18. Clay, *Hoffa!,* p. 66.

19. Rogers, *Trial,* p. 85.

20. Ibid.

21. Paul Jacobs, "The World of Jimmy Hoffa—I," *Reporter,* January 24, 1957, p. 16.

22. ABC News, "Close-Up," November 30, 1974.

23. Fraley, *Hoffa,* p. 59.

24. Ibid., p. 49.

25. ABC News, "Close-Up."

26. Ibid.

27. Ralph C. and Estelle Dinerstein James, *Hoffa and the Teamsters* (Princeton, N.J.: D. Van Nostrand Company, 1965), p. 107.

28. Dan E. Moldea, *The Hoffa Wars* (New York and London: Paddington Press, 1978), p. 33.

29. Ibid.

30. *Detroit Free Press*, September 13, 1941.

31. ABC News, "Close-Up."

32. *Playboy,* December 1975, p. 82.

Chapter 2

1. Ralph C. and Estelle Dinerstein James, *Hoffa and the Teamsters* (Princeton, N.J.: D. Van Nostrand Company, 1965), pp. 72–73.

2. *Time,* April 9, 1956, p. 37.

3. Lester Velie, "The Riddle in the Middle of America's Most Powerful Union," *Reader's Digest* (December, 1955): 91.

4. *Investigation of Racketeering in the Detroit Area,* Joint Subcommittee Report of Special Subcommittees of the Committee on Education and Labor and the Committee on Government Operations, 83d Cong., 2d sess., 1954, pp. 2–4.

5. *Investigation of Racketeering,* Joint Hearings before Special Subcommittees of the Committee on Government Operations and Education and Labor, House of Representatives, 83d Cong., 1st sess., 1953, pp. 312–14, 318.

6. Robert F. Kennedy, *The Enemy Within* (New York: Harper & Brothers, 1960), p. 52.

7. Ibid., p. 45.

8. Ibid., p. 8.

---

9. Jim Clay, *Hoffa! Ten Angels Swearing* (Beaverdam, Va.: Beaverdam Books, 1965), p. 94.

Chapter 3

1. John Bartlow Martin, "The Making of a Labor Boss," *Saturday Evening Post,* July 4, 1959, p. 53.

2. Jim Clay, *Hoffa! Ten Angels Swearing* (Beaverdam, Va.: Beaverdam Books, 1965), p. 83.

Chapter 4

1. Arthur M. Schlesinger, Jr., *Robert Kennedy and His Times* (Boston: Houghton Mifflin, 1978), p. 152.

2. *Newsweek,* July 29, 1957, p. 22.

3. Robert F. Kennedy, *The Enemy Within* (New York: Harper & Brothers, 1960), pp. 41–43.

4. Schlesinger, *Kennedy,* p. 153.

5. James R. Hoffa, as told to Donald I. Rogers, *The Trials of Jimmy Hoffa* (Chicago: Henry Regnery Company, 1970), p. 150.

6. John Bartlow Martin, *Jimmy Hoffa's Hot* (Greenwich, Conn.: Fawcett Publication, 1959), pp. 8–9.

7. James R. Hoffa, as told to Oscar Fraley, *Hoffa: The Real Story* (New York: Stein and Day, 1975), p. 94. Kennedy had, in fact, been a member of the Harvard Varsity football team a decade earlier.

8. *Business Week,* August 3, 1957, p. 109.

9. *Wall Street Journal,* July 29, 1957, p. 3.

10. Schlesinger, *Kennedy,* pp. 159–60.

11. *Hearings before the Select Committee on Improper Activities in the Labor or Management Field,* 85th Cong., 1st sess., pt. 13, 1957, pp. 5253–54.

12. Ibid., p. 5267.

13. Ibid., pp. 4950–51.

14. Ibid., p. 5215.

15. *Wall Street Journal,* September 27, 1957, p. 2.

16. Ibid., October 3, 1957, p. 1.

17. Ibid.

18. Fraley, *Hoffa,* p. 144.

19. Martin, *Hoffa's Hot,* p. 65.

20. *Wall Street Journal,* October 11, 1957, p. 6.

21. Ibid., October 14, 1957, p. 4.

22. Lester Velie, "Six Days That Shaped the Labor World," *Reader's Digest* (March, 1958): 119.

Chapter 5

1. *New York Times,* February 6, 1958, p. 26.

2. *Wall Street Journal,* August 7, 1958, p. 4.

3. Clark R. Mollenhoff, *Tentacles of Power* (Cleveland and New York: World Publishing Company, 1965), p. 298.

4. *Wall Street Journal,* October 8, 1958, p. 3.

5. Robert F. Kennedy, *The Enemy Within* (New York: Harper & Brothers, 1960), pp. 41–62.

6. Jim Clay, *Hoffa! Ten Angels Swearing* (Beaverdam, Va.: Beaverdam Books, 1965), p. 127.

7. *Hearings before the Select Committee on Improper Activities in the Labor or Management Field,* 85th Cong., 1st sess., pt. 36, 1958, pp. 13275–77.

8. Ibid., p. 13285.

9. Ibid., pt. 37, 1958, pp. 14061–62.

10. Ibid., p. 14065.

11. Kennedy, *Enemy,* p. 90.

12. *Hearings before the Select Committee on Improper Activities in the Labor or Management Field,* pt. 40, 1958, p. 15092.

13. Ibid., pt. 36, 1958, pp. 13636–37.

14. Ibid., p. 13635.

15. Kennedy, *Enemy,* p. 73.

16. Ibid., pp. 74–75.

17. Victor Lasky, *Robert F. Kennedy: The Myth and the Man* (New York: Pocket Book reprint, 1971), p. 119.

18. *Time,* September 29, 1958, p. 17.

19. *New York Times,* November 21, 1958, p. 21.

20. *Hearings before the Select Committee on Improper Activities in the Labor or Management Field,* pt. 13, p. 5189.

21. *International Teamster* (September, 1960): 16.

22. A. H. Raskin, "Why They Cheer for Hoffa," *New York Times Magazine,* November 9, 1958, p. 78.

23. Ibid., p. 75.

24. Ibid., p. 77.

Chapter 6

1. *New York Times,* August 30, 1958, p. 14.

2. *Time,* January 5, 1959, p. 22.

3. Walter Sheridan, *The Fall and Rise of Jimmy Hoffa* (New York: Saturday Review Press, 1972), p. 102.

4. *Time,* January 5, 1959, p. 23.

5. *Hearings before the Select Committee on Improper Activities in the Labor or Management Field,* 86th Cong., 1st sess., pt. 55, 1959, p. 19437.

6. Ibid., p. 19432.

7. Ibid., pp. 19432–33.

8. Ibid., p. 19434.

9. Ibid., p. 19439.

10. Robert F. Kennedy, *The Enemy Within* (New York: Harper & Brothers, 1960), p. 55.

11. Ibid.

12. Sam Romer, *The International Brotherhood of Teamsters: Its Government and Structure* (New York: Wiley, 1962), p. 47.

13. *St. Louis Globe-Democrat,* August 26, 1956, p. 2F:3.

14. Steven Brill, *The Teamsters* (New York: Simon and Schuster, 1978), p. 370.

15. *Initial Report of the Board of Monitors,* pt. I, Supplemental Report, May 27, 1958, p. 189.

16. Ralph C. and Estelle Dinerstein James, *Hoffa and the Teamsters* (Princeton, N.J.: D. Van Nostrand Company, 1965), p. 43.

17. *International Teamster* (October, 1962): 2.

18. Paul Jacobs, *The State of the Unions* (New York: Atheneum, 1963), p. 56.

19. *Saga Magazine* (March, 1959): 77.

20. *Newsweek,* July 10, 1961, p. 59.

21. *Wall Street Journal,* March 5, 1959, p. 10.

22. *New York Times,* June 14, 1959, IV, p. 3.

23. *Playboy* (December, 1975): 74.

24. The statement, which originally appeared in the June 1959 issue of the *Harvard Business School Bulletin,* was picked up by *Time,* which included it on page 16 of an August 31, 1959, cover story on Hoffa and thereby gave it considerable publicity.

25. *Time,* June 8, 1959, p. 59.

26. *Newsweek,* July 10, 1961.

27. *Wall Street Journal,* June 3, 1959, p. 3.

28. *New York Times,* May 21, 1959, p. 23.

29. Ibid., June 28, 1959, p. 48.

30. *Hearings before the Select Committee on Improper Activities in the Labor or Management Field,* 86th Cong., 1st sess., pt. 56, 1959, p. 19735.

31. Ibid., p. 19804.

32. Ibid., pp. 19836–37.

33. Ibid., pt. 54, p. 18915.

34. *New York Times,* July 8, 1959, p. 19.

35. Ibid., August 5, 1959, p. 1.

36. Ibid.

37. John Bartlow Martin, *Jimmy Hoffa's Hot* (Greenwich, Conn.: Fawcett Publications, 1959), pp. 104–5.

38. Victor S. Navasky, *Kennedy Justice* (New York: Atheneum, 1971), p. 454.

39. Kennedy, *Enemy,* p. 162.

40. Martin, *Hoffa's Hot,* p. 104.

41. Ralph de Toledano, *R.F.K., The Man Who Would Be President* (New York: G. P. Putnam's Sons, 1967), pp. 89–90.

42. Kennedy, *Enemy,* p. 320.

43. George W. Taylor, "Public Responsibility of Unions in Collective Bargaining," in *Labor's Public Responsibility* (Madison, Wisc.: National Institute of Labor Education, 1960), p. 20.

44. Select Committee, *Final Report,* pt. 3, March 28, 1960, p. 725.

45. *Newsweek,* August 10, 1959, pp. 20–21.

Chapter 7

1. *Wall Street Journal,* October 2, 1959, p. 4.

2. *Business Week,* May 7, 1960, p. 148.

3. Ibid.

---

4. Victor S. Navasky, *Kennedy Justice* (New York: Atheneum, 1971), p. 451.

5. *Wall Street Journal,* January 25, 1961, p. 4.

6. *Newsweek,* February 6, 1961, p. 29.

7. *New York Times,* January 26, 1961, p. 17.

8. *Newsweek,* February 6, 1961.

9. *New York Times,* January 26, 1961.

10. International Brotherhood of Teamsters, *Proceedings of the 18th Convention,* 1961, Third Day, p. 44.

11. Ibid., Fourth Day, pp. 113–14. Actually, this official record corrected Hoffa's grammar and changed the statement to "Hoffa doesn't have any machine."

12. Ibid., Fifth Day, p. 51.

13. Ibid., p. 52.

14. Walter Sheridan, *The Fall and Rise of Jimmy Hoffa* (New York: Saturday Review Press, 1972), p. 181.

15. International Brotherhood of Teamsters, *Proceedings,* Fourth Day, p. 85.

16. *New York Times,* July 7, 1961, p. 12.

17. Ralph C. and Estelle Dinerstein James, *Hoffa and the Teamsters* (Princeton, N.J.: D. Van Nostrand Company, 1965), p. 62.

Chapter 8

1. Statistics cited in this section, unless otherwise noted, are from American Trucking Associations, Inc., *American Trucking Trends,* 1961 edition.

2. Interstate Commerce Commission, *Interstate Commerce Commission Activities, 1937–1962,* Supplement to the 75th Annual Report, p. 145.

3. *Forbes,* May 15, 1962, p. 44.

4. Ibid.

5. Paul Jacobs, "The World of Jimmy Hoffa—I," *Reporter,* January 24, 1957, p. 13.

6. Ibid., p. 14.

7. Arthur A. Sloane, "Union-Employer Relations in the Over-the-Road Trucking Industry" (D.B.A. dissertation, Harvard University, 1963).

8. A. H. Raskin, "Hoffa'll Take Care of Hoffa," *New York Times Magazine,* March 26, 1961, p. 9.

9. *Transport Topics,* April 24, 1961, p. 3.

Chapter 9

1. Sumner H. Slichter, James J. Healy, and E. Robert Livernash, *The Impact of Collective Bargaining on Management* (Washington, D.C.: Brookings Institution, 1960), pp. 750–51.

2. Ibid., p. 751.

3. American Trucking Associations, Inc., *Proceedings of the Fourth Annual National Forum on Trucking Industrial Relations,* 1953, p. 13.

4. Ralph C. and Estelle Dinerstein James, *Hoffa and the Teamsters* (Princeton, N.J.: D. Van Nostrand Company, 1965), p. 168.

5. Arthur A. Sloane, Union-Employer Relations in the Over-the-Road Trucking Industry" (D.B.A. dissertation, Harvard University, 1963).

Chapter 10

1. American Trucking Associations, Inc., *Trucking Labor Relations Information Special,* February 5, 1961, p. 2.

2. Ibid., pp. 1–2.

3. *International Teamster* (March, 1961): 15.

Chapter 11

1. *Wall Street Journal,* February 20, 1962, p. 1.

2. *Newsweek,* May 28, 1962, p. 30.

3. Walter Sheridan, *The Fall and Rise of Jimmy Hoffa* (New York: Saturday Review Press, 1972), p. 222.

4. Clark R. Mollenhoff, *Tentacles of Power* (Cleveland and New York: World Publishing Company, 1965), p. 356.

5. Ibid., p. 363.

6. *Playboy* (December, 1975): 94.

7. *New York Times,* December 6, 1962, p. 47.

8. *Time,* January 4, 1963, p. 16.

9. Ibid.

10. Sheridan, *Fall and Rise,* p. 255.

11. *Wall Street Journal,* April 22, 1963, p. 1.

12. Ralph C. and Estelle Dinerstein James, *Hoffa and the Teamsters* (Princeton, N.J.: D. Van Nostrand Company, 1965), p. 219.

13. Hoffa was apparently both surprised and hurt by all five of these resignations and stonily refused to accept them. They became effective anyway.

14. Dan E. Moldea, *The Hoffa Wars* (New York and London: Paddington Press, 1978), p. 150.

15. Gibbons, for example, had apparently overheard Hoffa discussing this possibility. See Steven Brill, *The Teamsters* (New York: Simon and Schuster, 1978), p. 374.

16. House Assassination Report, pp. 176–77.

17. Moldea, *Hoffa Wars*, pp. 427–28.

18. John H. Davis, *Mafia Kingfish* (New York: McGraw-Hill, 1989), p. 406.

19. Ibid., p. 112.

20. Perhaps the two best of the breed are Davis's book and David E. Scheim, *Contract on America* (New York: Shapolsky Publishers, 1988).

21. Warren Commission Report, Exhibit 2980.

Chapter 12

1. *New York Times*, January 16, 1964, p. 30.

2. John L. McClellan, "These Labor Abuses Must Be Curbed," *Reader's Digest* (December, 1962): 98.

3. "Red" Medlin, the neighbor who had allegedly offered a bribe to juror James C. Tippens, requested and was granted a separate trial. The seven originally named defendants at Chattanooga thus became six.

4. *New York Times*, February 6, 1964, p. 36.

5. *Wall Street Journal*, February 6, 1964, p. 6.

6. *New York Times*, February 6, 1964.

7. Walter Sheridan, *The Fall and Rise of Jimmy Hoffa* (New York: Saturday Review Press, 1972), p. 330.

8. *New York Times*, February 26, 1964, p. 36.

9. *Time*, March 13, 1964, p. 25.

10. Ibid., p. 26.

11. *Wall Street Journal*, March 20, 1964, p. 12.

12. Ibid.

13. Robert F. Kennedy, *The Enemy Within* (New York: Harper & Brothers, 1960), pp. 114–15.

14. *New York Times*, October 24, 1965, p. 68.

15. Ibid.

16. Ibid., February 7, 1966, p. 40.

17. Ralph C. and Estelle Dinerstein James, *Hoffa and the Teamsters* (Princeton, N.J.: D. Van Nostrand Company, 1965), p. 375.

18. *Time,* July 15, 1966, p. 17.

19. Robert M. Cipes, "How They Got Jimmy Hoffa—or Did They?" *Atlantic Monthly* (November, 1966): 122.

20. *New York Times,* October 14, 1952, p. 38.

21. Ibid., December 14, 1966, p. 46.

22. *Nation,* January 2, 1967, p. 6.

23. Victor S. Navasky, *Kennedy Justice* (New York: Atheneum, 1971), p. 492.

24. *Wall Street Journal,* January 25, 1967, p. 12.

25. Ibid., January 18, 1967, p. 4.

26. Sheridan, *Fall and Rise,* p. 356.

27. Dan E. Moldea, *The Hoffa Wars* (New York and London: Paddington Press, 1978), p. 428. See also Sheridan, *Fall and Rise,* pp. 406–8.

Chapter 13

1. *Wall Street Journal,* March 8, 1967, p. 3.

2. James R. Hoffa, as told to Oscar Fraley, *Hoffa: The Real Story* (New York: Stein and Day, 1975), p. 182.

3. Ibid., p. 188.

4. A. H. Raskin, "What the 'Little Fellow' Says to the Teamsters Is What Counts," *New York Times Magazine,* May 30, 1971, VI, p. 12.

5. Fraley, *Hoffa,* p. 208.

6. Ibid., pp. 208–9.

7. Raskin, "What the 'Little Fellow' Says."

Chapter 14

1. The quotations in this paragraph are from *Newsweek,* April 17, 1972, p. 31.

2. Dan E. Moldea, *The Hoffa Wars* (New York and London: Paddington Press, 1978), p. 279.

3. *Wall Street Journal,* July 27, 1973, p. 10.

4. *New York Times,* November 10, 1974, p. 74.

5. James R. Hoffa, as told to Oscar Fraley, *Hoffa: The Real Story* (New York: Stein and Day, 1975), p. 233.

6. Ibid., pp. 13–14.

7. Ibid., p. 15.

8. Ibid., p. 24.

9. Ibid., pp. 234–35.

10. *New York Times,* November 22, 1973, p. 26.

11. *Playboy* (December, 1975): 83.

12. Christopher Davis, "Lord Jimmy," *Esquire* (March, 1975): 145.

13. Ibid., p. 146.

14. Lester Velie, *Desperate Bargain* (New York: Reader's Digest Press, 1977), p. 32.

Chapter 15

1. *New York Times,* August 2, 1975, p. 6.

2. Ibid., August 13, 1975, p. 14.

3. *Time,* August 18, 1975, p. 17.

4. Charles Ashman and Rebecca Sobel, *The Strange Disappearance of Jimmy Hoffa* (New York: Manor Books, 1976), p. 179.

5. Ibid., pp. 178–79.

6. *New York Times,* September 29, 1975, p. 36.

7. Steven Brill, *The Teamsters* (New York: Simon and Schuster, 1978), p. 42.

8. Ibid., p. 72.

9. Dan E. Moldea, *The Hoffa Wars* (New York and London: Paddington Press, 1978), p. 418.

Chapter 16

1. *New York Times,* January 15, 1989, p. 1.

2. Sam Romer, *The International Brotherhood of Teamsters* (New York: Wiley, 1962), pp. 41–42.

Index

Haggerty, James E., 260, 265, 271, 305–306, 309
Haggerty, Thomas J., 93, 95
Hall, Dallas, 293
Hall, Harry (Harry Haller, Hary Helfgot), 385–387
Hansen, John, 139
Harlan, John M., 323
Hastings, Al, 7
Hayes, A. J., 66
Healy, James J., 148
Hickey, Thomas L. "Honest Tom," 83, 87, 93, 95
Hobren Corporation, 260
Hoffa, Barbara. *See* Crancer, Barbara Hoffa
Hoffa, James P., 54–60, 70, 76, 285, 301, 334–335, 340, 348, 351, 356, 361–362, 364, 373, 376–378, 381–383, 385
Hoffa, James R. Children's Home of Jerusalem, 66–68
Hoffa, Jenetta, 2–5, 7, 60
Hoffa, John Cleveland, 2–4
Hoffa, Josephine Poszywak, 25–28, 54–55, 57–61, 63–65, 70, 84–85, 95, 108, 142, 150, 180, 259, 301, 329, 334–335, 338, 340, 345, 346, 348, 351, 353, 359, 361, 363–365, 369–370, 374–375, 377, 398–399
Hoffa, Viola Riddle, 2–6, 60–61, 383
Hoffa, William, 2–5, 16, 60, 90
Hoffman, Clare E., 42–46, 81, 172
Holmes, Alvin R., 209
Holmes, Robert, 8–9, 32, 36, 62–63, 65, 67, 346, 382
Holmes, Robert, Jr., 382
Holmes Transportation Service, 209
Holtzman, Joseph, 115–116, 124, 156–157, 161
Hooker, John J., 293
Hoover, Herbert, 91, 151
House Assassinations Committee, 284

Internal Revenue Service, 159
International Brotherhood of Teamsters (IBT), 9, 11–14, 19, 22–23, 25, 28–30, 35, 40, 46, 58, 60, 62, 65–66, 70, 78–79, 82, 87–89, 91, 96, 98–102, 104, 106–114, 117, 119–120, 123–124, 126–129, 131, 134, 136, 139–140, 143–145, 149, 152–153, 155–156, 159, 162–163, 167–169, 172–174, 179–181, 185, 192–193, 195, 198–199, 204, 206, 208, 210, 213–214, 218–221, 224–225, 232, 237, 240–242, 245–247, 252–253, 257–259, 269–270, 272, 276–279, 284–285, 290, 294, 297, 301, 304–305, 307, 310–316, 322–323, 331, 335–337, 341–343, 346–348, 353, 356, 361–365, 369, 372, 374, 377, 382, 394, 396, 404
Team Drivers International Union, 10
Teamsters National Union, 10–11
Western Conference of Teamsters, 22, 95, 363
International Laundry Workers Union, 26
International Longshoremen's Association, 39, 134, 154
International Teamster, 143, 146, 340
Interstate Commerce Commission (ICC), 188–189, 194, 196, 207, 325
Interstate System, 194
Iowa 75-Mile Rider, 202
Ives, Irving M., 50, 80, 82, 122, 160

Jackson, Henry M., 386
Jackson, Joseph R., 170–171
Jacobs, Paul, 146
James, Ralph and Estelle, 30, 187, 273, 318
Jefferson, Martha, 75
Johnson, David E., 62, 370–371
Joint Western Committee (JWC), 221–233

Katz, Michael A., 369
Kavner, Richard, 144, 280
Keathley, Ferguson, 144, 280
Keathley, Yuki Kato, 144, 280
Kefauver, Estes, 42
Kelley, Clarence M., 379
Kennedy, John F., 2, 50, 85, 122, 133, 154–158, 160, 163, 175, 214,

---

Reeves, Elmer, 378, 383
Reuther, Walter, 31, 40–41, 66, 146, 200, 341, 405
Ribicoff, Abraham, 175
Ricca, Paul "The Waiter," 84, 162, 403
Riddle, Steve, 61
Riesel, Victor, 81, 87
Roadway Express, 194
Rogers, Donald I., 338
Rogers, William P., 355
Romer, Sam, 402
Roosevelt, Franklin D., 18, 29–30
Ruby, Jack, 283–286, 328
Ryder System, 194

Safer, Morley, 387
Saffo, Peter, 144
Salinger, Pierre, 125
Sanson, Stanton D., 307–308
Scaradino, Sam "Frank O'Brien," 59
Schiffer, Jacques M., 271, 295, 297, 300, 302
Schmidt, Godfrey P., 107, 109–113, 135–136, 143, 152–153, 171
Schultz, Leonard, 379
Sears Roebuck Company, 16, 66
Seigenthaler, John, 260
Senate Select Committee on Im-proper Activities in the Labor or Management Field, 50
Shaffer, Charles N., Jr., 260, 262
Shea, Cornelius P., 11
Sheeran, Frank, 393, 398
Shelley, John, 92
Shenker, Morris, 330, 350
Sheridan, Andrew "Squint," 118
Sheridan, Walter, 176, 258, 260–263, 295–298, 301, 322, 326–327
Shiel, Bernard J., 66
Siegel, "Bugsy," 118
Silets, Harvey, 300
Skoglund, Karl, 18, 29, 31
Smith, Glenn W., 119, 152, 161
Smith, Wint, 45–47, 84–85, 120, 260
Snyder, Zigmont, 90, 162
Sobell, Morton, 337
Spector Freight System, 194

Spindel, 105, 300
Spock, Benjamin, 367
Steinberg, Lawrence N., 143–144, 214, 279–280, 288, 333, 337, 339, 341
Stewart, Potter, 323
Sullivan, Daniel, 364
Swanson, Warren, 264
Swygert, Luther M., 320–321

Taft, Robert, 133
Taft-Hartley Act, 213, 258, 260, 265, 313
Taylor, George W., 164
Teamsters Bar Association, 147, 179, 324
Teamsters Local 107, 109–110, 151, 178, 269–270
Teamsters Local 239, 176–177
Teamsters Local 245, 152
Teamsters Local 332, 116
Teamsters Local 500, 29
Teamsters Local 544, 29, 31
Teamsters Local 560, 167, 364–365, 379, 388–389, 391
Teamsters Local 574, 18, 22, 28–29
Teamsters Local 688, 140–141, 144, 363
Teamsters Local 705, 278
Teamsters Local 901, 327
Teamsters Local 929, 109
Teamsters Local 985, 42, 172
Teamsters Local 20467, ¡283
Test Fleet Corporation, 45, 84–85, 108, 259–260, 265, 272
Textile Workers, 161
Thomas, John W. Department Store, 161, 307
Tippens, James C., 261–262, 270
Tobin, Daniel J., 11–13, 18, 20, 23–25, 28–31, 34, 36–40, 168, 209
Trafficante, Santos, 282, 285
Triscaro, Louis M. "Babe," 46–47, 131, 186, 404
Trotsky, Leon, 18
Trotskyites, 19, 29
Truman, Harry S, 107

Tweel, Nicholas J., 270–271, 293,
    295–296, 301

Union Controlled Casualty and Life
    Insurance Company, 156–157, 402
United Automobile Workers
    (UAW), 31, 40–41, 66, 82, 86–87,
    146, 341, 347, 405
United Steelworkers, 41

Vinson, Fred M., Jr., 322
Vitale, Joe, 118
Vitale, Peter, 384, 391, 393

Wagner, Robert F., 135
Walker, James T., 293
Walsh, Maurice, 306, 309
Warren, Earl, 281, 323–324
Warren Commission, 286
Weiner, Irwin S., 284
Weiss, Abraham, 291
Wells, L. N. D., 107, 110–111
West Coast Truckers, 251
Western States Agreement, 226
White, Byron R., 321
Williams, Edward Bennett, 74–75,
    107, 110, 112, 122, 146–147, 157,
    163, 168, 179, 187, 279, 304–305,
    362
Williams, Paul W., 105
Wilson, Frank W., 292, 295–300,
    302–303, 312, 314, 327–328
Wisconsin Motor Carriers Associa-
    tion, 248
Woehl, Martin and Irene, 383
Woodcock, Leonard, 347–348

Zagri, Sidney, 144–146
Zapas, Gus, 119, 161
Zerilli, Anthony J., 385
Ziebert, Duke, 279